PROMISE &
ILLUSION IN
CANADIAN
POLITICS

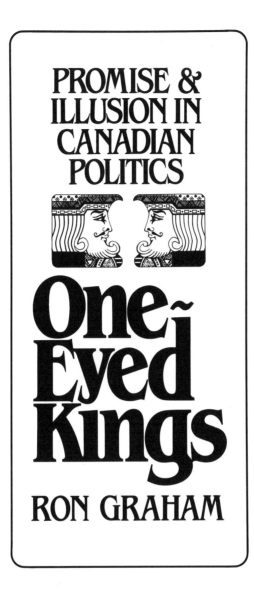

One~
Eyed
Kings

RON GRAHAM

COLLINS TORONTO

Canadian Cataloguing in Publication Data

Graham, Ron, 1948–
    One-eyed kings: promise and illusion in Canadian politics

Includes index.
ISBN 0-00-217642-4

1. Prime ministers – Canada.
2. Canada – Politics and government – 1979-1980*.
3. Canada – Politics and government – 1980-1984*.
4. Canada – Politics and government – 1984-   *.
I. Title.
FC630.G62 1986   971.064   C86-093225-7
F1034.2.G62 1986

First published 1986
by Collins Publishers
100 Lesmill Road, Don Mills, Ontario

© 1986 Ron Graham

A detailed research bibliography for *One-Eyed Kings* is available upon request from the publisher.

All inquiries regarding the motion picture or other dramatic
rights for this book should be addressed to the author's representative, The Colbert Agency Inc., 303 Davenport Road,
Toronto, Ontario M5R 1K5. Representations as to the dispo-
sition of these rights are strictly prohibited without express
written authorization of the author's representative and will
be vigorously pursued to the full extent of the law.

Quotation on page 117 reprinted from *The Collected
Works of F.R. Scott* by F.R. Scott. Used by permission of the
Canadian Publishers, McClelland and Stewart.

Quotations on pages 35-36 and 104 reprinted from *Cyrano de
Bergerac*, by Edmond Rostand, translated by Anthony
Burgess. Reprinted by permission of Holt, Rinehart and
Winston, New York.

Printed and bound in Canada by John Deyell Company

CONTENTS

*To my parents
and
in memory of F.R.S.
1899-1985*

The Triumph of Hope Over Experience

An Introduction

I

In October, 1984, I had a long breakfast in Ottawa's Four Seasons Hotel with an extremely knowledgeable Senator. The Progressive Conservatives had been in power with their massive majority barely a month, and we were speculating on what their first year would look like. We agreed, among other things, that a dramatic reduction of the federal deficit was unlikely; we predicted a startling growth of the Prime Minister's Office; and though we couldn't have guessed the details, we discussed the forces that would lead to rampant patronage, government subsidies and bail-outs to private enterprise, the expansion of Petro-Canada, the protection of Canada's sovereignty, and the renewal of tensions between Ottawa and the provinces once the honeymoon was over. These prognostications flew in the face of stated Conservative policy and the strong desire of Canadians for change. By the first anniversary of Tory rule, however, all of them had come to pass.

That isn't to claim a gift for prophecy. In fact, during the past few years I thought Pierre Trudeau would fight one more election, I lost $50 betting that Joe Clark would squeak past Brian Mulroney at the 1983 Tory leadership convention, I stated that Jean Chrétien had a chance to beat John Turner for the Liberal leadership in 1984, and for a week or so I even felt that the Liberals might win a minority government in the September general election.

The only consolation in this pathetic record is that I was wrong for the right reasons.

I had been paying more attention to the broad patterns of Canadian politics than to the vagaries of personality and party. In the broad patterns it was clear that Trudeau was stronger than any of his likely successors, Clark had a better grasp of Canada and his party than Mulroney, Chrétien had a better grasp of Canada and his party than Turner, and the Liberals were more comfortable with the winning formula than the Tories. As it happened, other significant but less fundamental factors—Trudeau the single parent, Clark the wimp, Turner the anglophone, or the Tories as fresh faces—obscured and overwhelmed the basic realities of winning and ruling Canada. Eventually, as the Senator and I told each other over breakfast, the realities had to surface and prevail. That's why Mulroney moved closer to Clark, Turner moved closer to Chrétien, and both Turner and Mulroney moved closer to Pierre Trudeau.

What are these patterns, these realities? Essentially they are a combination of Canada's political culture and the various pressures operating constantly on every Prime Minister and any party leader. By understanding how Canadians look generally upon politics, power, and the state and by judging the weight of the major interests that compete for influence and favours—including "the people" as well as businessmen, bureaucrats, union presidents, and provincial premiers—anyone can deduce what is likely to happen in the medium-to-long term, what the few options are likely to be, or at least why so many Canadian governments end up doing much the same things. In fact, in a relatively stable and cautious country such as Canada, there are only two "wild cards" that might upset the regular course of events: crisis and the particular will of a strong leader. If you decide that a crisis isn't imminent and the Prime Minister is more concerned with being liked, achieving harmony, and winning the next election than with asserting any particular will, then you can hold forth boldly at cocktail parties with some confidence that you'll be proven astute sooner or later.

The patterns of Canadian politics are not terrifically mysterious or complex. The society is young and small, power is concentrated in well-defined centres, and in the past twenty years there has been an abundance of academic studies, popular biographies, intelligent journalism, memoirs, diaries, royal commissions, and histories dedicated to defining how Canada works. Even the much-maligned daily press hits upon more truths than might be expected given the exigencies of deadlines, the temptations of herd reporting, and the natural duplicity of politicians. Often in writing this book, I had to stand on the shoulders of those who were taller or closer to the action than I, including George Radwanski and Richard Gwyn on Trudeau; L. Ian MacDonald on Mulroney; Christina McCall-Newman and Joseph Wearing on the Liberals; Jeffrey Simpson, Patrick Martin, and George Perlin on the Tories; Jack Cahill on Turner; Bruce Doern and Glen Toner on the National Energy Program; Robert Sheppard and Michael Valpy on the constitution; Louis Hartz, Kenneth McRae, and Gad Horowitz on Canada's political culture; and the authors of the three volumes of the Royal Commission on the Economic Union and Development Prospects for Canada.

Yet, despite this richness of material, I continually encountered well-connected and well-read Canadians trapped in the craziest beliefs, the falsest expectations, the darkest confusions. Brilliant businessmen wondered why Canada hasn't produced a Margaret Thatcher or a Ronald Reagan. Experienced politicos expressed surprise that the Tories have behaved so much like the Grits. Informed reporters announced with trumpets the re-invention of the wheel.

Ironically, part of the problem was the very surfeit of material. Twenty years ago it was possible to stay on top of the literature on Canadian politics. The important books were few, they were usually general in scope, and they often addressed readers who were assumed to be weak in Canadian history and political sophistication. Since then the shelf has become a library; there have been fat tomes devoted to such arcana as the constitution, the National Energy Program, and Bill Davis; and a lot of basic facts and ideas about Canada have become axioms rarely worthy of repetition. That is as it should be, a sign of Canada's maturity as a nation, but it's hard for most people to pore over scores of books in search of the broad patterns. Those who do often miss the forest for the trees.

My only excuse, then, in adding to the groaning shelves is to try to make clear in a single volume what has gone on, what is going on, and what is likely to go on in Ottawa. Though the King of France, the Loyalists, John A. Macdonald, Wilfrid Laurier, and a host of other historical personages make cameo appearances, my focus is the first half of the present decade, from the start of Pierre Trudeau's last term in 1980 to the end of Brian Mulroney's first year in 1985. This period has advantages beyond its immediacy. It was a time during which all the great issues of Canadian politics and government—the nature of the federation, the role of the state, the independence of the country—were raised and debated. At the same time many of the most contentious matters of Canadian history—free trade with the Americans, the use of French in Manitoba, freight rates, fish—resurfaced together as fresh disputes. Without much exaggeration it was as if the Confederation debates of 1867, Macdonald's National Policy of 1879, English Canada's rejection of Laurier in 1917, Mackenzie King's conscription referendum in 1942, Louis St. Laurent's pipeline crisis in 1956, the collapse of the Liberal Party under Lester Pearson in 1958, and the internal revolt against John Diefenbaker as leader of his party in 1966 had all occurred in the same five years. Those five years also saw the worst economic recession since the 1930s.

Such turmoil was particularly extraordinary for Canada, which tends to prefer its politics slow, civil, and rather mundane. In a land where prime ministerships are regularly measured by the decade, there were four Prime Ministers in almost as many years. One leader resigned after a humiliating defeat, withdrew his resignation shortly afterwards, and led his party back to power. Another leader resigned when he didn't have to, campaigned for his own job, and lost the convention to a man who had never been elected to public office. Another leader finally got to the top of the greasy pole after sixteen years of thwarted ambition and exile, resigned at once, and slipped right back into the Slough of Despond. There were two national elections, two federal leadership contests, a provincial referendum to decide if the province should negotiate its way out of the federation, a constitutional crisis, an energy crisis, an economic crisis, and major changes in the direction of almost every province. Small wonder the public-opinion polls taken during this time resembled the Mad Mouse ride at a local fair, or that many Canadians emerged from the blizzard punchy and confused by what had happened.

The greatest challenge in drawing the essential motifs of the period was also the greatest obstacle to most people's understanding of the times: the personalities of the leaders and the ambitions of the parties were so entangled with the realities of power that it was impossible to make precise distinctions among them. For example, how much of the economic bust that hit Western Canada in the early 1980s was due to the fact that Pierre Trudeau was Prime Minister, and how much was due to the Liberals' National Energy Program or the collapse in world oil prices? Similarly, how much of the improvement in Canada's economic statistics in 1985 was due to the fact that Brian Mulroney was Prime Minister, and how much was due to the Conservatives' budget policies or Canada's free ride on the American recovery? These sorts of questions are at the heart of every political quarrel in Parliament, on the hustings, or across the dining-room tables of the nation.

Since the leaders personify their parties and the parties represent policies that reflect the general situation, it seems natural and just that they all should rise or fall together. Not only can they not be separated easily, many partisans and ordinary citizens don't want to separate them. As is said over and over again, politics is perception. It is a game, a sport, a hobby, an entertainment. It is still the art of the possible rather than the science of the probable, being more concerned with myths and emotions than with truth and logic. It is, as Dr. Johnson said of the man who re-married immediately after the death of a shrewish wife, "the triumph of hope over experience."

Loving or hating the Prime Minister, pitting party against party, and distorting facts into symbols of good or evil are the stuff of politics. Unfortunately, they also stand in the way of any clear analysis. Focussing myopically on this leader or that party precludes examining the pressures that would make *any* leader or *any* party behave more or less in a similar fashion. The result is a cacophony of half-baked opinions, slogans, dogmas, cant—and the expression of perpetual disillusionment.

What makes this period from 1980 to 1985 so interesting and valuable is that there were enough leaders with different attitudes, enough governments with different approaches, and enough policies with different orientations for an objective observer to begin to see some of the common realities. Joe Clark's brief term in power (which petered out in the first six weeks of the decade) demonstrated, for example, that the wars between Ottawa and Alberta should not have been attributed solely to Trudeau's abrasive personality, and that the existence of Petro-Canada should not have been dismissed as merely Liberal interventionism. The return of Pierre Trudeau permitted the testing of a series of activist, centralist initiatives—for better or for worse isn't the point here—that would have otherwise remained vague might-have-beens in the minds of some political theoreticians. On winning the Liberal leadership, John Turner ceased to be Prince Valiant and was forced to adopt many of Trudeau's policies and advisers. And I know from experience that few of the prognostications that the Senator and I developed about the Tories in 1984 were credible to many people even months later. Yet, after Brian Mulroney's first year as Prime Minister, the patterns became more evident to everyone.

That isn't cynicism or determinism, but realism. While it is true that crisis and will can cause almost anything to happen, crisis isn't normal, by definition, and will usually exact a heavier political price than most leaders wish to pay. Ordinarily, therefore, the pressures are constant and the room to manoeuvre is minimal. If you assume that governments do one thing rather than another for a reason (even a bad reason), then you can assume that in most instances governments will do roughly the same things for roughly the same reasons. Trudeau once remarked that his biggest surprise on getting into power was the ease with which he and a tiny group of friends had been able to take charge of the party, then the state, and then the national agenda. Paradoxically, his second biggest surprise was the slowness and difficulty involved in changing the direction of the ship of state once he was in command.

Of course, different governments have different views, different priorities, different constituencies, and therefore different reasons for acting as they do. The most intriguing implication to emerge from a survey of the past five years is the hardening of those differences into two distinct visions of Canada and its politics. Traditionally the mainstream players have tried to avoid that by sharing the fuzzy centre. Elections have looked more like Tweedledum and Tweedledee's agreement to have a battle over a rattle than meaningful clashes over principles and policies. But there are signs that "the centre cannot hold," to borrow W. B. Yeats's phrase. The problems within the economy, the tensions within the federation, and the challenges to Canada's nationhood have already caused a dramatic tug of the centre to the left, as the first section of this book will explain; a strong and coherent set of beliefs has arisen on the right in reaction; and fewer and fewer analysts feel that the old techniques of muddling through the middle are either desirable or possible as this millenium draws to an end. Many think the only choice is crisis or will.

The handling of the crisis or the nature of the will can't be predicted with the same certainty as the consequences of muddling through. However, the two general directions that might be taken between now and the year 2000 can be described, their destinations can be imagined, and some of their advantages and disadvantages can be charted. It is not my purpose or my role as a reporter to conclude which road is better. I leave that to the politicians and the people. Rather, my hope is to serve as a clear-eyed guide who can remind them of what had gone before, point out the salient features of what surrounds them at present, and give a signal of what lies ahead.

II

Part of the confusion that many Canadians have about their politics can be blamed on the confusion surrounding such basic terms as liberal, conservative, and socialist. These terms are labels that are supposed to conjure up definite attributes—much as green, orange, and red do—but wear and tear have made them practically useless. If green were sometimes called orange and sometimes called red, there would be pandemonium at every traffic intersection; yet Trudeau is called a socialist, Turner is called a conservative, and Mulroney is called a liberal with cavalier randomness. The intent is to befuddle the competition, of course, but everyone ends up in a kind of mental gridlock.

A few key definitions will do more than establish my own use of the terms that appear throughout this book. They will introduce at the outset the fundamental aspects of Canada's political culture. Political culture is not a nebulous, quasi-academic fantasy, on a level with the feelings of plants. It is very real, very relevant, and very instructive. It is probably as crucial to sales at a Petro-Canada gas station as the price at the pump. A little knowledge of it would have saved Peter Pocklington the hundreds of thousands of dollars he spent running for the leadership of the Progressive Conservative Party in 1983. A country's political culture may be compared to a person's psychology, for both delineate general characteristics that cast light upon specific actions. At the root of every political culture are the two great questions of political ideology, political history, and political organization: *where* should power rest and *how much* should rest there?

The unique history and politics of Canada's provinces and regions suggest that Canada has a variety of political cultures. Though that is true to some extent (and helpful in explaining why the Liberal Party is a right-wing party in Saskatchewan and a left-wing party in Newfoundland or why the NDP is strong in Manitoba and weak in Alberta), polls and studies show that there are only two political cultures diverse enough to force special treatment: English Canada's and French Canada's. Despite an impression to the contrary, average Westerners don't think very differently from the people of Ontario and Nova Scotia in their attitudes toward power and government.

"There is a ton of views and beliefs that bind the country together," said Allan Gregg, the Tory pollster. "In some cases, where policy decisions affect regional vested interests, you'll see some differences in degrees or direction. But in terms of fundamental beliefs, values, and aspirations, there is a cohesive political culture in English Canada."

The differences between English Canadians and French Canadians, however, are wide-ranging and important, as might be expected from their origins. French Canadian society began as a transplant from feudal France in the seventeenth century. Therefore, feudalism set the prevalent norm as to how French Canadians regarded the relation between authority and themselves. In that seminal environment power was centralized at the top, order was more desirable than liberty, mercantilism regulated commerce for the benefit of the few, and the well-being of the collective whole predominated over the well-being of the individual.

Instead of being weakened by almost two centuries of political and economic upheaval since the British conquest of the small, remote French colony in 1763, the feudal values were reinforced by the society's fear of assimilation and by elites that benefitted from an obedient, hierarchical, superstitious, deeply religious, genuinely conservative community. Sovereignty was with God, not with the people, and a great deal of His command was vested in self-anointed agents in French Canada's colonial imitation of the Three Estates. Deference to the common good was essential if the religion, language, culture, and Establishments of *les Canadiens* were to survive.

In many ways French Canada remained an anachronistic fragment of pre-revolutionary France, caught by historical accident in English North America, until the middle of the twentieth century. Gérard Pelletier, the Quebec journalist who became a federal cabinet minister and Canadian ambassador to France and the United Nations, remembered a teacher who spoke fondly of the King (meaning Louis XVI rather than George VI) and even the language contained archaic echoes from the *ancien régime*. As for politics, Pierre Trudeau wrote as late as 1958, "French Canadians must begin to learn democracy from scratch." Certainly Quebec was still a claustrophobic, authoritarian, intimidated society heavy with incense and mothball patriotism when Trudeau was growing up in the 1920s and 1930s in Outremont, the verdant enclave of Montreal's French-speaking elite.

It was only after French Canada's political culture had taken hold that liberalism developed in France and England as a radical reaction to the privileged feudal order in both countries. Basically it was a revolt of the ambitious and the discontented against the entrenched and the satisfied. Therefore, in the ideological utopia of classic liberals the highest peak, the most revered goal, was the self-fulfilment of each individual. The vehicles to reach it were liberty, rationality, education, and self-discipline. The guides were Montesquieu, Locke, Tocqueville, and Mill. The routes were the paths of freedom, whether free thinking, free speech, free enterprise, or free trade. The landscape was a democracy in which the state provided the stability and services that its individuals couldn't provide for themselves but needed to flourish. To control the tendency of the state to oppress, everyone had the right and the obligation to participate in its operation to some degree. In other words, power had to be divided and decentralized, democratic freedoms had to be guaranteed, and government had to be an ever-adapting search for the Golden Mean between tyranny and selfishness.

The English colonies that became the United States of America were established just as the liberal ideas of the eighteenth century were battering against the conservative regimes of Europe. For the most part those colonies were dominated by those ambitious enough or discontented enough to quit English authority for the promise of liberty, equality, and individual happiness in the New World. From the start the political ethos of North America (with the exception of French Canada) was liberal. However, the liberalism of the United States, as expressed in the American Revolution, the Declaration of Independence, and the Constitution of 1787, turned out to be much more classic than that of English Canada. The obvious and often-cited reason was the influx into Canada of the Loyalists, those Americans who rejected the Revolution and wanted to maintain their allegiance to the British Crown. Their numbers and the timing of their arrival into the young, sparsely-settled colonies to the north made Loyalism the foundation of English Canada's political culture.

Loyalism is best described as conservative liberalism. Being Americans the Loyalists were fundamentally liberals —which would have become apparent at once if most of them had been dropped back into the broad politics of England in 1800—but for economic or emotional reasons they clung to certain aspects of feudalism, including a respect for elites, a submission to the law, a love of order, a suspicion of majority rule, a sense of collective community, and a trust in a beneficient state.

Throughout the nineteenth century various factors worked to reinforce this incipient political culture. The climate and the distances caused British North Americans to huddle together in tight, timid, hierarchical communities and scorn those who didn't pull their weight for the common good. Many new immigrants, especially the clannish Highland Scots and the former imperial soldiers, buttressed the bias toward obedience and community. The churches preached social duty above individual achievement. The great expense of commercial infrastructures such as canals and railways, the small domestic market, and the absence of old wealth required the state to take an early and active role in the economy. Class and foreign ownership stultified change and development. History and geography produced distinct regions with powerful local elites and strong identities, both of which emphasized groups instead of individuals in a "melting pot." That emphasis impeded the acceptance of majority rule as a democratic ideal at the national level and developed into an admirable toleration for minority rights as well as the rights of the individual. The most powerful minority was French Canada, of course, and its feudal ethos drew out the tory tendencies in English Canada's liberalism as the two cultures became entwined in makeshift alliances and ultimately the federation of 1867.

The Fathers of Confederation were a *mélange* of English-speaking conservative liberals and French-speaking bourgeois conservatives. John A. Macdonald had helped overthrow the Family Compact, the Toronto-based oligarchy that clutched to British supremacy as a means of keeping its privilege and power, and George-Étienne Cartier had been a successful Montreal solicitor with lucrative business connections and Anglicized ambitions. They even called their coalition the Liberal-Conservative Party (which remained the official name of today's Progressive Conservative Party until 1938 except for a brief interlude). The hybrid nature of their philosophy was also evident in their draft of the British North America (BNA) Act, by which three colonies united to form Canada. It incorporated such good liberal principles as parliamentary democracy, federalism, and religious tolerance with such good conservative traditions as the monarchy, an unelected second chamber of Parliament, and provisions for a strong central government. Power was dispersed and rights were guaranteed, but not to the extent of threatening peace, order, and good government as they had in the United States, where too much decentralization had almost split the nation in two.

Macdonald's dream had been to create a new *people* by binding the elites of the regions and the minorities at the national level, while using the constitution to safeguard their particular interests from the tyranny of the majority. In practice, however, Canada was too vast, diverse, and liberal-minded to be homogenized from above. For their part, Canadians were too dependent on authority, too submissive to their elites, and too attached to their communities to come together democratically as individuals. The functional compromise was to share power among the elites and use Ottawa as little more than the arbiter of trade-offs and deals. Even in Macdonald's day, with all his personal and political skills, the provinces became important power centres and various vested interests discovered the advantages of using them to check the central government when necessary. Efforts to unify the people, such as the National Policy, often created serious tensions among regions, language and religious groups, or economic Establishments. After Macdonald the decentralist trend accelerated as new and more remote provinces came into being, the Judicial Committee of the Privy Council in London delivered a series of liberal interpretations of the BNA Act, and French Canadians began to look on Quebec as the best protector of their collective security.

The genius of Wilfrid Laurier was to take Macdonald's national vision, loosen it somewhat in terms of provincial powers and minority rights, and direct it away from serving the comfortable few toward assisting the struggling many. After a youthful flirtation with radicalism à l'américain Laurier accepted Canada's less classic liberalism (including the mobilization of Ottawa's clout by means of alliances, horse-trading, and elite accommodation at the centre), but he gave it a progressive and democratic orientation. At the same time he began to transform the Conservatives' Anglocentric nationalism into a domestic one that wouldn't exclude his own people. In essence, he improved upon Macdonald's formula and changed the dynamic of Canadian politics in a way that kept his party in office for most of the twentieth century.

That change requires some explanation, for it clears up one of the most perplexing characteristics of English Canadians. If you plunk a bunch of average Canucks down among their equivalents in the heartland of the United States, it soon becomes evident that these northerners are more timid, more polite, more conscious of class, more attached to the status quo, less entrepreneurial, less opinionated, less litigious, and less political than their southern neighbours. In other words, much more conservative. But once the Canadians begin to open up in their clear, mid-Atlantic voices (punctuated by irritatingly tentative "ehs"), what radical ideas emerge: support for a state-owned broadcasting system and universal medicare, opposition to American involvement in Nicaragua and the testing of cruise missiles, pride in the state-owned oil company and the nationalized hydroelectric networks, acceptance of official linguistic dualism and multicultural traditions, and a lackadaisical attitude toward a socialist government in Manitoba and a separatist government in Quebec. In other words, these antediluvian tories are exposed as a cell of bloody un-American pinkos.

That seems to defy all reason until you realize that political ideology has a "looking-glass" effect not unlike the physical law which states that every action has an equal and opposite reaction. A strong right-wing ideology makes possible a strong left-wing ideology; a moderate right-wing ideology permits the development of a moderate left-wing ideology; and the lack of a right-wing ideology virtually assures the lack of a left-wing ideology. Far from being improbable hocus-pocus, the phenomenon makes perfect sense, because political ideology is simply the way people look at the key questions of where power should rest and how much should rest there. That's why centralized, authoritarian nations such as Russia and China were able to leap instantly from emperors to dictatorships of the proletariat by a quick, traumatic transfer of sovereignty from the emperor to the people; and that's why Catholic societies have demonstrated themselves more susceptible to Marxism than Protestant ones. Thus, the United States began as a classic liberal culture, with its values and myths in the individual and decentralized power, and it has more or less remained a classic liberal culture.

But English Canada began as a conservative liberal culture, applied that way of looking at power to progressive goals, and developed into a radical liberal culture. Its respect for authority, elites, community, and a certain degree of centralized power didn't prevent its leftward shift. On the contrary, that respect allowed that shift, because radical liberalism—or social democracy, since the two terms have become synonymous—required a respect for authority, elites, community, and a certain degree of centralized power. As concrete evidence, a protest party arose on the left and remained more vocal, more effective, and more permanent than any of the protest parties that arose on the right.

The evolution of Canada from a right-of-centre polity to a left-of-centre polity (with the centre, in this instance, being classic liberalism) was begun by Laurier and continued ever so cautiously by his successor, Mackenzie King, with the added assistance of urbanization, industrialization, immigration, depression, and war. King was always swift to decentralize and decontrol the moment the provinces and other vested interests started to squeal, but he proved adept at getting influential members of the different elites into the national government. He also introduced enough reforms and benefits to repel the challenge from the CCF, and by the time he retired in 1948 he had constructed the framework for today's welfare state. His longevity as Prime Minister was more than a simplistic matter of buying off the masses with election goodies: it reflected his understanding that Canadians liked to see themselves as compassionate, generous, tolerant, and reform-minded. King himself, however cautious and old-fashioned a figure, took pride in being the grandson of the old Upper Canadian rebel, William Lyon Mackenzie.

Unfortunately for the Liberal Party, Louis St. Laurent was less skillful as a political juggler. He could accommodate the elites all right, especially the business sector and the bureaucracy, but not without losing the party's reformist image. Though St. Laurent himself was seen as the benevolent Uncle Louis, his government soon looked arrogant, patrician, and reactionary, particularly in comparison to the populist alternative being offered by John Diefenbaker. The reasons behind the Liberals' loss in 1957 were the reasons for the social policies and party restructuring initiated by Lester Pearson in the 1960s, though Pearson was lucky enough to have political expediency and economic prosperity coincide with his own progressive spirit. The thrust was condensed into a truism by one of Pearson's chief organizers, Keith Davey, who went on to drill exactly the same message into the heads of Pierre Trudeau and John Turner, "Whenever the Liberals are seen to the right of the Tories, we lose." It was a variation on King's credo, "No enemies on the left."

As a result, the Liberal Party lurched hard to the left following every defeat by the Tories, after Macdonald's victory over Blake and Borden's over Laurier to Diefenbaker's over St. Laurent and Clark's over Trudeau. Each lurch was a move away from classic liberalism, which began on the left as radicalism, became the centre, and is now called the "conservative" right. In effect, the party that was defined at the end of the nineteenth century by its individualism, free enterprise, provincial rights, and free trade has become defined increasingly at the end of the twentieth century by its nationalism, *dirigisme*, centralism, and protectionism. The cause was plain: because Canada's political centre of gravity was on the left, the centre kept moving to the left and any party of the centre had to move accordingly.

Those who worried about their ideological principles insisted (correctly, I believe) that the transformation was merely a modernization of liberalism, not a rejection of it, because the basic unit of the state was still seen as the individual rather than as some collectivity such as class or ethnic group. Since the objective of the state remained the fullest realization of happiness and excellence within each individual, each individual had to have the freedom to realize his or her potential *and* the economic and social base on which to take advantage of that freedom. Those two conditions often required the state to intervene.

Each individual, moreover, had to be part of a community to be really complete. Neighbourhood, city, and province were such communities, but there was also a national community, which wasn't necessarily homogeneous but did share certain claims, values, obligations, and opportunities. Since the ultimate legitimacy of the national community lay in the fact that its individuals choose to live together, the national state was a contract by the people, not by the provinces, the elites, or any other intermediaries.

"Basically we've taken the liberal notion of individual self-realization and wedded it to the Aristotelian idea of community," said Tom Axworthy, who began as a protégé of Walter Gordon in the 1960s and ended up as Pierre Trudeau's last Principal Secretary in 1981.

That simple wedding had far-reaching repercussions. In effect, it linked the destiny of the individual to the common good, an activist state, majority rule, centralized authority, nationalism, and the will of the mass known as the people. Rousseau had pursued a similar line of reasoning away from Montesquieu and became the intellectual godfather of Marxism in the process. That isn't meant to suggest that English-Canadian liberals became Marxists; but it does explain why Canadian liberalism came to resemble social democracy of the CCF–NDP variety. The NDP itself is more liberal than socialist in its general emphasis of individuals over class. Indeed, part of the frequent misunderstanding about Canadian politics is in the notion, as taught to every first-year poli-sci student, that Canada's three main parties represent three separate ideologies—conservatism, liberalism, and socialism. As should be clear by now, in truth they represent changing varieties of liberalism appropriate to an essentially liberal polity.

While that provides an overview to English Canada's progression, it doesn't account for what happened in French Canada, especially Quebec. How did a feudal political culture develop into one that produced the Quiet Revolution, the Parti Québécois, or the Front de Libération du Québec? Not by the gradual evolution that occurred in English Canada, certainly. True, there were French-Canadian reformers and free thinkers in the early nineteenth century who picked up liberal ideas from Europe and the United States, agitated against the secular and clerical elites, and struggled for democracy; but the radical ideas of these *rouges* fell like seed upon stone or were crushed quickly under the feet of the dominant authorities. True, by 1900 French Canadians had begun to vote overwhelmingly for the Liberal Party under Wilfrid Laurier, who had been greatly influenced by *rougisme*, the classic liberalism of the British and the Americans, and the English-Canadian moderates; but they did so for reasons of collective safety and advantage. "French Canadians on the whole never voted for political or economic ideologies," Trudeau once observed, echoing Laurier's opinion, "but only for the man or group which stood for their *ethnic* rights." In fact, Trudeau went further in his analysis and asserted that French Canadians have had trouble absorbing the liberal democracy imposed upon them by their British conquerors because the survival of the community always prevailed over the rights and freedoms of the individual.

However, if the genuine conservatism of French Canada was far to the right of English Canada's right-wing liberalism in the nineteenth century, it permitted Quebec to go further and faster to the left than English Canada in the middle of the twentieth century. Once the feudalistic order began to buckle under the impact of urbanization and industrialization, and the blind obedience to the Roman Catholic Church was challenged by modern political and social ideas, then strong authority was transferred with astonishing rapidity from the paternalistic bosses to the servant state and from God to the people. Popular sovereignty, national will, majority rule, and collective action became the rallying cries of Quebec by the 1960s, and it didn't take long for charismatic leaders, interventionist governments, socialist policies, and a nationalism based on ethnicity to arise in the name of the people. The Quebec Liberal Party soon found itself bumped from the left to the right; the social-democratic leadership of the Parti Québécois entered a constant tug of war with its extremely powerful left wing; and Marxism found a constituency (albeit a small one) in Quebec that it never found in English Canada. This sharp, leftward jolt was checked, of course, by two hundred years of colonial rule, the infiltration of North American liberalism, the laws of the Canadian federation, the presence of a sizeable and potent anglophone minority, economic pragmatism, and a host of other moderating influences. What resulted, however, still tilted toward the community over the individual, regulation over liberty, and authority over free thinking.

Even within the federal Liberal Party there are more rural and small-town conservatives, radical reformers, and Quebec nationalists from that province than true grits. In fact, many of those French Canadians who arrived at liberalism intellectually tended to come through Catholic personalism rather than classic British individualism. Personalism, as espoused by Jacques Maritain and Emmanuel Mounier in France in the 1930s, joined liberal ideals to the doctrines of the Church for the sake of social progress and shaped the politics of such prominent Liberals as Gérard Pelletier, Marc Lalonde, Pierre Juneau, Claude Ryan, and Pierre Elliott Trudeau. By definition the whole *person* wasn't the same as the whole *individual* because personality wasn't distinguished from either its community or God. That difference, however subtle, opened the way for more collective authority than was ever implied by utilitarianism, as illustrated by the will apparent in the personalists' guiding motto, "Look! Judge! Act!"

The "looking-glass" transfer in French Canada's political culture had as much effect on Canada as on Quebec. From the 1960s on, French Canadians played an increasingly important role in the national government as cabinet ministers, as Members of Parliament, and as civil servants. Under Pearson, Trudeau, and Mulroney their numbers gave them enormous clout in the government caucus; their talent often ensured control of key departments; and their different perspective frequently changed how things were done and to what purpose. Indeed, "French Power" became a slogan to express what was right or wrong with Ottawa during the 1970s, from official bilingualism to cabinet committees to the metric system.

But "French Power" wouldn't have existed if these modern French Canadians hadn't found like-minded social democrats with a thirst for reform and justice among their English-speaking colleagues in the cabinet, in the party, and in the bureaucracy. Even before the "Three Wise Men" (Trudeau, Pelletier, and Jean Marchand) went to Ottawa in 1965, the Liberals had begun a sharp leftward shift in response to Diefenbaker's victories, as evidenced by their plans to extend the welfare state, the incipient debates over nationalism, and the "democratic" centralization of the party organization. Later, when many radicalized French Canadians moved into high-profile portfolios, they were backed by senior mandarins who had learned their arts in the activist years of the war or during the CCF regime in Saskatchewan, technique-obsessed control artists fresh out of the Harvard Business School, and not a few New Left veterans from the 1960s who had been turned on by ambition. Together they generally trusted the state more than private enterprise—in the spirit of *"L'État c'est moi"*—and they often thought of the central government as the first rather than the last solution to problems. Coming from opposite directions at vastly different speeds, Canada's two political cultures found a meeting of minds instead of the traditional marriage of convenience. They met in the "radical centre," as Trudeau called it.

This ideological momentum rarely operated at a conscious level. Indeed, most politicians of the centre like to think that they aren't ideological but *pragmatic*, just as most English Canadians believe that they don't have an accent. But pragmatism isn't the neutral, value-free, ideologically empty randomness it's generally portrayed to be. If the essential argument of this book is correct—that there are constant and well-defined forces impinging upon every party and every leader—then a series of pragmatic decisions will invariably develop into a consistent and coherent set of ideas. Everyone knows that it is pragmatic for the

Liberals to try to cut into the support of the NDP or for the Tories to try to steal the centre from the Liberals—that's "just good politics"—but such pragmatism has causes and effects that few people consider. Similarly, it may be pragmatic for a government to subsidize an unprofitable industry in a region of high unemployment, but there are ideological reasons which make that option more acceptable and desirable than moving the workers to productive jobs. Of course, sometimes unprofitable industries *are* closed down, but most exceptions are simply exceptions. Yet the fanatic preoccupation of politicians, journalists, and citizens with today's special event often obliterates the basic nature of the game. Many who remain mesmerized by the movement of the pendulum back and forth from left to right often miss the fact that the whole damn clock is on the back of a pick-up bound for paradise or hell.

It would be absurd to suggest that the unfolding of Canada's political history wasn't altered by such critical occurrences as the two world wars, the Great Depression, Keynesian economics, or a myriad of other developments that encouraged the centralization of power, state planning, huge bureaucracies, government spending, and so forth. But it would be equally absurd to suggest that Canadians responded to these occurrences with minds as blank as the Arctic snows. Just as churches are built from mortar and stones, so Canada's political cultures were constructed from things as real as winter, distance, population, resources, foreign capital, and war. Yet to look for the nation's soul only in the concrete details of its past would be as mistaken as to seek a church's divinity in its architecture alone.

III

This book is about an extraordinary place, a traumatic time, and four Prime Ministers. More than that, it is about the very nature of leadership. Its title comes from the British writer, H. G. Wells, who once said, "In the country of the blind, the one-eyed man is king." In my opinion, the blindness isn't supposed to impute stupidity or avarice. It merely recognizes the obvious fact that plain citizens are caught up in their own lives, their own work, their own regions, and their own goals most of the time. That isn't just understandable; it's unavoidable. Their blindness is in their narrow view, their short-sighted vision. To overcome that handicap for the sake of unity and direction, they commission their politicians to move among them, gather their views, seek expert advice, and evolve policies and programs that please as many as possible. Those who do best are chosen leaders. Their unique role in the society gives them a vision that most people trust as greater than their own. That is the promise of leadership.

However, the vision of politicians is highly imperfect— one-eyed, if you will. That too is understandable and perhaps unavoidable. For, despite the delusions that gather around them and in their own heads, leaders are simple humans. They cannot predict the future and have no monopoly on the truth. In fact, there are no absolutes in political affairs. To paraphrase Marshall McLuhan, "The art of politics is what you can get away with."

Realizing that, politicians tend to weaken their sight even further by becoming partisan. Often they turn a blind eye to the other sides of an issue, or to the long-term consequences of their short-term ambitions, or to any truth that might stand in the way of the power, respect, and spoils they seek. Sometimes they've been known to twist facts, hide data, misrepresent situations, and even lie as a result. And who in the country of the blind is to say that they're not telling it as it is? Other politicians? That is the illusion of leadership.

There is an overriding element, however. It was best expressed in another brilliant, jocular remark by McLuhan, "In the country of the blind, the one-eyed man is a lunatic." He meant, I assume, that people with a broader-than-average vision have been mocked and abused more than they've been honoured and rewarded. To the blind, the sayings of prophets and visionaries may seem the rantings of the deluded as much as the wisdom of the enlightened; and the people have been misled often enough by false prophets and charismatic types to retain some justified suspicions. Sometimes, rightly or wrongly, for better or worse, the instincts of the people take over. They demand a different direction or a new leader. They refuse to budge or to obey.

Leadership touches on promise and illusion together. It involves facts and myths equally. Yet, however intangible some of its qualities may be, leadership is grounded in, and may be judged by, the realities of a people's existence. By understanding those realities, more and more people can gain sight in one eye. That would make them better judges of their leaders. It might even allow them to start looking for those who have, if not perfect vision, at least both eyes open.

SECTION ONE

The Rouged Face of Power

I

"Well, welcome to the 1980s," Pierre Trudeau said to the thousand delirious partisans packed into the ballroom of Ottawa's Chateau Laurier Hotel. It was shortly after midnight on February 19, 1980, and Trudeau's Liberal Party had just won a majority of the seats in the Canadian House of Commons in the previous day's election. "Springtime this year is a little bit early," he went on in his shy-romantic mode, "and Valentine's Day a little bit late."

Political victory is always a sweet ecstasy, a high of such exotic euphoria that otherwise normal people sacrifice years of their lives to savour a few moments of it. But this one was made sweeter by the memory of the desperate night of May 22, 1979—just nine months before—when many of these same supporters had gathered in this same room to hear this same man concede defeat to the Progressive Conservative Party under Joe Clark, someone most Liberals thought unworthy to carry Trudeau's suitcase, let alone his mantle.

The 1979 election had ended sixteen years of Liberal rule, eleven of them with Trudeau as Prime Minister. At that time he said, "Let's keep on smiling and let's go on fighting and we'll see victory in the not-too-distant future." Even his most optimistic devotees recognized that was more rhetoric than faith, though some clutched to the small morsels of hope and consolation contained in the fact that the Tories had only won a plurality of seats. In theory—and the wildest flights of Grit fancy—the Clark

government could be tossed out of office whenever the
Liberals, the New Democratic Party, and the Créditistes
chose to gang up and force a new election. As spring
passed into summer and summer into autumn, the odds
of that happening became slighter and slighter, despite
Clark's initial confusions, persistent blunders, and rapid
decline in popularity. None of the opposition parties was
prepared for another campaign, least of all the Liberal Party.
Its leader grew a beard, wandered off to the Arctic and
Tibet, and spent a great deal of time bouncing and flipping
on the trampoline in the backyard of Stornoway with his
three young sons.

In truth, Pierre Trudeau had been in power too long
to be a good Leader of the Opposition. He recited the
attacks his speech-writers gave him, he displayed his outrage and indignation, but he knew the complexities of
governing too thoroughly to be simple and effective. He
even agreed with the thrust of "short-term pain for long-
term gain" in John Crosbie's fatal budget. "He wasn't in
agony about the defeat," said Trudeau's closest friend,
Gérard Pelletier, "but he didn't adjust to the job well. And
since he wasn't thinking of a comeback, what was the use
of staying?"

Throughout 1979, more and more Liberals had also
begun to wonder why Trudeau should stay. Though he
had been a major factor in causing the federal party to
sweep Quebec in the May election, he had been an equally
major factor in the party's virtual extinction west of Winnipeg and its precipitous fall from favour in Ontario and
Atlantic Canada. The evidence suggested that for a host
of reasons Trudeau was a spent force in English Canada,
and the current wisdom was that the Liberal Party could
be rebuilt more quickly and more solidly with a new, attractive, anglophone leader such as John Turner or Donald
Macdonald, both former Ministers of Finance who had
left Trudeau's cabinet to become corporate lawyers in Toronto. Under the party's rules, Trudeau would have had
to face a vote of confidence from the membership at a
convention, and the assumption was that he would have

to fight to keep his job. But Trudeau wasn't interested in the fight or the job. He was *"disgusted"* by the speed with which some of the party had begun to unsheath their knives behind his back; he wanted to spend more time with his children; and he harboured a fantasy that he might be able to save his marriage if he got out of politics.

Even when the polls began to improve for him and his party in the autumn of 1979, he told his advisers, "You still don't understand me. That only makes it easier for me to go." When they told him that the Clark government could fall by the following summer, Trudeau merely hastened his decision to retire, in order to allow his successor room to prepare for an election. On November 21 he announced his resignation. Tributes as flowery and forgiving as eulogies were paid to him in the House of Commons and analyses as long and sober as obituaries appeared in the newspapers. Pierre Trudeau was declared politically dead, what Marshal Tito of Yugoslavia once described as "the most terrifying death of all."

Yet here he was again, less than three months later, back not only as Liberal leader but as Prime Minister. The surprise was almost as great as the pleasure for his supporters. If Trudeau himself was as surprised as he should have been, he confined the display of his feelings to the quiver of delight at the edges of his mouth and the sparkle in his intense, blue eyes. It was usual for him to try to conceal his emotions behind a face as equanimous and ambiguous as a death mask. Since adolescence he had trained himself to suppress and control the oversensitivity that had caused him so many tears and insecurities as a boy. He had hardened his character with the same resolve he had brought to shaping his sickly body into muscle and grace, though his childlike joys and childish furies remained to be betrayed by his lips and his eyes.

His self-discipline contributed to his power and charisma as a politician. It lent him mystery, dignity, and an intimidating strength on which much of the public and most of his colleagues could place their hopes for the future, their fears in times of crisis, and almost any interpretation they chose. With the high cheekbones of an aboriginal shaman, the penetrating intellect of a Jesuit priest, and the unpredictable behaviour of a Zen master, Trudeau seemed to require mystical explanations. His fans spoke of him as a saviour or a sage; journalists called him a magus, a magician, and a sorcerer in order to account for his capacity to confound, enchant, and survive; and his worst enemies concluded that he was the very Anti-Christ because the licence of his Mercedes sports car was numbered 666, the sign of the Beast in Revelations. His astonishing political resurrection in February, 1980, seemed to confirm even the most far-fetched hypothesis.

Certainly Trudeau's supporters received his dramatically understated welcome to the new decade as if it were a portentous message of hope from the Beyond. Christ's disciples could not have been happier or more amazed when He showed Himself to them again after the Resurrection. Not only was the universe unfolding as it should, Trudeau implied, but it was unfolding as he had always known it would.

To a limited extent, to use the line of Buffon that Trudeau once quoted as a personal description, the style was the man himself. But Trudeau was both more and less than his style. He was more when he used his public persona as a disguise behind which he could protect his private nature. He was less when he came to believe in his own illusions. Either way there was a lot of artifice in Pierre Trudeau's style. He enjoyed being an enigma. Sometimes he deliberately created his own contradictions, such as pirouetting for the cameras behind the back of the Queen of England. Though he was proud of the consistency of his intellectual ideas, he often took contrary positions as a technique of Socratic dialogue. He made sport in the House of Commons and with the press by giving obscure answers to clear questions; he consciously manipulated his effect on people; and he brought his love of the theatre to the crafting, delivery, and body language of his major speeches.

If his followers were willing to suspend belief and credit

their leader with wisdom, spiritual powers, or divine fortune at least, the skeptics suspected mere cleverness, the cynics presumed blatant fraud, and the more hostile gained evidence that Trudeau was a satanic force that wouldn't stay dead until someone drove a wooden stake through his heart. It wasn't just that he resembled an evil figure from a German expressionist horror film in his grimmer moments; or that he and his advisers had a reputation for deviousness and chicanery; it was also that many Canadians considered him *too smart*.

"The people hadn't loved him since 1972," said the Liberals' pollster, Martin Goldfarb. "They respected him, they were prepared to follow him, they believed he wouldn't lead them astray, they trusted that he would know what to do in a crunch; all because they had a tremendous admiration for his intellect. But they were afraid of it too. They felt he could deceive them at his will. They wanted a smart guy at the top, but they don't like smart guys. This is a country that loves loggers and hockey players who can fight, not philosophers and artists. Trudeau was truly an intellectual, and Canadians didn't know how to handle him because he wasn't a part of their psyche."

Over the years this fundamental suspicion had gained currency from the number of instances in which Trudeau and his formidable, Machiavellian strategists seemed to have outwitted their opponents and even the electorate. Many voters hadn't trusted him since the 1974 election when a ferocious Liberal attack on the unpopular Tory proposal for wage-and-price controls made it inconceivable that the Liberals themselves would introduce similar controls by the end of 1975. As a result rumours arose that somehow Trudeau had plotted his own political demise in November, 1979, as an elaborate ruse intended to clear the way for his return to power.

According to this unlikely and rather paranoid scenario, Trudeau had learned from Goldfarb's polls that the Liberals could easily win an election against the Tories, and he foresaw the possibility of defeating the government on its December budget, which was expected to be a harsh one. The evidence usually cited was contained in a speech he made at the end of October, in which he said, "We've got to throw the government out as soon as we can and get back in again." First, however, he needed to lull the Tories into a false sense of security. Secondly, he needed to silence his critics within his own party and within the two other opposition parties, for whom his continuing leadership served as an impediment to their determination to bring down Clark. So, the speculation went, he resigned, confident that if the Liberals should find themselves in an election campaign within a month, they would call him back.

Even those who didn't believe that Trudeau, however brilliant, could have anticipated what happened after his resignation credited him with recognizing and exploiting the opportunity presented by the spontaneous momentum to overthrow the Tories. They conceded that Trudeau's resignation had been sincere but assumed that he seized with great skill and delight upon the chance to reconsider it. In fact, though his key advisers such as Jim Coutts and Allan MacEachen certainly manoeuvred to direct the accidental change of circumstance toward his advantage, Trudeau himself went along with events more than he instigated them. The urge to oust the Tories originated as a madcap, intoxicated adventure among the Liberal MPs during their annual Christmas party. It was sustained by their rekindled hopes and constant ambitions; it was received with sympathy by the NDP and the Créditistes because of details in the Tory budget; and it was achieved by an accumulation of small, deadly errors on the part of the Progressive Conservative government on December 13, 1979.

Far from having devised the outcome, Trudeau was faced with one of the most difficult choices of his career: whether to remain leader or cause the party to go through a leadership contest in the middle of the election. There were powerful proponents and arguments for both sides within his caucus and the party executive, and at the grassroots. On the one hand, a new leader would have had the benefits of a fresh face, a clean record, and lots of publicity, and the Goldfarb polls indicated that any Liberal leader could beat Joe Clark. "At least we can provide a leader. The Tories can't," Goldfarb told Coutts on the phone from Utah, where the pollster had been skiing Election Hill all day. On the other hand, his data showed that Trudeau was still the best candidate, and many were worried that a convention would be divisive in terms of party unity, chaotic in terms of party policy, and costly in terms of the time and money diverted from the national and local campaigns. While these debates raged around him, Trudeau was torn by conflicts within himself too. His duty to the party if it should want him to stay, his loyalty to his friends who were lobbying on his behalf, and his concern for the country on the eve of the Quebec referendum were checked by his personal indifference to being Prime Minister again and his overwhelming desire, as a single parent, to guide his sons through their formative years.

"Sometimes, in the furthest stretches of my imagination, I can imagine someone else being Prime Minister," he said with mock hyperbole during a long, intimate telephone call to Gérard Pelletier in Paris, "but I can't imagine anyone else being the father to my children."

Pelletier argued without compromise that Trudeau had no choice. "You're not free, Pierre. You have to stay."

At one point in the conversation, Trudeau confessed to a more selfish concern, his pride. "I don't relish the thought of being beaten twice in one year," he said.

The pride of winning was always a greater motivation within Trudeau than the lust for power, though observers often confused these two deadly sins because the cold-eyed competitiveness of one closely resembled the cynical tactics of the other. Trudeau was genuinely ambivalent about power. Seldom was it able to realize the principles and dreams he valued, and its perks hardly compensated for the loss of his most cherished possession, his personal freedom. Indeed, part of both his strength and his weakness as Prime Minister was the impression he gave that he could walk away quite happily at any moment from his colleagues, his party, and the Canadian people. Perceived as philosophical disinterestedness, that impression contributed to his charisma in the 1968 election. Perceived as lack of caring, it had almost destroyed him in 1972. However, as Trudeau himself noted after that near-defeat, "I don't mind leaving, but I don't like being thrown out."

His almost neurotic need to best everyone, whether in a debate or on a ski-hill, was the driving force that had kept him in office for eleven years. Losing power in 1979 had required some psychological adjustments (though more for the disruption of a decade of habits and comforts than for the loss of glory and authority), but the pain had been in the wounded ego.

Now the numbers and his own confidence assured him that he could win the election. However, his thirst to erase his humiliation by defeating Clark in a rematch only developed after his advisers, his caucus, and the party implored him to stay on as leader. Trudeau remembered a Chinese tale of a man who would only serve if the emperor asked him on bended knees three times. He made a similar condition, in order to be guaranteed full support and to be able to share the blame in case of failure, and he received the three petitions. Even then he had almost backed off, to the point of going into his press conference on December 18 with a statement of refusal alongside the statement of acceptance in his pocket.

If he hadn't returned for the sake of power or vengeance, he hadn't returned for the sake of history either. He believed he had done his best between 1968 and 1979; he had done better than he thought the opposition would have done; and he disliked looking backwards. "I've moved a few pieces of furniture," he said, "and that's enough." Few of his political obituaries agreed, however. They surveyed Trudeau's three terms and generally found them wanting. Some commentators found fault with what he had done: the creation of Petro-Canada and the Foreign Investment Review Agency (FIRA), the imposition of wage-and-price controls and the War Measures Act, the increase in the size of the bureaucracy and federal spending, or the introduction of the metric system and a tax on capital gains. Most concluded, however, that Trudeau had changed very little in a decade for someone who had come into office with so much new hope, so much good will, and so much strength. Even his major accomplishments, such as official bilingualism, an energy strategy, government reorganization, and a series of foreign policy initiatives, were either in jeopardy or in disrepute.

The notion that Pierre Trudeau had done too little must have come as a rude shock to those who thought him a rabid socialist and an autocratic centralist when they threw him out of office in 1979. Their thinking was rooted in some fact as well as a great deal of partisan bias, particular interest, ideological faith, and personal aversion; but the prevailing consensus was that Trudeau had been an intellectual who preferred to discuss rather than act, a pragmatist who opted for political expediency over national purpose, and a dilettante who threw away his chance to lead Canada to the greatness he seemed to have promised in 1968.

That consensus was shared by many influential Liberals during 1979 when they reassessed their time in government from the distant gloom of the opposition benches. They were haunted by all the time and opportunities wasted in cabinet committee meetings, federal-provincial conferences, consultations with business and labour, departmental task forces, and so on. They were angered by all the compromises that had weakened right actions and all the concessions for which there had been no thanks in the end. They were annoyed by the months of drift, the petty quarrels, the intellectual burn-out, and the periods when the Prime Minister himself was allowed to become overpowered by a strange kind of lethargy.

Even Trudeau, who wasn't given to hindsight or regrets, grew discouraged during the Clark interregnum by the vulnerability of the achievements that had mattered the most to him and to which he had devoted the most time and care, especially those in the area of national unity. He had entered federal politics in 1965 for two primary reasons: "One was to make sure that Quebec didn't leave Canada through separatism, and the other was to make sure that Canada wouldn't shove Quebec out through narrow-mindedness." Yet by 1979 the Parti Québécois government was preparing its referendum on sovereignty-association, Ottawa's two concerted efforts to bring full authority over the constitution home from Great Britain had failed, and the federal government had slipped out of favour as both a force for national cohesion and an instrument for social change. Meanwhile, the provinces had become powerful and fractious fiefdoms; Trudeau's long-standing desire for a constitutional charter that would protect individual minority and language rights forever had been blocked by provincial premiers wanting more powers; and restrictions on the status of English in Quebec and a bitter dispute about the use of French by air-traffic controllers had demonstrated the fragility of the national vision Trudeau had hoped to leave as his legacy.

"He had quelled much of the social unrest, but he hadn't put his changes into a lasting framework," said Senator Jerry Grafstein, a Toronto lawyer and Liberal advertising consultant. "It must have gnawed at him that he hadn't been able to reconstruct the legal structure as a means of reconstructing Canada's social values." Indeed, just before the 1979 election Grafstein had startled Trudeau by asking him over dinner at 24 Sussex Drive, "What are you going to be remembered for?"

II

There were countless practical factors to account for the terrible question—including the global economy, the explosion of Quebec nationalism, the effect of world oil prices on the Canadian West, and the personal unhappiness of Margaret Trudeau—but any understanding of the prelude to 1980 has to begin with the political philosophy of Pierre Elliott Trudeau. After all, he was an intellectual who valued ideas and had spent almost two decades nurturing them in the hothouse atmosphere of universities and small-edition journals. They were rare in Canadian politics for their clarity, their sturdiness, their balance, and their ambition.

Intellectually Trudeau was neither a socialist, a centralist, a nationalist, nor an autocrat. He was a classic nineteenth-century liberal who cherished the freedom of the individual, the decentralization of power, and democratic rights. His succinct summary of his ideology was, "Create counterweights." He even applied that to his own personality, in which his egocentric lust for liberty warred constantly with his strong sense of responsibility as a citizen and discipline as an individual. The emphasis he placed on deliberate counterweights went a long way toward explaining the many apparent contradictions in his character, his words, and his actions over the years. In fact, Trudeau was by temperament an individualist and an iconoclast well before he developed the philosophical reasons for being so. He liked to argue, to tease and provoke, and he liked to be different in his opinions and his style. Competing against himself was more attractive than team sports, and as a teenager Cyrano de Bergerac's famous braggadocio penetrated his heart and remained in his head:

> . . . But to go
> Free of the filthy world, to sing, to be
> Blessed with a voice vibrating virility,
> Blessed with an eye equipped for looking at
> Things as they really are, cocking my hat
> Where I please, at a word—at a yes or no—
> Fighting or writing: this is the true life. So
> I go along any road under my moon,
> Careless of glory, indifferent to the boon
> Or bane of fortune, without hope, without fear,
> Writing only the words down that I hear
> Here—and saying, with a sort of modesty,
> "My heart, be satisfied with what you see
> And smell and taste in your own garden—weeds,
> As much as fruit and flowers." If fate succeeds
> In wresting some small triumph for me—well,

I render nothing unto Caesar, sell
No moiety of my merit to the world.
I loathe the parasite liana curled
About the oak trunk. I myself am a tree,
Not high perhaps, not beautiful, but free:
My flesh deciduous, but the enduring bone
Of spirit tough, indifferent, and alone!

There was a lot of Cyrano de Bergerac in Pierre Trudeau: the intellectual and physical dexterity, the will to excel in everything, the delight in taking on a hundred armed men single-handedly, the self-hatred and self-doubt expressed as gratuitous aggression and marvellous eloquence, the fear of showing true feelings and being rejected, the pathos of finally risking love and losing, the irresistible charms and the disagreeable vanities. Above all, there was the self-conscious panache symbolized by the white plumes on Cyrano's hat and the red rose on Trudeau's lapel. Like the wild Gascon, Trudeau was quick to take offence and always ready to deliver a punishment more severe than the crime; but at heart he was a mushy romantic who used his fierce reactions to guard a very tender ego and loved to recite Rostand's sentimental alexandrines.

Essentially Trudeau was a loner, afraid to make commitments, too proud to ask for help or favours, and uncomfortable in any situation where someone seemed to have something over him. It was as if he never quite grew up emotionally after the usual stage of adolescent rebellion. He himself seemed to confirm that by linking his lifelong dislike of authority to the sudden death, when Trudeau was fifteen, of his much-adored father, a loud and colourful *bon vivant* who, Trudeau remembered, was himself compared to Cyrano by a friend. "Probably I lost the object of my revolt in the family and didn't have to fight my father," he told a BBC interviewer in 1975, "so I went out and fought other people like my teachers, or the church, or politicians, or whatever happened to be established." More likely, the loss placed a permanent rage in his soul against the unjust universe that had caused a shy boy such traumatic pain. It made him reluctant to ever again entrust so much love and respect to any authority that might prove as impermanent and hurtful as a father.

Whatever its psychological roots, Trudeau's personal instinct for individualism found its intellectual and political context in liberalism. At Collège Jean-de-Brébeuf he was heavily influenced by a Franco-Manitoban Jesuit, Father Jean Bernier, who introduced him to the writings of Locke, Tocqueville, Acton, and Jefferson and preached the liberal values of democracy, pluralism, federalism, rationality, and tolerance. At Harvard and the London School of Economics he probed into the tenets of American and British liberalism with all the enthusiasm and conviction of a religious convert. At the Sorbonne he discovered a way of integrating his new-found secular religion with his old faith through the Catholic liberalism of Emmanuel Mounier, the French intellectual whose concept of personalism closely resembled individualism with a social conscience.

During the 1950s he became associated with the Co-operative Commonwealth Federation (CCF), the forerunner of the New Democratic Party. He knocked on doors for CCF candidates, his essays showed up in books put together by prominent CCF thinkers, and he allied himself with a number of CCFers in a left-wing group called *le rassemblement*. But he never joined the party and he always seemed ideologically uncomfortable with it. He criticized its bias toward the centralization of power in the Canadian federal system. He worried about government bureaucracies, had a rich man's respect for the benefits of capitalism's marketplace, and often wondered about the efficacy of nationalization, to the extent of doubting the economic advantages when Quebec proposed to nationalize its hydroelectric companies in 1962.

On the other hand, he wasn't afraid to have the state intervene when necessary for good liberal reasons, such as providing the social conditions that would give weak individuals as much chance as strong ones to fulfil themselves. He had been impressed by the social security programs he saw in England, for example, and he understood the importance of an active, intelligent state in modern Keynesian economics. He also realized that the Quebec state could be particularly helpful in bringing French Canadians into the twentieth century, since they had so few strongholds in the private sector. When spoken in Duplessis's time these ideas made Trudeau sound a lot more socialistic than he ever was. In truth, though he never shook the radical reputation that resulted, he never bought socialism as a solution for Quebec or Canada.

Because Trudeau was obsessed above all else with making Quebec democratic, he tended to take his allies in that battle pretty much as he found them. "Democracy first!" he yelled in 1958, and it wasn't surprising that most of the people who rallied round his cry were union members, left-wing academics, journalists, English-speaking CCFers, and everyone else with little to lose by opposing Duplessis. In those days the federal Liberals promised little in terms of democracy and the provincial ones were soon caught up with Quebec nationalism. In Trudeau's eyes, they were "content to cultivate the ignorance and prejudice" of French Canadians and displayed either "brutal cynicism," "selfish docility," or trembling anticipation before "the rouged face of Power." On the other hand, the CCF in Montreal contained more Liberals-in-a-hurry and Tories-with-a-conscience than Marxists, and it offered such idealistic, open-minded, and brilliant personalities as Frank Scott and Eugene Forsey. By 1965, however, the NDP became soft on the issue of special status for Quebec, the federal Liberal Party had undergone a series of democratic and progressive reforms in the wake of its election defeats, and Trudeau felt it was time to counter the weight of Quebec City by joining Jean Marchand and Gérard Pelletier in the Liberal caucus in Ottawa.

If he felt awkward at all among those he had once called "trained donkeys," it may have been because his liberalism was actually purer than theirs. Classic liberalism and Canadian liberalism (as defined in the introduction) were like kissing cousins, obviously related, comfortable together at the family feast, but distant. Trudeau stood out immediately in Pearson's party. As a back-bencher his individualistic spirit was symbolized by his wearing sandals and ascots in the House of Commons. As Minister of Justice in 1967–1968 his ideals were epitomized by his famous phrase, "The state has no place in the bedrooms of the nation." He envisaged democracy as a contract between the state and each individual, not as the back-room cacophony of interest groups shouting their demands to elected representatives and wrestling each other for all they could get. Instead of justice, reason, and rights, Trudeau found the strong pushing aside the weak, the system muddling through from circumstance to crisis, and the many excluded from the process by the few who spoke only on behalf of their own interests. Too much power was concentrated; too many limits were placed on the principles of majority rule and popular sovereignty; and government had been reduced to playing the role of an unreliable Santa Claus.

For their part, many Pearsonian Liberals were suspicious of Pierre Trudeau once they got past his obvious intelligence and his useful Quebec bashing. All his talk of the individual, decentralized power, and the end of the nation-state may have come from the left in Quebec in the 1950s, but because of the differences in Canada's two political cultures, it certainly sounded as if it were coming from the right in English Canada in the 1960s. Many important Liberals, busy trading goodies among provinces, corporations, unions, and departments, must have thanked their stars that Canadians were screaming too loudly with Trudeaumania in 1968 to hear what the guy was saying.

"We are not promising things for everybody and we are seeing great visions," he told an interviewer at the time. "We are trying to make the people of the country understand that if they are to be governed well, they will have to participate in the governing; that there are no magic solutions; that there is no charismatic leader with a magic wand which will produce great solutions; that the solutions for this country will be as difficult as for any other country; and that if we want to sell our produce, if we want to progress in terms of our productivity, we will have to invent new things and we will have to find new markets and fight for them."

Yet Trudeaumania was a mass lunacy for a charismatic leader with a magic wand. English Canada and French Canada were expressing a desire to be led to goodness, if not greatness. Far from being frightened by his "socialist" background, they ignored his classic liberal tenets and fastened onto his strength, his commitment to social justice and minority rights, and his faith in Canada—all of which aroused their deference to authority, collective sharing, and national community. The Canadian political universe revolved around him. The people looked to *him* for answers; the party wanted access to *him* more than it wanted policy forums; and power became concentrated quickly and inevitably wherever *he* was. *His* agenda, whether official bilingualism or regional development or the recognition of China, became the national agenda; and *he* became the lightning rod for dissatisfaction.

"In Canada more than anywhere else," a political scientist wrote, "it is possible to define a party as being a body of supporters following a given leader." That was written in 1944. Television and centralized organizational techniques merely accentuated what was already there. Any Prime Minister controls the party policy, the party resources, and hundreds of senior appointments; he has all the information and prestige of the office; and since there is rarely a formal vote in cabinet meetings, he is the final arbiter of all important decisions. Though there is plenty of evidence that Diefenbaker and Pearson hoarded power more greedily than Trudeau, Trudeau looked more powerful because of his intriguing personality, his formidable intellect, his ferocious skill in argument, and his conviction about several critical issues such as bilingualism and law reform. Most of his ministers knew that they owed their seats in the cabinet and probably their seats in the Commons to Pierre Trudeau, and if that didn't make them deferential, they often deferred to his logic and knowledge.

Trudeau didn't cower from what was handed him. There were a few things he wanted to do and he set about doing them, using the good democratic argument that the purpose of government was to govern. "If you don't agree with me," he told Canadians, "you have to change your leader." He wanted to shore up the weakened central state, not by taking power from the provinces but by bolstering Ottawa's for the sake of preserving the union. He had been appalled by the haphazard, dysfunctional, undemocratic improvisations by which Pearson had ruled, making special deals in the hallways, greasing the squeakiest wheels, and putting off decisions. Trudeau wanted to introduce more planning and rationality into the process; but he knew from the start that he couldn't expect those reforms and any collegial consensus to relieve him from the task of making the toughest decisions. Thus, he launched a severe war against inflation and began the campaign for official bilingualism almost as soon as he got into office.

Nevertheless, the main thrust of his first term from 1968 to 1972 was the decentralization of power. Often that was obscured by his charisma, his passion for winning debates, his fondness for testing his will, and the presidential myths perpetuated by the opposition, the media, and disaffected Liberals; sometimes it was obscured by Trudeau's reluctance to alter course once a destination had been agreed upon. (Pearson had been a more unilaterial and arbitrary leader, but he changed his mind just as unilaterally and arbitrarily and so appeared the very soul of sweet conciliation.) In fact, Trudeau was uncomfortable in the role of leader. Most of his life he had purposefully avoided it. His election as head of the Liberal Party had caused him to laugh with shock and amazement, and he was acutely sensitive about his lack of experience and contacts in the party and across the country. Moreover, in his liberalism the leader should be an educator more than a boss, a guide who frequently takes his eyes from the horizon ahead to make sure the people are still close behind. "What do the citizens want?" he said. "That is the question a democratic government must constantly ask itself."

Many of his initiatives were exercises in pushing power away from himself and Ottawa. The fight against inflation centred on slashing the size and expenses of government. The provinces were given new authority, new responsibilities, and new money. Parliament was reformed in order to be more efficient and more relevant. The law reforms focussed on protecting and freeing the individual from the state. Every department became engaged in wide consultations, white papers, and task forces. To combat the centralizing effects of planning, the provinces were encouraged to establish their own planning tools, a host of intergovernmental agencies were set up, and Ottawa's internal system was democratized by changes to the cabinet and the bureaucracy.

In those changes, begun under Pearson, ministers lost some of their power and independence to a series of cabinet committees, while the committees in turn were checked by the active, well-briefed participation of the ministers who sat on them. Critical departmental decisions were to be reached collectively rather than unilaterally; trade-offs were to be done openly and rationally rather than secretly and arbitrarily; and the decision-makers were to be the elected officials rather than a cabal of civil servants (which had been invariably anglophone, Trudeau noticed). Every major issue, and many not-so-major ones, had to run a gauntlet of many studies, many voices, many debates, many *counterweights*.

"In the 1950s," said Senator Michael Pitfield, the former Clerk of the Privy Council, "the officials assumed a certain authority to make decisions. They didn't anguish about that; they just bloody well went ahead and did it. Under Mr. Diefenbaker the cabinet broke down. It was meeting two or four times a week from two in the afternoon until ten at night, all the ministers talked and they all went on and on, decisions weren't reached or the bureaucrats never found out about them. Based on his experience as a civil servant and as Prime Minister, Mr. Pearson launched a reform of the system, with the objective of putting ministers in charge of an orderly process. He got

too many cabinet committees, no one knew what was decided, and the ministers were overloaded, but 50 per cent
of what became known as the Trudeau system was accomplished and 75 per cent was designed under Mr. Pearson.
Mr. Trudeau continued with them, first as an act of faith
and then from conviction based on his own experience.

"By the 1970s the officials tried *not* to exercise their
influence but focussed on trying to get ministers to make
decisions. The potential capacity of a minister to participate
in collective decision making was never higher than in Mr.
Trudeau's regime. The potential of ministers to make their
own decisions was also greater, and ministers were encouraged to do so, though when in doubt (which was most
of the time) many of them preferred to get a collective
decision. The capacity of certain ministers to control the
agenda was consequentially reduced, but the reduction
was virtually exclusively with ministers of central agency
departments such as Finance and External Affairs. Even
then, if those ministers wanted to put their foot down,
they had the trumps to do it, and they were trumping and
trumping and trumping."

The new system even constrained some of the Prime
Minister's clout in favour of the ministers, for he had to
give up much of the private deal making and residual
decision making that had been the mainstay of Pearson's
power. More decisions were left to committees of which
Trudeau wasn't even a member; and when he was chairman, he often submerged his leadership beneath the tedious, time-consuming process of seeking a consensus
through well-reasoned and well-informed discussion.

"Despite his reputation for arrogance and authoritar-
ianism, Trudeau almost never railroaded his cabinet into
doing what he wanted," Gérard Pelletier said, echoing the
opinions of many other veteran ministers, including Marc
Lalonde, Donald Macdonald, and Jean Chrétien. "Pearson
was certainly less democratic. Trudeau wanted the *team* to
govern."

Pelletier's favourite example concerned an argument
in cabinet over the treatment of Chilean refugees after the

overthrow of Salvador Allende. Being leftists, many of them were having difficulties with Canadian immigration officers and the RCMP. Pelletier was pressing for a more lenient attitude, but he had to take on almost all his colleagues. It was so tough that he came close to resigning. Meanwhile, Trudeau gave no hint of his own opinion. Eventually Pelletier was able to prevail. After the battle was won, he asked Trudeau, "Would you have come to my rescue if I had been about to lose?"

"Yes," Trudeau replied, "but this is much better. You have built a consensus."

The operative slogan of the period was "Participatory Democracy." It was a vague phrase, promising more than it ever would (or could) deliver, but it reflected Trudeau's ideals. Somehow citizens were to put more into governing than a ballot every four years. The task forces, regional desks, white papers, and party conferences were to engage the grassroots in dialogues about government policy, with the Prime Minister himself at times playing the part of Socrates. Ottawa funded its own extraparliamentary opposition, from native associations to rebellious youths, to keep the democratic pot boiling. Even the expansion of the Prime Minister's Office (PMO), which was seen as a sign of Trudeau's presidential ambitions, was intended to serve as yet another counterweight. Other Prime Ministers had been able to use their contacts in the party, the government, and the nation to gather demands and satisfy them, and to balance the narrow views of the bureaucracy. To compensate for his lack of networks, Trudeau built a PMO to initiate and assess policies from a political perspective, offer alternatives, and be his eyes and ears to the people.

In practice, little of this decentralization worked very well. The PMO isolated Trudeau from inputs other than its own and soon entered into power struggles with the party executive, senior bureaucrats, MPs, and cabinet ministers. Few Liberals were interested in academic debates about policy, and those few rapidly became angry and frustrated when the government chose not to act upon their ideas because it had broader interests and other view-points to consider. As for the public at large, democratic participation didn't have much of a history in either En-glish-Canadian liberalism or French-Canadian conserva-tism. Those at the top—including most of the cabinet and Liberal brass—weren't too excited about it for obvious rea-sons, while those underneath didn't know what to make of it. They were accustomed to letting others run the show; they wanted answers, not provocative and complex mus-ings; or they wasted a lot of the taxpayers' patience with irresponsible shit disturbing. Not unexpectedly the only ones to rise to the challenge were those interest groups whose elites had clear positions to defend and some ex-perience in confronting governments. The results were increased political headaches, the appearance of chaos and indecision in Ottawa, and more talk than action. Mean-while, the cabinet committee system also became bogged down by too much talk, too many studies, and too many counterweights.

By 1972 Canadians were bitterly disappointed. In the euphoria of national pride and energy following Expo 67 and Canada's centennial, they felt they were giving an active, reform-minded leader a rare majority. They had expected much more than shrugs, sophistries that would have made Socrates himself reach for the hemlock, and a vicious jump in unemployment. The economy was starting to fall apart, the country was more divided than ever on linguistic and regional issues, and the Prime Minister only seemed interested in talking on a philosophical plane about the next century. Trudeau assumed that the reaction against him came because he had done too much. In fact, it came because he had failed to apply his power to progressive purposes. Most people weren't bothered by the growth of the PMO or the burst of government activity—indeed, Ca-nadians never showed more esteem for Trudeau than when he was his most dictatorial, dealing with the Quebec ter-rorist crisis in 1970—but they were angered by his abstract remoteness from their problems.

The gap between his ideals and reality came as a rude

shock to Trudeau when he barely got back into power with a minority government in 1972. During the campaign he had given what he considered some of the best speeches of his career, full of bold new thoughts and democratic principles, but no one listened until he began waving his arms around and behaving like a politician. "I'd almost say my faith in politics, my faith in the democratic process has changed a bit," he said shortly after that election. "I used to think it would be sufficient to put a reasonable proposition to a person, for the person to look at it reasonably, without passion, but that's obviously not true."

When Pierre Trudeau left the intellectual world for the world of politics, he consciously resolved to set aside the rules of the one game and take up the rules of the other. Apparently the new rules included a greater concentration of authority than he wanted, more elite accommodation than he cared for, more symbols and emotions than he knew, and more concern for winning than being right. "If I wanted to be right, I'd have stayed in university," he said. And, after assuring his shaken faith that this too was democracy, he set about to become a Canadian liberal.

For instruction he brought in from the cold Pearson's former campaign manager, Keith Davey. Davey started from the assumption that Trudeau "didn't know what the Liberal Party was all about," and he boiled his lesson down to three basic points: Trudeau had to act like a leader, Trudeau had to act like a progressive, and Trudeau had to act like a party man. That implied less long-term planning and more short-term benefits, less attention to ideals and eggheads and more attention to polls and patronage. In other words, "muddling through" was a perfectly legitimate, perhaps even desirable approach to public policy for a diverse country in a random universe.

As a result, the cabinet became more politically aware and the PMO became more politically preoccupied. Soon the entire government was bumbling along in the old, familiar way from concession to trade-off to crisis, though now it bumbled in collective committees and with more sophisticated rationalizations. It was called *pragmatism*, the philosophy of being practical; and in case Trudeau hadn't guessed its direction, the New Democratic Party showed him by holding the balance of power in the House of Commons between 1972 and 1974.

Spending his way to power or prosperity had never been Trudeau's preferred route. In his approach to public policy as in his personal life, he was more a parsimonious Elliott than a good-time Charlie. Even in the 1950s, when he was advocating a more active state, he had warned that "unless the economy is fundamentally sound, a strong, progressive social policy can be neither conceived nor applied." In 1968 he reaffirmed his belief that "we have enough of this free stuff." In his first term he froze government spending and cut 5,000 jobs from the public service, and his government proposed to end the universality of family allowance payments as a means of getting more money to the needy (until it was forced to back down under political pressure). Even as late as 1973 he said, "If a government wants to do the popular things, it will ruin the economy— real quick." It turned out, it seemed, to be the last, desperate cry of a man drowning in the pragmatic ocean.

After 1972 Trudeau—and his Minister of Finance, John Turner—spun round to stimulate the economy. Federal spending soared, deficits appeared, taxes were indexed to the rate of inflation and cut, ministers were judged by the expansion of their departments and their programs, and both pensions and family allowances were increased. In the same period the Foreign Investment Review Agency (FIRA) was created and, as part of the Liberals' response to the 1973 energy crisis in which the Organization of Petroleum-Exporting Countries (OPEC) trebled the world price of oil, Petro-Canada was conceived. Indeed, Trudeau's imaginative and confident handling of the energy crisis probably contributed more to the resurrection of his reputation than Ottawa's spending.

When the crisis hit, the cabinet flew around in circles trying to find consensus for a strategy. Finally Trudeau threw up his hands and said, "Well, you force me to do something. The Minister of Energy and I will go into a room and we'll produce a policy." There wasn't a whisper of protest—"because we were convinced of our impotence," one minister said. Trudeau had discovered the limits of collegiality. Huddled with his advisers, he also discovered that the situation demanded a highly interventionist solution, complete with price freezes, regional subsidies and public money for a pipeline extension and tar-sands developments, as well as for the state oil company. The package was nationalistic, progressive, thoroughly pragmatic, and extremely popular. It became a major factor in the re-election of the Liberals in July, 1974, with a majority.

Just as Trudeau was adapting to the old game, however, the old game was becoming harder and harder to sustain. Since the end of the Second World War it had been based on prosperity, growth, classic macroeconomic management, and social stability. In essence, there had been enough money to keep almost everyone happy. But after 1974 it was no longer possible for Ottawa to buy consensus and peace. Although the possible causes were hidden in the arcana of economic theory, the effects were obvious: double-digit inflation, climbing unemployment, declining productivity, mounting costs for new and inherited programs, diminishing investment, and rising debt. Even Keynesian fine tuning had broken down, and no one was certain what to put in its place. At the same time, upheavals involving energy, technology, and the environment threatened both jobs and profits.

Yet the public had grown used to a constant increase in services and benefits from their government. Businessmen wanted their grants and tax breaks; unions struck a record number of times for higher wages and job security; and women and students demanded a place in the work force. Meanwhile, the plight of the poor and the aged showed few signs of amelioration. "This revolution of rising expectations," as Trudeau once called it, added fuel to the fires of inflation, deficits, and political discontent already burning through the system. Trade-offs became tougher because now there were real losers rather than various degrees of winners.

"The structure was no longer capable of supporting the demands made upon it," said Michael Pitfield, who became the senior public servant in 1974, "not simply in terms of economics, but in terms of fundamental premises, techniques of public administration, manpower, and even tenets of political philosophy. The mechanisms became more and more incomprehensible and so, inaccessible and so, ineffective. Failing to produce despite skyrocketing costs, they simply laid the foundation for cynicism regarding 'big government.'

"Because the costs of these policies could not be met even by increased taxation, they also fanned the fires of inflation. This, in turn, undermined the wealth of the middle class and the confidence of everyone. The mid-1970s saw a classic explosion of inflation, a blowout of expectations followed by a fierce battle for shares. It had been building for decades. It had to come."

The most dramatic indication of the underlying muddle came in October, 1975, when Trudeau suddenly reversed his election position and imposed wage-and-price controls. He did it against his will and despite his pride, because he had been convinced by the Department of Finance that the traditional fiscal and monetary tools were unable to break the demand psychology of rampant inflation. He had been hoping that business and labour would agree to voluntary restraints, which appealed to his ideals of individual responsibility, social frugality, and decentralized power. Those elites, however, couldn't even be accommodated by John Turner before he resigned as Minister of Finance. So, as he had done in the energy crisis the year before, Trudeau went along with direct and rather heavy-handed intervention, though to ease his concerns about creating a bureaucratic monster and to retain some of his credibility, the controls were more limited in their range than the bureaucrats had first proposed.

Generally, while trying to get a national consensus on how to manage and direct the Canadian economy in a dark new world, Trudeau just floundered through his third term and got nothing. Wonderful industrial strategies were drawn up and discarded as impractical. Dramatic spending cuts followed dramatic tax cuts with little obvious effect or correlation. The government virtually stopped growing, pet programs were axed, the private sector was lavished with incentives and consulted regularly, but there were few new ideas, no will, and little understanding.

In fact, after getting a strong mandate in 1974 for showing the kind of leadership Canadians had wanted since 1968, Trudeau then took what one aide described as "a holiday for a year." Finally Gérard Pelletier had to send him a stern letter rebuking him for his lethargy. "Thanks," the Prime Minister replied, "I needed a kick in the pants."

Into the power vacuum created by Trudeau's abdication of authority had stepped two non-elected officials: Michael Pitfield, who was in effect the deputy minister of Trudeau's own department, the Privy Council Office (PCO), and Jim Coutts, a Pearson veteran who took charge of the PMO as Trudeau's Principal Secretary in 1975. Both were not yet forty when they assumed their jobs, both idolized the Prime Minister, and both dedicated themselves to serving him. In most ways, however, they were as unlike as Mutt and Jeff. Coutts was as short as Pitfield was tall, as blond as Pitfield was dark, as funny as Pitfield was intense, as street-smart as Pitfield was bookish, as folksy as Pitfield was patrician, and as young for his years as Pitfield was old. Together they made a formidable duo, with Coutts giving Trudeau the short-term, usually four-year, political "optic" and Pitfield providing the long-term, usually seven-year, bureaucratic perspective.

"But there was so much crossover that I couldn't say the PMO would only deal with ministers while the PCO would only deal with deputies," Coutts explained. "So I made an iron-clad arrangement with Michael. Both of us would cover the whole range, but we would tell each other what we were doing, so that there'd be no surprises. If the PMO wanted one thing and the PCO wanted another, we argued out our cases in front of the Prime Minister. It worked very well."

It may have worked well as far as they were concerned,

but both men were soon seen widely as the personifications of what was wrong with Trudeau's third term. While Coutts's good intentions had been to rebuild the Liberal networks and shape the PMO into a smaller, more efficient switchboard between the Prime Minister and all the other players, he quickly became the target of all those who couldn't get through to Trudeau, couldn't get Trudeau to their fund-raisers, and were fed up with Trudeau's aimless and cerebral inertia. To an extent, Coutts suffered the fate of every hatchet-man and food taster. He didn't help himself by developing an extremely partisan and rather ruthless fascination with gamesmanship. Beneath his elfish appearance and charming sense of humour, many people discovered a sly, tough-minded operator who was into everything. Since no one could be sure when he was speaking for himself and when he was speaking for Trudeau, the cautious deferred to him resentfully, the strong resisted him carefully, and the hostile attacked him as a safer way of attacking the Prime Minister.

Pitfield met a similar reaction for similar reasons. He was close to Trudeau personally as well as professionally, though closer in myth than in reality because of Trudeau's incapacity for regular friendship. Both were basically loners who had lost their fathers when young, children of privilege who were devoted to public life and social justice, and rationalists who were intrigued by abstract ideas. Both were slightly eccentric, sometimes aloof to the point of rudeness, sometimes delightful, and despite first impressions, essentially oversensitive and insecure. Trudeau, whose mind usually functioned more like a senior bureaucrat's than a politician's, was attracted by Pitfield's integrity, his hard work, his broad view, and his seriousness of purpose. They also shared a belief in systematic government and a vision of a united Canada.

Pitfield discovered endless ways to make himself useful. He took from the Prime Minister's shoulders many of the petty trade-offs and interdepartmental squabbles that had weighed upon Trudeau's predecessors. He helped to keep the cabinet united—a major preoccupation of every

Prime Minister—by coordinating and compromising in advance of decisions. He strengthened the voices of weak ministries against the strong, particularly the Department of Finance which never forgave him for absconding to the PCO with many of the planning and priority powers it had once held. Above all, he interposed himself between the politicians, whose interests were often self-serving and narrow-minded, and the bureaucrats, who had their own interests at heart.

According to Michael Kirby, who worked closely with Pitfield before both were appointed to the Senate, "The brilliance of Michael Pitfield was to provide the Prime Minister with a source of advice on all major issues that was distinct from that which emanated from either the cabinet or the bureaucracy. It was an objective analysis that prevented Trudeau from being the captive of either the public servants or the ministers who wanted to sell a particular point of view."

Brilliant perhaps, but it exposed him to criticism from almost every faction. Though Pitfield hadn't invented the cabinet committee system, he became one of the strongest defenders of its value for planning and coordination, for diffusing power and encouraging democratic responsibility. It accomplished most of its original purposes: more ministerial control over every decision, the better ordering of priorities among programs, and a government agenda with a more forward-looking aspect. The costs were great, however. Decisions were slowed down and diluted by the process. The plethora of new voices and new power centres created a destabilizing atmosphere. Strong ministers were outraged to see their former authority emasculated, and all ministers were harmed by spending more time in committees and on paperwork than in their offices and with their constituents. Few missed the fact that one of the chief beneficiaries of the "Pitfield system" in terms of power was Pitfield's Privy Council Office.

As the central clearing house for the government's activities and documents, it was able to influence the inputs and outputs by design or accident in a way that amounted to real decision making. Ministries felt their projects could be made or broken by the PCO, and some of them looked upon the bureaucrats in their committee meetings as "Pitfield's spies," even though the reforms had been heavily weighted to check bureaucratic power plays. In some cases planning and priority exercises pushed aside decision making altogether, until chaos sent the best-laid plans awry, forcing the system to resort to old-fashioned, Pearsonian crisis management.

"In the end politics comes down to debates about specifics," Michael Kirby said. "Broad statements of objectives that aren't themselves operational aren't much help. Yet to get a consensus we had to go to a level of generality that wasn't operational. Everyone could agree on the desire for a just society or equality for women or a fair oil price, for example, but once we got to the hard means, we discovered in the paper all the cracks that we had tried to cover over by going to generalities."

Jealousy and rivalry added the personal dimension to the flaws in the system. While ministers and departments slogged through the democratic ooze, all chained together and trying to get a consensus about where to go, they imagined Pitfield and Trudeau sitting in a comfy room beside a crackling fire and plotting the fate of the nation like two Fabian dons. Ironically, since no man revered democratic participation and an objective civil service with more conviction or sincerity, Pitfield was looked upon as mandarin power reincarnate and living proof of Michels's Iron Law, "Who says organization says oligarchy."

"Between a third and a half of that was a question of blaming the messenger," Pitfield said. "The rules were designed for the ministers to have their way in every respect over officials, but they always needed to convince their colleagues. When they couldn't do that, they blamed the officials. Also there was a strong Prime Minister whom no one was going to tackle. When you can't tackle the central man, the best thing to do is to tackle the people around him. Of course, officials do have influence, but maybe we would have served our ministers better if we had made more of the decisions. We were mindful not to."

In fact, the problem wasn't Pitfield's skulduggeries. Though he may have gone overboard in his respect for rational plans and wasn't beyond playing games for his own purposes, his intent had been liberal decentralization. If the bureaucracy had become politicized or the politicians bureaucratized, it was another triumph of pragmatism over ideals. In practice, the elected have to work closely and in harmony with their unelected officials. The former bring the needs and wishes of the people to a generally isolated bureaucracy, but the latter bring an extraordinary amount of information and direction to the implementation of those needs and wishes. Just as Trudeau found the limits to consensus in cabinet and learned to get his way, he found the limits to debate in government and learned to end-run his own regime.

"The objective of democracy," Pitfield said, "is to approximate the extreme where decision making is distributed among as large a number as possible in a decentralized system where the decisions to be made have been sorted and allocated according to weight and consequentiality. But that objective is forever eluding the system, because it's so hard to sort decisions, because people lust for power, because people huddle together around a man on a white horse when there's trouble. If you don't constantly set your shoulder against those tendencies, the whole history of civilization shows an inevitable narrowing to the other extreme where decisions are made by a small number of players in a highly centralized, highly discretionary system."

For much of his third term, however, Trudeau stuck to his principles and his lassitude. He really only roused himself when the very unity of the nation was in grave peril. National unity had brought Trudeau into power, it captivated his mind, and it touched his viscera. The 1976 election in Quebec of a government committed to the province's separation was the most serious threat, but it wasn't the only one. The new West, profoundly disaffected by its marginal status and made rich and brash by the energy boom, picked up Quebec's old cry for more provincial powers at the same time that its hostility toward Quebec's influence in Ottawa and official bilingualism reinforced the separatist arguments. Atlantic Canada, equally disaffected by its marginal status but poor and politically weak, joined the cry for more powers, more dignity, and more hope at the same time that it asked for more money from the rest of Canada. And Ontario, fat and smug in the centre of the country's economy and politics, was getting tired of being the milch cow of Confederation while it was attacked as the villain in everyone else's piece.

More serious than all the specific demands, quarrels, and discontents was the questioning of the underlying values that had allowed the various regions to come together in a federation in the first place: sharing, tolerance, linguistic dualism, and diversity subordinated to the well-being of the nation.

Trudeau's first reaction was to fight like fury for Ottawa on the letter of the law and matters of principle (such as refusing special status for Quebec or protecting the federal government's ownership of offshore resources), but give in to the provinces on demands for money. On the one hand, he wanted to safeguard the rules and powers necessary to keep the country prosperous and together. On the other hand, he thought that the provinces could do as good a job as Ottawa in many fields and that their electorates would keep them honest. Those counterweights satisfied his notion of federalism as a classic liberal ideal, in which individual freedom was promoted by dividing power between two different levels of government.

Many people saw Trudeau's hard-line defence of the national interest as a cause of strain in federal-provincial relations. Certainly the vicious logic of his debating techniques, which never admitted wrong and rarely pulled back from a kill, infuriated the premiers who were almost always at the losing end of his arguments. Some of them came to despise him; most of them approached a negotiation with him in the spirit of gladiators going into the arena with a lion. However patient, controlled, and understanding he tried to be, the least provocation triggered his compulsion to win and he became the Mr. Hyde of reason.

By the end of the 1970s, however, a good case could be made that the real strain had been caused by Trudeau's decentralizations. Between 1962 and 1978 Ottawa's share of public revenues dropped from 47 per cent to 32 per cent. Billions of dollars were handed over to the provinces to help them fulfil their responsibilities in areas such as medicare and post-secondary education, all without conditions so that Ottawa wouldn't interfere in their jurisdiction. As a result the federal government sacrificed most of its ability to establish national standards, while much of the money went into everything from roads to bureaucracies. Those bureaucracies soon learned to counter Ottawa's empires for their own advantage; and the premiers, on whom more political responsibility fell, reacted by demanding even more power and money. In other words, the federal government had to withstand the ferocious assault of enemies it had armed. Not only was it blamed for provoking confrontation, it was criticized for not controlling the third of its spending that it had transferred to the provinces.

"In the past," Trudeau observed, "there were lots of unoccupied areas of power, so those in power had room to grow without running into someone else. But as those unoccupied areas got filled up, we all started to squeeze together and collide."

His decentralist ideal had to be reconsidered. In his first term, for example, he had no qualms about giving the provinces the right to broadcast. In his second term he told a friend, "There will be one moment when we will say there is a bottom line, or the federation won't work anymore." In his third term he reached that bottom line.

The political and fiscal power of the provinces, already strengthened by the historical happenstance that made most of the important and expensive social programs provincial matters, had grown to an unprecedented degree. It threatened Ottawa's capacity to fine tune the economy, spread the national wealth to underdeveloped regions, and guarantee the free mobility of capital and labour. The premiers gathered like Shakespearian dukes around the Prime Minister at conferences that were frequently televised live across the country. In effect they replaced cabinet ministers as the spokesmen for their provinces in Ottawa and established the image of eleven equal governments running the nation collectively. Yet their appetite only became greater. Two all-out efforts to patriate the constitution (an apparently reasonable and necessary thing for a mature country to do) collapsed because agreement was conditional on more provincial power. Even in the wake of the unsettling, unexpected victory of the Parti Québécois in 1976, the "common front" of provinces wanted to put powers ahead of patriation. When Trudeau agreed in October, 1978, to discuss a transfer of powers, saying, "I've almost given away the store myself," virtually nothing could be decided.

"At one point I nearly offered them everything," Trudeau said in retrospect, "because I realized they would never agree to anything."

Since he didn't have the will or the support to act unilaterally, his prime-ministership petered out with the decade. Lost about how to answer all the questions he had raised, constrained by his character and his philosophy from imposing solutions, and distracted by the public breakdown of his marriage, he resisted the temptation to call an early election in spite of the temporary upsurge in Liberal popularity that followed the Quebec election. Instead, he drifted toward the end of his mandate as toward a cataract, directed by the flow of circumstance rather than the rudder of workable policies. When the end came— almost mercifully—in May, 1979, it was Trudeau's impotence that sent him plunging into history. Canadians had shown themselves willing to put up with a lot of his arrogance and foibles for the sake of his obvious qualities; but if they were to be led by the weak and confused, then at least Joe Clark was nice.

If that had been Pierre Trudeau's last election, as it

nearly was, he would have been remembered for what he might have been more than for what he was. His intelligence, his charisma, and his vision of Canada would have been noted along with a few ideas and a few pieces of legislation, but only in puzzling contrast to his uninspiring leadership. Despite his magnificent potential, he proved to be less purposeful than Macdonald, less charming than Laurier, less clever than King, less competent than St. Laurent, and less progressive than Pearson. If he wasn't quite the fizzled firework that Bennett, Meighen, and Diefenbaker had been, he didn't seem much more imaginative or significant than Robert Borden.

As he drifted toward defeat in 1979, however, he grasped as if by accident the deep-rooted truth that lay beneath the surface of Canadian politics. Disturbed by the rapacity of the provinces, distressed by the Conservatives' willingness to promote even more decentralization, Trudeau began to speak passionately about the national community and the national government. "Who shall speak for Canada?" he asked again and again, while his campaign slogan declared, "A leader must be a leader." He had his well-reasoned arguments, of course, but he also had patriotism in his voice and a gigantic maple leaf behind him on the platform. He used all three to attack Joe Clark's vague concept of Canada as a "community of communities." The issue of national leadership—as much Trudeau's improvisation as the strategy of his handlers—couldn't erase the public's dissatisfaction with the Liberals' economic record or their obnoxious smugness, but it was a major factor in depriving Clark of a majority government.

At first it seemed that the victory of the Progressive Conservatives was a defeat for the idea of a stronger central state. Yet Clark quickly ran into political trouble when he began to operate on that assumption. Most Canadians weren't happy with his proposal to privatize Petro-Canada, for example, and most of the provinces continued to quarrel for more power and money with every concession he made. The mean-spirited and greedy treatment of Joe

Clark by Tory premiers, particularly Peter Lougheed of
Alberta and Brian Peckford of Newfoundland, was an important lesson for Trudeau and the Liberals watching from
the opposition benches. Trudeau had been prepared to
admit that some of the tension between Ottawa and the
provinces was attributable to the partisan and personal
animosities built up between himself and many of the premiers over a decade. Clark's experience proved to him that
the heart of the matter was a conflicting vision of Canada.

That insight became a factor in Trudeau's mind when
he debated whether to stay as leader at the end of 1979.
"He reversed his decision to resign out of loyalty to the
caucus, his ministers, and the party," Jim Coutts said, "but
only after asking himself, 'What am I going back for? What
will I do if I go back?' "

Like Ebenezer Scrooge waking on Christmas morning,
delighted to find himself alive after witnessing his own
funeral and full of vows to be a better person, Trudeau
good-naturedly put himself in the hands of his political
experts for the 1980 election. He kept a low profile, as
advised, but recovered the compulsion to win which fatigue, vagueness of purpose, and marital turmoil had
blunted in 1979. He not only wanted to win, he wanted
to win a majority so that he could do what had to be done.

Since many voters neither understood or cared about
the constitution as he did, he deferred for once to those
advisers who cautioned him to play down the issue. But
its fundamental principles, such as unity and sharing, surfaced in the debate over energy prices and policies, something that concerned many Canadians in the light of the
second OPEC crisis and the unpopular provision in the
Tories' December budget to hike the price of gasoline by
18¢ a gallon. Using the details of a strategy developed by
a Liberal caucus committee while in opposition, he delivered a speech in Halifax that outlined a national energy
policy as the vehicle for communicating his vision of Canada.

"The energy policy that Trudeau announced during
the 1980 election," Martin Goldfarb said, "was designed

as a clear signal that we knew where we were going, that we knew what was best for Canada, that we will speak for the little guy."

The emergent theme was again national leadership. It spoke to Joe Clark's weaknesses as Prime Minister. It addressed the underlying fears about the upcoming Quebec referendum. It appealed to the sense of authority and community latent within the Canadian psyche. It stirred patriotic emotions. Though he announced this would be his last campaign (in fact, he had thought that every election would be his last), Trudeau also declared, "I'll stay until I've changed the flow of things." The cumulative result was the election of the Liberals in February, 1980, with the largest number of seats since 1968.

After entering the Chateau Laurier's ballroom on election night to the heroic, pugilistic anthem from the movie *Rocky* and after welcoming the crowd and the country to the 1980s, Trudeau said, "It is fitting and proper that less than two months into the decade, the people of this great nation should have been called upon to express their national will in a general election." It might have sounded like a platitude, but his references to the people, the nation, and the national will were important clues to the dramatic, almost revolutionary things to come.

III

"To witness those cabinet meetings in the summer and fall of 1980, compared to what I had witnessed between 1977 and 1979, was an absolute joy," said Tom Axworthy. "We had a group of tigers. In field after field they wanted to get things done. The cautious and the naysayers were remarkably few. The sense of reborn liberalism affected virtually everyone."

It was as if the flames of defeat had finally consumed that withered, exhausted thing known as 1960s or Pearsonian liberalism, and victory had produced from the ashes a cocky, energetic phenomenon instantly christened 1980s or Trudeau liberalism. In fact, it bore a startling resemblance to social democracy.

Canadian liberalism had taken another lurch to the left, directed there by the ideology of Canada's two political cultures and propelled by pragmatism. "In our view," Marc Lalonde said, "the Liberals had lost in 1979 for appearing to be a government that had run out of steam, out of ideas, out of leadership. We had been blocked by the provinces on the constitution. We had tried the gradualist approach in energy and always seemed to be behind events. We had engaged in extensive consultations with business and labour for nationally determined goals with no positive results. For the last few years we appeared to be running around in circles, administering but with no clear sense of direction. So, frankly, we told ourselves that if we were ever elected again, we weren't going to be defeated because of fudgy leadership or because we haven't indicated where we want to take the country. We'd rather be defeated for having done something than for having done nothing."

This sentiment was shared by English- and French-Canadian Liberals alike, though not universally, sometimes to varying degrees, and often for different reasons. By 1980 the party's right wing had been clipped in caucus and cabinet by the alienation of the West and the business community; anglophones and francophones radicalized by the 1960s were assuming positions of authority; the new Liberal constituencies of women, immigrants, and the young seemed less vulnerable to the Tories than to the NDP, whose voters, in turn, represented the party's only hope of penetrating the West; and the cabinet was full of resurrected veterans from the battles of the 1970s. Strangely enough, one of the last converts to Trudeau liberalism was Pierre Elliott Trudeau.

Trudeau had arrived at his classic liberalism by the force of his reason, and that force was greater than most men's. He knew too well how central authority could turn into tyranny, how the will of the majority could oppress the individual and minorities, and how constructive nation-building could degenerate into irrational chauvinism. He also knew that the two great counterweights he had envisaged in his writings to check the activist state, participation and consultation, were either irrelevant or dysfunctional. As a result, he retained a deep skepticism about authority and intervention: one had to convince him by hard evidence and persuasive logic that either was necessary.

Once convinced, however, he acted without compunction. Colleagues and the general public always noticed that he was at his best in a crisis—cool, decisive, resolute—as if released from his intellectual scruples and allowed to express his real self. That may have been true, in fact. After all, Trudeau's classic liberalism was a mental construct superimposed on his cultural background. His father was a French-Canadian Tory. His mother was descended from Scottish Loyalists. Trudeau grew up in a quasi-aristocratic society and played with a gang called *les snobs*. He was indoctrinated with a sense of superiority, righteousness, and will by the Jesuits. His Cartesian training gave him a love of abstract law and a respect for the order of things.

By birth, education, and choice Trudeau was a product of French Canada, which in his own analysis had had trouble absorbing British parliamentary democracy into its soul because of its feudal, Roman Catholic ethos. That's why, whatever his words or actions, many Canadians sensed that his meticulous, disciplined, neurotically competitive self was the stuff of dictators. The authoritarian side of his personality came through in dramatic flashes, when he called Members of Parliament "nobodies," when he gave demonstrators a rude finger, and most especially during the October crisis of 1970 when he told the press to "go on and bleed, but it is more important to keep law and order in the society than to be worried about weak-kneed people." After 1980, with a majority government, a firm grip on his cabinet, a will to do things, and no cares about getting re-elected, he seemed prepared to accept the autocratic image he had seldom deserved in the past.

His own resistance to authority, his bicultural home, his world travels, and his attachment to his intellectual principles had inoculated him against the extremes in French Canada's feudal culture and its radical reaction. Forced to act, however, he acted forcefully, on the grounds that a government has the right to govern, a democracy must protect itself, and a leader must be a leader. The significance of these notions only reached his understanding when he got into office. As a professor and essayist he found it easy to argue that power should be decentralized and authority checked. In government he recognized that the state had to be able to do its job. That is the normal difference between out and in. Trudeau himself wrote in 1951, "There nowhere exists a power which does not seek to increase itself: it's a universal law."

In this, he joined the entire Liberal Party in its tiptoe from decentralization to centralization. There's nothing like spending most of a century in power for discovering why power should be concentrated rather than curbed and dispersed, and it didn't take the Liberals long to detect the flaws in provincial rights when they were in charge of Ottawa and the provincial capitals were packed with Tories, NDPers, and the Parti Québécois. Trudeau was aware that this type of rationalization was also the road to totalitarianism, but he had to confront the *pragmatic* question of governing.

In general, he once explained, "when I centralize, it's because I discover it's the only way in that particular instance to get the thing done." This functional dynamic broke through most of his intellectual barriers and permitted what he called "a shift of gear."

"He finally said, 'I'm going to do it my way.' " Martin Goldfarb observed. "After participatory democracy and white papers and green papers, he began to feel that the government didn't need any more thinkers, it needed action and authority. My advice was, pursue the best interests of the nation. The country didn't want confrontation, but it was prepared to support federal authority. It felt that, in the crunch, it needed Big Daddy."

Moreover, after a decade of experimentation and fumbles, Trudeau finally understood the mechanics of getting things done. Indeed, he was angry with himself at having taken so long to learn. First, he needed a short but potent personal agenda. "People coming into power have to know on their first day what they want to do," Jim Coutts said. "They may not know how to do it, but they need a tremendous sense of political will or else the odds of doing anything are small. A government that comes to power without an agenda is a government adrift. During our months in opposition in 1979, we developed a policy thrust and a will to implement it."

Secondly, Trudeau needed to concentrate on that agenda. In the past he had been swamped, trying to keep an eye on the whole process. The thousands of details, meetings, reports, and consultations had stolen time and effort from the important and difficult problems. Now Trudeau understood he had to take more responsibility for the key issues and delegate the rest. By chance, his period in opposition had left him psychologically more comfortable about both responsibility and delegation.

"The greatest resource in town is the Prime Minister," Tom Axworthy said. "He's the *raw demon* of our government system. So, after 1980, we didn't want to get caught in the paper factory again. We cut down the size of the PMO and dramatically restricted what Trudeau would work on. We beefed up his meetings on primary subjects, we cut his meetings and memos on secondary subjects to nil, we spun off patronage and party affairs to the ministers, we pushed as much as possible out and kept as little as possible in. In other words, we ran a strategic prime-ministership."

What the PMO accomplished on the political side, the PCO repeated on the administrative side. Building on reforms that Clark had introduced, Pitfield turned the cabinet's Priorities and Planning Committee into an efficient inner cabinet under Trudeau's chairmanship. It focussed on the essential and broader issues, and, although it kept in touch with all the system's decisions, it left most of them to other committees of ministers, who were increasingly responsible for their development, their management and their financing. After 1980, therefore, the compromise between democracy and efficiency lay in greater centralization in a few essential areas and further decentralization in almost everything else.

All the strands of ideology, politics, personality, and know-how were ready for strong executive will, but Trudeau still might not have been able to act if there hadn't been an atmosphere of crisis. The first and greatest crisis came in May, 1980, when the Parti Québécois (PQ) held its long-awaited referendum. The question was convoluted and fell short of asking Quebeckers if they wanted to separate from Canada. It merely asked for a mandate to negotiate a vague form of sovereignty-association with Ottawa. A "Yes" vote, however, would have been an enormous boost for the independence movement and the gravest setback for national unity in Canadian history. Trudeau even suggested that he and all the Quebec MPs would have to resign because they would have lost the confidence of their province. Moreover, the qualified nature of the question increased the likelihood of a "Yes" victory. It could appeal to many Quebeckers as a tactic to get more powers and more dignity for their province. At the same time, it increased the risk for the Parti Québécois, since a "No" victory on such a neutral proposition would stop its cause dead in its tracks.

Before the referendum the PQ had followed a very sophisticated strategy of demanding a little more power here, a little more money there. Each small step seemed so reasonable and unthreatening that other provinces joined in making many of the same demands. Ottawa always had political difficulty in refusing, yet it knew that Quebec's strategy would eventually lead to the disintegration of the country if it was allowed to succeed.

Jean Chrétien, then Minister of Justice and in charge

of leading the federal campaign on the "No" side, said it was a very dangerous and very effective strategy. "I remember being told by Claude Morin, the PQ minister, 'We'll separate from Canada the same way that Canada separated from England: we'll cut the links one at a time, a concession here and a concession there, and eventually there'll be nothing left.' They began that by asking for new powers or an international presence, and the people bought it. That's why the referendum was their biggest mistake."

The battle mobilized the energy and determination of the Liberals, particularly Trudeau, Chrétien, and the Quebec caucus. The will latent within their ideology was awakened by the gravity of the fight and the conviction of being right. Conviction is usually a prerequisite for bold action and quick decisions. It had allowed Trudeau to act upon official bilingualism in his first term despite widespread hostility. While he was open to persuasion about energy policy or economic controls, he was certain that federalism offered French Canadians the best opportunities for progress and freedom. That certainty gave particular brilliance to his speeches during the referendum campaign. When the PQ had announced the date, Joe Clark was in power and no one could have guessed that Pierre Trudeau and his experienced Quebec members would be back by May. Instead of facing a weak, anglophone defence from Ottawa, the PQ encountered an aggressive, well-oiled machine. That machine probably tipped the balance in favour of the "No" vote, though most Quebeckers were already leaning away from sovereignty-association because of their fears about economic dislocation and their hopes for Canada. When 60 per cent voted "No" on May 20, 1980, Trudeau and his party emerged with greater potency, adrenaline, and purpose.

"Well, where do we go from here?" he asked Chrétien the morning after the vote. In fact, Trudeau had a good idea of where they were going. The referendum had finally brought his passion for constitutional reform to the top of the national agenda after a dozen years of provincial intransigence and public indifference. Trudeau wasn't going to throw away this rare opportunity.

It was ironic that constitutional reform became identified as Trudeau's issue. He had been one of the last Quebec intellectuals and Canadian politicians to think it important. In the late 1950s Gérard Pelletier had even teased him by saying, "You don't seem very interested in constitutional reform for a professor of constitutional law." In truth, Trudeau couldn't get very agitated about the transfer of powers to the provinces while court decisions and social evolution were augmenting provincial authority anyway. Matters that had been left to the provinces in the British North America Act as minor, parochial concerns, such as education and welfare, became major responsibilities that absorbed an increasing amount of the national revenue. Trudeau was content to let the momentum of decentralization run its course before suggesting that political energy be devoted to legalities. He saw patriation as self-evidently desirable and he always dreamed of an entrenched bill of rights, but he preferred to leave the rest to the give and take of cooperative federalism. That changed, however, when Pearson named him Minister of Justice in 1967. Pushed by the unrest of Quebec nationalism, the provinces had begun to look for a better deal and Ottawa was ready to talk. So Trudeau entered into the debate, late and rather reluctantly but with a resolve to see the issue through to its completion.

Even in the wake of the referendum, his failures in the 1970s didn't give him faith that he could achieve very much. He had had more first ministers' conferences than any other Prime Minister, only to receive longer lists of demands for power from the premiers. He had decentralized the federation to the edge of economic disequilibrium and national disintegration, only to be labelled a bully, a spendthrift, and an inept manager. He volunteered to divest Ottawa of significant authority in the fields of taxation, spending, trade, resources, law, and communications, only to see provincial legislation that, in effect, balkanized the country.

For Trudeau national unity took precedence over good economics or even good politics. What was a deficit compared to a country split in half? What were seats in the

West compared to the vision of a bilingual Canada? Lesser men, mere managers in Trudeau's eyes, might have administered the nation better, but preserving it was the stuff of statecraft.

The challenge was particularly great for him because it involved the continuation of an important experiment on which the future of world peace and prosperity might depend. He saw the Canadian federation as a prototype for viable states based on more than one ethnic or linguistic community, more than one *nation* in the French meaning of the word. Not only did federalism confront the modern curse of ethnocentric nationalism by allowing different cultures to flourish within a single territory, it allowed individuals to play one power against the other, decide whether certain responsibilities should be more local or more national, and be both part of a minority and more than it.

By 1980 he felt the provinces had gone from the legitimate protection of their turf to encroachment on Ottawa's. Class tensions were expressing themselves in regional conflicts; Ottawa was portrayed as the remote and inefficient tax collector while the provinces became the generous, competent sources of funds; and Trudeau no longer trusted them to do the right thing for their citizens. In his judgement it was time to re-establish the proper balance—to take a "sharp turn"—in order to restore Ottawa's ability to keep the country united.

He assumed he would have trouble. The Quebec government, dedicated to independence, could never agree to any deal whatsoever. Most of the anglophone premiers, with Tory affiliations or a history of antagonism toward Trudeau personally, would never give him or the Liberals even the small glory of patriation. "After ten years of thinking that he'd get this guy in place and then he'd get that guy in place," Goldfarb explained, "Trudeau said, 'Screw it, I'm never going to get them all in place, so I'll do what's right.' "

He had raised the possibility of some kind of unilateral federal action as early as September, 1976, and again during the 1979 election. He sensed, however, that the people weren't ready to back such a confrontation. Clark's experiences and the referendum changed his view. Publicly he vowed that, "following a 'No' vote we will immediately take action to renew the constitution and we will not stop until we have done that." Privately he told Chrétien, "We just can't fail again. This time we're going to do it."

As usual, he was bolder in image than in fact. Worried about the premiers and the support of the people—or, to put it another way, still sensitive to the classic liberal principles of federalism and counterweights—he was prepared to restrict any unilateral action to two initiatives: the patriation of the constitution with the amending formula that all the provinces had accepted in Victoria in 1971 and the entrenchment of a bill of rights limited to basic democratic rights and minority-language protection. The first merely corrected an historical anomaly. If it benefitted anyone, it benefitted the provinces by taking away Ottawa's ability to act unilaterally in the future. The second went some way toward guaranteeing individual freedom and the bilingual foundation of Canada; but far from being a centralizing initiative, it took power from Parliament and gave it to individuals via the courts. Trudeau saw language as a crucial factor in *individual* self-fulfilment as well as national unity. "The fire in his belly when he entered government," said Jim Coutts, "was to see a united country in which everyone could be accepted and play a part throughout it."

Chrétien, who hadn't fought the referendum for such a limited change, tried for one last deal with the provinces. He, his provincial counterparts, and all their constitutional advisers met throughout the summer of 1980 to find common ground in a twelve-item agenda that ranged from resources to communications, from regional disparity to Senate reform, from patriation to fish. It was a new game. All the concessions on spending, taxation, and powers that the Liberals had offered before 1980 were swept from the table. Instead, the federal government introduced a list of "powers over the economy" that it desired in return for new provincial powers. In addition, a "people's package" of patriation and rights was separated from negotiations over powers, so that democratic freedoms could no longer be bartered for provincial demands. And whenever the talks bogged down, Chrétien yelled, "Get the plane ready, boys, we're off to London!" as a reminder that Ottawa was willing to act unilaterally in the event of failure. By September, however, Chrétien and his advisers thought they were near a deal on most of the agenda. Some said there never would have been a deal on resources and communications, but a group photograph was taken for the history books, just in case.

At that point, the work of the ministers and the officials had to be passed up to the Prime Minister and the premiers for their consideration at a conference in Ottawa. Before the meeting even began, however, the premiers were enraged by a leaked federal document that suggested Ottawa was dealing in poor faith. Then Trudeau became furious at a provincial request that a premier co-chair the conference with him. A state dinner degenerated into unpleasant name-calling. "The whole thing broke down for personality reasons," Chrétien said.

Trudeau returned to his cabinet and caucus to reconsider the next step. If his willingness to settle for patriation and limited rights demonstrated a remarkable tenacity to classic liberalism after thirty years, his colleagues demonstrated how their thinking had evolved. After returning to power and winning the Quebec referendum, they weren't going to be satisfied with half-measures. Following the breakdown of the September conference, they wanted "to go Cadillac," as one Liberal MP phrased it. In other words, if they were going to be hammered for moving unilaterally, they might as well move with a first-class Charter of Rights. If language rights were included, why not rights for women or the elderly or the handicapped or the native peoples? In fact, some argued, it would be easier to sell a broad package than a narrow one that only served a few interests.

"If that is your will," Trudeau told the caucus, "I'm delighted to follow it." But he was neither foolhardy nor unaware of the risks. "We could lose the next election for taking on something so big. We could lose for a generation."

Going Cadillac meant confronting eight of the provinces, the opposition in Parliament, Quebec nationalists, alienated Westerners, a host of interest groups that wanted rights put in or left out of the Charter, the courts, and possibly the British Parliament itself. On the other hand, some believed that it could be good politics. "You'd raise a lot of hell," Tom Axworthy said, "but at least you'd go to the people having done something. Our problem in 1979 was that we had bloody few scalps in our belts. A good record tied to the concepts of nation and activist leadership for the national community could work."

The cabinet was even more gung-ho than the caucus. It wanted to shame the provinces into taking the high road toward patriation and a Charter of Rights. No more would they bargain, in Trudeau's words, "freedom against fish, fundamental rights against oil, the independence of the country against long-distance telephone rates."

No other issue ever took so much cabinet time—one source estimated more than thirty hours in one three-week period in the fall of 1980—and the ministers got involved in the very wording of the legislation. In fact, Trudeau had to check their enthusiasm. He wouldn't consider any unilateral transfer of powers to the federal government; he was reluctant to impose anything on the provinces; and he constantly challenged his colleagues with Socratic questions. At last the system seemed to be working as he always dreamed it might. He presided like a true philosopher-king over a cabinet that was engaged in a collegial discussion of monumental consequence, bound by a common resolve and clear vision. Their decisions involved the grand issues of government and nation, not the dreary routine of uninspired management that any set of politicians could have handled. They gave their political marching orders to a bureaucracy that was eager, on side, and brilliant with details and strategies designed "to take Moscow," as one senior official described the exercise.

"There was no Trudeau formula that had to happen," Jim Coutts said. "He only had a few fundamental principles: patriation, sharing, and the protection of minorities, which began as language rights but became very broad. As long as the principles were accepted, the nuts and bolts could go anywhere. His most devastating argument was that the federal package wasn't about more powers to either Ottawa or the provinces; it was about more rights to the people at the expense of all governments."

Perhaps, but that old decentralizing, individualistic ideal could only be attained by a centralist, community-oriented action. That was the contradiction at the heart of modern Canadian liberalism. It worked because of pragmatism and the impurity of liberalism in Canada and in the soul of Pierre Trudeau. In fact, the power of the national community, the social implications of the Charter, and the collective benefits for minorities all became more important to the debate than the freedom of the individual, though each had its intellectual roots in classic liberal theory.

The decision of the federal government to act alone was based on the belief that Canada is more than the sum of its provinces. It is a community formed by an understanding among all Canadians as individuals; and though the federation recognized the importance of the provinces by assuring them particular powers in regional matters, only the central government can determine and act upon the national interest because it alone represents all the individuals known as "the people" or "the nation." That relatively simple belief became the source of vicious conflict and unleashed a myriad of highly controversial and highly complex questions. Is Ottawa senior to the provinces rather than an equal partner? Does Ottawa have a direct relationship with the people other than the indirect one through the provincial capitals? Can Ottawa act on its own to break an impasse for the sake of the nation as a whole? The federal Liberals answered yes.

Most of the provinces, with Ontario and New Brunswick as the consistent exceptions, said no. They saw Canada as an understanding among the provinces, with Ottawa either their agent on broad matters or their equivalent in its own jurisdiction. Their belief meant that the "national interest" would be determined by Ottawa *and* the provinces. Provincial powers couldn't be pushed aside by the national will of the people (however *that* was decided), and any action as significant as constitutional reform required the consent of a majority of the provinces (if not all of them).

Thus, they rejected a federal constitutional draft that began, "We, the people of Canada." They proposed that a premier co-chair the federal-provincial conferences with the Prime Minister. They refused to refer to Ottawa as the *national* government instead of the *federal* government. They fought against language rights and the free mobility of labour and capital, in order to protect their own economic and social objectives. Quebec demanded that all equalization payments be made to the provincial governments rather than to individuals, and Premier Brian Peckford of Newfoundland declared that he preferred René Lévesque's vision of Canada to Pierre Trudeau's.

"Have you got a bag?" Chrétien said to Trudeau when he heard that. "I think I want to vomit."

The provincial position was actually closer than Ottawa's to the traditional, consociational liberalism by which Canada had operated for a hundred years. Its emphasis was on decentralized communities, elites, qualifications on popular sovereignty and guaranteed freedoms, and endless trade-offs. The union of 1867 had been a deal struck by delegations from the colonies that became the original provinces; federal-provincial conferences had been institutionalized to the point of vying with Parliament for the national spotlight; and as late as 1971 an agreement on patriation had collapsed because of the last-minute objection of a single province. Moreover, the provincial legislatures were assumed to be sovereign within their own jurisdictions, free from the interference of either the federal Parliament or the Supreme Court so long as they minded their own business.

Established by a happy conjunction of ideology and

circumstance, this arrangement continued to please the premiers who benefitted from it. The Quebec government claimed a special responsibility for the French-Canadian minority because it represented the only province with a francophone majority. The Western governments declared themselves the best defenders of Western interests because the federal Parliament was dominated by the political and economic power of Central Canada. And most of the Atlantic premiers used their positions at the bargaining table to get advantages their region couldn't have wrested from the system otherwise because of its small population, marginal representation, and economic misfortune.

Even though the federal constitutional package barely intruded upon provincial power, the dissenting premiers saw the dangers in its presumptions. If Ottawa was allowed to determine the national will, then the will of the people could supersede the will of the provinces. If a federally appointed court could override the provincial legislatures on issues that might arise out of the Charter of Rights, then the balance of power would tip toward the federal government. Ever since Chrétien picked up Ottawa's 1978 concessions and replaced them with a forty-six-page demand for more powers over the economy, the premiers realized they were involved in a crucial struggle.

"They went bananas at the notion that powers should be given *back* to Ottawa," said Michael Kirby, one of Chrétien's key officials. "So we said, 'Okay, let's not deal with powers, let's deal with the *people's* package.' Even the phrase, which had been dreamed up for marketing reasons, infuriated them. We came at them from such a totally different perspective that they didn't know how to play."

They played badly. However well-founded some of their arguments were, the "Gang of Eight" came across as a bunch of greedy warlords out on a power-grab. The Parti Québécois government would never agree to any change, yet the other seven premiers didn't hesitate to be seen in an alliance with the separatists. Their "shopping list" for additional powers became so extensive that Trudeau and Chrétien burst out laughing at one point, because there was almost nothing left for Ottawa to do; yet the premiers wouldn't give up any powers themselves. Even with the federal strategy paper in their hands, they failed to negotiate realistically and so gave Trudeau the excuse and the will to act on his own.

Most of the premiers assumed that he wouldn't dare move unilaterally in the face of such concerted opposition, but, as Coutts said, "they picked the wrong pussycat to fight." They underestimated the change that had taken place in his thinking, his cabinet, and his party. He and his Quebec MPs—who had just come out of the fight of their lives in the referendum—were appalled to hear premiers siding with Lévesque for personal, partisan, or parochial reasons. Still, the federal government dropped its desire for new powers over the economy and tried to set "reasonable limits" to the new judicial powers in order to protect the provinces' parliamentary traditions. It also accepted more than five dozen amendments to the Charter during a winter of parliamentary committee hearings. But Trudeau's patience was running out.

"First it was delay because of the substance," he told the House of Commons in April, 1981, "then it was delay because of the process, then it was delay because of the courts, and now it is delay because of the premiers."

Almost a week after Trudeau gave in to opposition demands and agreed to test his government's right to act unilaterally in the Supreme Court—a court decision that could have affirmed the dissenting provinces' vision of Canada and stopped Ottawa's course—the Gang of Eight issued its best counter-offer, which was hardly an offer at all: patriation, an amending formula in which provinces could opt out of any amendment with full financial compensation, and no Charter. Trudeau said it would lead to "a Confederation of five hundred shopping centres," and Chrétien called it "sovereignty-association by installment." Even Joe Clark was overheard to remark about the premiers, "Are we living in the same world as they are?"

The Supreme Court decision, when it finally came on September 28, 1981, gave a formal ruling on the three thorniest disagreements in the political debate. Yes, a majority of the judges concluded, Ottawa's resolution would affect the powers of the provinces. Yes, there was a tradition—"a convention"—that such a change would require a "substantial measure of provincial consent." But no, there was no legal impediment to Ottawa's acting alone in presenting its package to the British Parliament for approval. In other words, while the provincial vision of Canada had been the practice, the federal vision was the law.

Chrétien declared victory and announced that Ottawa was ready to proceed to London. Trudeau, however, was prepared to meet the premiers again in one last try for "substantial" provincial consent. He didn't expect much and, in his heart, was actually hoping that nothing would happen. Failure would allow him to go to the British Parliament without having to water down his package any further. Moreover, unilateral imposition wouldn't exclude Quebec from any deal. If London refused to act in that circumstance, Trudeau was ready to hold a general election on the issue. He couldn't risk losing that, if only because a loss would set the cause of constitutional reform back fifty years, so he had to be able to show Canadians that he had exhausted all efforts at finding a compromise solution.

Then, when he met with the premiers in November, 1981, his instincts showed him another possible route: if Ottawa and the provinces couldn't reach an agreement, let the people of Canada choose between two proposals by referendum. He had broached the idea of holding a referendum on constitutional reform, if necessary, during the 1979 election; his government had thought of conducting its own referendum to counter Quebec's in 1980; and there were two referendum provisions already in the federal package, one to let Canadians decide after two years if they wanted the federal or provincial amending formula, the other as a deadlock-breaking mechanism within the federal amending formula. While Trudeau had generally resisted the concept of direct democracy, he realized it could be an instrument of last resort to establish the political legitimacy of his reforms.

"Somebody has to be able to break a deadlock between the federal government and the provinces," Trudeau said, "and since there's no pope to say who's right, the people have to decide."

His enthusiasm was shared by all his senior ministers except Chrétien (who had seen the bitter divisions caused by the Quebec referendum and never wanted to "put on my running shoes" to fight another), by senior officials such as Michael Pitfield and Michael Kirby, by party advisers such as Jim Coutts and Tom Axworthy, and by the Liberal caucus. The Quebec referendum had reaffirmed their trust in the judgement of the people. It had proven that the popular will wasn't always the same as the views of the provincial governments, the media, the intellectuals, or any other elites. If the majority of Quebeckers could reject the soft question of the Parti Québécois, despite all the historical, social, cultural, and political factors working in favour of a "Yes" vote, Ottawa was confident that its national vision would carry anywhere. Indeed, the polls showed that most Canadians in all regions wanted the federal package even though they were unhappy with all the time and conflict involved in getting it.

Obviously the appeal to the national will and vision of a unified Canada was a useful, self-serving tactic in Ottawa's own power-mongering, for they strengthened the federal government's moral and political backing while diminishing the authority of the provinces. But they also illustrated the leftward shift in Canadian liberalism. They placed a new value upon a single community in which the majority ruled through its national government, sometimes even directly by plebiscite. Little could have been further from the old concept of doing things. It was as if, on the eve of entrenching individual freedoms, minority rights, and provincial protections, the federal Liberals were finally liberated from the dangers of constructing a collective and democratic nation. More significant, they found that most of the country was quietly in step, if not actually ahead of them. Canada, in its push-me-pull-you relationship with the Liberals, had taken much the same passage through the crises and changes of the 1970s as the party had, and it harboured a nationalism so powerful that Pierre Trudeau had trouble controlling it.

When Trudeau played his referendum card, all hell broke loose. Lévesque leapt at the challenge in the hope of overcoming the humiliation of the "No" victory, but the rest of the Gang of Eight panicked at the thought of facing their electorates on the wrong side of patriation and a Charter of Rights. Faced with their hostility and the doubts of his own supporters, Lévesque quickly retreated. However, Trudeau had achieved his strategic goal by shattering the common front. That enabled the federal side to open eleventh-hour negotiations and eventually discover a compromise solution, in which nine of the provinces accepted the Charter subject to certain modifications while Ottawa accepted the provincial amending formula without any financial compensation for opting out. Quebec alone, having gambled away its veto power when it joined the Gang of Eight in March, refused to sign the deal.

Trudeau wasn't delighted with the compromise. He didn't like the notion of opting out. He was worried about how the traditionally cautious courts would respond to the "notwithstanding" clause, a qualification inserted into the Charter to appease the provinces' concerns about the sovereignty of their legislatures. Most of all, he hated the last-minute forfeiting of the referendum clause in the federal government's amending formula. The ability of the people to arbitrate between their two levels of government was a formal and practical recognition of the principle of popular sovereignty that lay at the heart of the whole matter. If the people were sovereign, isolated individuals became part of a national community, their mass will took precedence over the narrow interests of elites and regions, and they looked to the centre more often for help and protection.

"We felt good about our achievement," Tom Axworthy said, "but there was some sense of loss at what we had given up, especially the referendum clause. It was the intellectual justification for the superstructure we had been building, and we lost it forever. The Charter will be a great instrument for national community, because Canadians will be looking to the Supreme Court every day, but we gave up the concept of popular sovereignty."

In the end, as Trudeau said, "a signed deal is better than a fight." He had become annoyed with what Chrétien had traded for the sake of an agreement, but his idea of holding an election evaporated when Premier William Davis phoned him on the eve of the conference's break-up. If Trudeau didn't accept the compromise, Davis said, he would lose his only provincial allies, Ontario and New Brunswick. Trudeau realized the jig was up. In fact, he had experienced the full force of the status quo in Canada and learned the enormous cost of trying to change it.

"The constitution has to be the greatest exercise of political will this country has ever seen," Michael Kirby concluded. "Not just by Trudeau, but by the whole cabinet, by Premier Davis of Ontario, and by Premier Hatfield of New Brunswick. If any of them had weakened their resolve at any point, the entire thing would have gone down the tube. It was kept alive in the face of unbelievable opposition and abuse, day after day, week after week, month after month for almost two years, by sheer will."

IV

"Are you people serious about this?" incredulous public servants kept asking Liberal cabinet ministers through the summer of 1980.

The object of their surprise was the new government's plan to introduce a comprehensive energy program in its autumn budget. It was the second item of the Prime Minister's short agenda. The broad political goals—a "made-in-Canada" oil price as opposed to the fluctuating world price, increased Canadianization of the oil and gas sector, and energy self-sufficiency—had been produced by the Liberal caucus in 1979 and outlined by Trudeau during the

1980 election. Back in power, Trudeau worked with Marc Lalonde (the Minister of Energy, Mines and Resources), Allan MacEachen (the Minister of Finance), and a small group of officials from the PCO and their departments to detail the regime of taxes, grants, and regulations that would achieve the goals.

"It was a textbook case of how the system is supposed to operate," Tom Axworthy said, "with the political arm setting the objectives and the bureaucracy working very hard to find the means to implement them." However, in bypassing the cabinet and the committee process as part of budget secrecy, it also exemplified what Trudeau and Pitfield had learned about getting things done. Later their efficiency would exact the price that collegiality had been designed to avoid. Ministers who usually ranted against the slowness and hassles of the Pitfield system would rant against the speed and lack of consultation in the energy decisions. They would point to the National Energy Program's political and economic mistakes and claim those wouldn't have slipped past full scrutiny. Not having been part of the decision-making procedure, many ministers would defend the National Energy Program (NEP) badly and soon agitate to modify it. Nor was cabinet solidarity strengthened by the jealousy that surfaced from the privilege, priority, and money Lalonde and his program had been accorded by the Prime Minister.

Like the constitutional reforms, the NEP was forged in an atmosphere of crisis. The Iranian revolution of 1979 had caused the world price of oil to double almost overnight. Since the Canadian price was set at 80 per cent of the world price, the financial implications for Ottawa, the producing provinces, the consuming provinces, the oil industry, and the manufacturing sector were tremendous. To take one example, the costs of the Oil Import Compensation Fund by which Ottawa subsidized energy costs in the East quadrupled to over $4 billion, while Alberta's Heritage Fund soared to more than $13 billion by 1982. Moreover, everyone was predicting that the world price would keep rising steeply. If that happened without a new federal-provincial arrangement, the Heritage Fund would surpass $150 billion by the middle of the new decade. In contrast, Ottawa would face larger deficits, be unable to make equalization payments to the have-not provinces (which would include Ontario before too long), and lose control over the general economy.

"The major factor behind the NEP wasn't Canadianization or getting more from the industry or even self-sufficiency," Marc Lalonde said. "*The* determinant factor was the fiscal imbalance between the provinces and the federal government in the scenario in which the provincial revenues would go up with the price of oil while Ottawa's share of the larger and larger pie got smaller and smaller. Meanwhile, our commitments to equalization payments and incentives to the oil industry would increase faster than our revenues. So we foresaw a situation in which the federal government would have no way of ever restoring the balance. Our proposal was to increase Ottawa's share appreciably, so that the share of the producing provinces would decline significantly and the industry's share would decline somewhat."

Thus, the NEP included a series of new federal taxes, incentives to encourage the exploration and development of federal lands, and the unilateral imposition of a new pricing and revenue-sharing formula on the producing provinces. Ottawa's share was projected to rise from about 8 per cent in 1980 to 24 per cent in 1983, while the provinces' share was expected to drop from about 45 per cent to 31 per cent.

Clearly this meant opening a second front in the federal-provincial wars in the middle of the constitutional debate, as well as taking on powerful corporate interests and the American multinationals. "These cats had received the rarest thing in politics, a second chance," Tom Axworthy said of the Liberals, "and by God they were going to make it count this time."

In many ways the fight over the NEP was a specific case-study of the abstract issues being negotiated in the constitutional conferences: where was power to be and how much was to be there? Though the two campaigns were waged simultaneously and often linked in the minds and emotions of the key combatants, they weren't linked in trade-offs or in federal cabinet discussions. They coincided only because the Quebec referendum coincided with the search for a new energy agreement between Ottawa and the producing provinces. The old one had expired in June, 1980, and the second OPEC crisis had demanded a radical change. However, in its complicated equations and computer projections the NEP was as preoccupied as the Charter of Rights with the questions of nationhood, sovereignty, freedom, economic union, and sharing.

Was it fair that all the costs of OPEC's arbitrary action be borne by Canadian consumers, while most of the windfall went to a single province with 10 per cent of the population? Hadn't Ottawa and the wealthy regions supported the West through its bad times, including paying higher-than-world prices from 1961 to 1973? Wasn't Canada founded on the ideal that those who are up should help those who are down, confident that if they too should ever be down, they would be helped? Trudeau was even trying to enshrine the principle of equalization in his Charter of Rights. The NEP was his attempt to restore the fiscal balance in practice.

"We hadn't been providing the leadership the Prime Minister wanted us to provide," Lalonde said. "We knew there would be a showdown with the West, but we felt the national government had a national responsibility that we shouldn't run away from. The old system was a recipe for disaster, so we had to work for the long haul."

In retrospect, Trudeau himself expressed surprise that energy policy came to overshadow all his government's other business except the constitution. The NEP proved the effectiveness of a strong minister allied to strong bureaucrats and a strong issue. Marc Lalonde was the perfect example of French-Canadian conservatism transformed into social democracy. Raised in a traditional Quebec farming family, liberated by personalism and a degree from Oxford, first attracted to Ottawa by the Tories (as was Michael

Pitfield, at the same time but from a very different direction), Lalonde brought authority, will, and a centralist state
to the cause of social reform and democracy.

His ascetic, bald head, with its prominent nose and
formidable countenance, resembled one in marble repose
on the tomb of a medieval abbot renowned for his intelligence, his worldly ambition, and his political cunning;
and when Lalonde suddenly smiled his big, joyful smile,
the impact was no less startling than if the effigy grinned.
In the name of the people, he established the presidential
character of Trudeau's first PMO as chief of staff between
1968 and 1972, pushed for massive and expensive social-
security reforms as Minister of Health and Welfare in the
mid-1970s, became an old-time boss of the Liberals' Quebec machine, and now moved forcefully on the energy
question. He was, in many respects, the worst person to
send in to deal with the business community and the West.

"He was an easy man to hate," one of his cabinet
colleagues admitted.

Peter Lougheed of Alberta and his allies saw Lalonde's
noble rhetoric as the crass ambition of the Liberals and
their Central Canadian supporters to grab the rights and
money that belonged to the hinterland provinces. In
Lougheed's opinion, the West had been kept down rather
than helped up by Central Canada. Alberta was paying
enough of its share through federal taxes and lower oil
prices, which he judged to have cost the government of
Alberta $50 billion since 1973; and the people of the pro-
ducing provinces had a duty to get as much as they could
from a resource that wouldn't last forever. He saw the
Liberals' moves on the constitution and energy as a two-
pronged attack on the West.

"They really want a unitary state where any decision
of substance is made in Ottawa," Lougheed said. "They
recognize they have to cater to Ontario and Quebec to stay
in office, but this select group cannot accept any other
province becoming moderately independent and not subservient to them for federal discretionary grants."

He articulated his own vision of Canada at a federal-provincial conference in 1978. "The only way there can be a fair deal for the citizens of the outlying parts of Canada is for the elected provincial governments of these parts to be sufficiently strong to offset the political power in the House of Commons of the populated centres. That strength can only flow from the provinces' jurisdiction over the management of their own economic destinies and the development of the natural resources owned by the province."

Lougheed's reaction to the NEP was swift and furious. Ottawa, he said, "without negotiation, without agreement, simply walked into our home and occupied the living room."

As he launched his counterattack, cutting back on Alberta's oil production and delaying the construction of two energy mega-projects, he found powerful allies in the multinational oil companies. They were particularly affected by the NEP's secondary purpose: to increase Canadian ownership of oil and gas production from 28 per cent to 50 per cent by 1990. To promote that purpose, the NEP discriminated against the multinationals in its incentive grants and used a 25 per cent "back-in" clause to claim a quarter of what they had already discovered on federal lands. It also proposed to build up Petro-Canada by acquisition of foreign-owned companies. The effect was noticeable: by 1984 Canadian ownership had increased more than a third to 38 per cent.

To some, this policy was simply the latest and most radical in a series of nationalistic, even anti-American initiatives Trudeau had introduced since 1968, including the Foreign Investment Review Agency, the Canada Development Corporation, and the Canadian Radio-Television Commission. To others, more familiar with Trudeau's writings, the NEP seemed a puzzling change of mind, whether welcome or not. Classic liberal that he was, Trudeau had always distrusted nationalism for subordinating the individual to the community. He especially abhorred ethnocentric nationalism of the Quebec sort. English-Canadian nationalism, as propagated by Liberals such as Walter Gordon in the 1960s and the NDP in the 1970s, hadn't struck him as much better: it tended to overlook French Canadians, it probably had an unnecessary cost, and it was often used as an emotional prop to bolster weak arguments.

"I don't like props of any kind," he said. "My father left me a lot of money when he died, but I preferred to hike around the world with only a knapsack and live in small, bare apartments because I didn't want to use money as a prop. In the same way, though I admit that tears sometimes come to my eyes when I hear the national anthem, I'm not impressed by appeals to nationalism without good economic or cultural reasons. For a long while I resisted those who wanted to change *Time*'s tax status in order to help *Maclean's*. Since neither magazine had any impact on my life, I couldn't see why I should hurt one or help the other."

However, Trudeau was aware that the individual must be an integrated part of a society, that a society must have a state with which to organize itself, and that the state must have all the power, freedom, and flexibility possible in the international game of states in order to protect and foster its society. Indeed, he once said it would be "a crime against humanity" if Canada were not preserved. Therefore, when presented with good economic and cultural arguments, he acted, just as R. B. Bennett had acted to establish the Canadian Broadcasting Corporation or C. D. Howe had acted to find an all-Canadian route for his pipeline. FIRA, the "Canadian content" rules for radio and television, and the elimination of *Time*'s tax privilege were minimal responses to the impact of American capital and culture on Canada.

"Foreign ownership wasn't a bother in itself," Gérard Pelletier said. "It is a fact of life that Canada's standard of living depends on foreign investment. But the constant preoccupation in the mind of anyone sitting around the cabinet table is, how long can a country remain master of its political decisions if the economic decisions that really affect it are made somewhere else? Is the Canadian government really governing or is it just the cherry on the cake?"

In 1970 Trudeau said, "We can't expect, without becoming much poorer, to control all of our economy. What we can do is make an effort to control those economic or financial institutions which are of greater importance in the free development of this society." But if a philosophical base existed for action, the practical pressures weren't great enough to cause significant change. Thus, when the first OPEC crisis in 1973 prompted federal intrusion into oil pricing and the establishment of Petro-Canada as "a window on the industry," Ottawa restricted its share of the pie to about 10 per cent. At the same time, it continued giving enormous subsidies to a predominantly foreign-owned industry, which obtained over 350 per cent more revenue in 1978 than it had in 1970.

The second OPEC crisis of 1979 had huge financial implications for the industry as well as the provinces. The multinationals were expected to grow so rich that the outflow of capital from Canada would become a serious economic problem. Their wealth would lead to further foreign ownership in this and other sectors, and their size would prohibit any opportunity for Canadian control in the future. Already their export of capital had reached close to $4 billion between 1975 and 1979, while their foreign ownership had caused public anxiety about Canada's security of supply in the event of a global crisis. Even the marginal amount of research and development done in the Canadian industry and the relative inadequacy of Canadian energy engineering were attributed to decisions taken abroad by companies whose first obligation was to their homelands. By 1980 seventeen of Canada's top twenty-five oil companies were foreign-controlled. They accounted for 72 per cent of Canadian oil and gas sales. By the same year Canada had moved to first place on the United Nations' list of countries with high foreign ownership, supplanting Nigeria.

"I've never defined myself as a strong economic nationalist," Lalonde said, "and the NEP wasn't economic nationalism for its own sake. It was a very special case involving a very strategic industry with very significant impact on the country and future generations."

That was the logic used to sell the NEP to Trudeau. The threats to Canada's freedom and flexibility, presented as pragmatism, overwhelmed his suspicion of blind nationalism. Therefore, restrictions at an international level, which he had opposed at an interprovincial level, were seen as constructive, nation-building tools. For him the nationalism of the NEP was functional, not narrow in its ambition, and a good compromise between letting the multinationals operate and strengthening the Canadian side.

While Trudeau bought the arguments of the Canadian nationalists who had come to the fore in the cabinet, the PMO, and the Liberal Party, he wasn't converted to their fervour. He only seemed to be because his concept of nation *vis-à-vis* the provinces coincided with their concept of nation *vis-à-vis* the United States. In other words, his nationalism had more to do with the national government and unity than with the national culture and sovereignty.

Ironically, the nationalism he mistrusted and played down became his strongest weapon in defending the NEP and fighting the producing provinces. It was the Canadianization aspects that most people in all regions understood and supported, while Lougheed's arguments about provincial revenues and control lost force for pitting the despised multinationals against the popular Petro-Canada. Even in the West at the end of 1981, according to a Gallup poll, most Canadians wanted 75 per cent Canadian ownership by 1985 and an expansion of Petro-Canada through an acquisition of one of the big four multinationals.

"Trudeau's never been a nationalist," Martin Goldfarb said. "His picture was that he had to bring some federal authority back to the table, because the country will fragment and disintegrate if we allow the provinces to fight for their own territorial self-interest. We sold the NEP to the public as a nationalist thing, but in Trudeau's mind it was something else."

Most people, including most Liberals, couldn't follow Trudeau's distinction between a maple leaf flag waved in support of the federal government over the provinces and one waved in support of Canada over the rest of the world. Indeed, Trudeau was fighting for his issue with one arm tied behind his back by even attempting to make the distinction, just as he had tried to fight Quebec separatism by reason instead of patriotic emotion. In practice, however, national unity and nationalism usually blur, because both are linked to a strong sense of community. As both English- and French-Canadian Liberals came to value the national community, they were lured into nationalist positions. Indeed, they often found themselves articulating the same view of society they had rejected *on principle* from Quebec nationalists: collective and centrist. Moreover, because Canada's east-west axis has never made much economic sense, Canadian nationalism has usually been accompanied by state intervention.

"Often Canada is running against the natural flows of the market," Tom Axworthy said. "Maybe you can never defeat the market, which may be the single most powerful force in the world except for religion, but if you want to change its directions, you need some big battalions. One ally is the nation-state."

In other words, nationalism encouraged the interventionism that modern liberalism was already practising for economic or social reasons. Just as Trudeau had been persuaded by the pragmatic arguments for wage-and-price controls and regional development, he now accepted the nationalist arguments for Petro-Canada and the Canada Development Corporation. If there were strong justifications why the individual should give up some powers to the state, there was room in Trudeau's ideology to do so—and there tended to be even more room in the ideologies of most other Liberals. On the whole, they preferred to leave the economy to the private sector, but if the private sector failed to produce jobs or innovations or significant Canadian companies, they didn't hesitate to use the state either directly or indirectly.

"The state is merely an instrument to serve the people," Marc Lalonde said. "There are instances when its intervention is positive or appropriate and instances when it is not. We didn't have the ideological pretension that the state was the source of all good, nor did we hold the ideological view that said the less government, the better. We looked at the cost-benefits, social as well as economic, and made a choice based on each case."

But after 1980, Lalonde admitted, there was a new factor in the choice. "Frankly we felt we had gone out of our way to accommodate the private sector, to help it along, and for all practical purposes we had been kicked in the teeth. So we proceeded to do what we thought was right."

Intervention came in various forms, to use the energy sector as an example. Petro-Canada had been set up as an alternative to nationalizing any of the multinationals, but in 1981 it bought Petrofina and in 1982 it purchased the refining and distribution assets of BP Canada. In 1981 the Canada Development Corporation acquired Elf Aquitaine. Tax and grant provisions in the NEP were designed to boost the Canadian oil companies—some of which were seen as "chosen instruments" for public policy—while incentives and regulations were introduced to influence the direction of business decisions. What the carrots couldn't accomplish, the sticks did, via pricing fiats, regulatory agencies, and strict measures like the 25 per cent back-in.

Behind all these actions were some common assumptions: the federal government had a responsibility to become a major player in this critical sector; the national community had a right to a fair share of the benefits accruing to an industry it had heaped with privileges and tax dollars; and only Ottawa had the mandate or the ability to arbitrate among the various interests that clashed with increasing force over energy issues. Ironically, Peter Lougheed in his words and actions showed he shared these assumptions, *except* he substituted the Albertan government, the provincial community, and Edmonton as the interventionists. More than once, he angered the oil companies by driving a stiff bargain "for the people of Alberta who own the resource."

The pros and cons of the NEP's intervention were hotly debated. Its opponents cited the drilling rigs that were moved to the United States, the anger of the Americans over the back-in, the loss of investment and exploration, the waste of money on the crown lands, and the cancellation of important mega-projects, all of which threatened the goal of Canadian energy self-sufficiency. Its supporters countered with the doubling of the federal share of revenues, more Canadian ownership, and greater energy conservation, all of which they claimed would have long-term benefits for the country.

The debate quickly became academic, however, when, to everyone's shock, world oil prices declined instead of rising, interest rates soared to over 20 per cent, and the North American economy fell into a severe recession. It became difficult to separate the effects of the NEP from the effects of these misfortunes, particularly since Ottawa made a number of tax and pricing concessions to the industry in the NEP Update of May, 1982.

In the universal scenario of rising prices, there would have been enough money to balance the federal budget by 1985, buy peace with the producing provinces, keep the multinationals exploring, build the mega-projects, develop an independent industry, make equalization payments and compensation grants to the consuming provinces, and possibly bring about a Liberal victory in 1984. Instead, in the reality of falling prices, the NEP began to be unwound, the industry struggled back to its former position, and most of the great controversies eventually passed over like summer thunderstorms.

Judged by economic standards, the NEP proved murky at best, and disastrous at worst. Politics rather than economics had been its main purpose, however, and in that respect the program proved more successful. Alberta was forced to bargain from a defensive position for a change, and this paved the way for an oil-pricing agreement with Ottawa in September, 1981. The NEP was popular across the country. Moreover, Lougheed's production cutbacks and his decision not to negotiate with Lalonde to save the Alsands project had hurt Albertans and the provincial industry more than anyone else, and the federal government seemed determined to go ahead whether Alberta agreed or not. Lougheed was a realist, and he even toasted Pierre Trudeau with a smile and a glass of champagne on the signing of their deal. ("It was a dumb thing to do," Lougheed admitted.) By conceding an increase in Ottawa's share, Alberta was able to protect its share at the expense of the industry and get higher prices generally.

Nothing better illustrated the ease with which harmony is obtainable in federal-provincial relations when both sides think they're going to get rich. Nothing better demonstrated how little the Alberta government's opposition to the NEP was based on a principled concern for its overtaxed, overregulated allies in the private sector. Indeed, with the Heritage Fund, the Alberta Energy Company, the Alberta Petroleum Marketing Commission, high provincial royalties unilaterally imposed since 1972, and a host of other state initiatives, Lougheed often displayed his own understanding of pragmatic intervention.

Lougheed had been correct in seeing Ottawa's moves as a raid on his province's till, but behind its baser motives the federal government believed that nation-building had to prevail over province-building. The power of that belief was mightier than any constitutional authority. Even at the height of the battle, virtually the same percentage of Westerners (58 per cent) as other Canadians (62 per cent) told a poll that their first loyalty was to Canada, ahead of their province. In other words, the majority of Westerners chose in the pinch as Quebeckers had in their referendum. Realizing that, the Western premiers had to allow Ottawa to become a wealthier, more influential player in the energy field, just as they had to allow patriation and the Charter of Rights.

V

"For four years," said one Liberal cabinet minister, "we left no turd unstoned."

Trudeau may have been off working on his own agenda, but Trudeau liberalism seemed to infuse the entire government with the spirit of national authority, innovative reforms, and the will of the people. "The spirit was to use the British North America Act to the fullest," Tom Axworthy said. "We weren't going to grab more power, but we sure as hell were going to provide activist leadership in the areas we had. Some say that the best way to govern is to keep the lid on, don't stir things up, only do what's necessary, but our ethos was activism and leadership. If you have serious problems, you can't just work at the symptoms or make them vanish by smoke and mirrors. You have to go to the underlying causes."

Thus, while the Trudeauites were battling the provinces on two fronts, they decided to launch a third assault. In his budget of October, 1980, Allan MacEachen gave warning that he was going to lop $1.5 billion from Ottawa's transfer payments to the provinces when the latest five-year agreement expired in 1982. These transfers, mostly in equalization payments and shared-cost programs in health, education, and welfare, now exceeded $10 billion. Moreover, under the 1977 agreement, the federal government had handed over cash and tax points that weren't tied to a special use. Basically Trudeau, still open to idealistic decentralization, had accepted the provinces' argument that conditional transfers distorted provincial priorities in matters of provincial jurisdiction. He had trusted that popular pressure would keep the provincial government honest even if their principles didn't. Once freed from the obligation to spend money in certain ways in order to get money from Ottawa, however, the provinces cut back on their own expenditures and used the transfers to pay for a greater portion of their social programs.

As a result, the provincial governments received more of the political credit while Ottawa received more of the bills. At the same time that Ottawa faced mounting deficits, it was losing the ability to guarantee national standards by its transfers. Yet the provinces were as shocked by MacEachen's proposal to take back money as they were by Chrétien's proposal to take back powers. Trudeau realized they couldn't have it both ways, with one hand reaching out for federal cash and the other hand trying to grab from Ottawa the powers and resources which provided that cash. Even the premiers of the poorer provinces, some of which relied on Ottawa for more than half their revenues, seemed determined to weaken the central state for the sake of their own power or political advantage. In the end, the provinces were able to wangle a 10 per cent increase from 1977, but the federal government still expected to save $6 billion under the new agreement. More important, as far as Trudeau was concerned, the dangerous decentralist trend was reversed.

It wasn't just a matter of money. Ottawa wanted a say in post-secondary education, because of the critical link between training and Canada's industrial development. It wanted uniform standards in medicare programs and even moved to penalize those provinces that sought to introduce extra billing or user fees. In general, it wanted to be able to establish a direct relationship between the federal government and the people through the money and services it provided. In that way, political credit would return to where it was due, Ottawa could keep better control of its spending and the value in that spending, and the conscious presence of the national government would foster the conscious existence of a national community.

Trudeau set the goal, then left his ministers to find their own routes there. According to Lloyd Axworthy, Tom's older brother and a Winnipeg MP who served between 1980 and 1984 as Minister of Employment and Immigration and then Minister of Transport, "Trudeau said to us, 'You run your departments, you make the decisions. If you have a bunch of policies, you put them through the system. Be my guest, I have other work to do.' Trudeau had been dismayed by the factionalism of the provinces, the regions, and the competing interest groups, and he saw Ottawa as the only repository of the national interest. It was almost Rousseauian in its way. So we were always asking ourselves how the federal government could become an active, involved, useful partner at the individual, local, and regional level, there not just to deliver the cheques but as a policy maker and a helpful manager."

As chairman of the Cabinet Committee on Western Affairs (established because of the lack of a Liberal caucus from the West), Lloyd Axworthy was in a good position to play policy maker and helpful manager. The committee determined priorities for the spending of the Western Development Fund, which the Liberals set up in the fall of 1980 in anticipation of the billions of dollars that would be flowing to Ottawa under the NEP. To try to reduce the sting of lost revenue in the West, the fund was to receive about $4 billion from the bonanza and send it back to the West as federal initiatives for economic development. Not only would a happy federal presence become visible in the West, so would happy Liberals, of course. Thus, as the West's regional minister, Axworthy found himself meeting every other week with Manitoba ministers and the mayor of Winnipeg to discuss what to do with the city's core.

As it turned out, that became a good example of the strengths and weaknesses of the Liberal thrust. On the one hand, some praised Axworthy for the money, enthusiasm, and high-level clout he brought to the project. On the other hand, some criticized his interventions as arbitrary, alien, and grossly partisan. Between the theory and practice of Jean-Jacques Rousseau there always yawns a chasm ready to plunge some helpful manager into the temptations of remote, presumptuous bossism. Even if he avoids becoming Big Brother, he often appears as a snooty, bookish boy scout from the city who feels compelled to drag his old but perfectly competent, small-town grandmother across a street she knows too well to want to cross.

The best example of the spirit that possessed the Trudeau cabinet in the 1980s was Jean-Luc Pepin's tackling of that sacred Canadian icon, the Crow's Nest Pass freight rate. The "Crow rate," in existence since Laurier's time, fixed the price that western farmers had to pay to send their wheat to market by rail. It had worked reasonably well until the 1960s, when inflation caused it to represent less and less of the true value of the transportation. In fact, Ottawa estimated that by 1995 the Crow would represent such a small percentage of transportation costs, it would be better economics to carry wheat free than to collect the charge. Linked to this basic problem were some serious side-effects: railways couldn't afford to expand their services, western farmers were worried that the rail lines would be taken over by those who could pay more, and the industrialization of the West was handicapped since it was cheaper to ship wheat than any processed products, including meat.

Enter Pepin, ebullient, energetic, emotional, a veteran cabinet minister who had been in and out of politics before returning in 1980. Immediately prior to that, he had been co-chairman of the Task Force on Canadian Unity with John Robarts, the former Premier of Ontario. Pepin hoped and expected that his two-year study of the constitutional issues would qualify him for a role in the patriation debate. But the Pepin-Robarts report had condemned him in Trudeau's eyes by accepting the principle that Ottawa and the provincial governments were equals, both sovereign within their own jurisdictions. For that "one cardinal sin," according to Pepin, he was completely excluded from any input regarding the constitution and banished to the Department of Transport. There he buried his frustration under a typical frenzy of work.

"I looked around the department and asked myself what the heck needed to be done," he said, recalling his war like a greying but still lively French resistance fighter. "Whether I was loved or hated, it didn't matter, I was looking for useful results, something dramatic, and personal glory, of course!" It didn't take him long to find the Crow. "This was a political job for a king to do! Certainly somebody had to do it, and what did we have to lose? Nothing! So we rose to the occasion."

He revved up his bureaucrats for the challenge, and together they emerged with plans for "three revolutions": to double-track the rail lines, to diversify grain production by eliminating the preference on wheat, and to encourage western processing by paying subsidies to farmers as well as the railways and eliminating the preference on grain as opposed to meat. "My arrogance was to try to tie transportation, agriculture, and livestock reforms together," Pepin said, "because I thought they were so intimately related that you could not divide them." In effect, the western farmers would have to pay considerably more for their transportation, but they would be able to transport more of more products at rates that were still heavily subsidized. Indeed, though the farmers would be paying for some of the costs of the reforms, the Western Development Fund was expected to make the reforms possible by providing over $1 billion to the railways for expansion.

"Then I had three people to conquer: Trudeau, Coutts, and Lloyd Axworthy," Pepin said. "Trudeau was easy prey. He always said that we were in politics to make the great changes that were necessary, not just to administer the daily affairs, so I simply played to his imagination. Coutts and Axworthy were against me—because there was no political benefit in the short term—but eventually Axworthy became convinced this was the right thing to do and he came along in spite of his fears."

Axworthy wasn't convinced by the transportation benefits, but he did see a chance to change the West's historical status as an exporter of unprocessed products. For their part, most of the western farm organizations, such as the wheat pools and the National Farmers' Union, opposed the new Crow package, though it had addressed some of their long-term concerns and contained some advantages, because they feared for their particular interests.

"The leaders chickened when they realized their troops weren't following them," Pepin said. "The pool leadership didn't dare make up its mind, so we had to be daring on its behalf." Therefore, he forged ahead. "I went to the cabinet, the Priorities and Planning Committee, the Economic Affairs Committee, and the Western Affairs Committee maybe twenty times. It was agonizing, and at some point physical stamina became more important than intellectual merit. Most normal human beings would have given up at the work, the patience, and the perseverance involved, but I was completely possessed by my objective and too far advanced to turn back."

Pepin got his first two revolutions through the system, but he hit a wall on the third. Quebec livestock producers were upset that encouraging the western production of meat might create competition that would hurt their industry. They lobbied their Liberal ministers and MPs hard. Pepin countered that western meat would serve a different market, but no amount of salesmanship was going to persuade Quebec pig farmers that something good for the West wasn't bad for them. Twelve Liberal constituencies in rural Quebec were thought to be jeopardized; about thirty Quebec MPs were threatening to quit the Liberal caucus; and Pepin and an irate Axworthy found themselves in a minority in the cabinet.

"I pleaded with Trudeau for two hours," Pepin said. "But he kept saying, 'In politics there are things you can do and things you can't do. If you can get some western farmers to support you, I'll tackle Quebec, but I can't tackle both.' He was right, of course. It was visible that he would have loved to back me, but he wasn't that crazy or reckless. It was difficult enough to take on the western interests, but it was impossible when Quebec was added to the fight. And to win over Quebec he would have had to tour the farm regions himself and explain the facts. In the end, the issue was important, but not as important as world peace."

"For twelve seats, which we lost anyway," Lloyd Axworthy concluded, "we gave up a lot and lost a lot of credibility. Canadians don't change very willingly. Yet once the hollering stopped, the Crow reforms were generally accepted and quickly became part of a new fabric. Napoleon warned against fighting on too many fronts at once, but we did exactly that. We pushed this country very hard."

While Jean-Luc Pepin was wrestling with the Prairie wheat pools and the Quebec pig farmers, to take one more example, Michael Kirby was assigned to wrestle with the East Coast fishing industry. Again the intervention was prompted by a sense of impending crisis; again Ottawa arrived in the guise of policy maker and helpful manager in the key sector of a regional economy; and again the solutions fell somewhere between autocratic boldness and political recklessness.

The crisis was the approaching bankruptcy of much of the industry. The small fishing companies couldn't survive in the international market against the large ones, while several of the large companies had overextended themselves financially in the optimism that followed the expansion of Canada's fishing waters to 200 miles in 1977. Their optimism had been broken by low prices, the recession, and high interest rates—not unlike what happened in the western energy sector—and they were on the verge of bringing down whole towns and hundreds of small creditors along with themselves. In January, 1982, after finishing his work on the constitution, Kirby was named chairman of the federal government's Task Force on Atlantic Fisheries. A year later it completed a report on policies for the industry as a whole and proceeded to the question of restructuring and refinancing the troubled companies, which composed about half of the vital regional industry that employed over 100,000 people.

"Our choice was to let the industry go bankrupt and then pick up the pieces or to step in and work with the companies and the provincial governments to find a solution," he said. "Many people in Ottawa were advocating the first option, as a way of increasing the role of government and their own power base, but neither the federal government nor the provinces could bear the unemployment that would result for six months, a year, or longer. So we sought a negotiated settlement with the owners and were willing to pay a small premium to avoid the dislocation of bankruptcy, just as Ottawa did when Dome Petroleum got into trouble with its banks."

The task force report had stated a couple of important policy objectives: economic viability was the industry's first priority, not jobs or Canadian ownership; and control should remain as far as possible within the private sector. The cabinet accepted these objectives before Kirby set off to negotiate with the owners, banks, unions, and provincial governments. But pragmatism soon had its own way. When economic viability above jobs meant the possibility of closing two redundant fish plants in Newfoundland in order to reduce the excess processing capacity and save $50 million, Ottawa was caught in a nasty confrontation with Premier Brian Peckford. In fact, the closures would have been only a small step toward making the industry a business instead of a social agency, since the restructuring proposal already intended to keep open a number of uneconomical plants in isolated Newfoundland communities that depended on them. Peckford, however, wanted all the plants kept open.

For a while Ottawa was prepared to act unilaterally, but ultimately politics prevailed, and a deal was made with Newfoundland in which the two plants remained open, subject to enough conditions to let the federal government save face and money. At the same time, the objective of private-sector control suffered a temporary, if not permanent set-back when Ottawa was forced as a last resort to make a $165-million investment in the shaky companies. They were already weighed down with loans, they couldn't be singled out unfairly for grants, and they didn't lure ordinary investors for obvious reasons. When the Nova Scotia company, National Sea, did attract a group of investors, the federal government reduced its holding to a minority position; but it was still the majority shareholder in Newfoundland.

"Trudeau preferred free enterprise," said Kirby, who also had opposed government equity at first, "but how do you solve a problem? Are you prepared to pay in social and public policy terms—not to mention political terms—the costs of bankruptcy? Traditionally Canadian governments of both stripes haven't, not because of ideology but because of pragmatism. The need to maintain *national* infrastructures and *regional* industries has led to government investment time and again."

For better or worse, therefore, the Trudeauites went to the rescue of Chrysler Canada, Massey-Ferguson, Maislin Transport, the textile industry, as well as Dome Petroleum and the East Coast fisheries, just as previous governments had gone to the rescue of the railways that became Canadian National, the steel industry in Nova Scotia, the aircraft industry in Central Canada, and scores of other faltering businesses. Even the Crow rate reforms were driven by the financial inability of the railways to double-track without hefty government assistance. Often the problems were structural rather than managerial, having to do with distances, limited domestic markets, and the world economy, and as a rule the emaciated private sector of the poorer regions has always needed Ottawa's help to survive.

In almost every case, businessmen and bankers put aside their typical anti-interventionist rhetoric and expected support. They displayed the same basic, self-interested, perfectly human contradictions that ran through federal-provincial relations, as they requested federal support through taxes, grants, rules, and partnerships for their expensive or high-risk ventures in northern oil exploration, offshore energy development, technology research, export programs, and so on.

"Mixed enterprises may be the wave of the future," Kirby said, despite his initial opposition to government equity in the fisheries. "All governments are underwriting their private sectors to some extent, and even the privatization of certain nationalized companies going on in the United Kingdom under Margaret Thatcher isn't completely that: the government is selling off 51 per cent but keeping the rest. Unless they are exceedingly profitable, many of Canada's big national industries are going to have to have the flywheel of some public participation."

If so, both government and industry share common concerns that neither knows how to answer. Is a mixed enterprise strictly a business operation or fundamentally a social vehicle? Should the general public be specifically rewarded for its investment or should the rewards go to the private shareholders alone? Do governments have any talent for backing the right horses, can they resist using their coercive powers and equity positions to force un-economical decisions on the companies, and will they ever get out of a business once they get into it? Should the private sector be allowed to pluck off the profitable areas of failing industries and leave the rest to public expense? Should mixed enterprises be favoured—or discriminated against—for government work? In the case of the fisheries, circumstances couldn't wait for the theories to catch up, and everyone had to bicker and elbow toward satisfactory improvisations.

The pragmatic impetus behind Canada's mixed economy was often missed by those who portrayed Pierre Trudeau as a socialist. On the contrary, he never thought highly of nationalization, he used to argue that it made more economic sense to move people to jobs than subsidize chronically depressed regions, his governments engaged in supply-side economics long before Ronald Reagan went to Washington, and he hardly achieved anything in redistributing wealth to the needy. Neither Chrysler Canada nor Dome were nationalized, for example, and the wealthy got the same share of national personal income in 1984 as they did in 1951.

In fact, most businessmen were hard pressed when asked to cite the specific legislation that fuelled their animosity. Capital-gain taxes, more rules and regulations, Petro-Canada, and FIRA were favourites, but their harm was almost always offset by tax concessions, decreased competition and hefty grants, protection for vulnerable Canadian industries, and lucrative government partnerships. More often and with more reason, business condemned Trudeau's general direction toward higher spending, higher deficits, bigger bureaucracies, and more intervention, but each condemnation was usually accompanied by demands for more favours to business itself. Between 1968 and 1983, to demonstrate the reality, the share of corporate taxes in national revenue declined from 17 per cent to under 14 per cent.

The most pertinent critique was also the most ethereal: Trudeau didn't inspire investment confidence. Its effect was very real, because confidence encourages investment, jobs, and growth, but its cause was as much in the realm of whimsy as in this world. Rumours about why John Turner left the cabinet were as important as what the budget said. Tales about the eggheads in the PCO were as significant as the Liberals' dependence on NDP support between 1972 and 1974. Many businessmen remembered Trudeau's 1975 television remarks in which he called his wage-and-price controls "a massive intervention in the decision-making power of the economic groups, and it's telling Canadians that we haven't been able to make it work, the free market system." Few remembered his reluctance to impose those controls.

If Trudeau bought John Kenneth Galbraith's analysis of the structural problems in the new industrial age, he didn't buy the famous Harvard economist's interventionist solutions, though pragmatism forced him to rent part of them. Yet the business community remained profoundly suspicious. It had never felt on sure ground with Trudeau. In closed, overheated boardrooms and clubs, the mildew of distrust had grown rapidly into a mould of hatred that gave an ugly hue to the plainest fact. Trudeau had tramped through Russia and China, therefore he was a Marxist. Trudeau had worked for the unions and the CCF, therefore he was an ideologue. Trudeau had long hair and sandals, therefore he was a queer. Trudeau had married a dope-smoking flower-child, therefore he was a dope-smoking lecher. The visceral hostility of the old Establishment toward someone who hadn't fought in the Second World War, hadn't dealt with a balance sheet more complex than that of an inheritance, and hadn't settled down by forty lent a distorting dignity to the private sector's views.

For his part, the Prime Minister came to have less confidence in the Canadian business community. In principle, as a classic liberal, he liked free enterprise, with its emphasis on individual initiative and decentralized power. An activist state was only intended to create the conditions in which everyone could have a fair chance to succeed. In other words, the state became a counterweight to check the stronger, more centralized corporations that had come to dominate the marketplace. In practice, however, he found the limits to entrepreneurship in Canada.

"The private sector resented Pierre Trudeau because he called its game," Martin Goldfarb said. "This country is divided into little groups that have all the wealth. They want the government off their backs so that they can keep their little club closed and get richer. But Trudeau kept asking them, 'Where are the jobs you promised? Why aren't you out selling to the world? When are you going to do it? And if you can't do it, why do you blame us?' He opened up China for them, but they seemed to expect him to go and sell their products door to door. He had no grand design to get government more involved in the economy. He didn't *want* that. But he felt he had no choice. And the private sector hated him for telling them to get off their butts. He really rubbed their noses in it."

With other interest groups, whether the native people or the trade unions, Trudeau felt he could get beyond their particular demands in order to initiate a dialogue about the national good or Canada's future. When he was dragged into a reception at the Toronto Club or the Mount Royal Club, however, he invariably found himself cornered by some chief executive officer who wanted a specific tax clause amended. Not only was the demand usually self-serving, it was often followed by cant about cutting back social services or deregulation. Moreover, he felt personally uncomfortable with businessmen. Perhaps they reminded him of his convivial, entrepreneurial father, around whom Trudeau had felt "so inferior." Perhaps he simply disliked sharing the spotlight with other powerful men, as he himself once speculated. Certainly they had come from different directions and were on different wavelengths.

The businessmen were obsessed by profits, good management, and the idea that they were the engine of the economy. The Prime Minister knew that government couldn't be geared to the bottom line, because its purpose was service rather than profit. Nor was national leadership the same as executive control, because it had elements of

vision, irrationality, and crisis that couldn't be put on a
flow-chart. Finally, while Trudeau recognized the unique
and important role of the business community, he saw
that it had to be treated as just another interest group in
the broad interplay of national forces. That was the worst
insult of all to a corporate elite who had been accustomed
to dealing with politicians as uppity, high-priced help.

Intellectually, Trudeau had an aversion to accommodating elites. After more than a dozen years as Prime Minister, he could remember by name the less than half-dozen
corporate lobbyists he had allowed into his office. John
Turner later argued that more stroking from Trudeau could
have secured a voluntary wage-and-price agreement from
business and labour leaders in 1975. To do so, however,
ran counter to Trudeau's aloof personality, his cold pride,
and his democratic theories. In fact, he took a perverse
delight in deliberately goading businessmen out of their
smugness, their self-righteousness, and their thickness.
Despite his background, his wealth, and his office, he never
felt part of any elite and never wanted to. As a result,
knowing he was driving his advisers to despair, he went
into meetings with newspaper tycoons and oil magnates
with Cyrano's spirit alive in his heart:

> . . . What would you have me do?
> Seek out a powerful protector, pursue
> A potent patron? Cling like a leeching vine
> To a tree? *Crawl* my way up? Fawn, whine
> For all that sticky candy called success?
> No, thank you.

Nevertheless, the old machine only functioned with a
lot of greasing, which meant consultation, conciliation,
and concession. Though Trudeau never developed Pearson's amiable, intuitive, experienced diplomacy, he went
through the motions more times than Pearson ever had in
government. "After 1981," Lalonde said, "we even opened
up the hothouse atmosphere around preparing the budget.
We said to the private sector, 'Come in with any idea you
want, but tell us the cost and how we're going to finance

it. Don't tell us to reduce the deficit and then hand us a list of demands.' "

Did Trudeau do enough and were the Trudeauites sincere before they announced the shortcomings of the marketplace? That was the hot debate. It was generally waged between those who believed that Canada's mixed economy was inevitable, moral, and beneficial and those who thought it was ideological in origin, costly in practice, and harmful in effect. Canada's political culture had always accepted and valued government intervention as part of its liberal ideology. Furthermore, only the fanatics on both sides denied that the mixed economy was both moral and costly. The real debate centred on whether it was beneficial or harmful in the long run. Since the proof lay somewhere in the vague future, the pros and cons were argued with equal amounts of conviction, statistics, theory, and political fog.

In the short run, however, public opinion on the matter began to change in the early 1980s. The recession, usurious interest rates, inflation based on rising energy prices, low prices for resources, dwindling markets for products, and chronic unemployment became linked to the simultaneous increase in government activity: more bureaucracy, more spending, and more deficits. While most Canadians didn't leap to the ideological conclusions of Margaret Thatcher or Ronald Reagan (whose classic liberalism was now on the right, and therefore erroneously pegged as conservatism), many began to wonder if the shift toward social democracy was functioning as expected. In other words, they didn't mind social democracy as long as it worked, but apparently it wasn't working very well.

Those doubts were only doubts. They opened the door to other ideas and approaches, whether decentralization, deregulation, or deficit-cutting, but they didn't close the door on interventionism *per se*. In fact, the worse things got, the more demand there was for government action. People wanted jobs, companies wanted bail-outs, and associations wanted industrial strategies. Provinces wanted transfer payments to meet the increased strains on the welfare "safety net." Everyone wanted money. Certainly it seemed a good idea if Ottawa made its bureaucracy smaller and more efficient, but no one wanted to lose services. Certainly it would be proper to balance the books, but no one wanted to be pinched. Certainly it would be refreshing to get the government out of the boardrooms, but no one wanted cutbacks in jobs, grants, industries, train stops, or clean air.

"Between 1980 and 1984," Allan Gregg said, "satisfaction with the government dropped from 50 per cent to 20 per cent, the lowest rate ever recorded. Yet there wasn't one scintilla of change in the belief that governments can wholly or partly solve the problems that concern people. They may have to do things differently, but the system can still work if changed."

In essence, the blame was focussed elsewhere: while social democracy may or may not have been working very well, Trudeau and the Liberals clearly weren't.

That catch-all blame had two advantages. It didn't require any intellectual consistency, and it could be solved simply and quickly by throwing the bums out. Many of the same people who applauded unilateral patriation and a Charter of Rights criticized Trudeau's conflicts with the premiers. Many of the same people who supported Canadianization in the NEP were bothered by Ottawa's alienation of Washington and American investors. Many of the same people who urged the Liberals to develop a high-tech industrial strategy for the future berated them for persistently interfering in the economy. What this approach lost in intellectual rigour, it made up in emotional gratification. Few felt obliged to sort through the complex mess and figure out how much of the country's woe was attributable to Trudeau, or the Liberal Party, or Canada itself, or, indeed, the Western world. As an explanation of what was wrong, ministerial arrogance seemed on a par with the deindustrialization of the Northeast United States.

Of course, Trudeau and his cabinet made themselves such easy targets. While ordinary people stood in danger of losing their homes, farms, and businesses, Trudeau was battling the premiers about the meaning of the word "not-withstanding" in the constitution. He seemed like a precious god sitting above the fray, acting out his destiny for abstract pleasure. Even uneducated minds could understand the risk to jobs in confronting the provinces, business, the multinationals, and the Americans at a time of economic crisis. Though they could agree with Trudeau's principle of nation-building, they knew that in the squeeze it would be their jobs, his principle. People were hurt and scared, yet all they saw among their leadership was disharmony and preoccupation. Trudeau's own agenda was full, and there didn't seem any place on it for the poor and the unemployed.

"If you're going to run a strategic prime-ministership, you better pick the issues right," Tom Axworthy said. "What you choose to concentrate on is crucial. When we were working on the constitution and energy in 1981, we weren't working on the budget, and that mistake may have lost us the 1984 election."

After 1980 there was a conscious decision to leave the economy off Trudeau's agenda. His credibility on the issue had been damaged ever since he had had to reverse himself on wage-and-price controls and there were only so many hours in the Prime Minister's day. Furthermore, both Coutts and Pitfield had become more sensitive while out of power to criticisms that the PMO and the PCO had interfered unduly in the affairs of the Department of Finance. So after the NEP budget in 1980, Finance was left to work on the economic priorities. Its canny, veteran minister, Allan MacEachen, was trusted to look after the political ramifications.

The result was a disaster. During the summer of 1981 MacEachen was persuaded by his officials to undertake a sweeping tax reform, in which the highest level of taxation would be reduced to 50 per cent but a whole series of tax loopholes would be closed. No doubt MacEachen was caught up in the same activist spirit that had seized the rest of his cabinet colleagues, and the reforms made some sense in the expanding economy that marked the first three-quarters of the year. By the time the budget was introduced in late November, however, the growth had stalled, the rate of unemployment had soared, and the public was looking for help and reassurance. Finance hadn't adapted to the new circumstances, so its restrictive, destabilizing measures fell like a bomb. Those hurt by the closing of the loopholes ignored any balancing benefits and yowled. Critics attacked the threat to jobs in the changes and the confusion. The public weren't the only ones unprepared for the massive jolt: the cabinet, the PMO, and the PCO were as shocked. Pitfield, for one, had been watching the budget presentation on television at home in his pajamas. When it was over, he got dressed, went over to the reception where all the Finance officials were congratulating each other, and said, "Don't you people realize you've just destroyed the housing industry, among other things?"

Trudeau and the cabinet had to immerse themselves in the deteriorating economic situation again. MacEachen was forced to backtrack on a number of proposals. A new budget was introduced the following June, and a program to curb inflation by voluntary restraints on wages and prices was instituted. Despite the relative success of the "6-and-5" program, the MacEachen budget shook the long-established assumption that, for all their faults, the Liberals were at least competent. Even party members began to question the judgement of their leadership in the wake of the fiasco. To an extent there was nothing any Canadian government could do in the face of international interest rates and world market prices, but jeopardizing some 40,000 jobs for the sake of an estimated $125 million in extra revenue was clearly making matters unnecessarily worse. In May, 1982, more Canadians said they were Progressive Conservatives rather than Liberals, and the Liberals ranked with the NDP as incompetent, impractical, and extremist.

By 1983 the cabinet, the caucus, and the party were as exhausted as the people of Canada from all the battles. They had spent most of their political capital on their activist agenda, and there was no money left to buy back favour. Timidity returned, and frustrated ministers started squabbling among each other for a piece of the billion or two Finance threw to them to use at their discretion as a way of diverting them from the real issues concerning the size of the deficit and unemployment.

"Some politicians think their only role is to spend money," said Marc Lalonde, who replaced MacEachen as Minister of Finance in 1982. "But we were forced to say there's no money. Governing and leadership required more finesse than before, when you could throw money at a problem and think you had achieved a great revolution. Now we had to invent things that didn't cost money or took money from somebody else. That was a frustrating experience for many ministers."

"It's a sick party," one close observer concluded after watching the Liberal cabinet growl and snap over goodies.

The atmosphere—part burn-out, part resignation to problems beyond control, part greedy desperation about getting re-elected—reminded some of the period leading up to the 1979 election. It was worsened by the distractions about whether Trudeau would stay on as leader or who should succeed him. Many Liberals looked at the polls and thought it was time for him to go. Far from sinking into his usual lethargy, however, Trudeau was showing more vigour and purpose than his ministers. In the fall of 1983 he launched a peace initiative that took him to capitals around the world and, as a happy side effect, boosted the popularity of himself and his party at home.

Votes hadn't been Trudeau's intention. He had been irritated by the number of government leaders who only spoke out strongly for nuclear disarmament *after* they had left office, and he wanted to re-emphasize his commitment to the international community before he retired. In fact, he undertook the peace initiative despite the warnings of those who thought it was doomed to failure and therefore potentially harmful to his reputation. The issue of world peace attracted him by its overwhelming importance and its intellectual challenge. It appealed to his belief that politics should be more than grubby pols agitating over post offices and wharves.

But while he was holed up in his office learning the intricacies of MAD (Mutual Assured Destruction) or huddled with his counterparts in New Delhi and Peking, his cabinet was tearing itself to pieces over the equivalents of post offices and wharves. In many cases, Trudeau no longer bothered to arbitrate among his ministers. He had higher matters on his mind, and his successor could concern himself with these petty feuds.

However, as the day approached for Trudeau to resign if he was to give the new leader time to prepare for the next election, pressure began to be applied by the loyalists for him to stay. Goldfarb told him that the numbers were beginning to shift in the Liberals' favour: another victory was possible. Jim Coutts and Tom Axworthy urged him to keep the momentum of activist leadership going in new sectors, such as pension reform, regional development, income redistribution, and post-industrial employment strategies. Now we know we exist as a nation, they argued, but what do we exist for?

"Trudeau wouldn't stay just to bail out the Liberal Party as he had done so often," Keith Davey said. "He had to have a purpose or a mission beyond keeping the party in power or retaining the trappings of power for himself. Why should he stay? What was there to accomplish? In the end, he couldn't find something that mattered that much."

He could always have found some excuse if he really wanted to stay, of course. But the negative factors loomed large as he took a long walk by himself in an Ottawa snowstorm on the night of February 28, 1984. There wasn't a consensus in the party about its future direction, and he could hear some knives being sharpened in the ranks. He could fight the guys in front, he thought, but he couldn't fight the guys at his back too. Then there was a personal factor: he didn't want his three boys to spend their teenage years at Sussex Drive or Stornoway. Most of all, he looked deep into himself and asked, "Do I have it in me to pick up the fight and go again? If I lose, do I have it in me to do the work that will have to be done to re-build the party?

Do I still have the fire in my belly?'' He discovered that
he didn't.

The next day, leap-day, he announced he was retiring
as Prime Minister and leader of the Liberal Party. He had
come a lot closer to staying than most people imagined,
but now someone else would have to stop John Turner.
The tributes that followed were rather more circumspect
than those after his 1979 resignation, as if no one was
prepared to count the man out until he was officially replaced in June. This time, however, he actually went.

<hr />

VI

<hr />

There were few tears when he left. Even those who
idolized him understood the appropriateness of his going.
He wouldn't risk the humiliation of defeat at the end of
his career, he wouldn't see the party turn against him, and
he wouldn't leave with the haunting sense of incomplete-
ness that had existed in 1979. If anything, many Liberals
and a great deal of the country wanted a respite from his
challenges and will. They wanted to forget the traumas of
the referendum, the constitution, the energy crisis, and
the recession. They needed to work on putting their economic affairs back in order.

"By 1984 there had been too much social change,''
Goldfarb said. "Trudeau had really shaken the country.
Every change had meant a fight, and the effect was a
massive culture shock.''

If Trudeau's record before 1979 had seemed scarcely
more significant than Robert Borden's, his last term made
him one of the few important Prime Ministers in Canadian
history. He passed Laurier in time in office, he changed
as much as King had done in many more years, and one
had to go back to Macdonald to find the same combination
of vision, action, and achievement. His strength arrested
the most direct threat to the union since Joseph Howe tried
to take Nova Scotia out of the young federation. His resolve permanently altered the country in terms of language, rights, regional sharing, and government. "He shook

the country out of the lethargy that probably would have led to its breakup," said Marc Lalonde.

In four years, in a time of crushing economic conditions, he undertook the most concerted effort at nation-building since Confederation. Though compromises were made to soften the blows, his thrust shattered most of Ottawa's traditional rules of conciliation, brokerage politics, and elite accommodation. It almost overturned the convention by which the federal government and the provinces had been abiding for more than a hundred years. It outraged the premiers, angered Washington, sent London into a tizzy, and fuddle-duddled the opposition. It broke the gentlemen's agreement under which the old boys of the business Establishment could consider their Ottawa bashing as they considered their martinis: a social habit passed down by Father, pleasant before lunch at the club, a bit excessive on occasion, but really nothing to worry about *yet*.

The costs were great. "If you continue what you're doing," a premier told Trudeau during the first ministers' conference in November, 1981, "you'll split the country."

"If the country splits because I'm trying to patriate the constitution and introduce a Charter of Rights," Trudeau shot back, "then it deserves to split."

Not unexpectedly, the greatest resistance came from the elites of Canada's decentralized power centres. They and their Ottawa colleagues were the principal beneficiaries of the old ways—as their very wealth and strength proved—and they understood the implications of Trudeau's changes. It didn't matter that many of the elites had never been more powerful than during the Trudeau years. The provinces had grown faster and richer than Ottawa, the premiers had become formal players on the national stage, corporations had never been as concentrated, the big banks had only become bigger, and, until the bust of the world price, even western businessmen and the oil multinationals had boomed to an unprecedented degree. All of them wanted more and were infuriated when Trudeau offered less.

Their complaints weren't really about the "back-in" clause or the "notwithstanding" clause. Those were just specific instances of the greater, yet more abstract issues: the principles of national community and popular sovereignty. People assumed that Trudeau was the only one absorbed by the philosophical questions, but the debates of his last term were as close as Canada has ever come to *The Federalist* letters of Hamilton, Madison, and Jay. Peter Lougheed got emotional defending the idea that Canada was a compact among provinces, not a contract among individuals. Sterling Lyon (the Tory Premier of Manitoba) and Allan Blakeney (the NDP Premier of Saskatchewan) got apoplectic resisting the idea that the courts could overrule their legislatures. René Lévesque wanted to divide the country because of his adherence to majority rule. Everyone recognized that giving in on their principles would mean, sooner or later, giving in on their powers.

"I realized that if our cause was right," Trudeau said in his farewell speech to the Liberal Party, "all we had to do to win was to talk over the heads of the premiers, over the heads of the multinationals, over the heads of the superpowers to the people of this land, to the people of Canada."

It was a crucial realization. More than anything else, it was inspired by the Quebec referendum. For almost twenty years the spectre of separation had hung like a sword over Ottawa's head. Concession after concession had to be made, or else Quebec would separate. Each concession had to be given to every province, or else Quebec would have special status and be on its way to separation. Finally, the threat was faced in a sudden-death drama, and despite a question so soft that Trudeau himself could have voted "Yes" with reason, the people voted for Canada.

Nothing was the same after that. Not only did the steam go out of the Parti Québécois, the bluster went out of the arguments of all the premiers. No Canadians were more in love with their region, more sensitive to the interests of their province, or more legitimately concerned with the preservation of their identity than Quebeckers. Yet they remained virtually indifferent when patriation and a Charter of Rights were imposed on them without the consent of their provincial government, even though that meant the loss of their veto. No matter how loudly the elites yelled about Trudeau's *coup de force*, most Quebeckers wouldn't have rejected him as they were to reject John Turner. If they had turned at all, it would have been for change, for the economy, and for an end to the bickering, not because of Trudeau's direction.

The same was true in most of English Canada. It was the bruising pace of Trudeau's actions that angered people, not the direction or even the distance. Urban life, mass communications, economic integration, and frequent mobility had created a new sense of national community. While everyone bitched about taxes, red tape, and intrusive legislation, few actually wanted Ottawa to do less for them. Cautious, gradualist, consensus leadership in Ottawa had been the safe and sure means of governing, because the elites wouldn't surrender anything without a fight and every fight had a political cost. Yet it had barely welded the country together since 1867 and didn't satisfy the nationalist, centralist, collectivist elements usually dormant within Canada's two political cultures. Indeed, Trudeau had tried the old methods until the country began to fall apart in his hands.

Compelled by pragmatism, often because he had "no choice," Trudeau advanced with trepidation from his classic liberalism and then from 1960s liberalism and stumbled upon the majority of Canadians waiting for him to catch up. During the 1979 and 1980 elections he found as if by chance that, in Tom Axworthy's words, "the single most visible constituency in this country is nation, leadership, activism." During the constitution battles he learned to differentiate between the loud, almost hysterical voices of the premiers and the barely audible, more sensible attitudes of their citizens. During the NEP fight he discovered the latent force of Canadian nationalism. Indeed, one could have asked of Trudeau's move what the essayist Junius had asked in the eighteenth century: "Is this the wisdom of a great minister? Or is it the ominous vibration of a pendulum?"

In effect, when Trudeau swung with Canadian liberalism to the left, he struck a response because the new ideology almost precisely mirrored Sir John A. Macdonald's ideology. In other words, Trudeau liberalism was as far to the left of classic liberalism as Macdonald's conservative liberalism had been to the right. From different sources and for other goals, both saw Canada as a new experiment among the states of the world, more than the sum of its parts, to be protected and nurtured by a strong central government and a necessary amount of intervention in the economy. Both were based on Canadian concepts of authority, community, and national will. In essence, both shared a remarkably similar view of where power should be and how much should be there.

As a result, most Canadians adapted quickly to Trudeau liberalism. There was a perceptible shift in what was normal, what was possible, and what was desirable. That didn't mean there wasn't a political price to pay for offending the elites, provoking confrontations, and jolting the nation. Just as Macdonald's Conservatives had paid a heavy price for warring with the premiers and upsetting French Canada, so Trudeau's Liberals alienated the business community and the West. It's not inconceivable, as Trudeau warned his caucus, that the federal Liberals could suffer the fate of the Tories after Macdonald for much the same reasons. The power-brokers of the nation have found "the Canadian way" to govern to their advantage, and in the end they weren't fundamentally weakened by all the compromises that they forced Trudeau to make. However, once the dust settled, the people themselves found it hard to see their society in the traditional way. The voters may have turned from the Liberals and disliked Trudeau's attitudes, but anyone who confused that with a general rejection of the national state would soon find themselves in political trouble.

In this respect, Trudeau's last term can be compared

to Franklin Delano Roosevelt's impact on American government during the Depression. Crisis prompted and permitted a major shift to the left in both cases. The reforms were structural in nature and long-lasting in effect. The people wanted to pause for breath and to let the stragglers catch up, but most had kept up. However, far from being loved by the masses and hailed as the saviour of the nation by the intellectuals and media, Trudeau left office despised by those he had hurt and hardly missed by the rest.

He didn't have a world war with which to heal the wounds he had inflicted, of course, but mostly Pierre Trudeau lacked the human qualities that allowed people to forgive Roosevelt his sins. "Trudeau couldn't do what he did and be loved at the same time," Tom Axworthy said. "He didn't have the personal skills, the little arts of democracy, to make people feel at ease. He was a Catholic intellectual, a rather private thinking man. He could inspire people by his depth of vision, he could attract people like a magnet, but he couldn't make them feel part of a cohesive team. He constantly challenged people, so that they were left feeling uncomfortable, and he constantly challenged Canada without giving much of himself."

There were practical effects to this inadequacy, such as his inability to bring the elites into the national arena as Macdonald and King had done or charm his enemies into submission. More important, however, were the strange psychological effects. He scared people with his cold reason, his rigid discipline, his impatience with human weakness, and his *panache*. Canadians were ready for centralization, intervention, and leadership—in fact, part of their psyches longed for them—but Trudeau and Trudeauism got so entangled with them that there seemed something frigid and menacing about Ottawa and national unity. To an extent, that was a reaction based on the classic aspects of English-Canadian liberalism. A strong leader might be necessary and even satisfying, but eventually "the King must die." The ritual slaying of the temporary kings was the people's only real check against tyranny. Yet it seemed particularly necessary in Trudeau's case. He had led the nation hard and fast, his ways had worked to his own delight, so all the more reason to depose him. Indeed, his natural aloofness resembled contempt, as if the people had become another authority to be mocked and resented.

"Prejudice sometimes seemed to replace argument," Donald Johnston observed of the government in which he had been a minister. "The private sector seemed to be tolerated, not supported; provincial governments were seen as selfish, obstructionist, and not to be trusted; big government and crown corporations were seen as good, foreign investment as bad. Surprisingly for many, Trudeau himself was not doctrinaire on any of these issues. Unfortunately, a number of ministers were, or at least seemed to be."

An absence of tolerance, a tendency to overgovern, a deliberate narrowing of the base of appeal among Liberals were personified by Trudeau's absence of warmth, his tendency toward bullying, and his deliberate narrowing of his circle. As Saint-Simon once wrote about Louis XIV, "He was a prince in whom no one would deny good and even great qualities, but he had many others that were petty or downright bad, and of those it was impossible to determine which were natural and which acquired." Certainly power didn't do much good to Pierre Trudeau's ego, his competitiveness, or his private character.

> Pierre, suddenly challenged,
> Stripped and walked into the rapids,
> Firming his feet against the rock,
> Standing white, in white water,
> Leaning south up the current,
> To stem the downward rush,
> A man testing his strength
> Against the strength of his country.

These lines by F. R. Scott, the poet and constitutional lawyer, were written long before Trudeau became Prime Minister, yet they caught his fatal weakness. The flaws that marred his spirit—pugnacity, vanity, and indifference—wouldn't allow him to harness his strength *with* that of the country. There was no doubt that he was a superior man, in the Chinese sense of the term. He had trained his mind and his body to be strong and precise instruments, and he had developed himself into an elegant and complex person of principle. But if in his youth he had passed his forty days in the wilderness and withstood the first temptation, in maturity he succumbed to the earthly kingdom below and thereby lost his soul.

Just as the ascetic who loved bare rooms and solitary journeys gathered a taste for marble desks and yachts in the Adriatic, so the shy intellectual acquired a talent for cynicism, opportunism, connivance, sarcasm, and public rudeness. Coarsened by public life, captured by his own rationality, rarely able to translate his thoughts and visions into emotions that might stir the hearts of a cold and reasonable people, he couldn't civilize the nation that longed to be uplifted by him. Isolated by power and his own habits, he had spent more time studying statute books than the lives he shaped.

"There was acre upon acre of farmland," he said in a speech in Strathroy, Ontario, in October, 1983, after nearly fifteen years as Canada's leader, "and all we could see— though I pressed my forehead against the cold window— all we could see were little lights here and there. And I was wondering what kind of people lived in those houses? And what kind of people worked in this part of Canada? And lived and loved here?"

If he was curious and ignorant about them, they remained curious and ignorant about him. In the end, though they had come far together and retained a wary respect for each other, Pierre Trudeau and the people of Canada could only love each other as abstractions.

SECTION TWO

The Who's Farewell Tour

I

Joe Clark began the 1980s in tears, and things were going to get a lot worse before they got better. It was a few days after the February election. Clark was in the office he would soon have to vacate, and he had been on the phone thanking party workers around the country for their help and apologizing for the loss. "What did I do wrong? What did I do wrong?" he started repeating at one point, and that's when he began to cry.

As Prime Minister he had been responsible for the debacle the previous December, when clumsy management and poor judgement had permitted the defeat of his government on its budget. As leader of the Progressive Conservatives he had been the Liberals' most devastating argument in the subsequent election. "Canadians were embarrassed to have Clark as their Prime Minister," Martin Goldfarb said, so the Liberals' strategy had been to play down their own controversial leader and concentrate on Clark's deficiencies: his awkward and uninspiring personality, his inadequate expression of national leadership, and the blunders of his 259 days in power. In the end, more Canadians hoped Trudeau had learned a little humility than expected Clark to have acquired a little competence.

Ever since his election as Tory chief in 1976, at the age of thirty-six, Clark had suffered in comparison to Pierre Trudeau. Trudeau was what Canadians wished to be— suave, intellectual, worldly, independent, and spontaneous. Clark was what Canadians feared they were—earnest, nice, honest, predictable, and rather dull. As a young man Trudeau had wandered the earth from adventure to adventure; as a young man Clark had cut short a visit in Europe to return and write pamphlets for the Diefenbaker government. Of course, many people hated Trudeau and loved Clark for the same reasons. "Joe" was one of them, ordinary but trustworthy, sympathetic and decent, neither a threat nor an arrogant sophisticate, a dedicated and open-minded human being with his own brand of complexity and courage. Old ladies smiled on his small-town polite-ness and veterans admired his clean-cut perseverance. However, many more Canadians reacted against this fum-bly, pompous reflection of themselves. Joe Clark just wasn't good enough to make them greater.

Progressive Conservatives also wanted to be some-thing greater. Having tasted power after sixteen years of famine, they were driven half-mad by being deprived of it so quickly. They craved victory again. Clark had done a commendable job of narrowing their distance behind the Liberals during the 1980 election campaign, and once the shock and despair of defeat wore off, he led an effective and constructive attack on the government's constitution and energy legislation. But many Tories remained con-vinced that Joe Clark was Joe Btfsplk, a born loser, an eternal wimp, condemned forever to be a figure of tragedy or fun.

Under the party's constitution, the delegates to a gen-eral meeting can vote by secret ballot to hold a leadership convention. In 1981 a third of them did so. The remaining 66.4 per cent was much more than the simple majority Clark needed to carry on, though less than the support he had hoped for. "Go downstairs and thank them," said Clark's close friend and adviser Senator Lowell Murray, when asked what to do about the poor showing. "What the hell else can you do?" However, the degree of discon-tent reinforced the dissatisfaction with Clark inside his own caucus, which Murray described as becoming un-governable. Every caucus meeting was like a fight for sur-

vival. East fought West, right fought left, old guard fought
new guard, and everyone was obsessed by the leadership
issue. To keep the peace after the 1981 vote, Clark more
or less promised to reopen the issue if he didn't do appreciably better at the next general meeting in January,
1983, in Winnipeg. All through 1982 his organizers worked
to ensure that pro-Clark delegates got there. Meanwhile,
his enemies were recruiting delegates of their own.

"In 1981 there was a genuine 33 per cent who had a
real sense that I had let them down or couldn't win again,"
Clark said. "But 1981 demonstrated to people who wanted
to make mischief that they had a vehicle for doing just
that. The leadership review was a way to get to me. Winnipeg was less indicative of the grassroots party and more
manipulated and calculated."

Certainly the opposition in Winnipeg was more organized and better funded. There was even a secret informal committee, headed by Frank Moores, the former
Premier of Newfoundland, and partially funded by mysterious overseas sources ("strange money people," Clark
called them), to coordinate strategy for the various anti-
Clark forces. Besides those who thought him a loser, a
jerk, or both, there were others who never forgave Clark
for not putting them in the cabinet, not distributing the
spoils of office quickly and abundantly enough, and above
all not hanging on to power. There was an orchestrated
presence of right-wing ideologues, a loose *mélange* of Amway distributors, members of the National Citizens' Coalition and the Right-to-Life movement, extremist youths,
and those inspired by Ronald Reagan and Margaret
Thatcher. The majority of them were new to the party.
They saw it as their only plausible vehicle to power and
they hated Joe Clark for being a progressive or "Red" Tory.
Their numbers may not have been great, but their press
coverage increased their influence and their vocal demonstrations against Clark fuelled the feeling that he was
too divisive to stay. Finally, there were those with ambitions of their own. Clark's Minister of Finance, John Cros-

bie, had been plotting a leadership campaign since March, 1981, and close colleagues of Brian Mulroney had been rounding up anti-Clark delegates across Quebec.

Clark and Mulroney had met as active, young Tories in 1961, when both were twenty-two years old and ardent Diefenbaker supporters. They apprenticed in party organization more than party policy, turned on Diefenbaker and supported Dalton Camp's campaign to get a leadership review in 1966, and backed Davie Fulton for leader in 1967. Though Mulroney didn't find Clark "a fellow you'd go fishing with" and Clark admitted they wouldn't "choose to spend Saturday night watching a hockey game together," they maintained the cordial relationship of brothers-in-arms, Clark as an MP, Mulroney as a Quebec organizer. In 1976, however, Clark—"Joe *Who?*"—unexpectedly came from third place at the convention to replace Robert Stanfield and beat Mulroney for the leadership. In public Mulroney made great professions of loyalty and continued raising money for the party. In private he was extremely bitter and a good deal less complimentary about Clark's qualities. He went off to lick his wounds and learn about the private sector as president of the Iron Ore Company of Canada, declined to run for Parliament in either the 1979 or 1980 election, and bided his time. After the Tories' defeat in 1980, Clark became vulnerable. Mulroney began making major speeches across the country, while his friends captured control of the party's Quebec executive. Soon an unofficial committee began working on how to make Brian Mulroney the new leader of the Progressive Conservative Party.

As the Winnipeg general meeting drew closer, however, Mulroney got cold feet. The struggle for the leadership review was becoming personalized in the press and in the party. If Clark fell in January, everyone would point to the bloodied knife in the hand of Brian Mulroney, who didn't need to be reminded of the hatred and ostracism that had been Dalton Camp's reward for bringing down Diefenbaker. Moreover, because of the efforts of Clark's organizers in Quebec and elsewhere, with all the resources available to a party leader, it was far from likely that Clark would fall. Even if he only got two-thirds of the delegates again, Clark was told by Mulroney, "Well, Joseph, if 66 per cent was good enough in 1981, it's goddamn well good enough today." So, ever prudent, Mulroney decided to "get out of the traffic" in early December. At a well-publicized meeting with Clark at the Ritz-Carlton Hotel in Montreal, he reaffirmed his personal support for the leader. At the same time, with much less publicity but with Mulroney's knowledge, his friends continued their surreptitious labours.

Mulroney always insisted his declaration of support had been sincere. "I even met in my home with a group of Quebec organizers and asked them to back Clark," he said. "Some did, but some couldn't. I wasn't the goddamn Pied Piper who could deliver them all. I told Joe that. And one thing's for sure, he would have received a lot fewer votes from Quebec if I hadn't supported him."

But, in light of what happened, Clark always remained suspicious. Many believed he was conned by Mulroney's clever duplicity. By accepting Mulroney's loyalty so publicly, Clark relieved him of any responsibility for the third of the Quebec delegates who voted for a leadership review.

As early as March, 1982, Clark was told that he would have trouble getting his numbers to an acceptable level by January. There was also a caucus revolt in the making, spearheaded by Elmer MacKay, the Nova Scotia MP. Some advisers urged Clark to make a pre-emptive strike by turning Winnipeg into a leadership convention. That would have meant resigning as leader, however, just at a time when there were hopeful signs for the party. The Tories had pulled ahead of the Liberals to 49 per cent in the polls, and though Clark lagged behind it in popularity, the Conservatives had an excellent chance of winning the next election if only they would unite. That was the fundamental message Clark took to Winnipeg in January, 1983. But despite a strong speech, he managed to increase his support by only half a point, to 66.9 per cent.

This time when he asked Lowell Murray what he should

do, Murray said, "It isn't enough. You won't be able to hack it. The dynamics are such that the caucus will force you out in a couple of months. They'll take the initiative and make life utterly unbearable."

Even if the caucus could have been reined in by the hope of victory, the press would have leaped on any hint of disunity, the review forces would have remained active, and the party would have gone into the election divided and crippled. Clark had to put the differences into a context that would resolve them. So he resigned, called a leadership convention, announced he was a candidate for his own job, and left the general meeting among tearful loyalists who cried, "We'll get those bastards!"

In effect, Clark was asking the party for authority to discipline it. That itself was held up as another example of his weakness and bad judgement. Who ever heard of a politician risking his office because he had only two-thirds support? Some of his own followers felt betrayed, and many others never understood why 51 per cent at a leadership convention in June would be better than 67 per cent at a general meeting in January. Brian Mulroney was astonished that Clark didn't cling to power, as he himself would have done, and Premier Richard Hatfield of New Brunswick (who didn't believe in the principle of leadership reviews) thought Clark's decision a mistake and withdrew his support for the rest of the campaign.

One night Joe Clark woke up and wondered if he had made the right decision. He thought about it for a moment and recognized that he had had no choice. He had to force his opponents out into the open, and he had a good chance to triumph over them. He would survive this test of fire stronger and with a stronger party, or he would destroy himself trying. Then he went back to sleep.

II

It was a cool, rainy April morning in Smiths Falls, a farming centre between Ottawa and Kingston, Ontario. At the legion hall, a grey-haired lady in red slacks was playing

"Let Me Call You Sweetheart" on the piano beneath a portrait of the Queen. A local party panjandrum in legion blazer, regimental tie, and medals escorted a slow trickle of senior citizens toward the chairs and fussed around the doughnuts and coffee at the back of the room. He frowned when a parade of squealing schoolchildren was herded in, causing an abrupt drop in the dignity and average age of the small crowd. The kids squatted on the floor at the front. They were on a field trip to see a rare bird, Canada's only living ex-Prime Minister at the time, but since everyone else had read about nine-year-olds being allowed to vote at delegate-selection meetings in Montreal and Toronto, all the oldsters made the same joke about Clark packing another hall with Tiny Tories.

There was a commotion at the door, a swirl of news crews and junior reporters from Ottawa, and Joe Clark entered as if propelled out of a quickly spinning revolving door. The pianist burst into "Hello Dolly." Back straight, more belly than chest out, face flushed, precisely groomed, Clark shook hands in a workman-like fashion, said "Hi, hi, hi, how are you, hello, hi, hi," moved efficiently down the aisle except for tripping once on a child, and threw his head back in laughter at the least excuse.

"Ladies and gentlemen! Boys and girls! The next Prime Minister of Canada: Joe!"

Clark began by informing the children that he failed grade one in High River, Alberta, and telling a cute story about his six-year-old daughter, Catherine. Then he turned serious, explaining to the adults why he had to call the leadership campaign. "The squabbling in our party would have been *the* issue of the next election," he said. "It would have put us on the defensive, and we just can't afford that vulnerability. We have to get our act together. Let there be a choice after a fair and open contest, and then let there be the three Ds: discussion, decision, discipline." He talked about renewing the spirit of federalism, which had been damaged by Ottawa's confrontations with the provinces. He advocated rescuing parliamentary democracy from the effects of Trudeau's "presidential" system, by allowing

MPs to vote freely on the merits of most bills. And he called for a return to faith in individual enterprise after the Liberals' bureaucratic statism. His basic message was that the party had to be broad based in its appeal, moderate in its policies, and national in its scope. "Respect all the candidates," he concluded, "but vote for me."

Then he invited questions. The first was about a plot by the Liberals to make the honour rolls of the war dead in the parliamentary chapel *bilingual*. The second was about the Liberal plot to force the metric system on Canadians. The third was about the Liberal plot to reduce Canada's military commitment to NATO. One of the schoolchildren, no doubt impatient with the pettiness of the grown-ups' concerns, asked point-blank if there was going to be a nuclear war. Clark, though obviously addressing the elders, spoke directly to the little girl about the preservation of free societies, the Geneva disarmament talks, and Canada's obligation to test the cruise missile.

"Why do you want to be Prime Minister so much?" a little boy suddenly asked.

"Ha, ha, ha," Clark laughed. "Catherine thinks it has to do with swimming pools. If I win the election, I get a swimming pool. But, seriously . . . " He carried on about infinite challenges, but it was evident that the boy thought the swimming pool enough of an answer.

Clark searched for an adult to put the meeting back on track. He found two, very earnest Tory youths who had questions to ask on behalf of "young Canadians": should a gas station selling gas by imperial measure be prosecuted and what about the monarchy? Maybe they weren't the meatiest topics of the minds of young Canadians, but at least Clark earned the biggest applause of the morning for stating baldly that the Tory Party stood staunchly behind the Queen.

"How did you become leader?" a boy piped up, without a trace of intentional malice.

"An act of God," Clark responded with his stilted laugh. His composure was wearing a little thin. He looked again among the old faithful and pried out a few desultory quer-

ies about the civil service, pensions, and compulsory retirement. But a little girl wasn't to be put off so easily.

"Is metric a bad way to measure things?" she asked.

Clark wasn't going to touch that in this crowd and he
admitted defeat. The pianist led everyone in "O Canada,"
the meeting broke up, Polaroids were taken and auto-
graphs received, and Joe Clark was whisked away in an
organizer's lime-green Lincoln to give the same speech to
the same sort of people in Renfrew, Deep River, and
Pembroke.

These good, decent, law-abiding people represented
the backbone of the traditional Progressive Conservative
Party, to be found in farming villages and small towns
across the country. Most of their ancestors, only two or
three generations back, were Scottish immigrants who
carved farms out of the forests, had their lives portrayed
in the popular Glengarry novels of Ralph Connor, and
voted for their eloquent kinsman from down the road in
Kingston, John A. Macdonald. Thus, the descendants assumed a rather proprietary view of power and the political
culture of English Canada, not to mention the party. One
could imagine their shock and annoyance if they realized
they had come to represent what was wrong with the
Tories, a negative image once caricatured by the party's
pollster, Allan Gregg, as old, narrow-minded, cranky, slow,
not with it, not chic, not successful, not competent, and
not for women, labour, or minorities.

Time had passed them by, and like proud aristocrats
confined to a couple of small rooms on a crumbling estate,
they weren't quite sure what to do about it except complain
about the modern world. Metrication became an obsession
because it was the most concrete metaphor for the loss of
the old, comfortable ways. What was sacred if the familiar
twelve-inches-to-a-foot by which the Empire had buried
its dead and dug its battle trenches were replaced arbitrarily by the foreign and incalculable metre? Clearly a
government that would impose such a change was itself
something foreign and incalculable. Filled with Frenchies,
Catholics, and Harvard-educated eggheads, it seemed in-

tent on ramming French and republicanism down the throats of those whose forefathers were supposed to have won the battle of the Plains of Abraham in 1759 for the purpose of keeping Canada English-speaking and loyal. Ottawa was only an hour's drive away, but it might as well have been someone else's capital as far as these people were concerned.

As Macdonald Conservatives, more or less, they weren't opposed to the idea of government. They had a strong concept of the national community, however antiquated in terms of its British associations, and they wanted to be protected from the Americans. Though they weren't happy about having their taxes wasted on bureaucracies and metric conversion, they weren't averse to having the state own or subsidize the railway if that's what was needed to get their products and shoppers to Toronto. In other words, they were conservative liberals, in that they constrained their individualism and freedom through their collective view of society, respect for the past, and desire for an orderly social structure. But since the central state had apparently fallen into the wrong hands, the outs discovered new virtues in provincial rights, private enterprise, and all sorts of anti-government issues.

At heart, however, they didn't buy the philosophy of the new American right, with its evangelical rhetoric about the free individual operating in the free marketplace. That was little more than nineteenth-century *laissez-faire* liberalism, which was now called conservatism by those who wanted to conserve the frontier spirit and the Horatio Alger myth in the face of a liberalism that argued that the complexities of modern society require extensive state intervention. Whatever it was called, it was more at home in the American Republican Party than in the Progressive Conservative Party of Canada. As Gad Horowitz, the Canadian political scientist, once wrote, "A Republican is always a liberal. A Conservative may be at one moment a liberal, at the next moment a tory; he is usually something of both."

Macdonald himself, for example, had been a Conservative who recognized the role of unions, spoke about "progressive ends," and formed a coalition of moderate Tories, Reformers, and French Canadians into the Liberal-Conservative Party.

"Macdonald recognized the reality of the country and he devised a party to reflect it," said Flora MacDonald, a Clark supporter who had been Secretary of State for External Affairs in his government. "The party was founded by a mix of Highland Scots and French Canadians, who shared a way of looking at society, the family, and their responsibility toward others. Macdonald's clan consciousness was evident in his direction of the party, and it was reinforced by his correspondence with Disraeli, who saw the negative effects of the industrial revolution and reminded Macdonald that there would always be groups to be looked after in society."

Macdonald's vision was taken by the Liberals, who slowly transformed it into a winning formula. The British aspect to the Tories' vision of the new Canadian nation enabled Laurier to pull Quebec from their coalition, and the left-of-centre shift in English Canada's political culture allowed King to attract large numbers of workers, farmers, and immigrants to the Liberal flock. It wasn't long before the Tories became a minority alliance of traditional voters, disgruntled outs, and business, which slipped naturally into its anti-government positions once it lost control of the state. Though they were returned to power periodically, their stays were short, as if their victories were merely warnings by the voters to the "governing party" to keep it on its toes. In fact, the Tories seemed to realize they had to catch up to the Liberals and steal their amended vision back.

Arthur Meighen, though an arch-imperialist and notorious for jailing the Winnipeg strikers in 1919, became seen as a dangerous radical by the Montreal and Toronto financiers for his attacks on moneyed interests. R. B. Bennett, despite or because of being a rather autocratic Conservative, set up the CBC and the Bank of Canada and tried to introduce massive government regulation to deal with the Depression. In 1942 a party think tank met in Port Hope, Ontario, to reconcile the belief in private enterprise with the role of the state and the need for social reform. It paved the way for the acceptance of the Progressive Premier of Manitoba as the party's leader. John Bracken even got the party to change its name to accommodate him. But his failure to make gains against Mackenzie King and the CCF discredited the reform wing and left the Progressive Conservatives as an Ontario rump, which picked a former Ontario Premier as its leader. George Drew accomplished even less than Bracken, not surprisingly. His Establishment image, Loyalist background, army record, and private-sector emphasis played to the party's weaknesses: it looked like an old-fashioned, exclusive, unilingual, business-controlled, Ontario-centred old boys' network led by wealthy lawyers or chubby colonels who were probably just puppets for the tycoons. (Ironically, and prophetically for Canadian Tories, when Colonel Drew was premier, he launched an extremely progressive program of social and economic reforms to undercut the CCF. It set the stage for the Ontario dynasty, William Davis, and indirectly Brian Mulroney, as will become evident.)

In 1956 the dominant clique permitted John Diefenbaker to become leader despite his reputation as a Westerner with a radical bias, either because it was desperate for a winner or because it could be forever rid of his irritating presence if he lost. Diefenbaker was a bizarre blend of classic liberalism, Prairie populism, and Anglophile toryism. It was a combination that accidentally—but with huge significance—touched the political subconscious of the nation, for it promised to satisfy and reconcile all the contradictions that raged within the Canadian psyche: imperialism versus nationalism, individual rights versus minority identity, regional community versus unhyphenated national unity, fiscal restraint versus social justice, and free enterprise versus state intervention. Diefenbaker seemed to have resolved them all in his own mind, so perhaps he could resolve them in fact. Once he used his party's Ontario strength to win in 1957, he parlayed that victory into a national landslide in 1958. Then, of course, he was unable to act on his promise and everything began to come apart again. All the factions of the country warred within his bosom as much as within his caucus.

His leadership, however, had two lasting effects. The most immediate was to bring the West into the party for the first time since the 1930s, and with the West came support from Canadians whose backgrounds were neither British nor French. By forgetting his original debt to the Ontario old guard, Diefenbaker changed the balance of power within the party. The second effect was related to that, but not as perceptible at the time. Beneath all the pro-British rhetoric and all the Sir John A. Macdonald stories that appealed to the right, John Diefenbaker was a radical liberal. He believed in a national community of individuals, a collective vision, the popular will, majority rule, and anti-elite reformism.

"Drew and the traditional people couldn't conceive of a different future," Clark said. "By instinct and accident Diefenbaker proved that we could be more than we were and that we had to change. Diefenbaker pushed us forward and he kept us back. He had many talents, but he didn't have the talent of putting it all together. Stanfield began to do that as he had run Nova Scotia, by creating an elemental consensus and then applying that consensus to progressive purposes."

Robert Stanfield, however much he resembled a patrician from an established Maritime family, had learned how things worked as Premier of Nova Scotia. He was, in essence, a 1960s liberal. After being elected federal leader in 1967, he embarked on a modernization plan, designed to open the party to the young, the urban, and the upwardly mobile, as well as to French Canadians and immigrants. In other words, he wanted to get the Progressive Conservatives to the left-of-centre position where the Liberals were, because that was the only position from which to win and because it coincided with the viewpoint of modern Tories. He achieved a kind of palace revolution and almost won the 1972 election as a result, but the old

guard in the party and the Diefenbaker loyalists in the
caucus made his leadership a living hell. In 1976 he gave
up. Joe Clark, however, was determined to carry on Stanfield's work. In fact, his surprise election as leader occurred
because he was the compromise choice of the progressive
majority at the convention.

"I arrived in the House of Commons at the same time
as polling," Clark explained, "which caused us to understand the electorate in its component parts. Polling made
us realize that there were deliberate as well as charismatic
ways of appealing to the larger electorate and knitting the
country together."

In the 1980 election, for example, the Conservatives
won only one of the twenty ridings in Toronto with large
immigrant minorities. Partly the New Canadians felt a debt
to the Liberals for having allowed them into the country;
partly the very word "conservative" suggested the reactionary regimes many of them had left behind; and partly
the Tories had been content to appeal to their entrepreneurial instincts without giving much attention to their
ethnicity. But polling revealed that a businessman of Greek
origin might value his Greekness as much as his trade.
That revelation led to an internecine battle in the Toronto
riding of Broadview-Greenwood in 1983, when a Greek
captured the party nomination from a well-known, right-
wing newspaper columnist.

"That battle was an important watershed in the life of
the party," Clark said. "It radicalized people who were
unhappy with the change in the party, the city, and the
country. They saw that I was determined that the party
was going to be a broad one, and they didn't like that.
Nor do I have any regrets about what we did in York
Centre. That riding is 40 per cent Jewish and 40 per cent
Italian. Yet the party executive had been consistently Anglo-Saxon, with an association of thirty or forty members
who wouldn't allow Italians to join. We went in with five
hundred people, mostly Italian, and they elected an executive that precisely reflected the composition of the
riding."

Clark's strength had always been in organization. In April, 1983, during the first phase of the leadership race in which about two thousand of an estimated three thousand delegates were elected by party associations across the country, his Toronto team recruited numerous immigrant groups to pack the riding meetings and elect Clark slates: hundreds of instant Italian Tories in Davenport, Koreans and Vietnamese in York West, Greeks in York East, Armenians in Don Valley East. Clark argued that this would broaden the party base for years to come, but the principle was clearly as self-serving as it was generous and many traditional party workers were outraged.

Broadening the party base went hand in hand with liberalizing the party policies. Some argue that it's futile to search for any principles or even thoughts that bind the Progressive Conservatives. "If you're for hanging, you're a Tory," an MP once remarked, but neither Joe Clark nor Brian Mulroney was for hanging. Certainly the years in opposition meant that many outsiders were attracted to the party for purely negative reasons. But there has always been a core with a vision of what the party had been in Macdonald's day and where it should proceed.

"Sometimes I've been criticized for being too much a party man," Clark said, "but that's from those who don't understand parties. Party experience is not learning how to hold back-room meetings. It's learning the various parts of the country and how to bring them together. Roosevelt may not be a Canadian Conservative hero, but he was able to create a new coalition of hope by bringing the 'antis' together. And Mackenzie King understood that there always has to be a party where the country is. We haven't been it, and we can only become it by careful design and hard work."

Clark's pragmatism was forged by two decades of party organizing and nine months as Prime Minister. The uproar that followed his government's promise to privatize Petro-Canada, for example, made him cautious while other candidates were vowing to sell off the CBC and Air Canada. Instead, Clark usually spoke in generalities about incentive, restraint, initiative, and confidence. When pressed by one young man for details, he gave a frank insight into politics. "There are dangers in spelling things out," he said. "If you propose a change, those who are threatened by it will remember it, while those who will benefit just dismiss it as another political promise."

His caution was increased by a new and rare circumstance. The speed with which the Liberals had moved leftwards since 1980 seemed to have given the Tories a chance to grab hold of the consociational, reformist liberalism that had been victorious since Laurier's day. Eventually Canadians might adjust to the new norms introduced in Trudeau's last term, but in the meantime they appeared war weary and nostalgic for the peaceful approaches of the past. "The Liberals have left us a big hole right in the centre," Lowell Murray said almost gleefully during the leadership campaign. "We're fools if we move to the right. Most of the delegates may be right-of-centre, but they also work hard for provincial Conservative governments that have stayed elected by hogging the middle of the road. We should grab the centre and stay there."

Hence, Clark's praise for Roosevelt and King; his promises to renew federalism, Parliament, and free enterprise without undermining the national government, strong leadership, or social programs; and his worry about the impact of the new right. "Ambition, frustration, and ideology are threatening our victory in the next election," he told a group of delegates in Brockville, Ontario, the day after his visit to Smiths Falls. "The forces of confusion are rising up just when the country is ready to accept us. The forces of the ideological right prey on the naïve of the party. They don't understand the country. The Progressive Conservative Party isn't a debating society. And we can't sit on an extreme, because the country doesn't."

Later he would expand on that thought in Kamloops, B.C., where the party's delegate-selection meeting had been overrun by Amway representatives. "The role of national political parties is to draw Canadians together, to give them a sense of confidence and a sense of direction," Clark said. "Our purpose is not to divide people by ideology. We have enough divisions already in Canada." Then he sang the praises of both Macdonald's National Policy and C. D. Howe's "glorious" post-war reconstruction period as examples of the collective effort based on private enterprise that could usher Canada into the age of technology. This wasn't the absence of ideology, of course: it was an affirmation of 1960s liberalism.

As Clark saw it, the ideological right would learn better if it stayed in the party. Pieties about balanced budgets and privatization would eventually have to give way to realism. (For example, Peter Pocklington, the millionaire entrepreneur from Edmonton, political novice, and darling of the Amway set, quickly discovered how poorly his attacks on government spending and state-owned companies were received in the Maritimes, where many family incomes depended on both.)

Generally, the major leadership candidates shared Clark's moderation and made their unpleasant fiscal prescriptions more palatable by a lot of sweet talk about social justice. John Crosbie emphasized the private sector, government restraint, and his own autocratic manner, but he didn't hide the fact that he had been the father of medicare as a Liberal in Newfoundland. Brian Mulroney liked to play to the right by emphasizing his experience in the "real" world of business and claiming that Canada could be run like the Iron Ore Company, but his Irish lyricism wafted easily from hymns of individual initiative to sentiments of compassion for the poor, the sick, and the elderly. Michael Wilson stressed the fiscal side, David Crombie stressed the social side, and if they had been one person, neither too tall nor too short, neither too boring nor too exuberant, they might have swept the convention.

John Crosbie once argued that Clark had made a bogyman out of the ideological right for tactical purposes. That was true, to an extent. If the threat had been significant, Clark as a practical politician would have tried to undercut it by moving toward it. Though the party as a whole may have been somewhat to the right of the country, Clark was confident that most of its delegates could stand comfortably in the new centre. But there was cause for some concern. The simplistic, well-financed, widely publicized arguments of the new right jibed with the anti-Ottawa sentiments prevalent among the outs, the business community, and the new generation of students. The more those arguments infiltrated the minds of party members and the media reports on the Tories, the more the party would frighten off the general electorate.

Clark's challenge was to attack the Liberals' use of the nation-state without raising false expectations or catering to reactionary emotions. He knew too well that pragmatism in Canadian politics meant a mixed economy. He said that Trudeau was out of touch with the country, but never malicious. He wanted to clear away the most controversial legacies of Trudeauism, such as FIRA and the NEP, but warned that attacks on the bureaucracy would cost votes in almost every riding. He expected growth to cut most of the deficit and defended universality in social programs. As a result, his economic policies sounded rather soft, rather vague. The buzz-words were right enough (in both senses), but Clark constantly qualified them with conditions, complexities, and exceptions. It was as if his time in power had left him incapable of taking a definitive stand on any issue.

Nothing appeared to have awed John Crosbie, on the other hand. While Joe Clark was mealy-mouthing his way between Smiths Falls and Brockville, Crosbie went blustering through the same region of Eastern Ontario as boldly as his campaign bus, the *Jessie and Ches*, named after his parents. Crosbie buried his conditions, complexities, and exceptions in a heap of turgid policy papers that few delegates bothered to read, just as he buried his degrees from Queen's (University Medalist in political science), Dalhousie (University Medalist in law), and the London School of Economics beneath his folksy Newfoundland persona. As plump and amiable (when he cared to be) as a grey papa seal, Crosbie blasted into Carleton Place, Almonte, and environs like a travelling preacher who had worked his serious message into an entertainment and had a few quick cures to flog at the door.

The serious message was all about the economy. The government owned and controlled too much of it. Individual freedom was threatened, the collective wealth had declined, the huge national deficit eventually meant increased taxation or raging inflation, and the loss of investment caused a loss of jobs. The panaceas involved restoring investor confidence, giving incentives to the risk takers, securing access to the American market, and reducing the deficit through growth and (less loudly) taxes. "This is a crusade," he said, "a conservative crusade to reverse the decline and deceit and get Canada moving again."

"That's right, that's right," a woman kept interrupting from the back of a living room in Almonte—a scene from the life of Diefenbaker on the wall, three old ladies munching tomato sandwiches on the sofa, the host pushing his kids toward the candidate in full oration for a photograph—as if she were at a revival meeting.

Of course, Crosbie's ideas were much closer to classic liberalism than to Macdonald Conservatism. Sir John A. must have rolled in his nearby grave to hear a Tory talk about moving toward free trade with the United States; the old ladies on the sofa weren't expecting to have their pensions reduced as a way of lowering the deficit; and no one had been happy defending Crosbie's policy of "short-term pain for long-term gain" during the 1980 election. Still, he seemed so full of conviction and bashed the Liberals so amusingly that everyone applauded warmly. Though his campaign was a crusade, he admitted in an aside, it was also fun, or "foon" as he pronounced it in his St. John's English.

Half the fun was to listen to his heavy accent roll through a half-hour performance of one-line witticisms, corny puns, rhetorical flights, and thesaurus-like variations on key nouns and verbs. Drawing a similarity between the Liberals and the NDP, he called their leaders "Pierre Trubent and Ed Broadeau." Attacking the government's management of

Canadair, he said, "Its name should be How Can They Dare." Addressing the membership's preoccupation with metrication, he suggested the Liberals' theme song was "Nothing Could Be Sweeter Than to Introduce the Litre." His Dale Carnegie lessons weren't wasted.

"Soon Marc Lalonde will be Marc Lashort," he bellowed. No one could possibly have known what that meant or why it was funny, but everyone laughed anyway. In fact, it sounded like something Diefenbaker might have said: it seemed clever on the surface, it was deliciously partisan, and it only worked by mispronouncing a French name.

If Crosbie conjured up the Chief in his anti-Grit barbs, his mock-heroic flourishes, and his hinterland fellowship, he avoided the economic illiteracy that had led Diefenbaker to lose power almost as quickly as he had gained it. Indeed, under the slovenly, jolly exterior, Crosbie radiated George Drew, too, through his Establishment family background, his autocratic personality, and his plutocratic message. Even though he wasn't from Ontario, he seemed to hold out hope to the men in the Carleton Place legion hall and to the old ladies on the sofa in Almonte that they could get their party back, if not their country. Clark was a nice enough lad, full of good intentions and respectful of his elders, but he had these modern notions, had brought in these new people, and had been bullied by Lougheed. Worse, in the blunt words of a woman in Pembroke, he was trying too hard "to suck up to the froggy-froggies." Nothing gave the old Tories more admiration for and confidence in John Crosbie, despite his somewhat American ideas, than his complete and unapologetic unilingualism.

"People want economic growth and jobs no matter what language they speak," he said. "Quebec wants the same things as Newfoundland, and Trudeau has been a perfect failure in both languages."

Fluent bilingualism was one of the characteristics that made many traditional Tories suspicious of Brian Mulroney. It, along with the cut of his business suits, the polish of his Gucci shoes, the mellifluousness of his rhetoric, and the fashionable beauty of his wife created an aura of urban, trendy slickness—exactly the type of impression guaranteed to make a true-blue Conservative check on his wallet and his daughters. In fact, Mulroney looked like a *Liberal*. More than anything else, his slickness had torpedoed his leadership campaign in 1976, when Mulroney had zoomed around the country in a private jet, dropped a bundle of money on his media-oriented hoopla, and generally peddled himself like a new brand of deodorant. He had learned from the mistake. Now he conducted a "frugal," "underground" campaign, designed to let him meet the delegates in informal, private sessions where his oozing charm and bountiful promises were more effective. To this end, he avoided the media at the beginning, ducked all public debates but one, and rambled from town to town by commercial aircraft and borrowed cars. In fact, his tactic was so obviously manipulative, so patently false, so widely reported that few were taken in by it. He might as well have travelled more comfortably and speedily.

In other words, his image was still a problem in 1984. If Clark had an image as weak as his chin, Mulroney seemed to have too much of both. His image was the first thing to come through the door; it dominated the room while he was talking; and it was the last thing to leave the memory. It exaggerated his strengths (cleverness, hard work, lack of pomposity, and amicability) and his weaknesses (summarized in print by one columnist who had known him for years as sleaziness, trickiness, dubiousness, and shallowness). Finally, it brought to mind Bertie Wooster's reservations about Tuppy Glossop: "Nature, when planning this sterling fellow, shoved in a lot more lower jaw than was absolutely necessary and made the eyes a bit too keen and piercing for one who was neither an Empire-builder nor a traffic policeman."

"Brian's always loved conniving and scheming," Flora MacDonald said with some amusement in her voice. "At one time we picked up some dirt about a Liberal organizer in Nova Scotia, and Brian thought the priests at St. Francis Xavier should hear about it. So he went down to tell them. Later he called me and said, 'It's 007 reporting.' "

On the other hand, in the words of Michel Cogger, a Montreal lawyer who went to Saint Francis Xavier University with Mulroney and managed his leadership campaign, "Brian's always been seen as a slick Liberal, ever since college. His style often overcomes his message, but there's nothing he can do about it. The image feeds on itself. If Flora says it's raining, that's compassion. If Brian says it's raining, that's ambition."

In essence, Brian Mulroney came across as an Irish Duddy Kravitz, an electrician's son from Baie Comeau who had climbed his way to a stone mansion on the top of Westmount by hustle, street smarts, blarney, and self-made luck. His delight in himself and the world was infectious when it wasn't too gushy, and his devices were often forgiveable because he seemed incapable of hiding his real emotions and ambitions. But small-town Tories were usually raised to distrust the smooth patter of well-heeled vacuum-cleaner salesmen. They detected something of that in Mulroney's smiles, his songs, and his moving speeches. He boasted about his charity work and announced every family anniversary and first communion with a rather tawdry lack of subtlety. After his fancy orations, all twinkly eyes and baritone sincerity, he chain-smoked furtively, sought approval shamelessly, and glanced rapidly about the room for the better chance. Once alone with his advisers, his warm *bonhomie* frequently vanished into cool plottings, nervous insecurity, fits of rage, and vows of vengeance.

"Those myopic, incestuous bastards!" he once shouted about the Ottawa press corps. "They're skeptical because they don't know me. Believe me, their time will come!" In fact, many journalists were skeptical because they knew him better than most Canadians. They had seen his joviality turn on and off with their television lights. Not a few of them had received furious phone calls from him in the middle of the night, and most of them had witnessed the jarring transformation of the idealistic man-of-the-people into an icy, mean-spirited, cynical politician.

Because the party didn't really know him either, it had its own skepticism about the candidate. Except for his work in the back rooms of the Quebec organization, Mulroney only seemed to show up for leadership campaigns. He had never run for a seat in Parliament, he was an unknown factor as a political leader, and he seemed to have a greater loyalty to his own career than to the cause of the party. Moreover, the last time he had come round he sold himself as a progressive; this time he was selling himself as a corporate CEO. In between he had gone from being a labour lawyer to being a company president, of course, but his change of view seemed either a blatant appeal to the new right or proof that Mulroney was in the pocket of Conrad Black and Paul Desmarais.

"Canada is about hard work, sacrifice, and reward," he often said, citing the example of his father who had laboured under the toughest conditions to build the North Shore of the St. Lawrence River into a thriving region. In contrast, Pierre Trudeau had been the darling of the socialists in the 1950s, his Liberals had "Swedenized" Canada and left a trail of damage and sadness, effort had been penalized rather than honoured, entrepreneurial genius had been thwarted, and the soul of the nation had been scarred. Mulroney vowed to restore the private sector as the generator of wealth and jobs, to reduce the national deficit without harming any necessary social programs, to increase Canada's trade and productivity, to welcome foreign investment, and to trim the size of the bureaucracy by handing out "pink slips and running shoes."

Mulroney's economic message was similar to Crosbie's in most respects. The two men were competing for the same anti-Clark delegates, after all, including Amway representatives, neo-conservative youths in Ontario, and disaffected businessmen. They also appeared to be competing for a prize for the one who could embellish his right-wing pitch with the most humour, verbiage, sentimentality, and exaggeration. Mulroney often won that contest, with his natural gift for hyperbole and his infatuation with his own voice, but he was also more skillful in doubling back to appease the left. He achieved this apparent impossibility by keeping away from specifics. While Crosbie talked bluntly about free trade with the Americans and issued fat economic manifestos, Mulroney stuck to promising nothing and everything. Though he hadn't had Clark's experience in government, he had hung around Tory politics long enough to know its tricks.

In Ontario, for example, most active Tories realized that their provincial party, which had been in office since 1944, kept power by using the same left-of-centre formula as the federal Liberals. Just as Premier Davis had supported Trudeau's constitutional package and taken Ottawa's side in the energy battle with Alberta, he shared a belief in active government, state participation in the economy, progressive social measures, and a formidable bureaucracy. He wasn't as bold or experimental as Trudeau, but he earned the support and even the praise of the Ontario New Democrats while leading two minority governments in the 1970s. While the provincial caucus, executive, and organization were no doubt to the left of the membership in Smiths Falls and Almonte, their numbers and influence made their thinking more important. On the whole, they preferred Clark's realistic moderation to the more dramatic utterances of Crosbie and Mulroney.

However, they had other problems with Clark himself. The provincial party had helped him win Ontario in 1979, but relations between the two Tory governments deteriorated at once. There were clashes of personality, there wasn't a Toronto representative in Clark's inner cabinet, and Davis warred publicly against Clark's energy policy, which was seen to favour Alberta's producers and revenues at the expense of Ontario's consumers and Canadians in general. That war lost Clark the 1980 election, because the provincial machine stayed home and the Ontario electorate turned against him.

Despite all that, Davis liked to consider himself a party

loyalist. Immediately after the Winnipeg debacle he had been helpful to Clark in private and encouraged one of his own organizers, a Toronto insurance broker named Bill McAleer, to supervise Clark's leadership campaign. However, Davis chose to remain neutral in the race and he almost gave in to the pressure to enter it as a candidate himself. The hawks around him were hungry for federal power, and many in his party were desperate for a candidate who would restore Ontario's pre-eminence at the national level. One hawk, knowing that Davis was reluctant to abandon his Brampton bungalow and Florida condo, even tried to convince him that he would have to stay only two-and-a-half days a week in Ottawa if he won.

Davis was smarter. He learned that his candidacy would divide an already fractious party by rousing the active wrath of Alberta's Peter Lougheed and Saskatchewan's Grant Devine, and he figured that he couldn't win anyway. Too many delegates had been tied down by March. Even if Davis took two-thirds of Ontario's nine hundred votes, he would have only 20 per cent of the convention and not enough room to grow in the other parts of the country. His desolate troops scattered among the existing candidates.

Clark picked up some of them. Besides his Toronto slates, he drew on the loyalty of the federal party organization he had begun building in Ontario once he saw how risky it was to rely on the provincial machine. That federal network had never really come together, but it did leave him with supporters in small towns and in the financial Establishment. Bay Street heavyweights such as John and Doug Bassett, Hal Jackman, Don McDougall, and Ted Rogers, all of whom had backed Brian Mulroney in 1976, now swung to Clark because of his experience and perhaps because of their own aversion to change.

"What board of directors would change its president just when it was beating its competitor and a big contract was coming up for bids?" Rogers, a cable magnate, asked the three hundred Tories crammed into his Forest Hill mansion for a Clark reception. He, Joe, and Maureen were on the grand staircase amid a swarm of news teams. "What team would change its coach when it was ahead in the fourth quarter and on the verge of another touchdown?"

"The Argos!" someone yelled. The Clarks had been an hour late and everyone was feeling the effects of the heat, the congestion, and the free bar. Rogers persevered. "As Churchill [sic] said, 'We have nothing to fear but fear itself.' "

These people saw Clark as a broad-based consensus builder, someone who could win across Canada and bring it together. But others never forgave him for remarking that Bill Davis could be seen as a "regional" candidate if he ran. However true that observation was, the heart of Ontario was not to be won by treating it as less than the centre of the universe. At an all-candidates debate in Toronto's Massey Hall on April 30, a dozen Koreans did dances reserved for an emperor, beat drums, and waved red banners with slogans and Joe Clark's picture on them outside in the rain, while inside Clark was booed for speaking French. "I've worked hard to build a party in which French would not be booed!" he reacted fiercely. "A party open to everyone! This is not the time to play with the destiny of the party and lose the base we've worked so hard to build!"

Afterward, across the street in the Eaton Centre, he joined his delegates and organizers for a light beer. "I was embarrassed to be part of that crowd," one Tory said sadly. "I was ashamed to be a member of the same party."

The next afternoon, in a suite in the Ramada Inn beside Montreal's Olympic stadium, a wound-up Brian Mulroney read the *Sunday Star*'s headlines ("Crombie, Mulroney stars of Tory debate—Clark under attack") and bubbled, "Look at that! What about the hostility of that crowd! That's what I hear from P.E.I. to British Columbia! They weren't booing French, they were booing *him*! They hate that guy and they want him out! He's got eight hundred votes on the first ballot and then he's out!"

III

"Why should the nation support you when you don't even have the support of the delegates from High River?" an aggressive CBC radio reporter asked Clark in Calgary.

"We'll have to see how those delegates vote in the end," he replied hotly.

But it was true that more than three hundred instant Tories had turned up at the Bow River constituency meeting in High River, Alberta, and elected as delegates three "Concerned Conservatives" who believed in God, country, free enterprise, and a "fresh wind" in politics. Bow River wasn't Clark's riding—he had been denied it in a bungled public feud with Stan Schumacher in 1976 and had had to seek the nomination next door in Yellowhead—but losing the symbolic support of his home town was a cruel blow.

The "Concerned Conservatives" were part of the right-wing, anti-Clark movement that was particularly successful in southern Alberta, though it surfaced in Edmonton, British Columbia, and Ontario. Inspired to get involved politically by Canada 2000 Project Ltd., a company owned by Peter Pocklington's former employee Bill Campbell, it rallied networks of Amway distributors to elect slates in the same way that Clark had used the Greeks and Koreans in Toronto.

The Amway ("American Way") Corporation may not have been involved directly, but the billion-dollar, U.S.-based soap and cosmetic distributorship was indoctrinating its 100,000 Canadian merchandisers with the same fundamentalist buzz-words it uses to support the Republicans in the United States. Not surprisingly, the message seemed to be received more widely in Alberta, with its strong links to Texas, Oklahoma, and the American frontier mythology. But it was still the message of an ideological minority, whose success had more to do with its organizing capabilities than with the political culture of most Albertans. Thus, most of the "Concerned Conservatives" at the delegate-selection meeting in High River had been recruited from the suburbs of Calgary, thirty miles away.

Like Joe Clark, High River is fastidiously neat, deliberately up-to-date and open-minded, cautiously amiable, self-confident, self-reliant, and proud. Most of its main blocks have been renovated, the old stone railway station is now a heritage museum, and the only unpleasant sight in the spring of 1983 was a long, white trailer parked in the middle of town. It turned out to be a travelling Government of Canada promotion. "Programs to help you realize your goals," its loudspeaker blared, in French and English, "and enjoy Canada more!"

But the town had made a point of realizing its own goals. It designed and financed the Pioneer Square redevelopment, for example, after a federal funding scheme fell through. "Best thing that ever happened to us," said Mayor Lucille Dougherty. Primarily a service town for ranchers and farmers, it was incorporated in 1906, six months after the founding of the province of Alberta and two months after the founding of the *High River Times* by Clark's grandfather. The earliest settlers remained within the British tradition of law and mutual responsibility. In general, the law (in the form of soldiers and the North West Mounted Police) arrived before the mass of settlers did, and the *garrisons* shaped the political and social consciousness of the region as thoroughly as the *frontier*. "We weren't shooting each other, like they were across the border," the mayor remarked one evening in the large new library just before a screening of the National Film Board's anti-nuclear documentary, *If You Love This Planet*. "And there's nothing individualistic about those Amway people. They're following someone."

"When I was a boy in High River," Joe Clark often told his audiences across the country, "I used to lie in the fields and study the heavens. And I noticed a very peculiar thing about birds. They had two wings, a left wing and a right wing. And if they had only one wing, they would fly around in circles."

If Clark exaggerated the impact of the new right, he did so partly because it had struck closest to home and been so personally abusive to him. Fierce youths had greeted him with buttons proclaiming "The Who's Farewell Tour." The Diefenbaker veterans from the West were among his thorniest critics in caucus, because he was a Red Tory and had left them out of his cabinet. He was accused of having no backbone, of watering down his principles for expediency (unlike Ronald Reagan, the latest folk-hero of the western right wing), of being little better than the "socialist" Trudeau.

Even though he was the first western-born Prime Minister, he never enjoyed a favourite-son status. And although he had been one of the strategists in Peter Lougheed's first campaign, the Alberta Premier always seemed contemptuous of him, undermining the Clark government's energy policy, not bothering to show up in Winnipeg and deliver the votes that would have boosted Clark's percentage, and quietly favouring Brian Mulroney during the leadership race. While one old Conservative in Vancouver suggested that Winnipeg had been a conspiracy to bring control of the party back to the East, many more in Calgary said that Joe Clark had always been in Ontario's pocket. After all, he was against world prices for oil and capital punishment, and he spoke French!

Some argued that Clark wasn't macho enough in his image or his rhetoric to be seen as a western spokesman. Clark had a more analytical explanation for his lack of a base. "Alberta changed dramatically with Lougheed," he said. "I was part of that change at the beginning, but I made a conscious decision to go into federal politics, so I was less and less involved physically and psychically with what was going on. That new base, largely urban and energy related, created some tensions with the older base, which was mostly rural and agricultural. I belonged to the new group, but I had separated myself from it. I didn't spend time developing a regional base in an organizational way, except in my constituency, and the psychological base was taken by the Lougheed movement. That's not unusual, but I did miss having it. On the other hand, it's arguable that given the fortress mentality that developed, I couldn't have been comfortable there and still been an effective national politician."

As a boy Clark had been brought up in a wider world. His father, Charles, whose own father had been an Ontario Scot and whose mother had been an American, was High River's editor, which meant he travelled, entertained visitors from across the country, and followed world events as well as local ones. He was also an active Conservative in the days of Social Credit. His uncle, Colonel Hugh, had been an "unrepentant, unregenerate Ontario Tory MP," according to his great-nephew. But Charles's wife, Grace, a strong-minded Irish-Catholic school teacher, had flirted with the CCF in her youth and was one of the three known Liberals in town. (It's often forgotten that aversion to the Liberal Party in Alberta didn't start with Pierre Trudeau.) So Clark grew up with a broader view of society and the nation than most Albertans. "We were always afraid of provincialism," his mother once said.

Clark's fate was set in 1956 when a public-speaking scholarship sent him to Ottawa with the Rotary Club's "Adventure in Citizenship." There he met George Drew, saw Fulton and Howe in the pipeline debate, and returned home smitten by national politics and national issues. In 1957 Diefenbaker visited High River with his populist magic and "made it easy for a seventeen-year-old from the West with a sense of national community to be a Progressive Conservative," as Clark put it.

Diefenbaker didn't lure the West into the Progressive Conservative Party by appealing to free enterprise, individualism, or provincial rights. On the contrary, his attractions were his egalitarian populism, his multiculturalism, and his patriotic vision of Canada as a single community tied to British traditions. Most of all, he spoke to the region's sense of alienation, which was rooted in history, geography, and economics. Many Westerners felt like second-class Canadians. Their provinces had been created after the original union of 1867. Their economy was based on selling their resources and produce cheaply to the East and paying dearly for the manufactured goods that were shipped west in return. Their political power in Ottawa was handicapped by distance, a small population, a rural constituency, and the wealth of Central Canada. By presenting an opportunity for these outsiders to get into power, Diefenbaker was able to collect them from their protest parties—the Social Credit and the CCF—and make them federal Tories.

Predictably Diefenbaker's promise was exposed as a romantic, messianic delusion as soon as reality intruded. He couldn't change distance or population, he couldn't revolutionize the West's hinterland status, and he couldn't ignore either the moneyed elites in Ontario or the growing discontent in Quebec with the unilingual, Anglocentric patriotism of English Canada. Like all dashed expectations, his failure only increased the West's bitterness. As the Liberals regained power, with little need for western seats, Westerners left a rump of Diefenbaker relics in the federal Parliament to represent them and turned back to their provincial governments for protection. This coincided with Ottawa's efforts under Pearson and Trudeau to defuse the separatist agitation in Quebec by creating genuine Canadian symbols, introducing bilingualism throughout the federal public service, and recognizing the country as a bicultural entity. Many Westerners saw these efforts as mere concessions to Quebec by those whose political fortunes depended on French-Canadian votes. Ukrainian had more relevance as a second language on the Prairies than French, and the need to speak French became simply another impediment to the influence of Westerners on their national government.

The alienation of the West from the Liberal Party and Ottawa was deeply felt and profoundly significant, but it was often equated wrongly with a regional rejection of state intervention and national unity. After all, three of the four western provinces had NDP governments in the 1970s and western separatism attracted more reporters than voters. "Why should I sell the Canadian farmers' wheat?" Trudeau once asked as a prelude to a speech, and his own answer was completely obliterated by the hysterical indignation that he should have raised even the question. The variations in English Canada's political culture are most evident in Alberta, where different periods of settlement, the economy of ranching and then oil, strong north-south ties, and the spread of fundamentalist religion accentuated the *laissez-faire*, classic liberal elements of Loyalist liberalism; but the differences are more in the rhetoric than in the action.

In fact, as the federal government became more antipathetic and remote, all the western provincial governments became more powerful and active. They went through a kind of Quiet Revolution of their own. Irrespective of party label, their spending grew faster than Ottawa's, their bureaucracies blossomed in size and competence, and their legislative clout began to be exercised in their economies through taxation, grants, planning, and regulation. Oil and gas made most of them extremely wealthy, and with wealth had come a new class of western politician: urban, well-educated, modern, aggressive, and determined to break the East's grip on their region. Just as the same class had arisen in Quebec in the 1960s and latched onto independence as the quickest and most satisfying way for them to take the place of the English-speaking bosses, so the West's new professionals seized upon provincial rights and powers as the handiest way to fulfil their own ambitions at home.

Indeed, Quebec's premiers showed the Westerners the advantages and methods of playing hardball with the federal government, while Trudeau's refusal to countenance a special status for Quebec meant that all the provinces benefitted from the concessions the Quebec government was able to obtain from him. Thus, Peter Lougheed was able to say after the election of the Parti Québécois in 1976. "Quebeckers have a desire to be master in their own house. I have empathy with that feeling."

As Clark pointed out, Lougheed came to represent this new class, not just in Alberta but throughout the West. As macho as the football player he had been, as sharp as his Harvard Business School training, as bullish as his swift and surprising rise to power in 1971, Lougheed personified the spirit as well as the interests of the new West. Even his eyes, his voice, and his posture conveyed the chip-on-the-shoulder mood of the western elite. The entire West seemed to share the stern, wistful desire to regain a paradise lost that was poignantly symbolized by the story of Lougheed's father drinking away the fortune and estate of his own father, Sir James Lougheed, millionaire, friend of the Prince of Wales, and once Premier of Alberta.

Lougheed's basic program was simple: the resources of Alberta belonged to Alberta, Alberta had to get the best deal possible for these finite resources, and the government of Alberta had to direct a good portion of its patrimony toward creating an industrial and technological base for the day when the province's resources would be depleted. From this everything else followed—the demand for world prices, industrial strategies, provincial ownership or regulation in certain sectors, and of course the battle against the constitutional package and the NEP. The simplicity and plain justice of the program made Lougheed a formidable leader. Prosperity, excitement, and pride were the immediate results, and if the rest of Canada wasn't happy with Alberta's attitude, then "Let the Eastern Bastards Freeze in the Dark," as the popular bumper sticker phrased it.

There was a fatal flaw in this, however, which became apparent as time went on and the confrontations with Ottawa increased. When push came to shove, the West remained a minority and the federal government retained the preponderance of power. Lougheed's insensitive, uncompromising negotiations over energy prices with his former aide, Joe Clark, may have come close to success, but they also provoked the federal Liberals to counter harshly and unilaterally with the NEP. The NEP was possible because Ottawa had the political and legal authority, perhaps even the moral authority, to override the narrower interests of a particular region and a particular sector. By focussing on their provincial governments, the western elites in effect had abandoned their influence within the greater

power centre. Not only did the federal Liberals have virtually no seats to lose by bashing them back into line, but
after 1980 the old bluff about western separation no longer
worked. If the majority of Quebeckers chose Canada over
the vivid ambitions of their elites, Ottawa was certain that
the majority of Westerners would do the same.

Some Westerners, among them Joe Clark and Lloyd
Axworthy, recognized that reality. Their reasoning was
similar to Trudeau's, in fact, when he used to tell French
Canadians that the anglophones in Ottawa "have been
strong by virtue only of our weakness." Power was up for
grabs there, Trudeau saw, and by breaking out of the defensive confines of the province, by going to Ottawa with
good people and in great numbers, Quebeckers could gain
control of the whole country even though they were a
minority. Then he and a small vanguard proceeded to do
just that. Of course they were called *vendus*, sell-outs, because they had to forge alliances and make compromises,
but ultimately "French Power" triumphed by its persistence. In contrast, Peter Lougheed turned down two good
chances to become leader of the federal Progressive Conservatives, in 1976 and 1983, even though winning the
leadership would probably have made him Prime Minister
of Canada.

In fact, entering the larger arena would have demol-
ished the simplicity of his viewpoint, on which depended
his conviction, his outrage, and consequently his forceful
image. Whether he had won or lost the conventions, he
would have had to come to terms with the complexities
of the country: the interests of the energy-consuming provinces, the fiscal requirements of the underdeveloped regions, the causes of the federal deficit, the protectionist
demands of Canadian industry, and the very reasonable
request of Quebeckers that their Prime Minister at least
try to speak French. "And thus the native hue of resolution
is sicklied o'er with the pale cast of thought," Shakespeare
observed, and Lougheed decided to stay with the ills he
knew in Edmonton rather than fly off to those he didn't
care to know in Ottawa. If the Trudeau Liberals laid waste

the West, as Lougheed later claimed, he was partly responsible for having destroyed Joe Clark and handing them the reins of government so as to keep pure his own righteous indignation.

While that purity allowed Lougheed to be honoured as Alberta's great protector (even though it could be argued that he lost the energy battle in September, 1981, as badly as René Lévesque lost the constitutional battle a few months later), Joe Clark's compromises seemed to have stripped him in western eyes of his western roots. Using national contacts and his national base as an MP, he had achieved something rare as a Westerner, the prime ministership; but like so many Westerners who gained power in the front benches and back rooms of Ottawa, he was seen to have gone to the other side—to the East—to get it. Naturally Clark didn't agree with that view.

"Provincial politics was exciting at the start," he said, "but I saw that my particular role was to understand *both* where I came from and beyond where I came from. That was the root of the idea of 'community of communities.' It was to draw identity locally but express it nationally."

Clark once described his job as a politician in terms of his father's job as a small-town newspaper editor. "If Lew Bradley, the saddlemaker, was being honoured by the Rotary Club or whatever, Dad would write the speeches, because he had made a point of figuring out what Lew Bradley and others were about and he had the gift of being able to express it better than they did. So his job was a job of understanding and interpretation." Clark's own job was to take a similar sort of understanding and interpretation to the national level.

Clearly his strong sense of community came from High River. "You might not agree with everybody, you might not even like everybody," he said in a speech he gave there when he was Prime Minister, "but this community knew that when you had to build a flood dike or fight a fire, the community would come together. It was there when you needed it. Of course there is an independence in this part of Canada, a willingness to go out and do things. Without that there would have been no town, no West, no oil discoveries at Turner Valley. But independence needs a base to build on. It is instructive to me that the people who did the most for themselves also did the most for their community."

That vision, as neat a revelation of Canadian liberalism as his Tory father marrying his Liberal mother, also shaped his national perspective. Regrettably he was never able to translate his sense of national community into a living political sense of nation, though he talked in every speech about nation-building and national unity. He fervently believed that local loyalties were legitimate, essential, and could strengthen Canada if tapped, not drain it as Trudeau seemed to think, yet Clark couldn't convey an image of Canada that was as precise and stirring as Trudeau's. In fact, his image of a "community of communities" was seen as an attack on the national government. In power it seemed to have meant no more than giving the provinces the lotteries and caving in to their demands on energy policy. It exposed Clark to Trudeau's devastating question, "Who shall speak for Canada?" Tory attacks on Petro-Canada, FIRA, and the CBC, along with a call for closer trade relations with the United States, created the impression that nationalism was dead in the party of Macdonald, Borden, and Diefenbaker. In fact, "community of communities" was just another way of describing the consociational democracy of 1960s Canadian liberalism: power was to be shared among many power centres and articulated by the elites of each community. The Tories had shifted toward this decentralist concept because, as perennial losers, they were susceptible to notions of limiting power and because, dependent on the victorious Conservative premiers for help in federal elections, they were vulnerable to provincial-rights pressures.

"For years there was no Conservative provincial government except in Ontario," Flora MacDonald said, "so Ontario could maintain its pre-eminence in the federal party. Then that changed, in New Brunswick, in Nova Scotia, in P.E.I., in Manitoba, in Newfoundland, and in Alberta.

Suddenly there was a proliferation of Progressive Conservative parties, so the tensions that are endemic in Canada moved much more into the federal party. Tensions between East and West moved into the party with Diefenbaker's victory, but they weren't entirely the product of the party. They were brought in by strong premiers too."

Clark knew better than most of his party that excessive decentralization wouldn't work in Canada. It went against the political culture as well as the party tradition; it threatened national unity as well as the operation of the federal government. Even a brief time as Prime Minister had taught him about the greed of the provinces, the desire of most Canadians for strong national institutions, and the growing weakness of Ottawa's macroeconomic management.

"We must face the fact," he said at the start of the 1980 election, "that the federal government is not as able as it should be to manage the national economy, to help overcome regional disparities, and to conduct major national policies. There has grown up a serious fiscal imbalance, not only among the provinces but between the provincial and federal levels of government."

But Trudeau had taken the successful national vision that had once been Macdonald's, so Clark couldn't just say, "Me too," particularly since his own party was beginning to fill up with those premiers, businessmen, and ordinary outsiders who had been bruised and wounded by the Liberals' policies in the 1970s. "Community of communities" was vague enough to satisfy most Tories, but it turned out to be too vague for most Canadians. It made Clark look like "the head waiter" to the provinces, it indirectly cost him Ontario, and it kept him from reaping both an energy deal and the historical glory that Trudeau grabbed for reforming the constitution. In fact, Clark knew the Tories couldn't oppose either patriation or the entrenchment of democratic rights, so they had to focus on attacking the process by which the two were achieved.

Early one Saturday morning during the leadership race, in an airplane over the Prairies, Clark tried once more to explain his concept. He had just flown out of Calgary, and a display of branding irons in the airport had brought back memories of his childhood in High River. Though he hadn't been able to pay a quick visit home on the first anniversary of his father's death, his mother and some friends had driven up to the fund-raising luncheon where he had delivered his standard speech.

"I too am worried about how much the federal party relies upon the provincial parties in some regions," he said. He was tired, his chipmunk cheeks drooped, and his voice barely rose above the hum of the engines. "One of the reasons I'm interested in federal institutional reform is that it would be healthier to have regional desires expressed effectively through channels other than the mouths of premiers. They have their legitimate powers, of course, but they have acquired excessive power through the default at the centre.

"That isn't inconsistent with a 'community of communities.' Our definition began by understanding what we were against, which was Trudeau's centralism. It's very powerful and it has no understanding of the regions. A strong national government like King's had Jimmy Gardiner making sure that the interests of Western Canada were reflected, for instance, but now we have a strong central government that is absolutely out of touch. It's not a choice between the national community and the local communities. It's a choice between the capital and the country.

"I've had an awful time defining 'community of communities,' but I believe there's something there and we have to define it. The national community has to incorporate the elements of the local communities within it, but there's still a strong national sense. And that idea could become the encompassing perspective that the National Policy was in Macdonald's day."

IV

"Joe! Joe! Joe! Joe!" a thousand people shouted in the dining room while a wandering Italian orchestra played

"Blue, blue, my heart is blue" and Joe Clark and Maureen McTeer entered waving. It was not an unusual campaign scene except that the enthusiastic crowd was French-Canadian and the setting was a fifty-dollar-a-plate Sunday lunch in east-end Montreal. In 1976 the two Quebec candidates for the Tory leadership, Claude Wagner and Brian Mulroney, had been defeated by an unknown MP from Alberta, and that had been perceived as another signal that Quebeckers weren't welcome in the Progressive Conservative Party. In the 1980 election the party's standing in the province stood at one seat and 12.6 per cent of the popular vote. "In fact," Brian Mulroney often said with disgust, "in the seventy-five Quebec ridings, fifty-four candidates lost their deposits. In thirty-nine seats we ran third behind the NDP, and in two seats we even ran behind the Rhinoceros Party." The reasons were old and complex, but Mulroney didn't hesitate to finger Joe Clark.

Clark's reincarnation as a Quebec candidate was one of the few surprises of the campaign. It was rooted, predictably, in organization. Clark's strategists figured that he needed at least 200 delegates from Quebec to win the June convention. That meant electing pro-Clark slates as quickly as possible to prevent Brian Mulroney from walking off with most of the 750 delegates. Mulroney and his team had more or less taken charge of the Quebec wing's election machinery after Wagner went to the Senate, and some of his organizers had already mobilized an anti-Clark network for Winnipeg. But Clark had done some counter-manoeuvring in Quebec to dilute the review forces, so he was able to activate his own network as soon as the leadership campaign was called. The result was a series of "dirty tricks," "irregularities," and squabbles in which the Clark and Mulroney teams tried to outnumber each other at delegate-selection meetings by recruiting children, skid-row drifters, and other instant Tories. The party's Quebec membership jumped from five thousand in August, 1982, to thirteen thousand just before Winnipeg to well over thirty thousand by April. These tactics offended long-time Conservatives across the country, but Clark merely chided

the press for dwelling on the rough-and-tumble and missing the real story, which was the influx of Quebeckers into
the party. The other part of the story was that Clark had
tied up about 40 per cent of the Quebec delegates in the
first week.

Joe Clark was preoccupied with making a breakthrough in Quebec, for the party as well as for himself,
though he saw the two as going hand in hand. Winning
in Quebec was like winning in the immigrant ridings of
Toronto. There were practical, philosophical, and moral
reasons for doing so. The practical was best expressed by
Brian Mulroney, who had a wonderful talent for finding
the most convincing argument on any issue and then finding the most convincing way to articulate it. He also had
a wonderful talent for equating the national interest and
that of the party with his own by promoting the advantages of a fluently bilingual, Quebec-born leader. "There
are 102 ridings in Canada with a francophone population
of more than 10 per cent," he said everywhere he went,
"and in the last election we won only two of them. Give
Pierre Trudeau a gift of 100 seats and he'll beat you ten
times out of ten!"

The causes of that imbalance were a whole catalogue
of Tory sins against Quebec, kept fresh by constant ad-
ditions: the hanging of Louis Riel in 1885, Macdonald's
procrastination over the threat to Catholic schooling in the
West, conscription in the First World War, imperialist jin-
goism, conscription in the Second World War, and the
reaction against official bilingualism. The party had no
more success finding another Cartier than it did finding
another Macdonald, so Laurier led the disenchanted French
Canadians into the Liberal Party *en masse* and Lapointe,
St. Laurent, and Trudeau kept them there. Meanwhile,
the Conservatives drifted further and further from the sen-
sibilities of Quebec. The anti-Catholic, pro-British element
became even more influential in the wake of the French
Canadians' desertion. R. B. Hanson, the party's interim
leader in 1940, even refused to read anything translated
from French on the grounds that if something were im-

portant enough it would have been written in English in the first place.

In 1938, desperate for power, the party held its nose and made a special effort to woo Quebec by making R. J. Manion its leader. Manion was a magnetic ex-Liberal of Irish descent, married to a French Canadian. Using the carrot of victory to maintain unity in Ontario, he moved the Conservatives toward reformist policies and sought an electoral alliance with Maurice Duplessis's Union Nationale. But the war and conscription defeated that idea and Manion resigned after the disastrous results of the 1940 election. His successor, George Drew, proposed the alliance with Duplessis again in the 1950s, using provincial rights as the common bond. However, nothing took place on any organizational level until 1957, when Duplessis gave some quiet assistance to Diefenbaker, and 1958, when the Union Nationale and all Quebec jumped on Diefenbaker's steam-roller. That marriage of convenience quickly disintegrated in the early 1960s. Duplessis died, the Liberals came to power in Quebec, and the Quiet Revolution exploded in the middle of Diefenbaker's term. Already insensitive to the feelings and aspirations of French Canadians, Diefenbaker reacted by becoming even more so. His respect for individual rights and multiculturalism couldn't distinguish francophones from any other ethnic minority, and his old-fashioned Canadian nationalism precluded both Quebec nationalism and a vision of a bilingual, bicultural Canada.

Robert Stanfield made a valiant effort to correct the image of the Progressive Conservatives as bigoted Orangemen. He recruited high-quality Quebec candidates for the 1968 election, but they were defeated by Trudeaumania. He pressured most of his caucus to support the Official Languages Act in 1969, but seventeen MPs defied him, including Diefenbaker and his western cohorts. Stanfield made Claude Wagner his Quebec lieutenant, refused to allow Leonard Jones to stand as the Conservative candidate in Moncton because of the former mayor's anti-French views, made contacts among key opinion makers, stumbled through the French language, and showed up in a toque at winter carnivals. But the party won only three seats and 20 per cent of the Quebec vote in 1974. More than any other of the raucous divisions that tormented Stanfield and cost him the leadership, the struggle to drag his party toward an understanding of Quebec broke him.

Joe Clark was able and willing to build on Stanfield's work and good name. Helped greatly by his wife, who had grown up in a bilingual town in Eastern Ontario and developed a credibility of her own as a campaigner in Quebec, Clark learned French, established a new party machine in the province, and began the laborious process of earning the confidence of French Canadians by conciliation and good will. However, the election of the Parti Québécois in 1976 abruptly forced everyone back into traditional hard-line positions. English Canada saw conciliation as weakness; French Canada saw it as impossible.

Quebec elected only two Conservatives in 1979, and Clark could acquire a credible French-Canadian member of his cabinet only by bringing in a senator. In 1980 he dropped to one Quebec seat. At the same time, part of his loss in English Canada was attributable to the perception that Trudeau would be a better champion for Canada in the upcoming Quebec referendum, since Clark had decided to take a hands-off approach as Prime Minister. Clark preferred to portray the referendum as an internal issue, to be resolved by Quebeckers, but that was clearly a case of trying to make a virtue of necessity. The Tories just didn't have the troops or the credibility to engage in the debate.

Then Trudeau's unilateral reform of the constitution gave Clark an issue with which to dramatize his party's change of heart. Virtually alone at first, he persuaded his caucus to stall the government's constitutional package and search for a less confrontational deal. In time he won a series of concessions, and—as he described it—Conservatives in Quebec were able at last to hold their heads high at Montreal cocktail parties. Not coincidentally, the huge Montreal fund-raiser that cheered Clark during the leadership campaign was held on the first anniversary of the patriation ceremonies in Ottawa.

Brian Mulroney had supported Trudeau's action at the time. "Brian tends to be pretty simplistic when it comes to strategy," said Lowell Murray, who had gone to university in Nova Scotia with him. "He goes for the big splash. He supported Trudeau's constitutional position not because he had thought about it for five minutes, but because he was so thrilled by the sheer bravado of it all. That position would not have served us very well."

But Mulroney didn't believe that Quebec would be won by the nuances of the British North America Act or conciliatory gestures to Quebec nationalism. Like Trudeau, he hated separatism with a passion and distrusted the PQ, many of whose leaders he had known at Laval University as a law student. He had no expectations that they would ever be satisfied by any federal solution. He believed, on the other hand, that Quebec could be won by a *chef*, a native-born leader whose very selection as leader would lead French Canadians back to the Conservatives in the same way that Laurier had lured them to the Liberals and Diefenbaker had lured the West into the Tory Party. Of course, he himself was the only such candidate.

"French Canadians are *your* salvation," he said to English Conservatives across the country, all of them hungry for power. "Eight million French Canadians are crying out to be welcomed into the Progressive Conservative Party. All they need is a bicultural, bilingual leader who can reach out and say, '*Vous avez un foyer chez nous*, you have a home with us!' "

Whatever their customary attitude toward the "froggy-froggies" and the French language, many party members in Saskatchewan and P.E.I. couldn't resist the appeal because it made such practical sense. Mulroney always softened the message by restricting it to self-interest and electoral numbers. His first concern, he constantly emphasized, wasn't the constitution or cultural survival; it was jobs, jobs, jobs.

Joe Clark didn't have Mulroney's given advantage as

a Quebecker, so he had to approach the party's practical need to win seats in Quebec from a more thoughtful direction. Nor did he have Mulroney's private-sector experience as a reason to play up the economic questions, so he had to focus on his own experience and interest in the broader questions facing the nation. "Unlike the other candidates," he said, "I believe that *the* most important issue is national unity. I define it differently than Trudeau, but finding the common chords to give the country a sense of working together remains the essential issue."

So, unlike Mulroney, Clark made a point of emphasizing that English Canadians had a moral duty to understand and receive Quebec. And he put Quebec into the same ideological context—diversity, moderation, and community—as he put everything else. He argued that the party couldn't assume, as Mulroney and Crosbie seemed to, that its entrepreneurial, economic message would carry the same weight in Quebec as elsewhere without being linked to questions of language and ethnicity. Nor was he convinced that Quebeckers, with their conservative, nationalist, and radical traditions, were as hostile to state intervention as many English-speaking Tories were thought to be. Finally, his sense of community made him sympathetic to Quebec's nationalist feelings, though never to separatism. That became the outstanding difference between him and Brian Mulroney.

"There's no miraculous way to win votes in Quebec," Clark said, "not even by the sonorous quality of your voice." He knew the attraction of Mulroney's style in the province, but it grated on him to imagine that only a Quebecker could speak to the desires of Quebec. Besides, he had reservations about Mulroney's tactics. Bashing the Parti Québécois, as Mulroney could do as a native son, might have pleased the dissatisfied Liberals in Quebec, but Clark judged it a short-sighted approach. Eventually the Liberals would return to the fold, and the Tories would be back where they started.

Clark believed that the Progressive Conservatives should take the more arduous route of building a new coalition in Quebec among the traditional anti-Liberals, including the Union Nationale, the Créditistes, and the Parti Québécois. "*Mériter*," he said, "not *hériter*." That meant appealing to the nationalists and giving them a federal option that wasn't as centralist or rigid as Trudeau's. It meant understanding that most Quebeckers usually regarded their province in a different way from French Canadians in Ottawa and were angry at the Liberals, not Canada. After all, Maurice Duplessis's clientele had come from among the Quebec Tories, *les bleus*, who had fled the Conservative Party without really feeling comfortable with the Liberals.

As Clark explained, "Brian has the old party organizers and those who can deliver, and he has people who have known him personally—a crony factor—and ambitious people who want to get into federal politics and believe that Brian can deliver. They've probably never voted PQ and they identify with the traditional, often anglo elite. My people are more nationalist and more rural. They're part of another elite, which is francophone and associated with the PQ but isn't necessarily separatist. It's in the *caisse* movement, for example, and it gravitates more to Quebec City than Montreal."

Mulroney described it another way. "I have the real Tories, and he has the rest. There is no Quebec loyalty to Clark. He was leader for seven years and had control of the $7-million PC Canada Fund, which he used effectively."

But Clark's stand on the constitution did attract some support that went beyond plain organization. In fact, the presence of PQ organizers in Clark's team caused a backlash in English Canada, despite Clark's claim that he had converted them to federalism by his policies. ("A little bird came down and told me," Mulroney said after he read about those organizers, " 'Brian Mulroney, you're going to be the next Prime Minister of Canada.' ") Without a sizeable Tory base in Quebec, it was inevitable that all the candidates would get support from people who generally voted differently, but the Liberals tended to go to Mulroney and the nationalists to Clark. One reason was image: Mulroney's slickness worked on the Liberals, while Clark

styled himself *"le petit gars de* High River" to attract the
small-town, small-business, and rural constituencies. Another was the resurfacing of the constitution debate during
the leadership campaign in the form of an argument over
financial compensation for provinces opting out of constitutional changes that affected provincial jurisdiction.

Though that had been part of the Vancouver amending
formula accepted by eight provincial premiers (all except
Davis and Hatfield, in fact), and though it had been part
of the Tory caucus's position during the constitution debate, Clark was the only candidate courageous enough or
foolhardy enough to defend it. The formula was to apply
to all provinces and to limited areas of existing provincial
responsibility, but Clark was accused of being a patsy to
Quebec for the sake of convention votes. Meanwhile, Brian
Mulroney was on the phone saying that Clark had cooked
up a deal with René Lévesque and that financial compensation was a sell-out to the PQ. By implying that Clark
was soft on separatism, Mulroney also hoped to deflect
the party's criticism that he himself had been soft on Trudeau's constitution. Finally Robert Stanfield, fearing the
kind of distortions that had harmed the party in 1968 when
Trudeau twisted its *"deux nations-*two nations" concept,
called Mulroney and said he would oppose him publicly
if he didn't desist. The issue died shortly after.

"The Vancouver formula may have been all right in
the middle of negotiations," Mulroney said in a conversation in his Westmount home, "but not out of the blue
two years later. I was offended when Joe stood up in that
east-end meeting and gave his cards away to Lévesque.
The PQ must have been in heaven. No wonder they have
such nice things to say about him. Before I give away a
plugged nickel, I want to know what Lévesque is going
to do for Canada. Why should I give away the ace of hearts
when he wants to destroy Canada?"

Mulroney told a Montreal press conference that "we'll
find a serious and eloquent formula to meet Quebec's legitimate and historical responsibility to safeguard its language and culture." When challenged repeatedly to be

more specific, he scribbled a nine-point statement of principles on a Quebecair barf bag while flying into Mont-Joli. "Canada is a great country and Quebec is an integral and important part of it," said the first principle. The ninth declared, "My past is a guarantee of success in the future. Wherever I have gone in my professional life, I have sown harmony and understanding." Despite an aide's urging that a ten-point program would be more memorable, Mulroney couldn't think of another "parameter."

Actually Mulroney didn't think that constitutions would cut much ice with the Quebec delegates anyway. He seemed genuinely surprised that all Quebeckers (particularly the nationalists) didn't rally behind one of their own. He was obviously jealous of Clark's support among the intellectuals and from *Le Devoir*, but he couldn't imagine that any issue would outweigh his own home-grown, anti-intellectual, sentimental personality. In the end, he seemed to have been right. Quebec has usually preferred to keep its nationalism at home while sending strong, federalist native sons to Ottawa, and a leader's network of friends and hangers-on is often firmer than any patchwork of principles and alliances. That's why Mulroney talked so openly about patronage throughout the leadership campaign, not only in Quebec but across Canada, pointing to hordes of future senators and promising he'd only appoint a Liberal to a job when there wasn't another living, breathing Tory left to reward. "If anybody thinks that kind of talk hurt me," he said, "then he doesn't know the Conservative Party."

Certainly, there were many Quebec delegates who opposed Clark solely because he had been so slow and negligent about dispensing the rewards of power when Prime Minister. At the time, however, Clark was equally adamant that his own approach would be best in the long run. "In the past there was no substantive reason to be a Conservative in Quebec, except anger at the Liberals and the prospect of reward. We were on the sidelines because Quebec is an idea-oriented province and we weren't involved in policy.

"Most of our Quebeckers were waiting for the federal party to win elsewhere so that they could collect in Quebec. The movers and shakers were looking at it as a spoils system. Brian's people, by and large, are spoils politicians. They don't really think we can win down there. Brian talks about winning because it showcases his bilingualism, but I don't think he believes we can win in any significant way. But I believe we can win and that it will endure."

Between them, Clark and Mulroney made winning in Quebec the pivotal issue of the campaign. Poor John Crosbie, trying to talk about economic problems, found his unilingualism becoming as much of a problem in Edmonton as in Quebec City. "Would you be here tonight," Joe Clark used to ask his English audiences, "to listen to a French Canadian talking to you through a translator?" Though the diehards still appreciated Crosbie's jokes and temper tantrums about the French language, and though some members of the Parti Québécois considered him the perfect candidate for their own Machiavellian purposes, his campaign effectively ended on the May evening when he compared French to German and Chinese.

"What would you do if Quebec voted to separate?" he was asked at a Montreal news conference.

"As Winston Churchill said, I was not elected to preside over the dissolution of the British Empire," Crosbie bluffed. Then he deflated himself by adding, "Of course he did do just that."

Meanwhile, Joe Clark and Brian Mulroney were competing throughout Quebec for delegates, the future of the party, and a concept of Canada. One Saturday in May, while Clark was heading to Sherbrooke and Trois-Rivières, Mulroney was trying to relax at home after another gruelling week of campaigning. But the phone rang all morning with aides in a panic about two polls that placed Clark ahead in Quebec and in the country. Mulroney reassured them with his soothing, confident baritone, slightly hoarse from fatigue, speech making and du Mauriers. By noon he was still in his silk dressing gown, moving in a slow, edgy way between the phone and the breakfast of beans and eggs Mila had prepared him.

"I'm neck and neck with Clark on the first ballot," he said, finally regaining the public enthusiasm that usually hid his personal lack of security. His habit was to suppress his doubts and worries beneath a smooth torrent of blarney, optimism, and exaggeration. The gap between what his thin, tense body was expressing and what his smiling, easy-going words were saying partly accounted for any impression that he wasn't sincere or trustworthy. "Their eyes are going to pop out! Crosbie is behind by 600 votes! I've got the polls and I promised the boys two weeks ago that I've got 1,060 coming out of the gate! It's going to be an eye-popper!"

V

In the middle of May, Joe Clark was sent to the Maritimes. The campaign was in its second phase: consolidation and expansion. The delegates had been selected. Their preferences and the degree of their commitment had been registered in twelve categories in David Small's computer in the Ottawa headquarters, and the "key switchers" had been identified for a phone call or a visit from the candidate. "Hard" and "soft" supporters had been given chores in the campaign as a "babysitting" device, and attention had been paid to the third of the delegates who weren't elected by party meetings: MPs, MLAs, and all sorts of party VIPs. Small coordinated his information with the touring committee, the touring committee made arrangements with the priority ridings, and Joe Clark found himself on a Sunday night with Halifax-area delegates at the Brightwood Golf and Country Club in Dartmouth.

On Monday morning he was driven to Antigonish in a cavalcade of four cars, one for him, one for local party officials, and two for the journalists assigned to track him during the last weeks of the campaign. En route he stopped at an Irving station. He took off his sweater and put on his jacket, went into the coffee shop, shook hands with all the surprised customers, sat on a stool, and had a cup of coffee. Returning to the car, he changed back into his sweater and invited Val Sears of the *Toronto Star* for an interview.

"Where do you get your stamina?" Sears asked as they rolled along the highway.

"At night my spirit leaves me," Clark replied. "But instead of wandering up the Nile, it does push-ups."

In Antigonish, home of St. Francis Xavier University, where Lowell Murray and Brian Mulroney had been president and secretary of the PC Club, Clark met delegates, organizers, and a couple of distant relatives in the executive suite of the local Wandlyn Inn. Since everyone was sardined uncomfortably into the small living room, Clark confined his remarks to a brief explanation of the need for the leadership race and a defence of his own record. "I'm a *national* candidate with national *experience*," he said, without comparing himself to Crosbie or Mulroney by name. "I've had to make the tough decisions, and I've been right more times than I've been wrong. The party is stronger in significant areas of the country, and there's no guarantee that the painstaking lead we've built can be transferred to another leader."

Joe Clark spent much of the campaign running against himself. More than economic policy or social responsibility or even Quebec, the issue on most delegates' minds was Joe Clark's judgement as Prime Minister. The fiasco involving his retracted promise to move the Canadian embassy from Tel Aviv to Jerusalem, the confusion about his Petro-Canada policy, the unresolved quarrel between Alberta and Ontario over energy prices, and the harsh budget measures which brought down his government were mentioned again and again. They had lost him the 1980 election, and that loss became still another error to wonder about.

He confessed his mistake about Jerusalem, but he wondered why he received no credit for helping the American diplomats to escape from Teheran via the Canadian embassy. He straightened out his thinking about Petro-Canada, and he stressed that he had been about to conclude a negotiated settlement on energy pricing when his government fell. He defended the budget as necessary at the time and even better in retrospect. As for his government's defeat in the House of Commons, he recognized it had been a gamble. The Liberals were virtually leaderless, and their threat to bring down the Tories sounded like big talk. The Créditistes were demanding another billion dollars in expenditures, which seemed a lot for six votes. Besides, it would not have served Clark's Quebec strategy to strengthen a party the Conservatives wanted to absorb. Finally, Clark's advisers had been certain they could win if an election were forced. But the abrupt fall had left him with a record that looked worse than none at all. His only defence was that he had learned from his mistakes.

"He's no world-beater," Lowell Murray said, "but he's usually right on the important issues."

To which Brian Mulroney liked to reply, "He may have been right on most issues, but he was wrong on the big one. He lost the government. If that's political experience, I wouldn't brag about it."

But experience was still Clark's strongest card against Mulroney. "The main question is judgement under pressure," he told the delegates in Antigonish. "I bear the bruises of a guy who's been through seven years of war."

Certainly he had picked up a lot of knowledge. For almost two hours, sometimes balancing a plate of sandwiches on his knees, sometimes stretching backwards with his hands cupped behind his head, he sat among his dwindling listeners in the Wandlyn Inn and answered questions about DREE (the Department of Regional Economic Expansion) and Quebec and NATO and freight rates. Appropriately in a college town, the meeting became a seminar: long and considered answers about complex matters, deepening voice and serious expression, and no small talk. He was interesting, frank, and articulate, but his views tended to get lost in the details and complications. He left the impression of a thoughtful, reasonable person who talked too much, listened poorly, refused to take a simple or dramatic position, and was smarter than imagined.

Twenty-four hours later he was in Charlottetown, Prince Edward Island. In the meantime, he had attended a garden party in Truro, given a long interview to the *London Free Press*, delivered a rambling speech in Kentville, and then returned to Halifax for the night. The next day he had had breakfast with the Nova Scotia Tory caucus, flown to Charlottetown, had lunch with the P.E.I. Tory caucus, met with Premier James Lee at the legislature and youth delegates in his hotel suite, had a moment's "down time," talked on the phone, talked to the press, talked, talked, talked. That was his job. While others plotted and laboured in operations committees and themes committees, Clark was the front man—or, as he preferred, the symbol—for the "modern, moderate, national" party. That's why his image was so important.

"Bad judgement" was often an excuse for bad image. Nova Scotian MP Elmer MacKay compared Clark to a dog food that wouldn't sell. What he said and did seemed overwhelmed by the stubby chin, the funny strut, the animated hands, the odd vocabulary, and the grand-old-man pretensions. For all his frankness and in all his analyses, he never confronted the "wimp factor" adequately because it wasn't a problem within his soul and because there was nothing he could do about it except change his hairstyle and make self-deprecating jokes.

The problem was compounded by his public-speaking style. His honesty kept him from the exaggerations of demagoguery, and he never lifted audiences to emotional heights. Keeping his own emotions in check, he seemed separated from crowds whose notion of a leader was Macdonald or Diefenbaker. There was little that was extreme in his content, just as there was little that was extreme in his personality. Nor had he learned the technique of speaking to each individual in the audience, plainly and directly, as he could in private. He had to win his support person by person, because on the platform he often became strident, his voice indignant, his posture tense, his thoughts clichés. His hands chopped and pointed so much that one worried what bizarre message he was inadvertently sending out to any deaf-mute present.

At the nighttime reception in the ballroom of the Hotel Charlottetown, his standard speech fell flat again. The organizers of the reception had failed to provide chairs, and tradition in P.E.I. dictates that if you're sitting you're quiet, but if you're standing you talk. So most people were bunched around the bar at the back, chattering with old acquaintances and leaving an enormous gap in front of the microphone all through Clark's speech. In that gap the *Journal* crew clumped and clattered. Meanwhile, Val Sears was loudly clanking a spoon against his coffee cup to menace the tape-recorder of a more diligent colleague, and the sound carried to Clark, who was already intimidated by Sears's threat to yell out the punch lines of the all-too-familiar stories. Finally Clark brought his dull rhetoric to a sudden finish, asked for a beer, and invited questions.

"Throw out the metric!" a woman called, but it took a while to find someone who had been paying enough attention to ask a question about the economy. The back of the room remained in an uproar while Clark tried to speak intelligently about the NEP, FIRA, tax incentives, capital punishment, the technological revolution, electrical rates on the island, the fishing industry, defence, Quebec, and food production. A lesser man might have asked, "How in hell did I get here and what on earth am I talking about and who cares?" But Joe Clark merely said, "I guess if you can't beat them join them. So I'm going to get involved in some of those conversations back there."

Later, as he flew by small plane to Charlo, in Northern New Brunswick, he remarked, "That wasn't one of our better meetings."

His reluctance to complain, his endurance, and his solid confidence were commendable. He loved campaigning, because it took him out of Ottawa and gave him the mood of the people, though he rarely mingled in any natural way. He was working hard, drawing on all his strength just to get through each day with all its pressures. There was almost a sadness in how cut off he seemed from others. His gesture in asking for a beer was a futile attempt to connect, and his awkward jokes with the press only accentuated his alienation. Everyone seemed to be having a good time around him, and his efforts to be one of the boys proved he wasn't.

There was something boyish about him, though—his quick stride, his nervous whistling, his love of Coke and movies and detective stories—but he tried to suppress it by gravity and convoluted phrases because he had been described as a boy among men. Though he had grown up with Bob Dylan, he liked to be seen as the "Old Chieftain," and his constant reminders that he had been Prime Minister increased his distance from his peers. Generous to his enemies, he was accused of being weak. Accused of being weak, he tried to act tough, often at the oddest moments, such as during the Jerusalem debacle or the Winnipeg convention. Getting tough about electing his slates, he damaged his greatest asset, his reputation for honesty and fair play. Portrayed as a wimp and a jerk, he built a shield that guarded his natural friendliness and trust. He designed a public persona with the same care and hard work he used for the party's image. Trying to be all things to too many people, he was seldom himself.

"Joe Clark," one of Crombie's team observed, "thinks that being nice is a strategy."

That was perhaps unjust, but there was a deliberateness in his behaviour that explained the tremendous gap between his public and private effectiveness. Obviously sincere on a one-on-one basis, he was evidently less so in front of a crowd. Though he never read from a text, he repeated the same sentences word-perfect over and over again so that he wouldn't risk being misinterpreted. He had formula answers ready for most questions and, if he were asked something provocative, he learned to be "inventive" in his evasions so that no vested interests would be aroused.

All politicians do the same, of course. Mulroney and Crosbie, in particular, put on performances in public. In private Crosbie's famous humour often vanished into shyness or arrogance, while Mulroney's charming sentimentalities were pale disguises for insecurity and hostility. But Joe Clark had neither a delightful accent nor the gift of the gab to coat his cautious platitudes. However, his presence improved as he grew into his public self. Older, plumper, a littler greyer, he appeared more comfortable with his design, and therefore more sincere. Admitting he had been inexperienced in the past, he felt he was coming into his full powers, and everyone noticed a new command in his manner.

"What have you ever done for real?" a young man had shouted at Winnipeg.

"I've been Prime Minister of Canada!" Clark shot back. He finally had an answer for dropping out of law school.

His brief months in power must have often returned to him like a suppressed fantasy or recurring nightmare. In such a glorious, terrible, foreshortened time he saw (with the full force only known to those few individuals who have sat in the Prime Minister's chair) what Pierre Trudeau had seen in eleven years. Clark had the advantage of entering office as a 1960s Canadian liberal rather than with a headful of cherished ideals, but he quickly discovered how slight that advantage was. Whether on major or minor levels, the old ways that he had learned from Fulton and Stanfield were faltering.

The second OPEC crisis revealed the weaknesses of the world free-market system and Canada's place in it. It provoked a dramatic exposition of the strains in the federation. After every concession Clark made, the premiers only wanted more power and more money. The private sector wanted less regulation but more assistance—to the extent where multinational oil companies came to the defence of Petro-Canada because of the services and profits it provided in partnerships. On energy policy and Jerusalem and the budget, Clark learned the difficulties of accommodating the bureaucracy while maintaining political control. Meanwhile, the public's attitude to "short-term pain" was tested by the ultimate poll, an election, much more immediately than anyone imagined. When Clark tried to take the high road, by not doling out patronage after the writs were issued or by making some good non-partisan appointments, he soon found the cost.

It was easy for many people to see these events as evidence of Joe Clark's incompetence. Another leader, a better man, could have made the old ways work. Clark himself was able to attribute many of them to inexperience, atrocious luck, and bad press. Trudeau and the Liberals, watching from the opposition side, saw them differently, however, and were preparing a different approach for when they regained office. The Tories had to wait a while longer before they could try their approach again.

In the meantime, ever optimistic or dumb, Joe Clark pressed on. The night after the unhappy meeting in Charlottetown something rare happened. The day had been a long one, from breakfast in Campbellton to lunch at the Portage Café in Chatham, from Chatham to Pokemouche by air and from Pokemouche to Paquetville in a startling gold Mercedes, a speech in French in rustic Paquetville's community centre, and on by air to the Howard Johnson's Motor Lodge in Moncton. But the sun came out after the snow in P.E.I., the countryside was beautiful in the spring light, and Clark's heart had been warmed by the sight of unshaven Acadian workers putting on Clark stickers. It affirmed his hope that the party, through his efforts and with the help of Premier Hatfield's work, was ready to sprout in Liberal preserves. He remembered coming into this region in 1974 to give his first speech in French. Jack Horner, the strong-willed Albertan MP, was opposing Stanfield's rejection of Leonard Jones at the time, and Clark was sent to Tracadie, New Brunswick, as a signal that all Westerners weren't anti-French. He had assumed that would remain his contribution to the party's evolving attitude to French Canada, and it pleased and touched him to have become a major interpreter of Quebec's nationalism since then. This, he felt, would be his historic and enduring contribution to the party and to national unity.

So he was in good spirits when he spoke in the gaudy

red Anchorage Room at Howard Johnson's that night. He skipped his usual stories and told the audience about Tracadie, the mishaps in getting a French text to him in Alberta, his awful accent, and the local Tory candidate losing his deposit in the next election anyway. He was enjoying his own story as much as his listeners were, laughing at it and stroking the back of his head, a habit normally reserved for private moments when he was at peace.

"After that speech Maureen and I went to a pizza parlour for dinner," he continued, remembering something else. "Well, a couple of years passed and I won the leadership, to most people's surprise though not to mine. After the convention Maureen and I went back to our little house, and we were wondering what we had got ourselves into when the phone rang. 'Aha,' I said. 'It must be the Prime Minister of England or the President of the United States calling to congratulate me.' But it was the woman who owned the pizza parlour in Tracadie. She had just lost her liquor licence, and since she couldn't get through to Hatfield, she wondered if I could help her now that I was leader of the Progressive Conservative Party! It was a rude introduction to what was in store for me."

Relaxed by laughter or the sun or fatigue, he moved into his speech without becoming stiff and earnest. His message was not different, but the words were remarkably clear and his feelings showed through. "In seven years we have built a modern, moderate, national party," he said. "We have risen to 52 per cent in the Gallup Poll, and I will take credit for forty-eight of that. That wasn't achieved by accident. We *built* it by making people feel comfortable with us. We did it with the Greeks in Broadview-Greenwood. We did it in Timiskaming, where we went into French-Canadian homes in French and into NDP homes committed to social justice, and we won that riding for the first time in fifty-two years. And we did it in Quebec, where we are up to 40 per cent in the Gallup. We did it because we are a certain type of party, of which I am the symbol.

"All the candidates agree on the basic issues of the

economy. What's at issue is a leader who can attract support across the country for years to come, not just the anti-government vote that will turn against us later, and a leader who can bring out the best in this country by encouraging its regions and its individuals to realize their potential.

"I've been leader for seven years. There are easier jobs, there are other things to do, and I've had the title and the office. I'm here because I've invested time and effort in this party and this country and I have the experience to know what is needed. I'm an old man at forty-four."

VI

Three minutes before the start of the vote that would destroy his hopes in the prime of his life, Joe Clark was singing fervently. His eyes were closed and the long hands that had poked and bothered through so many speeches were clapping a determined beat. "Oh, we ain't got a barrel of money! Maybe we're ragged and funny!" he hollered. "But we'll travel along, singin' a song, side by side!"

Maureen McTeer, Grace Clark and her other son Peter, Robert Stanfield, Duff Roblin, Davie Fulton, MPs such as Flora MacDonald and Don Mazankowski and Roch La-Salle, organizers such as Lowell Murray and Finlay MacDonald and Bill McAleer, hundreds of friends and supporters were hollering along with him. "But we'll travel the road, sharin' the load, side by side!"

The road had taken most of them through the coup of 1976, the glory of 1979, the tragedy of 1980, the humiliation of 1981, and this final challenge which had begun in Winnipeg 135 days before. It had led them at last to the sweltering arena in Ottawa, June 11, 1983, high noon. All the meetings and receptions had been organized, the speeches given, the deals done, the money raised, the strategy laid. Now there was nothing left to do but sing like hell. "Through all kinds of weather! What if the sky should fall? Just as long as we're together, it doesn't matter at all!"

The old-fashioned song, evoking small-town picnics and innocence, added to the nineteenth-century atmos-

phere that permeated the convention in spite of the television cameras. The men sweated in their shirt-sleeves,
the women fluttered "I am a Clark fan" fans, and the
reporters pressed in with their notebooks open. Clark himself had taken off his jacket. The reserve of his public
persona had wilted in the heat and the tension. Like a
Holy Roller, he bellowed the song to prepare himself for
the moment of truth. "When they've all had their quarrels
and parted," sang the Right Honourable Charles Joseph
Clark, "we'll be the same as we started! Just travellin'
along, singin' a song, side by side!"

"If Goofy wins," a John Gamble supporter said of him,
"then we're all going back to Disneyland."

"Clark's dying hard," a grim Mulroney organizer said.

"Give me a J! Give me an O! Give me an E!" the Youth-
for-Clark yelled. "What have you got?"

Exactly, thought the Anybody-but-Clark delegates as
they headed for the first ballot. He wasn't Joe Who anymore; he was Joe Why. Seven years of bad luck were more
than enough. Some didn't want a broad-based party and
hadn't liked Clark's methods of achieving it. Some didn't
want a moderate party and believed the country needed
strong right-wing policies. Some didn't want a national
party if that meant cosying up to the separatists. And after
all the agony and the millions of dollars spent in the campaign, the Progressive Conservatives would look foolish
if they woke up Sunday with Joe Clark still the leader.
Overthrowing him was much more exciting than keeping
him, and this was the last chance.

Besides, the Anybody-but-Clark people *hated* him. Their
anger stemmed largely from their anger at themselves for
electing him in 1976. He had made that accident their dis-
grace, for which they had suffered ridicule and defeat.
They were determined to correct it, no matter what the
risks. So there wasn't anything he could say against that
vitriol. His promise of party unity became "my way or the
doorway," which simply enraged his enemies more. His
claim to experience only reminded them that he had used
the party and the nation as a training ground and that they

had paid for his mistakes. No argument that the party was on the verge of victory could convince them that Joe Clark wasn't a loser. In fact, the closer they got to victory, the less they wanted to give Clark the occasion to bungle again.

It was impossible to argue that Clark's image was a bum rap, because image is almost everything in politics. Clark had laboriously built careful designs for himself and the party, but in the end they looked laboured and designed. In his pragmatic, organizational, poll-taking approach there was no excitement, no soaring vision, no magic. Even if Clark could have proved himself a better manager, and even if Canada would have benefitted from plain, collegial management after the Trudeau years, the country's spirit desired more boldness, more flamboyance, and more leadership.

So did the party's spirit. The momentum was for change, and Clark's "kamikaze" campaign (as Michel Cogger called it) had to come close to victory on the first ballot because there was so little chance for growth. As it turned out, Clark got and held the third of the delegates he had convinced, but all the other candidates and almost all the undecideds ganged up against him. Even David Crombie, who had campaigned somewhat self-righteously with his uncompromising dedication to moderation and national unity, furled his yellow umbrellas, put on the button of the unilingual Crosbie after the second ballot, and then changed hats to end up in Mulroney's camp along with Peter Pocklington after the third. He had never forgiven Clark for not putting him in the inner cabinet.

The question became whether Mulroney or Crosbie would reap the whirlwind for change. There was a favourable tilt toward Crosbie, helped by his organization and the media, but it was checked by the obsession with winning in Quebec. After the second ballot there were attempts to have Clark throw his lead behind Crosbie's third-place position to stop Mulroney, but they quickly came to naught. Although Mulroney had been a shadow nemesis for seven years, Clark wouldn't stop him. Crosbie later attributed that to Clark's being "ardently stupid," but his pique merely demonstrated his failure once again to understand Quebec. Even if some of Clark's Quebec organizers might have gone to Crosbie, because they knew they were finished with Mulroney's gang and because Crosbie would require their help, Clark knew that the party would be destroyed in Quebec if he caused the election of a Drew-like anglophone by conspiring against the only candidate other than himself acceptable to French Canadians. He had to put aside his personal feelings for the good of the party and watch Brian Mulroney win the leadership in a fourth-ballot showdown.

What made the result slightly easier for Clark to take was his knowledge that Mulroney came out of the same moderate, pragmatic, and conciliatory Conservative tradition as he had. However useful Mulroney's Iron Ore Company hype had been in the campaign and as a device to allow him to attract Wilson and Pocklington's support at the convention, his victory was not a victory of the ideological right. It was, above anything else, a victory for electoral opportunism. Faced with a final choice between Clark and Mulroney, most of the delegates went with the one who looked more like a winner. In fact, they overcame their aversion to cosmopolitan slickness and went with the one who looked more like a Liberal.

Whether John Turner or Jean Chrétien replaced Pierre Trudeau as expected, the Tories had found a challenger who combined the two of them in one presentable package: a North-Shore Quebec working-class federalist who lived in Westmount, wore blue suits, and talked about the bottom line. Indeed, Brian Mulroney was from a Liberal family, had become a Conservative at university more by accident than conviction, and admired Trudeau. (Nevertheless, despite reports usually attributed to Mulroney himself, Trudeau never offered him a cabinet post over dinner at 24 Sussex Drive. Indeed, when the reports circulated, Trudeau couldn't even remember having dinner with him.) At that same time, however, he combined Diefenbaker's populist instincts and fuzzy contradictions with Reagan's mediagenic likeability. His skills at Iron Ore were public relations and labour negotiations, and those were precisely the skills the party hired. If image had been the problem, then the Tories meant to solve it with a vengeance.

It wasn't quite a perfect image, though. Mulroney's victory was no joyful love-fest. It was a negative vote, a choice among three flawed men. Some were appalled by the crudeness of Mulroney's ambitions. During the convention, for example, David Crombie invited him for a drink at the Crombie tent in downtown Ottawa. Mulroney showed up with a busload of supporters and a horde of media, so taking advantage of the hospitable gesture that he left Crombie organizers in tears of rage. During the voting, between the third and fourth ballots when John Crosbie's people had to choose between Mulroney and Clark, Mulroney positioned himself near Crosbie in the stands and deviously made a polite wave become a handshake and then a grasp, as if an endorsement, all for the sake of the cameras.

Mulroney's essential flaw, however, was his trustworthiness. He struck some Tories as a snake charmer, and 45 per cent of the delegates preferred Clark with all his weaknesses, including about 265 Crosbie supporters who just couldn't vote for Mulroney on the last ballot. Even his own "boys" must have had some reservations about his credibility when, instead of coming out of the gate on the first ballot neck and neck with Clark with 1,060 votes, he popped no eyes with 874, 217 votes behind. Mulroney's wild exaggerations were part of his exuberant charm, but they often left a trail of suspicion, contradiction, and broken promises. It wasn't that Mulroney lied. He said everything with heart-felt, oozing sincerity; he really believed what he said as he said it; but in another room a moment later, he could say the opposite with the same heart-felt, oozing sincerity, the same real belief.

Then there were the doubts about how he would behave under pressure and how he would perform in the House of Commons. (In fact, several Clark organizers who knew Mulroney well had been seriously worried about what he might do if he lost the convention. They feared, to the point of putting a contingency plan in place, that he would do something so rash that it would damage Clark and the party in public. Mulroney, of course, would prove to have greater steel and resiliency than even his closest friends suspected. Indeed, he had pondered the possibility of losing and merely concluded that Ronald Reagan had taken three attempts to win the Republican nomination.) The more common doubts were about how he would unite the various party factions to whom he had sold himself as one of their own.

Though he knew as well as Clark that the left-of-centre position was the winning one in Canada, he now carried the party's right wing like a monkey on his back. When he was first introduced to the House of Commons from the gallery after his victory, he had Peter Pocklington with him; and he had debts to the unimpressive collection of Alberta and Ontario rednecks, dinosaurs, and odds and ends who had made up his support in the caucus. Meanwhile, the real talent and experience lay mostly among Joe Clark's MPs. It would take almost a year, all of Mulroney's negotiating skill, and the heavy smell of approaching power to reach a *modus vivendi* that resembled peace and solidarity. He was helped by the fact that Clark's people were generally the sane and decent members of the caucus, less likely to have made the mischief that Clark had had to put up with from the Mulroney supporters.

"I can't hold the party together by blaming others," Joe Clark once lamented, "but it's extremely annoying that the people who were the architects of my problems then exploited the wounds in my carcass."

Mulroney's victory created an important psychological shift in the party's energy, away from the leadership issue and toward winning the next election. But it didn't change the philosophical direction of the Conservatives. In fact, Mulroney simply continued Stanfield and Clark's work. As he surrounded himself with many of the same colleagues and advisers, as he faced the same fundamental tensions from the leader's viewpoint, as he honed his image and ideas, he sounded less like the former president of the Iron Ore Company and more like the former Prime Minister from High River. He even came to recognize that thoughtful policies might be as necessary as spoils and cronyism in winning French Canada, and so he even reached his own accommodation—however rhetorical and mercenary—with Quebec nationalism and Parti Québécois organizers.

Clark himself, devoted to public life and apparently immune to personal humiliation, stayed on in the Tory caucus as a significant policy maker. Mulroney might have found his victim's presence somewhat uncomfortable, but Clark had done a great deal of the groundwork that permitted Mulroney's subsequent success. Whether Clark's philosophical alliance with Quebec nationalism would have developed into a firmer and more lasting base than Mulroney's expedient one, whether his appreciation of Canada as a "community of communities" would have proved a more effective national vision than the one Mulroney took from Trudeau and watered down, whether Clark's apprenticeship would have blossomed into a more active and substantial return to power than Mulroney's first year in office—those were the untested possibilities that haunted Joe Clark. Seeing them erased from history was more bitter to him than the loss of the top job and his official residence. He believed in them, and he believed that he had finally come to a unique capacity to shape the destiny of his party and his country. Instead, Brian Mulroney picked up Clark's basic principles, modified them to be even closer to the Liberals' winning formula, and marched into power.

"If Joe wins this convention, that's fine," said Frank Moores over a drink in Mulroney's hospitality room at the Chateau Laurier the night before the leadership vote. "He'll have earned it. But he had to go through this test of fire."

A test of fire is supposed to be a cathartic experience, a purging of sins and a cleansing of self. In that sense, however scorched, Joe Clark didn't fail it. He emerged with his ideas more clearly articulated and deeply felt than before, and he himself gained dignity by the cruel ordeal. He persevered, he seldom flinched, he did his duty as he saw it. And in the end he was joined by the people he had most admired in the party. Against all expectations, his third of the delegates stayed with him through all the ballots, when there was no more hope and at the cost of their own careers, and supporters who had begun in Winnipeg out of a sense of loyalty or sympathy finished by weeping tears of genuine love.

"He just didn't deserve this," said one sobbing organizer.

He was still disconcertingly ordinary as he stood at the podium in the final moments of the convention and urged his party to be loyal to Brian Mulroney. His body was still stiff and funny-looking, his voice slightly irritating, his very generosity and fortitude like weaknesses. Abused and mocked, betrayed by his own colleagues and discarded by the party that had been his life, he had come back for another whipping, until one hoped he would be himself at last, release his emotions in a fury of disappointment, and send all the schemers and liars and traitors to hell.

But he *was* himself, now singing "O Canada" with his arched back at attention and his hands finally at rest. His face was cauterized by pain and his mouth was determined not to tremble on the lyrics. He was an awkward kid from High River at the end of his big dreams. His old-fashioned virtues of honesty and public spirit and good will had been battered and sometimes lost in the dirty game of politics, but he had been toughened, trained, made steadfast like the unheralded surveyors who had methodically charted a new nation across the West. He looked as valiant and foolish as the small-town boys who had strutted whistling to their deaths in the mud of Europe for their own vague and noble principles, a brave little soldier to the end, just an ordinary Canadian.

SECTION THREE

Mano a Mano

I

In the late afternoon of May 10, 1984, on a chartered bus travelling the Macdonald-Cartier Freeway between Trenton and Toronto, John Napier Turner pretended that the aisle of the bus was a thin tightrope. His jacket off, his arms stretched wide for balance, with a frown of determination, he placed one foot in front of the other ever so cautiously and demonstrated his skill at walking a very fine line.

The demonstration pantomimed his vision of politics, of business, of government, perhaps even of life itself: a high-wire act of balance, determination, and cautious progress above the abyss of conflict, failure, or eternal damnation. Even his personality was a methodically achieved balance between his obsessive fears of failing or making a mistake and his heroic conceits about his ability to influence people and get things done. His fears were constantly tested by his ambition, his assumption of superiority, and the expectations of others; but any arrogance was checked by his insecurity, his sensitivity to criticism, and the humility ingrained by his Roman Catholic faith. Small wonder John Turner always looked tense.

Like any good high-wire artist, he radiated magnificent self-confidence from a distance. His classic beauty, his falcon stare, his stern voice, his athletic postures, his tailored suits, his preppy family, his important connections, and his record of achievement all contributed to the impression of great assurance. Up close, however, he was as tightly strung as one of his beloved tennis rackets. He spoke as if each phrase were a ball being thwacked across a net; he listened as if each question were a serve from John Mc-Enroe. From nervous worry and excessive adrenaline, he was forever clearing his throat, adjusting the knot of his tie, licking his lips, barking at his own jokes, chewing a breath mint, and scrunching his eyes. "For heaven's sake, shut off the baby blues for a while, John, and let's talk," he was told by a woman who had known him for more than twenty years; and friends wanted to shake him by the shoulders and yell, "Come on, John, relax! You don't have to impress me." Yet Turner seemed incapable of relaxing because there was always his God, his mother, and himself to impress.

The balancing act on the bus from Trenton had been to impress the half-dozen or so reporters accompanying him that day on his campaign to succeed Pierre Trudeau as leader of the Liberal Party and Prime Minister of Canada. It had come in reply to a question about how he could create the reality and appearance of newness while stuck with most of the policies and faces of the Trudeau regime.

Turner's initial campaign strategy had been to establish some distance between himself and Trudeauism from the start and then to widen it as the June convention approached, so that he could fight an election as the new leader of an improved party. It had seemed like an appropriate strategy from the thirty-eighth floor of a bank tower in Toronto's financial district, where Turner had worked as a corporate lawyer since resigning as Minister of Finance in 1975 and where Trudeau was looked down upon as a cold-eyed socialist. Once Turner left his Bay Street cocoon, however, he discovered that the Trudeau legacy had found greater acceptance than he had supposed from listening to his friends and clients rant over long lunches at Winston's, the Toronto restaurant where he had a regular table and a salad named after him. To win the party—and later the country—he had to draw closer to Trudeau, in fact, while sounding fresh, innovative, and sympathetic to the discontented. Hence, the tightrope; hence, the nervous worry.

There must have been a lot of times during his leadership campaign when John Turner woke up in some strange hotel room and wondered what the hell he had got himself into. Life had certainly looked neater, simpler, and brighter from his skyscraper window than from the back of a rented bus rambling past drunks stretched out on city sidewalks or tar-paper shacks littering the hinterland. He had had an enviable career, a substantial income, a beautiful mansion, time for tennis and the theatre and his children, hordes of friends, privacy, and the esteem fitting for a man everyone expected to be Prime Minister someday. More than that, he had had all the good answers and clear solutions for what ailed Canada that had delighted the bankers and chief executive officers over cigars at the Toronto Club.

When Trudeau announced his intention to retire on February 29, Turner was basking in a metaphoric sun as well as the real one over the exclusive resort in Jamaica where he was vacationing. He was enjoying the kind of peace and glory the gods permitted a hero in a Greek tragedy just before hubris and fate brought him down. Indeed, like a tragic hero who only understood the happy half of a message from the oracles, Turner heard the voices telling him that he was going to be Prime Minister at last. Though he was fully aware of the difficulties the Liberals might encounter in winning the next election, he couldn't have known that destiny was to elevate him briefly merely to make his fall greater.

Despite all the expectations and rumours to the contrary, Turner wasn't certain he would run and he had no organization at the ready. The previous summer, while on holiday at the family's cottage on Lake of the Woods and after watching the outcome of the Tory convention on television, he had weighed the pros and cons of his candidacy, but he hadn't come to any decision other than to allow some of his closest friends to meet informally once a month for discussions.

"I was never convinced Mr. Trudeau was going to step down," he explained, "and I'm not the sort of person who makes decisions when they don't have to be made. So there was no campaign in flow, no policy prepared, no people in place, because one can't practise law and fulfil one's business obligations if one has something else on one's mind."

Especially if one were John Turner, with a mind like a filing cabinet of hermetically-sealed compartments to be opened and closed at will. He always tried to give his total attention to whatever he was doing, wherever he was, and whomever he was with—which explained all the scrunching of eyes and the laborious time he took to sign an autograph. In fact, part of his problem when he finally decided to go for the leadership on March 16 was that he couldn't make a clean break from his law firm and his business affiliations. For much of the race he—and the nation— seemed genuinely confused as to whether he was a lawyer, a board director, or a politician; and because he had trouble psyching himself into his political persona after more than eight years away from it, everyone noticed how rusty his speeches and his manner had become.

Worse, when he opened the dusty drawer marked "Politics," he found his file cards out of date and incomplete. Though he had kept abreast of major economic issues and federal-provincial relations, there were dozens of current matters he hadn't followed and couldn't digest as thoroughly as his opponents had done during years in the cabinet. He wasn't even up on the buzz-words, the changing lexicon that allows a politician to deflect or obfuscate potentially dangerous issues. During the campaign, for example, he persisted in referring to reporters as "the gentlemen of the press," "the boys," or "guys," even though there were women on the bus. He couldn't say he didn't notice them: one was so aggressive in her questioning that he barked, "Down, girl!"

These disadvantages might have worried a lesser candidate, but they terrified John Turner. All his life he hated being unprepared. To avoid being bested or surprised he had been hard-working, conscientious, and scrupulously organized. As a schoolboy in Ottawa he was expected to stand at the top of the class. If he came home with nine

A's and one B, his mother wanted to know about the B. "She wasn't domineering or oppressive," said Turner's sister, Brenda Norris, a Montrealer as bright and beautiful as her brother, "but Mummy believed in striving for excellence. Not for fame or money or ambition—which is rather *déclassé*, isn't it—but for excellence." At the University of British Columbia, Chick Turner was coordinator of activities on the student council and applied his talents to ensuring that athletic, social, and literary events didn't occur at the same time. As Minister of Finance he kept notes of his conversations on file cards.

For a person who talked so fervently about rewarding risk, he was remarkably careful. His heroic side let him take his family canoeing in the Arctic each summer—"Only the venturesome will ever try it," he wrote—but the trips were planned like military manoeuvres. His heroic side let him get involved with a venture-capital company—"I have first-hand experience of how small business has been savaged"—but his involvement was minimal. And his heroic side let him enter the leadership race—"Politics makes small business look like a sinecure," he declared on the bus from Trenton—but the real question was whether he would win on the first or second ballot. He never went out on a tightrope without carefully assessing what would happen, and his tightropes were usually as wide as the aisle of a bus.

Thus, even before Trudeau resigned, John Turner took a briefing book to Jamaica. Prepared by his informal committee of friends, it summarized seventy-four key issues. "You're trying to wreck my holiday," he muttered. "Who cares about this goddamn stuff?"

His holiday was wrecked anyway by Trudeau's announcement. Then there was another unexpected development. Turner had never discussed his committee or his possible candidacy with his wife, Geills. Now that he did, she had some questions: Are we going to be poor? Will the kids and I ever see you? Will we have to move to Ottawa? Eventually her answer reached the committee in Toronto, where it was operating from a couple of rooms in the Royal York Hotel and waiting for the signal to launch the campaign: "Her Highness says no." That seemed to be the end of that. However, when the Turners flew home from their holiday, they were greeted by a horde of cheering supporters and the media hoopla. Apparently Mrs. Turner enjoyed the experience. And so, from a standing start and this inauspicious lurch, the Turner juggernaut set off.

Turner's doubts and insecurities at the start of the campaign were real enough, but against them he had two great advantages. First, the Liberal Establishment seemed eager to welcome him back to its bosom because he looked like a winner. Second, he had a brain like a sponge—he could absorb extremely complicated material, assess it and find in it the heart of the argument and most of the pitfalls. That's the talent for which he was best remembered in the Department of Finance, and it made his legal opinion much sought after when he joined McMillan, Binch in Toronto, even though he rarely concerned himself in the details of cases. In one corporate matter involving a Canadian company in Australia, he distilled sixty hours of material into a twenty-minute presentation before the Australian cabinet and made his point.

"But he doesn't get comfortable with an issue cerebrally," said William Macdonald, Turner's partner at McMillan, Binch and one of his closest advisers. "He gets comfortable by getting in touch with people and getting a feel of things through them. As a brief he's fast, but he's not fast at acclimatizing himself to new situations. He has his own pace for getting comfortable."

So even if he could get up on most of the issues by studying his thick, black briefing books through horn-rimmed glasses at the back of buses and small planes, Turner had to touch and feel as many Liberal delegates as possible, *mano a mano*, hand to hand, as he liked to phrase it. It bothered him that most of them had never seen him in action and that he didn't know who they were, for Turner was a Rolodex politician with a filing-card network that was a legend. He boasted, with some justification, that he knew more people on a first-name basis in Canada than anyone else in the country, and he kept track of hundreds of friends via birthday cards and get-well telegrams. For eight years, though, he had been tracking his legal, business, and personal contacts. He hadn't even been faithful to most of the so-called 195 Club, the group of supporters who had stayed with him to the last ballot when he ran for the Liberal leadership in 1968 and was beaten by Pierre Trudeau. Until he filled in a lot more cards with political contacts, he wasn't going to feel in control of the issues. And until he felt in control, he wasn't going to have any *fun*. "It's important to have *fun*," he liked to remind people out of the blue, as if suddenly remembering what a camp counsellor once told him never to forget.

The press always seemed to be having fun, drinking the candidate's beer before noon, littering his bus with their newspapers and cigarettes, guffawing about the time in St. John's when he put the sou'wester on backwards, or gossiping about whether he had been the mysterious MP in Shirley MacLaine's memoirs. Turner may not have been certain whether all this was important fun, but he understood that "the boys" would be boys and their job was as fundamental to parliamentary democracy as his own.

Away from politics, refusing almost all interviews and rarely speaking in public, Turner had become mythic as Prince Valiant in exile. That image had been fostered by the press because it was an effective device with which to hammer Trudeau by comparison. In the golden glow of nostalgia, Turner became a demigod of touchy-feely politics, of the House of Commons, of the Department of Finance, of the 1974 election campaign. Turner the quitter became, in retrospect, the shining example of Trudeau's inadequacy with people. From time to time Turner assisted in his own deification by taking shots at the Trudeau record from various podiums or, more frequently, over Scotches with selected media owners and journalists. But he always suspected that, good as he had been, the press would be rougher than boot camp once he returned to the arena—

a suspicion confirmed a few hours after he stepped off the bus from Trenton.

Considering how scared John Turner was, his opening press conference at the Chateau Laurier in Ottawa on March 16 had been an act of bravery—as he himself pointed out later. There, alone, he faced the dishevelled horde that is the parliamentary press gallery *mano a mano*, elegantly answering their questions in both English and French. One frustrated reporter asked if he wasn't worried that his campaign seemed "too pat, too perfect." But many others were disappointed. Turner's nerves were a surprise and his speaking style was both jolting and dull.

Then everyone jumped on his response to a question about French-language rights in Manitoba. He implied that they were a provincial matter, that a political solution was better than a judicial solution, and that the federal government ought not to intervene. Those implications defied Liberal policy and the bilingual passion behind Pierre Trudeau's national vision. In the subsequent furore Turner was forced to clarify what he had meant. There was a distinction between minority-language *services*, which are a provincial matter—he said—and minority *rights*, which are guaranteed by the constitution. Thus, while he hoped that the services would be provided by finding a provincial and political solution, he agreed that any abused rights should be remedied by the courts and, if necessary, by the intervention of the federal government.

Turner's advisers insisted that the clarification had been the answer his briefing book had told him to give and that he had delivered it incorrectly at the press conference. But his fudgy, common law, legalistic opinion fit his initial strategy by distinguishing him from Trudeau. It signalled to the West that bilingualism would be pursued, as one of his advisers put it, "with less enthusiasm." It suggested that the provinces had jurisdictions that would be respected, that political consensus would be valued more than impositions from above, and that constitutional questions would have a lower priority than economic issues.

However, from the first day of his campaign Turner learned the dangers of that strategy. Many of the Quebec MPs and party organizers who had declared their support for him before he uttered a word, in order to get a good seat on the winner's bandwagon, were shocked by his apparent deviation from one of their basic principles. Some even threatened to turn on him if he didn't issue the clarification to conform with Trudeau's thinking.

Then, on April 11, Turner learned his second lesson. During a chaotic press scrum in Montreal, he was asked if he approved of Bill 101, Quebec's language charter, which placed severe restrictions on the public use of English in the province. He answered, *"En principe, pour la charte, oui."* In his mind there was again the distinction between services and rights, but his "yes" drew outraged editorials that wondered where he really stood. For weeks, to whomever would listen, Turner insisted he had been shanghaied. "I was getting on an elevator when I began my answer, but before I could explain it, boom, the doors closed. I didn't have a chance." Reporters who were present denied that they were near any elevators, however, and Turner's own transcripts showed he gave a long answer that courted misinterpretation by its vagueness. Once more Turner had to move back toward Trudeau to protect himself.

John Turner always protected himself; that was part of his caution and his reserve. He didn't give up his corporate directorships until he was certain he had won the leadership. He had learned from C. D. Howe and Jack Pickersgill never to write a memo in case it ended up on the record—a lesson he forgot to his embarrassment at McMillan, Binch when his name appeared on policy assessment papers critical of the Liberal government. He was a private man who didn't enjoy talking about his personal life or his philosophy. Even his gregariousness served to hide what was in his heart. As a minister he was noted for giving out very little information to the opposition and the press; yet he took pains to soothe them with attention—"We had meals together, we did sports together, we played poker together," he said—so that they never really held it against him.

By 1984 the rules of the game had changed. "We'll have to have a drink together, eh guys?" he said to two reporters in the Montreal airport before a swing through Atlantic Canada. It was impossible. From the beginning he was forced into a prime-ministerial tour because of the number of media people on his trail. He didn't know whom to trust. He discovered that reporters had no scruples about listening in on his private conversations. He knew that every drink he took during a flight could be material for a "campaign notebook" column, and he sat in terror through a meal in Saskatoon because it required him to pick up meatballs with a pair of chopsticks while the photographers waited for him to fumble.

As a schoolboy he perfected short answers to exams because his left-handedness had made him a slow writer. As a candidate he had been told to answer no questions of substance during a scrum. He probably reached the peak of his form in Halifax when, of three questions, there was one he wouldn't answer because he had already answered it, one he wouldn't answer because he would answer it later, and one he wouldn't answer because it needed further study. Most of his meetings with delegates were closed to the media, despite his promise in 1968 that he would never hold such meetings *in camera* because the public had a right to know what he was saying. He gave almost no lengthy interviews for the first two months of his campaign; and when he did give them, he mostly repeated by rote the answers he had memorized from his file cards.

If his tactics seemed to contradict his pledge of an "open, accessible, and accountable" government, Turner had two (short) replies. First, when the press became as important as a single delegate, he would give it some time. That may have been frank and reasonable, but it cast doubt on his reputation as a master political masseur and confirmed the impression that his friendliness was in direct proportion to one's immediate usefulness to him. Second, he said, "I want the media to be informed and I want to be open with them, but I don't want to be left vulnerable. If I can come to some terms of reference that are mutually respected, I'll be happy. But if the media want to be confrontational, then I'm going to have to protect myself and my government will have to act accordingly."

As soon as Turner's fears met the media's aggression, relations between Prince Valiant and the people who created him deteriorated. The more aggressive the press became, the more guarded the candidate became. The more guarded he was, the more frustrated the reporters were. The frustration increased the aggression, the aggression increased the fears, the fears increased the guardedness, and so on. By the time his campaign bus rolled into Trenton on May 10, Turner had the look of a man under siege. He kept to the back, consulting his briefing books, filling up his index cards with notes, issuing commands, soaking up instructions, or staring lost in thought at the passing Canadian landscape he loved so much, while beyond two rows of assistants and a no-man's-land of empty seats the notebooks and electronic gadgetry of the fourth estate lay ready to pounce the moment he dared move.

II

Just before lunch the bus pulled up at the Ramada Inn, which sat outside Trenton beside the Toronto-Montreal highway, and everyone trooped into the Harvest Ballroom. There, in front of a garish mural photograph of autumnal woods, Turner stood at stiff attention and sang "O Canada" with two hundred area Liberals. He toasted the Queen, bowed his head during the grace, and headed for the buffet.

Because of all his defences John Turner struck most people as an extremely complicated being. He looked like an architectural facade disguising some dark dwelling and he sounded as if every thought were working its way through a secret labyrinth. In truth, he was the sum of every summer-camp, private-school, varsity, junior-bar, model-citizen, and parish-church virtue he had been taught. Be prepared. A strong body makes a strong mind. To the swift goes the race. It's not whether you win or lose. A friend in need is a friend indeed. Leadership, team spirit, duty to God and country. True patriot love, traditions, public service, Sunday Mass, family, even *fun*—there wasn't a platitude for which John Turner wouldn't go to the wall. If at times he imagined elevators or got mean with whisky or strayed from the path of righteousness, well, to err is human, man is a miserable sinner, and tomorrow is another day. He was every mother's dream, the apple of every father's eye, a dedicated paterfamilias, a loyal friend, a devout Christian, and an all-round Canadian. He was Kipling's "If" and the Nicene Creed in the body of a Roman consul.

The only unexpected thing Turner had ever done in his life was resign from the government in 1975—which made that act the object of endless fascination—and then he worried whether the Canadian people thought he had let them down. Early in his development he locked himself into the attitudes of postwar, Anglo-Saxon Canada. Believing in events and not destiny, he set his course for a Rhodes scholarship, Oxford, the Sorbonne (to master French), and corporate law. On and off for ten years, between the ages of sixteen and twenty-six, he considered becoming a priest. "If he can't be Prime Minister, he can always be Pope," his mother said to his sister. At thirty-three he was drawn into public life—the second-highest calling in his opinion—with the same sense of mission and service.

"Life is a trust," he said, "and one has a fiduciary obligation toward one's country to put back into it what one has received. I've received a great deal, and I believe that a free society only operates properly if the best men and women offer to serve."

He picked up some of these ideas from the masters at Ashbury College and from the priests at Saint Patrick's College as a boy in Ottawa during the patriotic, altruistic years of the Second World War. But his greatest influence was his mother, Phyllis Gregory Turner Ross, a beautiful and brainy miner's daughter who propelled herself from Rossland, in the B.C. interior, to the University of British Columbia, Bryn Mawr College in Pennsylvania, and the London School of Economics. In London she met and married a handsome, rather mysterious fellow named Leonard Turner, variously described as a journalist and a gunsmith. They had three children in as many years—John in 1929, Michael (who died shortly after birth), then Brenda. Leonard Turner died at the age of twenty-nine from hyperthyroidism, perhaps the effect of catching malaria on an adventure in Sumatra. His widow returned briefly to her family in Rossland with her two small children before going to work in Ottawa as an economist. She was with the Tariff Board and then the Wartime Prices and Trade Board, where she became the country's senior female public servant. Everyone remembered her brilliance, her charm, her vivacity, and her high standards.

Phyllis Turner always set time aside for John and Brenda (a discipline her son practises with his own four children); her friends, from R. B. Bennett to C. D. Howe, often dropped in for dinner; Turner went to camp in the summers and was busy with his studies, athletics, and school activities in the winters. By the time he was a teenager most of his friends' fathers were away at war, so he didn't feel the lack of a father as strongly as he might have. But several of Turner's closest associates have suggested that his sense of purpose and vulnerability came from his being "the little man" of the household. Surrounded by expectations, he seemed to have missed a real childhood.

Not that he was ever lugubrious. He absorbed postwar optimism along with postwar determination, and he remained an upbeat, enthusiastic person who didn't like to complain or lament. At the University of British Columbia (UBC) he was even known as a "funnyman" for the jive talk in his sports column ("Klahowya, freshies!") and his repartee at Beta Theta Pi dinners. His four years at UBC seemed to hold for him the magical memories that college days are supposed to hold. His later rah-rah style suggested that he never recovered from being coordinator of activities on campus. University was a good time for John Turner. He was a track star heading for the Olympics and a prize-winning student heading for Oxford. His mother had just married Frank Ross, a Vancouver millionaire who showed new horizons to his stepson.

Herb Capozzi, a Vancouver businessman who was a UBC football hero during Turner's years and remained a friend, remembered Turner's driving ambition. "John was destined for posterity, if not greatness," Capozzi said with a twist of mischief. "He became a competitive runner because he needed a sport to get a Rhodes scholarship, and he used to *work* on his sense of humour. He was a big Catholic. He went out with girls with good references, and though he had lots of opportunity with his looks and his money, he was less likely to make out than to make good. He was interested in making saints, not devils."

Turner stayed true to the old values and the traditional institutions. He was, to use the phrase of his law partner, William Macdonald, a "sociological conservative." He had simple, though expensive, tastes. The highest praise he could bestow on his former deputy ministers was to call them "good steak and martini men," and the highest compliment he could bestow on his famous waltzing partner, Princess Margaret, was to call her "an interesting chick." In his speech in Trenton, as in many others, he talked about the privilege of democracy, the centuries of British parliamentary tradition, the stability of the family unit, the wholesome life of rural and small-town Canada, and the bountiful land blessed by God from sea to sea.

This is standard fare for every after-dinner speaker, of course, but it seemed to stir John Turner. Unfortunately, his delivery kept him from stirring anyone else. On business confidence he sounded confident; on cost-efficiency, efficient; on education, instructed. When he spoke of the heart and soul of the state, however, he sounded like a high-school debater trying to put conviction into clichés memorized in civics class. Day after day he repeated the same trite ideas with the same choppy earnestness, while the reporters recited them aloud like an echo from the back of the halls. An open, accessible, accountable party. A progressive, populist, reformist government. To rebuild the party in the West. To restore the confidence of Canadians in themselves. To reward risk. To put the young to work. Equality of opportunity for women and New Canadians. Consensus, harmony, and peace. All politicians have their scripts, but Turner's reluctance to answer any question for which he hadn't prepped that day left the press growling for its daily feed.

After his speech in the Harvest Ballroom, Turner took questions about agricultural policy, federal-provincial relations, and education, but he refused to answer one on rising interest rates. "That's worth a fifteen-minute discussion," he said, and went off to meet delegates in private.

Waiting for him to emerge for the trip back to Toronto, the reporters stood in the May sunshine and bitched. At least Jean Chrétien, said one, always gave you a story. What a wasted day, said another. They laughed at the way Turner, presented with a local cheese, had said, "Hey, what a great cheese!" They mocked his speech pattern and compared it to an army colonel's parade address, a football coach's pep talk, and a chief executive officer's annual report. And they imitated his walk, which one reporter observed could be accomplished only by pressing the cheeks of one's ass together as tightly as possible. They speculated about his clumsy organization, his appreciation of good whisky, his income, his marriage, even his sexuality. When Turner was ready to leave, after a quick hike around the parking lot to exercise his limbs and consult privately with an aide, they started teasing him.

"What's this plan to grow bananas in Ontario?" asked the *Toronto Star*.

"What's all this stuff about the wholesome life of villages?" asked the *Globe and Mail*. "When did you ever live in a village?"

Turner's humour was unreliable if he hadn't got the upper hand, and he was clearly put out. His grin, which was often a sudden baring of teeth, was slow and forced, as if someone were pulling back his ears. "If I have one mission on this campaign," he said, "it's to make you guys at least a bit less cynical."

Did cynicism win two great wars, build the most blessed nation on earth, or make the twentieth century belong to Canada? Did cynicism take Turner's grandfather from Nova Scotia to British Columbia in search of a better life, lift his mother from a mining town to the Lieutenant-Governor's residence in Victoria, or put her son on the verge of becoming the Prime Minister of Canada? John Turner was patient with sinners, however, and he had always been attuned to criticism. When he arrived in Parliament in 1962 he quickly realized that his brash ambition didn't endear him to his colleagues, and he learned the reserve, caution, and patience that marked his political style ever since.

His greatest discomfort came when he was thrown into a game before he had a chance to assess the rules and the other players in order to adapt himself to them. But getting on the bus in Trenton he knew exactly what was required. He suppressed his irritation at the cynicism and the hostility, pushed it down into that deep black hole where he confined all the remembered slights, wounding grievances, and repressed outrages that sometimes surfaced in foul-mouthed fits, and boarded the bus determined to do a little stroking.

How else to explain what happened? Why else was he soon standing in the centre of the bus, jacket off, *mano a mano*? These visits from the back were a regular event, but they had always been breathtakingly inane. Despite his legend, Turner didn't perform this campaign duty very well. He was so uncomfortable, stumbling from impenetrable coldness to intimidating hotness with few moments of natural warmth, that many reporters came to dread his lurking above them and wrecking their travelling party. The day before, for example, en route to Stratford, he had been so dull that the *pro forma* chat had petered into awkward silence. "Hey, so Fred Astaire is eighty-five," he blurted, grasping at a newspaper headline for something to say.

But now the sun was shining, the passing countryside looked beautiful, and one of the reporters was Val Sears of the *Toronto Star*, who had been an editor of the *Ubyssey* when Chick Turner was writing sports. "Hey, Val," Turner asked, "are you going to the class of '49's thirty-fifth reunion in October?"

Then Tom Walkom of the *Globe and Mail* had a more serious question of his own. "Now that we have fifteen minutes, Mr. Turner, what *do* you think of the rise in interest rates?"

Turner's answer turned out to be neither very complex nor controversial—basically, cut the deficit and trust the Governor of the Bank of Canada—but for some reason he was willing to say on the bus what he hadn't been willing to say in the Harvest Ballroom. Directly or indirectly that reason was connected to the security he felt believing that this form of casual conversation was off-the-record and for background only, as it had been in the good old days when Turner used to hoist a few pints with the boys. One question led to another, and soon the focus came round to the perennial mystery: why had Turner resigned from Trudeau's government in 1975? It must have been difficult as Minister of Finance, a reporter probed, to have been caught between friends in the business community calling for government restraint and cabinet colleagues wanting to spend more. That wasn't why he quit, Turner said. Four years in Finance had been enough and, besides, when the "chief executive" didn't support him, it was time to go. Turner went on to explain that he had been close to a voluntary agreement with business and labour for wage-and-price controls, but the agreement had collapsed because Trudeau hadn't been supportive. So it hadn't been "useful" for him to stay on.

"And you weren't offered another portfolio?" he was asked.

"Only the Senate or the bench," he replied with disdain.

Later, when he finished showing off his prowess on the tightrope, he flashed his cute-and-don't-I-know-it grin, raised his arms like a victorious boxer to grab the overhead

racks, and searched for applause and sympathetic understanding in the faces of the reporters who were, by necessity, looking up to him. Their eyes *did* sparkle and their
smiles *were* broad, but not for the reasons Turner assumed.
They knew what he hadn't yet realized: by attacking Trudeau so sharply and so candidly, he had given them a
front-page story and taken his worst tumble from the high
wire of his campaign.

When he entered the race, he promised his advisers
that he would never say more than "Pierre Trudeau is the
most remarkable Canadian of his generation." It was an
ambiguous compliment, since it could imply remarkably
bad as much as remarkably good, but Turner only smiled
tightly when asked to explain his statement further. Given
his coy evasions and the media's growing frustration with
them, it was perhaps sad and inevitable that his rare can-
dour on the bus from Trenton didn't have a happier result.
Sad that he could speak his mind only if he assumed the
public would never hear it. Inevitable that the press would
seize its chance on the technicality that he hadn't said,
"Off the record, boys."

By midnight Turner's attack on Trudeau had been
broadcast; by morning it was headlines; and by the following evening the furious Prime Minister had issued a
statement declaring, in effect, that John Turner was a liar.
"Trudeau was just in a bad mood," a senior Turner aide
said to dismiss the matter. "He was about to lose the perks
of office and he'd just found out that Margaret was preg-
nant by her new husband." Meanwhile, cabinet ministers,
labour leaders, and editorial writers leaped into the debate
as to whose version of history was correct. The result was
a standoff, partly because there could be no clear-cut proof
until the cabinet documents from 1975 became public, partly
because the historical question was pushed aside by the
fresh squabble.

Turner never complained openly about what he considered the breach of confidence on the bus, but in response to it he demonstrated that his recall of even
immediate events was less than perfect. He said that his

statement about not having been supported by Trudeau had nothing to do with his resignation, but had come in reply to a question about mandatory wage-and-price controls. Furthermore, he assured the Prime Minister that "he had not discussed in any way the conversation which took place between them on the occasion of his resignation." When, then, had Trudeau offered him the Senate or the bench?

III

The Trenton bus controversy would have become a small piece in an intricate puzzle for some future historian had Pierre Trudeau not issued his rebuttal and thereby barged into the matter of his succession. Though John Turner was essentially right to insist that his 1975 resignation was a media obsession of no interest to any delegate, the old and new conflicts between himself and the Prime Minister touched upon all the critical issues at the heart of the Liberal Party, the government, and the nation.

Those issues were often ignored for the more obvious differences between the two men's personalities: Trudeau the solitary, ascetic, almost eccentric rationalist, wavering between flamboyance and inscrutability, European graciousness and gutter one-upmanship; Turner the gregarious, worldly, neurotically normal operator, wavering between heroism and timidity, North American chumminess and locker-room aggression. They shared a serious Catholicism, the premature loss of their fathers, a love of canoeing in the wilderness, and a broad outlook, as well as a need to take control of themselves and the environment in which they functioned. Their looks, their intelligence, and their reputations gave them the habit of controlling their surroundings and assured that they would clash once mutual advantage had been exhausted.

At the start of Trudeau's regime he couldn't have been delighted with the presence in the cabinet of an ambitious, popular, and powerful minister whom everyone was calling the heir apparent. Nor could Turner have easily extin-

guished his resentment that he wasn't in Trudeau's chair.
Though he had run for the leadership in 1968 not so much
to win as to build a power base in the party, John Turner
wasn't accustomed to being denied whatever golden apple
he reached out to pluck. It must have galled him to lose
to this novice, this academic, this dilettante who had travelled around the world adventurously, flirted with socialism and scores of women, and stolen the affections of
Lester Pearson, while Turner, the hard-working goody-
goody, had been assiduously climbing the greasy pole.
"What's this guy got anyway?" Turner asked of Trudeau
in 1968. One could almost hear the plaintive, "And where
can I get some?"

The strength of these all-too-human factors ought not
to be underestimated, but there was an intellectual tension
too. Trudeau had been educated by the Jesuits, had devoted years to political theory, and had worked as a professor of constitutional law. His training, therefore, had
left him susceptible to ruthless Cartesian logic, grand plans,
great codes, big ideas, and a second-hand understanding
of the practical world. Turner had been educated by Oblate
fathers (a down-to-earth missionary order ready to adapt
to any circumstance) and had spent the first eight years
of his career practising commercial and tax law in the courts
of Montreal. Moreover, his liberalism wasn't a late-bloom-
ing, ideological overlay on his native political culture, as
was Trudeau's. Turner had learned it at his mother's breast.

Though Phyllis Turner may have been a Tory like her
father or her ardent suitor, R. B. Bennett, she raised her
son in the playground of Canadian liberalism. He picked
up its tenets when Mackenzie King was demonstrating his
own great skill on the tightrope, walking the unstable line
between an effective national government and provincial
rights, the social good and individual freedoms, East and
West, French and English, rural interests and urban demands, protectionism and free trade. The trick lay in balance, flexibility, and slow progress. Things were to be done
at the centre when they had to be, but power was to be
shared enough to keep everyone appeased. If a depression

and a war forced Ottawa to act, King intruded into provincial fields and intervened in the economy. At the same time, he made sure he had strong ministers to protect the interests of their regions and he pushed for "orderly decontrol" once the crises passed.

John Turner learned more than the theory. From his mother's circle of powerful friends and then in "the kitchen of government" (as Pearson called it), he learned how Canada functioned in practice. In committees and caucus, in opposition, on the back bench, and eventually in the cabinet, he saw that spouting off in the House of Commons and giving good speeches on the hustings were not what mattered. Throughout society there were centres of power— the cabinet, the bureaucracy, the provinces, business, labour, the universities, the media, and so on—and in those centres there were men who could get things done. Things got done quietly, behind the scenes, by connections, by trade-offs, by a slap on the back. "It matters not what you know but who you know" became Turner's operative thought. Who you know eventually becomes what you know in any case.

Wherever he went—to Montreal or Moncton, to Washington or Canberra, to a locker room or Buckingham Palace—Turner hunted down those in charge, zapped them with his two-handed clasp, and caged them forever in his filing system. He prides himself on being a "people person" as well as a man's man, able to stride into any room and find common ground; but he's most at home among those who exercise power and therefore are of use to him. A wall in his office at McMillan, Binch, was covered with photographs of Turner with the mighty, and every campaign speech contained the brag that he would put his influential contacts to the service of Canadians. His old friend, George Shultz, the American Secretary of State, would no doubt solve any problem for John, just as John would be happy to help George.

The efficacy of networking is nothing new in a country in which "the vertical mosaic" is a cliché, of course, but John Turner must have been the first Canadian politician to raise it to the status of a public virtue. Some said that this only revealed his insensitivity after eight years on Bay Street, on a par with his persistent reference to the Prime Minister as the chief executive officer. In fact, networking described his realistic assessment, based on broad experience, of Canada's political system long before the concept of using people became as fashionable as sushi.

But networking for what purpose? For political stability and success, in the manner of Mackenzie King. For good, cost-effective management in the manner of St. Laurent and C. D. Howe. And for reform, in the manner of Lester Pearson. The reforms of the 1960s were social programs, such as medicare and pensions. The reforms needed in the 1980s, Turner believed, were economic: industrial growth, jobs, international competitiveness, technological change, and training. That didn't represent, in his mind, a shift from left to right; it was merely a shift in what the government's priorities should be.

"The key area is the restoration of national confidence," he said. "That means psychological leadership. That means assuring the business community that the rules are going to remain predictable, that there's going to be a stable economy and a climate for investment where risk and reward are equated. We must achieve recovery in the private sector in order to achieve our employment goals, though in the short term there may be a youth job corps and a national apprenticeship program."

Turner's preoccupation with the business community, his grey suits, his Monte Cristo cigars, and his talk about fiduciary obligations made even his supporters wonder if Bay Street hadn't turned his head. In the 1960s, as Minister of Consumer and Corporate Affairs and then Minister of Justice, he was considered to be on the left of the party. He had joined the Liberals—"It was like committing oneself to a church"—because they believed in equality of opportunity. He absorbed the activist jargon and reformist spirit of the times and declared himself "restless" to close the gap between the rich and poor, to reach out to the disenchanted and the dispossessed. And he introduced progressive changes in the regulation of business and the legal code, while always able to defuse dissent among the lobbyists and the opposition.

"His instincts are reformist," said Senator Jerry Grafstein, who had been Turner's executive assistant in 1966. "He wants to open up the system, and he always wants to make things work *better*."

But making things work better is not the same as divisive, costly, or hasty progress. Turner developed an appreciation for King's gradualism, and—particularly in economic affairs—he remained worried about the effects of dramatic change. As a young man vacationing in St. Andrews, New Brunswick, he had seen his stepfather and C. D. Howe helping each other out and recalling the glory days of the Second World War when businessmen, politicians, and civil servants had worked as one. That remained John Turner's very human, rather simple idea of things working better. Government would provide stability, confidence, tax breaks, broad directions, and a well-trained work force; it would consult with the private sectors on every issue that affected them; then business would produce jobs and prosperity.

Even in 1968, in his book *Politics of Purpose*, Turner warned against the growth of government and the centralizing of power. He accepted the balancing mechanisms of Keynesian planning. He accepted the costs of a social safety net to protect the poor, the old, the ill, and the unemployed. He accepted that there are occasions when governments have to intervene actively, as shown throughout the career of C. D. Howe, one of Turner's many father-figures and a major influence in directing him toward politics. However, Turner held to the Canadian liberal view that the government should serve as a referee or a facilitator rather than be a player in the marketplace.

"I come from the mainstream of liberalism in this country," he told the Liberal audience in Trenton. "I believe in free enterprise under a mixed economy and with a heart, and I believe in a progressive, populist, reform party in the tradition of Laurier, of King, of Pearson, and"—here he mumbled, as if choking—"of Pierre Trudeau."

Actually he didn't believe that Trudeau's liberalism was in the mainstream at all. Its idealistic, classic basis was more appropriate in a university common room than in the kitchen of government, and it led to such aberrations (in Turner's opinion) as the cabinet committee system, the flood of discussion papers and the subsequent morass of talk, the participatory exercises that were wasteful of time and money, and the general confusion in leadership and direction of Trudeau's first term. As a strong, gung-ho minister he particularly disliked the new constraints that collegiality placed on his authority, his energy, and his department's decisions. Meanwhile, he saw the Prime Minister's Office swell in size and clout, and as Trudeau's successor in the Department of Justice, he probably felt the Prime Minister's close watch on his work. After all, Trudeau had initiated most of the Criminal Code reforms that Turner developed into legislation, he had a long and passionate interest in the constitutional reforms that Turner proposed to the provinces, and he had a special commitment to the Official Languages Act that Turner introduced in the House of Commons.

Any closeness in collaboration only served to widen the differences in their thinking. Turner worried about Trudeau's overly logical intransigence toward Quebec nationalism, for example, and he reacted against the insensitivity with which Trudeau imposed bilingualism on the federal government and dusted off the War Measures Act during the October Crisis of 1970. Grand plans based on abstract political theories, the weakening of ministerial responsibility, and occasional acts of cold-blooded will didn't jibe with the liberalism John Turner had imbibed as the Canadian way.

The tensions between the two men grew worse when Turner became Minister of Finance in 1972. The cabinet committee system became more than just an irritation: by spreading out decisions that involved government spending and by shifting power to the coordinators in the Privy Council Office, it directly diminished the traditional authority of Finance. Turner and his officials had to fight constantly to maintain their control of spending and their influence on planning.

"The Pitfield system didn't centralize power with the Prime Minister," Jim Coutts said. "It simply moved the centres of clout from Finance and External Affairs to the Privy Council Office and the Treasury Board. The reason was to move to a broader view with more voices. And plainly the PCO had a better overview than Finance, which had its own axes to grind. Obviously the vanquished didn't like the victors."

At the same time, after the harsh, anti-inflationary restraints of Trudeau's first years, Ottawa burgeoned with people, programs, and pep. French-Canadian radicals and English-Canadian progressives were appointed to important posts in cabinet and the civil service; ministers and bureaucrats were judged by their innovations; and the federal government seemed flushed with money because of inflation. Everyone seemed turned on by the intellectual excitement Trudeau had brought to the sludge of governing at the national level. As Minister of Finance, concerned with taxes, deficits, and the money supply, Turner found himself throwing cold water on much of the reformist zeal he had helped ignite.

In many respects the business community becomes the "constituency" of every Minister of Finance, and Turner moved quickly to restore (in his phrase) "the working relationship between business and government." New confidence would mean new investment and new jobs, and the fastest way to instil confidence was with cash. In his first budget in May, 1972, Turner proposed to slash the corporate income tax from 49 per cent to 40 per cent at the start of the following year. But the election intervened in October. Because Turner's proposal added to the right-wing economic image of Trudeau's first term, it was effectively attacked by the NDP's campaign against the "corporate welfare bums," and was therefore a factor in the

Liberals' near-defeat. Turner only got it through the House of Commons in June, 1973, with the help of the Tories and at the cost of some political sweeteners, including a reduction in income taxes, the indexing of income tax to the cost of living, and an increase in old-age pensions and family allowances.

In fact, staying in power between 1972 and 1974 proved to be very expensive. The NDP had to be satisfied, cabinet ministers who had spent the first term setting their agendas or frustrated by the restraints were now eager to accomplish something, and the Prime Minister's political advisers were urging him to butter up the voters for the next, imminent election. The pressure was on the government to spend in spite of inflation and business confidence, but the pressure didn't come from Pierre Trudeau. It came from the important progressive side of the Liberal Party, and from most of the old Pearson politicos who were brought back in from the cold to save Trudeau's skin. It also came from pragmatism. If Trudeau had resisted that pressure with the kind of obstinate will he showed in his first fight against inflation or in his imposition of official bilingualism—as economic reason, long-term planning, and the Department of Finance suggested—John Turner probably would have landed on an opposition back bench in 1974 ranting about the leader's political stupidity.

This was the period in which Trudeau learned to modify his classic liberalism and understand the Canadian variety. The expenses that followed were less the result of the Privy Council Office, the committee system, and the eggheads in the PMO than of short-term expediency, ministerial self-interest, and the election organizers. Turner knew the realities as well as anyone. Indeed, his job was all the more difficult because he was aware of the consequences of saying no to his colleagues, the opposition, and the voters. That wasn't the way to make friends, and John Turner was much more concerned than Pierre Trudeau with making friends. The significant thing wasn't that many ministers were pressing for new programs. After all, most ministers of all labels think that's what they're elected to do. The significant thing was that Trudeau supported any cut or restraint that Turner put forward. "All the fiscal decisions were John's," said Marc Lalonde, who bore the scar to prove it. As Minister of Health and Welfare he developed, at the Prime Minister's request, a sweeping reform of Canada's social security system, including a plan for a guaranteed annual income; but in a head-to-head clash between Lalonde and Turner over the costs of the plan, Trudeau backed his Minister of Finance and the scheme was abandoned. Certainly Turner had a useful weapon in Trudeau's legendary stinginess, however annoying and expensive he had found that character weakness when forced to pay every tab run up over dinner with the Prime Minister.

They also shared a similar viewpoint on whether to introduce mandatory wage-and-price controls as a means of checking inflation. The Liberals fought the 1974 election by opposing the Tories' suggestion of such controls, and the only critic more effective in the campaign than Turner was Trudeau. Something had to be done as wages chased prices in an upward spiral, however, and after winning a majority government the cabinet decided that Turner should seek a voluntary controls agreement with business and labour. The Prime Minister strongly preferred that option, as much to save his credibility as to avoid a disruptive intervention in the marketplace. In that sense he was right to argue in 1984 that Turner had had his full support. But Turner knew that the old-style elite accommodation of Canadian liberalism required more than intellectual approval. It usually required the Prime Minister to invite the labour leaders for a drink at 24 Sussex, say, or to slap the backs of the chief executive officers while preaching to them about their duty to the nation. That's what John Turner would have done, but Pierre Trudeau was never comfortable using the prestige of his office to achieve his goals. So, in Turner's eyes, he didn't go the full distance in the "confidence exercise." It was in this sense that Turner felt Trudeau didn't back him enough to bring in the voluntary agreement.

Moreover, Trudeau didn't share Turner's bouncy conceit that he could bring the boys on side after a few ribald jokes, a little football patter, and a couple of whiskies. The traditional methods of Canadian liberalism were becoming harder to use. There was less money available to buy alliances—partly due to the fact that the government was receiving the stiff bills for Pearson's generosity—and the new scarcity was causing every sector to scramble doggedly after its own interests without lowering its expectations. Backed by many officials in Finance, Trudeau came to believe that a voluntary agreement was impossible in this atmosphere. His reading of Galbraith's analysis, which argued that the power of big corporations and big unions to manipulate prices and wages marked the end of the free marketplace, seemed to fit the situation in which inflation, unemployment, interest rates, and deficits were all rising together. Meanwhile, the first OPEC crisis threatened the economic stability of the entire international system, and foreign competition and technological revolution were shaking the very foundations of Canada's industrial structure. It looked obvious that increased government involvement in the economy would be more effective than inviting the boys for a drink.

Turner thought Galbraith's ideas bunk, and he sensed in cabinet that he was no longer debating Trudeau so much as Galbraith. "I'm against the Galbraithian and technocratic overlays," he explained in 1984, "the laying out of plans that pay less attention to the vagaries of human behaviour, to the differences in provincial jurisdictions, and to the legitimate self-interest of people. My style is to motivate that self-interest in the national interest and to harness forces rather than to dam them up and deliberately re-channel them."

Increasingly he believed that the problem wasn't with Canadian liberalism and the free marketplace; it was with Pierre Trudeau. A more open-minded and sensitive man could have made both work better.

When Turner resigned from the cabinet on September 10, 1975, it was not because of his failure to reach an agreement with labour, though that was a discouragement, or because of a plan to set up an economic advisory group in the PMO, though that was infuriating. Nor did he resign because of any promised $1.8 billion in spending cuts being reduced by a third, though he claimed that was the final straw, or because Trudeau hadn't invited him often enough for dinner or urged him forcefully to stay, though Trudeau could perhaps have delayed the departure. And, though they were important factors, he didn't resign because of his young family, or his desire to make money, or his fatigue and frustration. "I can't speculate," he once said, "but if Mr. Pearson had been in a similar circumstance I would still have been in government." He resigned, in other words, because he mourned the passing of his liberalism.

"The style I'm trying to replace had consequences in national unity and on the party," he said in the leadership campaign. "There have been strains on the fabric of the country—in federal-provincial conflicts, in business-labour tensions—that have to be eased. Leadership is less a Cartesian master plan than a human procedure. The technocrat is an impatient type, but we mustn't forget consulting, communicating, winning people onside. We have to restore ministerial accountability. We have to simplify the structures of the public service. We have to revitalize the role of the party, a good deal of which has been usurped into the leader's office. And we have to recognize the legitimate role of the provinces and of other sectors in the economy. My skills are people skills, and those are the skills required to put a human face on technology and government. If those are the skills of yesterday, well, we'd better look to yesterday to solve tomorrow."

For almost a year before his resignation, Turner had been advised by close friends to quit unless he wanted to commit political suicide. When at last he did leave, it wasn't to save his political hide for a future return. He thought his public life was over and he knew that many in the party would never forgive him. But when he went into exile in McMillan, Binch, he kept one small door open: if an unsolicited pressure built for him to return to politics, he wanted to be free to consider it. In 1979, when Trudeau first resigned, Turner recoiled from running even though he presumed he could win the convention. His family was still young, his law practice was growing, there wasn't an irresistible groundswell, and the party Establishment wanted a public *mea culpa* for his having left. Nor had the country yet seen the NEP, the constitution fight, or the worst of the recession. Turner assumed that the leadership would pass to Donald Macdonald, another Bay Street lawyer, or that power would pass to the Conservatives under Joe Clark. Either result would have brought about the harder economic choices and softer political approaches that Turner felt were needed. In 1979, said his friends, Turner proved that his ambition had been tamed.

By 1983, however, things had changed. Trudeau had stayed on. Macdonald was at the head of a royal commission, and the likely successors looked second rate in Turner's view. Meanwhile, the Tories had replaced Clark with Brian Mulroney, an unknown and inexperienced leader. If the Tories had selected Peter Lougheed or Bill Davis or former Ontario Treasurer Darcy McKeough or John Crosbie, Turner wouldn't have seen the need to run himself. They were Turner's friends, he admired them, and in effect they would have done his job for him. Then, when Trudeau resigned the second time, the Liberal Party Establishment began to pressure him. Corporate friends, many of whom had put him on their boards because he was the heir apparent, leaned on him. And his duty called him to give up his comfortable life, his interesting and lucrative work, his summers of tennis and canoe trips with the family, to undo the mess of the Trudeau years. His heart wasn't in it, but hearing the cry for a true 1960s Canadian liberal, John Turner stepped forward to restore, renew, and revitalize.

IV

However much the Liberal Party of Canada wanted to win the next election and expected John Turner to do just that, it still admired Pierre Trudeau and wasn't ready to throw out the policies it had defended so painfully while Turner was off making money and playing tennis.

"The Liberal Party will never take John Turner," Pierre Trudeau said in 1983.

The Old Guard of advisers and organizers clung particularly tightly to Trudeauism. It was a way of maintaining their clout, of course, but it was also a reflection of their experience in the party and the country. By leaving politics in 1976, Turner had missed all the significant events that signalled the breakdown of the old ways, from the election of the Parti Québécois to the second OPEC crisis, and the consequent change in the party. The Old Guard didn't believe the either the party or the country *could* go back. Brokerage politics didn't work, to take an obvious example, when one of the provincial governments was dedicated to independence; and how would Turner have patriated the constitution, entrenched a bill of rights, or struck a deal with Lougheed? It was easy to say that personality would have made a difference, but it couldn't have made all the difference. In fact, a root of Peter Lougheed's hatred for the federal Liberals went back to 1974 when the Minister of Finance, John Turner, disallowed the deduction of provincial resources royalties when companies paid federal taxes. To Lougheed, that was a revenue grab which also happened to break a promise Ottawa had made to him.

Moreover, the Old Guard didn't think the party *should* go back. Keith Davey's rule about playing to the left still held sway, and many were worried in political terms when Turner returned sounding more serious about the deficit than John Crosbie and less flexible on social spending than Brian Mulroney. Turner got his first demonstration of the Liberals' fidelity to the Trudeau record at a Liberal convention in Toronto two weeks after his entry into the race. All the leadership candidates spoke, but the biggest ovation went to Tom Axworthy, then Trudeau's Principal Secretary, who gave a vigorous and partisan defence of the government's actions since 1980 and a convincing argument that the future "market" of the party lay with women, youth, New Canadians, and the disadvantaged—"an almost social democratic core," in Axworthy's terms. That meant taking seats from the NDP in the West and Ontario, and it meant being perceived as standing to the left of the Conservatives. It didn't mean going to bat for Bay Street or looking like Robert Winters reincarnate.

That message continued to be delivered to Turner by the unexpected momentum behind Jean Chrétien's campaign. Chrétien had come close to not running—he even drafted a letter to that effect—though he had been toying with the idea of succeeding Trudeau since 1979 and had done some preliminary organizing before Trudeau's resignation in February, 1984. He was discouraged by the instant media hype that assumed the June convention would be merely the coronation of John Turner and that Turner was the party's only hope to beat Brian Mulroney. Then, too, there was the spectacle of cabinet ministers, MPs, and officials rushing to save their careers by getting close to Turner before he even opened his mouth. They included some who had said they would never forgive Turner for quitting in 1975; some who had said they could never live with his right-wing policies; and some who had promised their help to Chrétien.

Most of all, there was the Liberal tradition of alternating between anglophone and francophone leaders. It appeared to Chrétien as scandalous that, after fighting for the Charter of Rights, he should be denied any chance of victory on the grounds that he had been born a French Canadian. Worse, the clear discrimination was being defended most fiercely by many of his Quebec colleagues, who saw it as a protection against a succession of English-speaking leaders or as a boost to their own leadership ambitions once Turner retired.

"I don't understand those of you who are supporting a guy who's made a career out of knocking Trudeau in the last eight years," he told the Liberal ministers from Quebec. "You guys owe everything to Trudeau. I'll go and happily defend Trudeau and his policies, because I believe in them. When I leave politics I'll leave by the front door.

Nobody will ever be in a position to say that Chrétien's a prostitute.''

Despite the odds against his winning, several factors persuaded Chrétien to run anyway. Trudeau told the caucus that the tradition of alternation wasn't a fast rule. It wasn't why he had won the leadership in 1968, and it shouldn't deter anyone from backing the best candidate. Then, those who felt that it was important for the party to have a French Canadian in the race began to add pressure, as did those who sensed that Chrétien would be the only candidate who could stop Turner or at least deny him an unexciting, first-ballot victory, and those who thought that Chrétien would be more likely than Turner to keep Quebec Liberal in the face of a strong challenge from another native son, Brian Mulroney. Three junior Quebec ministers and more than forty Liberal MPs got behind him, and Chrétien had reason to believe that all the other candidates would choose to come to him rather than go to Turner at the convention. Then, on March 16, Turner gave his opening press conference, and Chrétien saw the weaknesses.

''Turner wanted to create three fundamental impressions,'' he said. ''One, that he had nothing to do with Trudeau. Two, that he was to bring the Liberal Party to the right, closer to the business community. Three, that he was to be soft on the language issue in order to attract votes in the West. I knew that being against Trudeau was an error. I knew that trying to move the party to the right wouldn't wash very well. And I knew that it was dangerous not to take the party line on language rights. Also I figured that the press had been too good to him. It would start to feel guilty within a month, and what had built him would destroy him.''

The day before Turner entered the race, Chrétien had accidentally encountered him in Toronto's Royal York Hotel. Turner was having his shoes shined and was trembling. To Chrétien he looked like a man on the eve of his execution, almost shattered by fear and anxiety. The impression was a shocking contrast to the heroic image being pushed by the media and growing large in the fantasies of the party, but it fitted what Chrétien remembered of a cautious, not very decisive Minister of Finance. All through the campaign, whenever he was asked why he was running, Chrétien replied, "Because I *know* Turner." It was a disturbing answer, revealing nothing but implying the worst, and it caused some second thoughts among those delegates who were already wondering why their Prince Valiant was screwing up.

"I always told them that Turner is a good man but he's not as good as you think he is," Chrétien said. "He's better than Mulroney, but I thought I was better still, otherwise I wouldn't have run. And because the public, at that time, saw Turner as better than Mulroney, I used to say to the delegates, 'Let me beat Turner, and Brian Mulroney will be small potatoes.' It was my way of answering the common argument that only Turner could win the election."

Put together, all these bits and pieces gave Chrétien some hope. That was all he needed to declare his candidacy on March 20. As he once told Joe Clark, when Clark was wondering whether to contest the Tory leadership in 1976, "One thing's for sure, Joe: if you don't run, you won't win." Jean Chrétien loved a tough challenge, he loved entering as the underdog, and he had never lost an important fight. Not only did he want to be leader and Prime Minister, he wanted to prove wrong those Quebec colleagues who had always looked down on him as an undereducated hick from Shawinigan, those close friends who had deserted him after all he had done for them, and his own nagging sense of inferiority.

Jean Chrétien had never been seen as a leftist in the cabinet. During the 1968 Liberal leadership campaign he supported his mentor, Mitchell Sharp, who as Minister of Finance was on the party's right, though both Sharp and Chrétien rallied behind Trudeau just before the convention. As President of the Treasury Board in 1974 he did John Turner's dirty work by slashing more than $1 billion from the government's spending and earning himself the nickname "Dr. No." While Minister of Industry, Trade and Commerce and then Minister of Finance he often spoke up for the interests of business, favoured foreign investment, battled the deficit, and backed the virtues and efforts of private entrepreneurship. As Minister of Energy between 1982 and 1984 his goal was to appease Canada's oil industry following the trauma of the NEP and the failure of world prices to rise. Nevertheless, despite much of his record, Chrétien had a public image of being on the left.

The image came mostly from his style as a rough-hewn, earthy, frank populist who spoke street French and fractured English. The style came partly from his background, partly from contrivance. His father had been a machinist in a paper mill in Shawinigan, an industrial town on the St. Maurice River, which flows into the St. Lawrence at Trois-Rivières, northeast of Montreal; his mother had had nineteen children, of whom nine survived. Jean, born in 1934, was the eighteenth. He didn't grow up in abject poverty, but the continual struggle to make ends meet was made harder by the ambitions Wellie and Marie Chrétien had for their children. Wellie held three jobs at once and Marie skimped all her life to pay for decent educations.

"The will!" Wellie Chrétien once exclaimed, thumping his chair with a fist, when asked how a machinist had raised two doctors, three businessmen, and a senior cabinet minister. "When something has to be done, you go ahead and do it. I looked around me and I saw that it was better elsewhere and I wanted my kids to have the chance to go there."

After a rocky academic start at various boarding schools, where he was more familiar to the teachers for his mischief and his scraps than for his grades, Jean Chrétien studied at Laval University in Quebec City and returned home to practise law. But he had known from an early age that law was just a way into politics for him. His father and his father's father had been Liberal organizers; he himself had handed out Liberal pamphlets as a boy and defended the Liberals with his fists and his clever tongue in the local pool room as a teenager; and at university in the 1950s he became an active president of the Liberal Club, a student protester, and a keen party worker.

Though politics was a family tradition, a competitive sport, and an obvious road out of Shawinigan more than it was a set of principles or policies for the young man, Chrétien absorbed the romance of *les rouges*, the nineteenth-century Quebec radicals who had formed the seed of the Liberal Party in the province. Reformers and free-thinkers, hostile to the power of the traditional French-Canadian Establishment and the Roman Catholic Church, preoccupied with democracy, they had picked up liberal ideas from France, England, and the United States but carried them in a direction that diverged sharply from both classic liberalism and the tory liberalism of English Canada. Influenced by Rousseau and the revolutionary programs that swept France in 1848, many of the youthful, early *rouges* didn't distinguish among liberalism, socialism, and even communism any more clearly than their enemies did. They were less interested in freeing the individual than freeing "the people." Their economic solutions were often more extreme than those of English-Canadian progressives; and they opposed representation by population, the federation of 1867, and George Brown's Ontario Grits, in order to defend their ethnic collectivity.

However, by the time Chrétien's grandfather refused to confess to Monsignor Laflèche, the Bishop of Trois-Rivières and an arch-Tory, for having handed out liquor for Liberal votes in the 1896 election, there wasn't much left of *rouge* radicalism except legend and just that type of symbolic gesture. Most of its nationalist element had settled for the provincial-rights platform of Premier Honoré Mercier (only to reappear with a vengeance decades later under Jean Lesage and René Lévesque), while its democratic, reformist, anti-clerical element had succumbed to Wilfrid Laurier's sunny ways for the sake of power in Ottawa. Basically, Laurier adopted Canadian liberalism, much as Trudeau did in the 1970s. That allowed the *rouges* to ally with English-Canadian moderates, while its moderation took some of the heat out of his opponents' attacks in Quebec. Laurier's attraction to French Canadians wasn't his liberalism, however. It was in his native-son roots, his wonderful personality, and his vision of Canada as the best guarantor of their survival as a people. It was those aspects, more than any economic or social policies, that had made Laurier an idol to Wellie Chrétien.

Still, just as William Lyon Mackenzie King derived some glory from being the grandson of a famous Grit rebel even when he was working for the Rockefellers, Jean Chrétien got some satisfaction and some support for being a true heir to those feisty, anti-Establishment radicals. It was an easy myth for a young, scrappy, working-class Liberal in rural Quebec to assume in the late 1950s. Maurice Duplessis held tight control over a paternalistic, repressive provincial government with the assistance of a corrupt party machine, a backward and authoritarian church, and the anglo business elite; John Diefenbaker was in power in Ottawa with a huge majority, thanks in part to the Union Nationale; and the Liberals were depending more and more on progressives, from union leaders to leftists academics, to restore their energy at both levels.

Certainly the union vote was crucial in Shawinigan when Chrétien first ran for the federal party in 1963. In the previous election nine months earlier, the incumbent Liberal MP had been defeated by the Créditistes largely because they had been able to articulate the worries and dissatisfactions of ordinary people in plain language, entertaining imagery, and basic ideas. Chrétien learned from the success of their populism and then used their own style—part slang, part humour, part sentimentality, part horse sense—to trounce them. He did it again in 1965 in the face of strong challenges from both the Créditistes and the NDP. With the style went a lot of allusions to "the people" and a lot of digs at the elites up above.

There was a certain amount of artifice in this, of course. Though he could afford to live in a better part of town, he deliberately moved to a working-class neighbourhood. Though his mother had made sure that her children learned to speak French properly, he preferred to give his speeches in the working-class idiom; and as for his distinctive broken English, he often said, "Maurice Chevalier and I worked hard to keep our French accents." Even after more than two decades as an MP in Ottawa and seventeen years as a cabinet minister, he didn't ignore the small tricks of his political image: his main constituency organizers were always working-class guys and never lawyers, he resisted a brief fancy to own a Cadillac Seville, and his wife remained a faithful customer to a local butcher and a local dressmaker.

Like an actor who becomes the character he's played so often, however, Jean Chrétien grew into the image he had designed. There's little that's false in him, except perhaps the knowledge that if he had chosen another role— such as the smooth, sophisticated Montreal lawyer in which Brian Mulroney and countless other small-town, working-class Quebeckers had cast themselves—he would have had the talent to pull it off equally well. He remained committed to his image long after it had served its original purpose, and even when it developed into a liability in some regards. It suited his personality. His origins, the facial paralysis that came from having been born deaf in his right ear, his place in the large family made worse by the precocity of his younger brother gave him an early but lasting complex which later became translated into an identification with those who see themselves as outsiders.

"Some people find it hard to believe," he said, "but I've always had an inferiority complex. Kids used to tease me about my face, and even today the cartoons and seeing myself on TV can hurt. Michel was the youngest, but he grew faster than I did. He was bigger, better at sports, and when we were in the same class he always came first while I slipped further and further behind. So I've had to work hard to build up my confidence."

Power and popularity didn't erase that feeling completely. He lived in a stylish house in Ottawa. His daughter, France, married a son of Paul Desmarais, the wealthy chairman of Power Corporation, which owns the mill where Wellie Chrétien laboured for fifty years. He hunted quail with Texas oil millionaires and hobnobbed with the Royal Family so often that the Queen once greeted him in Buckingham Palace with "What! You again?". Yet he never became totally comfortable among the elites, and most of his closest friends remained the people he grew up with. His idea of heaven remained his tiny cottage on Lac des Piles outside Shawinigan and he continued to view much of the world from that corner of it.

If that view became less important in getting him elected locally once he was established, it helped him as a minister and then as a leadership candidate. Keeping close to the people on Rue Principale gave him the confidence to make rapid decisions in government and spontaneous policy statements on the campaign trail without getting into too much trouble, because he always had a well-based instinct for what average Canadians wanted—or at least what they were willing to buy. For as soon as Chrétien arrived in Ottawa and picked up enough English to understand what was going on, he learned pretty much the same thing as that old watered-down *rouge*, Wilfrid Laurier, had: the best way to accomplish reforms and advance the cause of French Canadians was compromise, pragmatism, and Canadian liberalism. To be a liberal, in Chrétien's opinion, was to be in the centre, balancing East and West, French and English, business and labour, the whole jumble of interests and desires; but whether he was aware of it or not, the centre was moving to the left and he moved with it. His pragmatism and his instinct, not his youthful radicalism, took him there.

Though he quickly earned a reputation as one of the impatient, progressive "Young Turks" on the Liberal back benches, he was smart enough not to let his romantic outlook get in the way of his education about how Canada operated in the 1960s. Under the tutelage of Mitchell Sharp and Sharp's senior Finance officials, Chrétien discovered the intricacies of the cabinet, the bureaucracy, federal-provincial relations, and the economy. Some thought he had gone over to the right, as in fact he had in his loyalty to Sharp, but once Trudeau appointed him Minister of Indian

Affairs and Northern Development in 1968, he used his knowledge to great effect as an activist reformer. He knew how to get money out of the cabinet system, mobilize his bureaucrats, and accommodate the provincial governments, business lobbies, and other Establishments that got in his way.

It's not surprising that Chrétien could remember that he was with that department six years, one month, three days, and two hours or that he called them his best and most creative years. Since the native peoples come under exclusive federal jurisdiction, he could deal with their social and economic problems directly and with a thoroughness he couldn't have brought to the problems of Shawinigan. He had such freedom to act over a huge territory that he sometimes referred to himself as "the last emperor in North America." Here, then, one caught glimpses of the French-Canadian radical released from the genteel minuets of Anglo-Saxon elite accommodation. He went to the people, visiting every Inuit village but one, often being the first minister ever to listen to the complaints of the Indians on their land. He funded native associations to organize and publicize their opposition to his own government's policy papers. He helped the Crees of Northern Quebec fight the provincial Liberal government in court to get compensation for the land taken by the James Bay hydro development. And more than a decade before the Quebec referendum and the constitution fight, he discovered that the best way to break a deadlock with a provincial government or any other vested interest was to appeal directly to the people. When he wanted to create national parks in Quebec and British Columbia, for example, he got local associations to pressure their provinces into agreeing. If public opinion went against him, as it did when an inquiry he established to rally support for a pipeline down the Mackenzie River valley got everyone calling for the scheme to be abandoned, he had the savvy to give in.

Once Chrétien made up his mind about the right or necessary course, however, he could be more stubborn than Trudeau. "The will!" Wellie Chrétien had exclaimed, and his son often exhibited the same trait as a minister. Though he gave native groups money to fight him, he fought back when they demanded more than he could concede. "That's where I learned to say no," he said. "There's nothing worse than raising expectations and not delivering. They always knew where I stood." He showed the same determination when creating ten new national parks, one in the Arctic by calling for a map and drawing a large, arbitrary circle. Indeed, he prided himself that his management style was speedy and decisive.

"He has the strength of simplicity," one of his former deputy ministers remarked. "Ask him a question and you'll get an instant decision, and he's right more times than he's wrong. He once said to me, 'I play politics like I ski: fast but with no style.' In fact, he has great style, but it's sometimes frightening for a bureaucrat. Simplicity is more often found in a politician of the left or the right."

Another former deputy minister remembered presenting Chrétien with forty-two problems. "Give me the three most political ones," Chrétien said, "and solve the rest yourself." Normally he delegated all details and technicalities, rarely read a long memo, and never wrote one. He preferred oral synopses over which he swooped, dove to the heart, plucked out the political implications, and flew on. The abruptness was sometimes taken as high-handedness, shallowness, or even rudeness; often it was simply experience, indifference, or his instinct for the centre.

He took the same ministerial blend of democrat and autocrat into his next three portfolios, but none of them did much for his popular image. Treasury Board was where he became "Dr. No" on account of his attack on government spending. His brief term at Industry, Trade and Commerce seemed mostly concerned with subsidizing business. And as Minister of Finance between 1977 and 1979 he had to face an economy in disarray, with the dollar floating downward, interest rates floating up, and unemployment and inflation rising in tandem. At the same time he got dragged into two unpleasant political squabbles. One was when he was betrayed by the Parti Québécois's Minister of Finance, Jacques Parizeau, over a deal to lower every province's sales tax as part of the federal budget. The other happened when the PMO played a power game and got Trudeau to announce a $2-billion cut in spending without consulting Chrétien. He survived, certainly better than John Crosbie and Allan MacEachen were to do. His officials found him on top of the subject, the Bank of Canada was satisfied with his performance, and the business community could hardly fault him for the efforts he made to satisfy it. But his style had become a disadvantage.

For one thing, his management techniques didn't fit well with the methods of Finance. Its bureaucrats are notorious for their careful studies, macroeconomic jargon, thick dossiers, and computer print-outs, all of which make them believe they are engaged in a science. Chrétien knew he was engaged in politics, and wouldn't allow himself to be snowed under by all the paper. He wanted concise oral briefings, clear and essential alternatives, and a good idea of what it all would mean for the people of Shawinigan. At one time, for example, he was involved in the delicate and complex matter of when to lift wage-and-price controls. The computers worked overtime to analyze the thousands of factors pertinent to setting the date—contracts, trade cycles, seasonal fluctuations—but the endless permutations were leading nowhere. Finally Chrétien simply chose an early, arbitrary date. He impressed the department even more by holding to it despite pressures from some of the cabinet.

If his officials got over their initial doubts, much of the public didn't. Jean Chrétien just didn't look like a Minister of Finance was expected to look. He hated reading the long, technical speeches that came with the job. Often he just told his jokes, summarized the text, and swung into his usual patriotic rhetoric. The clarifications that followed from his officials increased the suspicion that he didn't comprehend the material. While the bankers heard the skeptical naïveté of the people in his voice, the people heard the cold-hearted mumbo-jumbo of the bankers. As a result, everyone was rather confused about Chrétien's real principles. He became a prisoner of his own creation, his political image. He had worked so hard to seem ordinary that no one could believe he wasn't.

"The first day I came into Mitchell Sharp's office," he often told his audiences, "there was a big meeting there, the Governor of the Bank of Canada, the Deputy Minister of Finance, all those big shots, you know. For an hour and a half they discussed bond issues, interest rates, balance of payments, and what not. At the end of the meeting Mitchell came to me and said, 'Jean, this meeting was very secret and you should not talk to anybody about what you have heard.' I said, 'Mitchell, don't be worried, I have not understood a goddamn thing at all!' "

However delightful the tale and the telling, his self-deprecation sparked criticisms as much as it defused them. Doubts about his competence became entangled with questions concerning the inefficacy of the nation's economic structure and the breakdown in traditional Keynesian logic. As pragmatic as any shrewd small-town lawyer, Chrétien had dedicated his considerable energy and his sharp mind to making Canadian liberalism work in his economic portfolios, but he discovered its new weaknesses. Despite or because of the growing scarcity business, labour, and the provinces were demanding more and more from Ottawa. Often they received it. Yet business fought against increased government intervention, labour resisted many of the technological and regulatory changes required to boost productivity and compete in the more aggressive international markets, and the provinces were hampering the federal government's ability to influence macroeconomic forces. In essence, the elites of Canada's various power centres were engaged in a series of virulent battles in which greed, selfishness, and short-sightedness threatened the authority of the central government and the supremacy of the national interest.

Nothing epitomized the situation more clearly for Jean Chrétien than when he, as Minister of Finance, asked the executives of the Sun Life Assurance Company to postpone their decision to move their head office from Montreal to Toronto, so as not to give another symbolic argument to the Parti Québécois on the eve of its referendum. They refused, claiming that it was a private-sector decision. Chrétien was outraged, particularly because he knew it had been a Liberal government's law that had limited the foreign ownership of Sun Life and therefore protected the positions of those same professional managers.

"These *private servants*," he fumed, "more narrow-minded than any bureaucrat, weren't in power by divine right. They were in power because of a government action. But still, they wouldn't accede to a reasonable request from an elected cabinet minister during a time of national crisis."

So he was ready to make the radical shift that Trudeau, the cabinet, and the Liberal Party underwent after the 1980 election. Indeed, as Minister of Justice in charge of the federal forces in the Quebec referendum and later the constitutional reforms, Chrétien was a major factor in that shift. Justice was "the last goddamn thing I ever wanted to do," he said. As the traditional portfolio for French Canadians, it seemed like a backward step after the power and prestige he had had as the first French-Canadian Minister of Finance. His practical mind fled the abstractions and technicalities of the law, but mostly he was terrified of bearing the responsibility for the result of the referendum. Normally he welcomed tough challenges. This one, however, could have destroyed more than his career. Failure could have destroyed his country.

"You can't understand Jean unless you understand that he is, first and foremost, a great patriot," a friend once observed. "Canada is in his heart."

A vision of Canada was what Laurier and the Liberal Party had meant to Wellie Chrétien. A vision of Canada was what had lured his son into federal politics and kept him there, despite several tempting opportunities to run in Quebec and perhaps even be its premier. The principles underlying all his portfolios were to be found in issues of national unity, sharing among regions and individuals, and minority-language rights rather than in questions of economic policy and social programs. Taking on Justice enabled him to expose those principles with a clarity and force unmatched even by his term in Indian Affairs. It also made him a much more significant contender for the leadership in 1984 than he would have been in 1979.

Many Canadians first took Jean Chrétien to their hearts during the Quebec referendum campaign. He described it as his "greatest mission," and it did have the aura of an evangelical crusade. For eight weeks Chrétien scampered among the "No" coalition and throughout the province, dampening fires, spreading the message, and waving the Canadian flag. Trudeau and Claude Ryan, the austere, ponderous former editor of Le Devoir who was leader of the Québec Liberal Party and head of the "No" team, were barely speaking to each other. A "disaster gang" of thinkers and strategists around the Privy Council Office was upsetting the cabinet and the caucus with its Chicken Little talk. Advisers and the media were questioning the ethics and the legality of Ottawa's multi-million-dollar advertising campaign. Meanwhile, the Quebec government had launched its own advertising blitz, and it seemed to Chrétien that "every old ladies' tennis association was suddenly getting money for new tennis shoes." Every evening and weekend, after racing back and forth between the cabinet in Ottawa and Ryan's committee in Montreal, he travelled from town to town with a small federalist roadshow to deliver his funny, peppy, emotional speeches. Freed from Finance's dry statistics and in contrast to the language of the PQ's many intellectuals, his populist style was again effective. "The Rockies are my Rockies," he shouted, "and my St. Lawrence River belongs to all Canadians!"

By May 20 he had lost ten pounds off his lean frame, his face was twisted by fatigue, his voice was almost gone, and he seemed on the edge of collapse. But, more than Ryan or the Quebec MPs and MNAs or even Trudeau, he emerged with the lion's share of the credit for the sixty-forty victory. "I had been saying all my political life that, when it came to the crunch, the people of Quebec would choose Canada," he said months later on a night flight to Ottawa from the West. But there had been times during the campaign when that hadn't seemed so certain. "What if I had failed?" he suddenly asked, staring out the airplane window at the remote villages that sparkled like stars in a vast, empty darkness. Then he covered his eyes with an arm and moaned "Oh, God" at the thought.

That flight had occurred in November, 1980, shortly after the Trudeau government decided to move unilaterally for patriation of the constitution and a Charter of Rights. The referendum was primarily an exercise of the heart, the constitution was primarily one of the mind. Chrétien had never taken much interest in the subject as it dragged its byzantine, tedious, and frustrating way through the 1960s and 1970s. "Constitutional law wasn't the big problem in Shawinigan," he said. "The biggest problem for lawyers was their fees." However, given the challenge and Trudeau's promise to Quebeckers that a "No" vote wouldn't be a vote for the status quo, Chrétien demonstrated an intellectual range, a mental agility, and a negotiating talent that surprised many people.

During the summer of 1980 he juggled twelve major items among eleven governments as the travelling committee of ministers laid the groundwork for the disastrous first ministers' conference in September, and he and many of his colleagues thought they would have had a deal if their work hadn't been tossed away by the acrimonious relations between the premiers and the Prime Minister. Then Chrétien guided the "people's package" through its rocky course in the House of Commons, which required him to testify for more than a hundred hours on its intricacies before a committee. He shook with nerves every morning, knowing that what he said would be examined by academic specialists and learned judges, but he had the advantage of having lived through all the conferences. At one hearing he was asked why a clause read one way rather than another, and he realized it was because he had been feeling stubborn the day it was written.

Finally, in November, 1981, he worked out with Roy McMurtry of Ontario and Roy Romanow of Saskatchewan a last-minute compromise that allowed nine provinces to agree to a modified federal proposal. Though he was sorry to see Quebec left out and sorrier to see Lévesque give up Quebec's veto right, outfoxing the Parti Québécois was a special triumph for him. Many of its leaders were the kind of urban, sophisticated intellectuals who had always looked down on his style and his brains. Partly they reflected the snobbery about education, language, and manner that exists in Quebec's bourgeois circles; partly they attacked his slang, his jokes, his sentimentality, and his lack of polish because they knew how popular he was and how effective he was against their cause. During the ongoing talks Claude Morin, the PQ's wily Minister of Intergovernmental Affairs, was able to fluster Chrétien unlike anyone else, because Morin's disdain stirred up Chrétien's inferiority complex.

"I'm from rural Quebec," he said, "and I've always had a chip on my shoulder about Montreal. The intellectuals and everything. Even though I've been minister for all these years, with all the experience and success, I still feel that way, as if they're superior, as if they're looking down on me. People say I talk about it too much, that it's not rational. But it's a feeling and I have to get past it."

So, with patriation and the Charter of Rights, Chrétien savoured a personal vindication as well as a political one. "Morin's such a big intellectual," he said in 1980, "but even with our strategy document in his hands he helped us. The worst thing for us would have been a near-miss at the first ministers' conference in September, but Morin made sure it was a disaster. I just love to see him begging the Queen and the British Parliament to protect Quebec's rights! I really laugh to see those intellectuals begging London to keep us a colony!"

The sweetest moment came the morning Chrétien informed Trudeau that they had a deal with nine provinces. "To think that Lévesque and Morin believe you're not educated enough!" Trudeau said with marvel in his voice.

"And to think they believe you're *too* educated!" Chrétien replied.

Their relationship was intriguing, for if anyone personified the rich, suave Montreal intelligentsia that gave Chrétien the heebie-jeebies, it was Trudeau. Indeed the

Prime Minister was reported to have had reservations about Chrétien's capacities in Finance. But their intense and successful collaborations on the referendum and the constitution apparently dispelled any of his doubts about the Minister of Justice's brains. For his part, Chrétien initially wondered if Pierre Trudeau wasn't too academic and rational for his own political good. When they differed, it was often because Trudeau became stuck on some overly logical, intellectually precise detail while Chrétien wanted to barge ahead with what was workable. Compared to Chrétien, Trudeau had more patience for consensus-building cabinet discussions, was more susceptible to the theoretical plans of the bureaucrats in the PCO, and seemed more willing to lose a point in practice so long as he had won it in debate. Chrétien chafed against the cabinet committee system for taking up time and favouring the lowest common denominator; he mocked the high-falutin' irrelevancies that absorbed the interest of the technocrats; and he thought Trudeau conceded too much power and money to the provinces merely for the sake of his classic liberal ideals about federalism. While Trudeau's pleasure came from thinking and listening, Chrétien's came from doing and talking. While Trudeau was generally open to fresh ideas and good arguments, Chrétien listened very poorly, as if his deafness had caused a personality distortion similar to his facial paralysis, which was caused by the lifelong habit of pulling his mouth toward his good ear so that he could hear himself talk.

"We're really the opposite of how we're perceived," Chrétien once remarked. "He's very patient and he's often more flexible than I am. He was even ready to accept the Vancouver amending formula if it was the only thing standing in the way of a deal."

In fact, Chrétien frequently showed more will and took more risks than the Prime Minister. He wasn't encumbered by Trudeau's philosophical superstructure. Usually he drew his political thoughts from his own experiences, to the point where he half-jokingly claimed to oppose abortion because, as the eighteenth child, he wouldn't have stood a chance of being born. He also had a better grasp than

Trudeau of how the political system worked and what the Canadian people would tolerate. "Trudeau knew he could give me the tough jobs and I'd get them done," Chrétien said, and indeed Trudeau once praised his minister for teaching him that if he insisted on perfection, nothing would be accomplished.

Sometimes that meant Chrétien urged Trudeau to give up some special intellectual fixation, and sometimes it meant Chrétien told him to hold firm. Though Chrétien had pushed the Prime Minister to try for another round of constitutional negotiations with the provinces just after the referendum, in order to get a fuller reform than immediate unilateral action would have allowed, he was ready to proceed to London as soon as the Supreme Court ruled the federal package legal. It was Trudeau who advised the precautionary step of holding another first ministers' conference. Chrétien went along and became more willing than Trudeau to make compromises, but he vehemently opposed Trudeau's new notion of holding a series of referendums on the reforms in the event of an impasse. Chrétien had nothing against the principle of popular sovereignty, of course, but he considered in this case that an appeal to the people was divisive and unnecessary. If the conference failed, Ottawa should just have acted and let the chips fall where they may.

Nevertheless, Trudeau was consistently seen as the Bad Cop and Chrétien the Good Cop. Occasionally that was justified, but it really had more to do with their characters. Those who experienced one of Trudeau's "Socratic dialogues" seldom forgave him the grilling even if he gave them what they wanted in the end. Chrétien's honesty, frankness, and humour often made people say, "A hell of a guy," even after he had kicked them in the pants. Trudeau was a mystery, a threat, an egoist. Chrétien always made time for a beer, a baseball game, or a little buttering up. He and his opponents got to know each other as people. If John Turner valued his own "people skills," he never used to invite his ministerial chauffeur into important meetings as Jean Chrétien did, just so the poor guy wouldn't have to sit out in the car. Chrétien fought the premiers, the CEOs, and the separatists every bit as fiercely as Trudeau, but his style rescued him from Trudeau's unpopular image. Even in Western Canada, where a French-Canadian Liberal was generally less welcome than a plague of grasshoppers, he managed to keep his credibility and good will by talking about his maternal grandparents who moved to Alberta in 1907, his 250 western relatives, and his own sense of being an outsider.

"The feeling may be irrational and petty," he said, "but it is as strong among people from the Mauricie or Cape Breton or Northern Ontario as it is among Westerners. All of us are made to feel that we lack sophistication and culture because we are still close to our rural roots compared to those who have made it in the cities for several generations."

After listing what the Liberals had done for the West, whether the Syncrude project or the super-depletion allowance, he added, "Those things are no help to the people of Shawinigan. But nobody talks about that, nobody remembers those things. There's a real problem of alienation when the provinces are seen as the givers and the feds are seen as the tax collectors. It's a stage in the evolution of the West. It's not a question of money anymore. The West has the money now, but the feeling remains that things are happening somewhere else. They don't have the confidence yet that great things can happen there."

Chrétien wasn't arrogant, he wasn't inaccessible, and he was a superb salesman. He had the ability to take a complex issue and find a way to express the government's position—by a personal anecdote, by common sense, by passion—so that it was easily understood and often convincing. He also had awesome stamina. "I worry about him," an old woman said when she saw him dash through an airport terminal one day. "He always looks so tired on TV." But his wife said he looked like that when he was seventeen, though television did accentuate the dark rings of his deep-set eyes, the gothic effect of his large cranium, and the distortion of his mouth. When he took up a difficult campaign he usually pushed himself to exhaustion, but he had the ruggedness and determination to withstand it. He moved the way he talked—quickly, directly, roughly—and the odd combination of exhaustion and energy gave him the look of either a marathon walker or a man on amphetamines. It provoked numerous articles headlined, "What makes Jean Chrétien run?"

Though he may have been still running to catch up to his brothers and sisters, or only because he was often late, his wife suggested another reason when describing the thrust behind her husband's career ever since law school. "It was always to advance, to keep moving up. It was never to stay at the same level."

That thrust made it almost inevitable that he would run for the Liberal leadership, however bad the odds. He ran with particular gusto because, this time, he was running not for the party or a policy but for himself. Sometimes it seemed as if he were trying too hard. His ambition gave a kind of crazed frenzy to his pace. He repeated his spiel so often in a single day that he couldn't be certain he wasn't repeating himself in the same interview or speech. He bore down on delegates like a typhoon, his loud laugh became louder, and his famous voice sounded more and more hoarse. Far from apologizing for the Trudeau record, he defended it passionately, countering hostility to it with his jokes and personality. On national unity, central government, social justice, and the will of the people there would be more or less a continuation of Trudeau's policies; but in place of rationality Chrétien offered passion, in place of federal-provincial conflict, patriotism, and in place of a magus, his warm, trustworthy, frank self.

Why would he promise to slash the deficit when he knew that wasn't possible? Why would he promise the end of tensions between Ottawa and the provinces when he knew that was unlikely? "Promises don't win elections," he said. "I learned that in my first campaign against the Social Credit in Shawinigan. They were promising everything. I couldn't compete, so I just said that I would do my best, and I won. Politics has become a question of confidence, so you have to be very careful about what you promise. That's what hurt Clark. He raised expectations that he couldn't meet. I try never to make promises. But if I say I'll do something, I make sure I do it. My father taught me to always keep my word."

Instead of promises, Chrétien's instinct told him to offer a vision to the new centre. His old patriotism found a response in Canada's latent nationalism. "The social policy is mostly in place," he said. "What is necessary is to build a new patriotism, based on unity and sharing. And that is a good issue. The centrifugal forces are great in Canada, the West has rejected Trudeau emotionally, but it will help the Liberals to be seen as the party of unity because, in their hearts, most people know that Canada is the best."

It would also help Jean Chrétien to be seen as the candidate of unity. Indeed, in policies and fervour, his patriotism passed into a Canadian nationalism that Trudeau himself never accepted. Considering how far behind the starting line Chrétien had been, and considering the prevalent assumption among the media pundits and party gurus that the Liberal Party's only hope for victory was with Turner and alternation, the Chrétien challenge proved to be remarkably effective. He had the enthusiasm, he had the momentum, and by the time of the convention he probably had more of the elected delegates than Turner.

"Ultimately" he said, "I was offering the Liberal Party a real choice as well as an exciting convention. The Liberals hadn't been led by a populist since Wilfrid Laurier. Suddenly there was a populist on the scene defending the Liberal heritage and appealing to 'Main Street, not Bay Street.' Because I had stayed in politics I was in touch with Liberals across the country and I knew their thoughts and concerns well enough to reflect them."

In fact, whenever John Turner tried to question the principle of universal social benefits or the size of the deficit or the back-in provision in the NEP, he found Chrétien, the Old Guard, the radical Liberals, and the legacy of Pierre Trudeau breathing down his neck. One knowledgeable official guessed that two-thirds of Turner's support was based on his presumed electability, only a third on his policy direction. Three weeks before the convention, another insider said that even the Liberal Establishment wanted to deny Turner a first-ballot win "to teach him that he can't walk away with the party."

V

At five o'clock in the afternoon John Turner got off his campaign bus from Trenton and entered the men's room in Montecassino Place, a large banquet hall in the Toronto suburb of North York. Still unaware that the press had dashed off to file its reports about his unguarded attack on Trudeau, the candidate stripped off his jacket, tie, and shirt to shave.

"This is going to be hand-to-hand combat," he said, referring to the upcoming reception for local multicultural organizations. "Are you having *fun*?"

The hall looked like the ballroom of a Holiday Inn. It had peach walls and colossal mirrors. The several hundred guests packed themselves into a dense and frenetic swarm around Mr. and Mrs. John Turner for a slow shuffle across the floor to the rhythm of a Culture Club tune played by a steel band from Jane Junior High. Italians, Portuguese, Greeks, Caribbean blacks, African blacks, Chinese, Koreans, old men in turbans and young men in yarmulkes, a multiracial baseball team—everyone pressed in for an autograph, a photograph, or a two-handed clasp.

"Thanks for coming, glad you could come," Turner said repeatedly. To a lady wearing an exotic hat he said, "Hey, looking good!"

Normally, in the more subdued crowds of Vancouver or Halifax, the men and especially the women hung back to clear a circle around the candidate, as if he were royalty or a sleek carnivore on loan from the zoo. Then, one at a time, each would receive the slightly intimidating Turner treatment: the X-ray stare, the scrunch of the eyes, Turner's left hand gripping the stranger's right elbow, and the firm handshake that usually lasted for the entire conversation. Often Turner merely rattled the hand he was holding while he listened intently. Sometimes he jabbed it with his left index finger to make his points. He showed respect with old people, college spirit with students, tenderness

with women. With every man he made a private deal. One
could see why he was so effective in closed meetings with
delegates or at lunches with reluctant clients at Winston's.
Wherever he went, he grasped for a personal connection
to prove his empathy. In Moncton, the centre of one of
the most depressed regions in Canada, he remembered
some great parties at the nearby Shediac Yacht Club in the
1950s. In Halifax he noted that many of the young lawyers
working at McMillan, Binch were graduates of the Dalhousie Law School and that Anne Murray was one of the
firm's clients. And in St. John's he hoped to sway a young
Chrétien supporter by saying, "I used to play tennis with
your mother."

Unlike Trudeau, Turner always said the proper things
and never got nasty in public; but at least when Trudeau
deigned to be pleasant one felt it was genuine. Turner's
advisers noticed the scepticism among people meeting
Turner for the first time. They thought it unfair and unfortunate, but consoled themselves that his icy presence
contributed to his prime-ministerial image.

At Montecassino Place, Turner hadn't played tennis
with the mothers of these New Canadians or been to parties at their yacht clubs. Grasping for a connection, he
reached rather far to observe that he, too, had been an
immigrant, coming to Canada from England as a baby.
These people were treating him like a movie star not because he was another immigrant, however, but because
he belonged to them as another Liberal. Under Trudeau,
not only had command of the party passed to new circles
but the grassroots had been changed as well. Women were
now a sizeable force, youth played a major role, and New
Canadians made up a crucial component of the key metropolitan ridings, while the proportion of well-educated,
upper-income supporters had diminished with each election since 1968. As Tom Axworthy put it, "When some
Liberal traditionalists used to meet in places like the
Chateau Grill to complain, 'It's no longer our party,' they
weren't being disloyal, just astute."

At the outset of his leadership campaign Turner knew
about this transformation in theory and fretted about the

inadequacy of his file cards. On the road he discovered the full implications. Not only did he have to adjust to meeting crowds and giving speeches again, he had to adjust his thinking, or at least his words. For eight years his preoccupations had been those of his law partners, his board colleagues at Canadian Pacific and Bechtel, and his clients. He denied that he had been isolated—"travelling the country and the world, picking up new experiences, honing my talents, understanding the complexities of how this world works"—but he had moved among elites in specialized, protected environments. There he had had to listen to the constant recitation of Trudeau's socialist sins. Often his own critical voice had been the loudest.

Now, in adjusting to the realities of the campaign, Turner became more insecure and cautious. If progressive policies hadn't been his reason for returning to politics, he soon seemed more open to considering them, often after sharp behind-the-scene battles in which the activist ministers who had joined Turner's campaign coalition to be with the winner took on his Bay Street advisers, such as William Macdonald at McMillan, Binch. "It was a period of high learning for Turner," said Lloyd Axworthy, the former Minister of Transport, who later admitted to regrets about not having run himself as a candidate of the left and the West. Even the dapper lawyers and blow-dried hustlers who rode the Liberal gravy train worried about Turner's image, for they knew what kinds of Canadians kept them in the chips by voting for the party. Yet however far Turner's pragmatism and realism brought him back toward Trudeau, his stubborn display of class seemed provocative.

For most of the campaign he demonstrated a *Gentlemen's Quarterly* fondness for seersucker and striped shirts, and his own band followed him through convention week playing "Puttin' on the Ritz." While stressing job retraining (and trusting "the climate of investment" to provide the jobs, which sounded a lot like trusting the weather), he often joked—as he did in Montecassino Place—"If I can be recycled for the third time in my life, anyone can." But that joke could be funny only in a political party whose members *didn't* laugh when a policy forum was interrupted because a lady lost her Christian Dior glasses.

How could John Turner possibly equate his life with that of a miner laid off in Flin Flon or a kid who'd never held a job in Campbellton? When Turner went from an eminent law firm in Montreal to the House of Commons, his stepfather used to phone Pearson and ask when John was going to be in the cabinet. When Turner left the government in 1975, William Macdonald flew from Toronto to offer him a partnership in McMillan, Binch. When Turner left that firm as a shoo-in for the prime ministership, a number of his wealthy friends (including Ralph Barford, then a director of Argus Corporation, and Warren Chippindale of Coopers and Lybrand) formed a secret committee to ease his financial transition into public life. Though Turner wasn't told of the plan and denied its existence, his friends were willing to pay for the education of his children as the least controversial or detectable way of slipping him support.

If his joke about retraining suggested a rather narrow view of reality, it also suggested his belief in the equality of opportunity. "That's why I'm a Liberal," he told the crowd at Montecassino Place. "With guts and a little luck, young men and women can go all the way to the top. I want to make equality a state of mind in Canada. No distinctions! No barriers! No elites!"

No elites? Turner might be thought to have been carried away by his own enthusiasm, except that he usually promised to *abolish* them. That was a tactical response to all the grumblings within the Liberal Party about the backroom boys who had grabbed power from the hands of the party executive and the policy conventions under Trudeau. It held out hope to those who had felt outside. But elites were fundamental to Turner's entire *modus operandi*. If Trudeau could be defined by "The style is the man himself," Turner was defined by "A man is known by his friends." The elites must be open to brains and talent, they must consult broadly, they must be accountable to some elected authority, but they must exist. When Turner spoke of party reform, he wasn't talking about another experiment in participatory democracy. He was aware—certainly more aware than Trudeau had been—that the leader and the cabinet are responsible for their decisions not to the party executive or membership but to Parliament and the people of Canada. Therefore, some informed and cohesive group at the top is necessary to sort out the competing demands and interests, arbitrate among them, and get things done. That's exactly what Trudeau had discovered as he passed from classic liberalism to Canadian liberalism to social democracy.

Trudeau entered power dreaming of making the Liberal Party a "mass party which would be the focal point of all the dissidents" in the country. He continued Pearson's efforts to shape a more open and democratic organization, less bound to its financial backers and local satraps. The nominating procedure for constituency candidates was reformed; limits were put on campaign spending; policy conferences and regional desks were set up to get input. Ultimately, however, organization again bred oligarchy.

"That is a general problem for all parties," Jim Coutts said. "How do you make a political party effectively part of an administration? The leadership is responsible to the party that brought it to power for a number of reasons, but it has to avoid the favouritism of bringing in activists who weren't elected to run the country. So how does the political wing play a bigger role in articulating ideas and directions?"

Coutt's own solution—to create an efficient and powerful "switchboard" in the PMO—merely made him the villain in the piece. Within the party he was denounced by an alliance of the new wave (who, beneath their rhetoric about democracy, could have been bought off with a job in the PMO) and the Pearsonian Liberals (who never recovered from their anger and sorrow at seeing the new gang take over *their* party). Turner and many of his chief advisers belonged to the latter group.

In fact, Turner never really meant to abolish elites. As a traditional Canadian liberal he meant to replace Trudeau's more authoritarian gang with a new gang that would consult more frequently, subject itself to occasional accountability sessions, and work at achieving a better rapport between the leader and the party.

However, if there had been problems with Trudeau's strategic prime ministership, there were also problems with old-style elite accommodation. The process is often bilateral and secretive (who's phoned, whose calls are returned, and what is said?). It's often static (people consulted by a Prime Minister are usually powerful, comfortable, and eager to remain so). It must keep expanding (new elites demand attention while old elites expect it). Moreover, the process functions best when the country is divided into decentralized power bases (whether provinces or economic sectors or even multicultural associations) spoken for by elites, not when it's geared to national unity, equality, the will of the people, or centralized planning. If Turner rejected such institutional changes as the reform of the Senate and the restructuring of the party, preferring instead more "human" contact, *mano a mano*, who would get Turner's hand and how? The man was renowned for his consideration and loyalty to his friends. What would he do if his friends asked for a favour? And what if his friends remained the corporate leaders, bankers, and lawyers, with an occasional union chief or orchestra conductor thrown in for effect. "My client has become the country," he said at his first news conference, but what unemployed immigrant would be invited to lunch at Winston's?

Turner was not a snob; his contacts were numerous and varied; but he had a weakness for high-powered company, useful connections, and old friends. Even his campaign team was founded on cronies from his political past, members of private clubs from Halifax to Vancouver, preppy youths, figurehead women, and the party Establishment. At the start he had a plethora of committees, advisers, and provincial offices, but their power soon faded because key decisions weren't getting made and little was happening efficiently. Authority gradually gravitated to the "boys" who had Turner's ear. Before long, a group of western supporters extracted a promise of a western council and a Westerner in the PMO from him, because they sensed the oligarchical direction in which things were drifting. As for the accountability of the leader, Turner already hated the all-candidate policy sessions the party had arranged for its members in various cities. He thought them a waste of time.

"No elites! No rainmakers!" he cried, referring to the nickname of Senator Keith Davey, the archetypal back-room boy. He didn't mention that Davey had been one of Pearson's election organizers and had been called back to the smoke-filled rooms in 1972 in order to teach Pierre Trudeau Canadian liberalism; nor did he mention that in the deep shadows Davey was quietly helping the Turner campaign. In a matter of months, however, the whole country would see John Turner publicly call back "The Rainmaker" again in order to learn about Trudeau liberalism.

Ultimately it was the members of the elites who made Turner the leader of the Liberal Party. Some decided he was a winner (as Marc Lalonde did); some decided they needed an anglophone (as Allan MacEachen did); and some decided that Jean Chrétien wasn't polished enough to be Prime Minister. While his style may have struck a chord in the hearts of Canadians, many of whom shared his rawness and felt his sense of inferiority, many Liberals preferred to see themselves as they often were: winners, intellectuals, sophisticates. They talked a great deal and in glowing terms about the common people, but they weren't sure they wanted to be led by one of them. (It was a discrepancy that went to the centre of the general perception of the Liberal Party as hypocritical, opportunist, and fraudulent. Many voters would soon punish them for just that discrepancy.)

In reality, of course, there was little common about Jean Chrétien, but he couldn't alter his style without betraying his followers and himself. It was his greatest strength and his worst handicap. As Joey Smallwood, the former Premier of Newfoundland, explained the problem in his own inimitable fashion, "Canada has not been cheated out of her due and fair and just and proper share of jackasses. Jackasses expect a Prime Minister to have a prime-ministerial appearance, look, sound, stance. Jean Chrétien doesn't look or sound like a Prime Minister. But what are you hiring? A TV star? And didn't John Turner dance with Princess Margaret? What better qualification!"

Oddly perhaps, his little-guy-from-Shawinigan persona met more resistance in Quebec than it did in English Canada. The West had a long history of folksy populists; Ontario and Atlantic Canada often responded to the rousing patriotism and the happy, unthreatening Quebecker; but many French Canadians seemed more particular about the class of person to represent them on Sussex Drive and the world stage.

In many ways Chrétien was the perfect embodiment of the *embourgeoisement* of the upwardly mobile Quebec businessmen, plump lawyers, and self-satisfied engineers who had used the Liberal Party as one means to the American dream. Unlike many of them, however, he hadn't buried where he had come from under a deep Florida tan, a gold neck-chain, or a lot of pretentious phrases about the *nouveau Beaujolais*. Their old social habits and new social ambitions had taught them to defer to a *chef* like Trudeau or Lalonde—brilliant, hard, aloof—and their self-esteem was offended by Chrétien's jokes, his slang, and the way he was received as a pet frog by English Canadians. If all that didn't cause them to pause, Marc Lalonde sent orders to the Quebec machine that no one was to organize for Jean Chrétien.

"It was terrible," Chrétien said. "At one point I had nobody, because everyone who knew the party had been blocked at the top." People who had worked closely with him during the referendum were threatened with various punishments if they helped him; others for whom he had campaigned or raised money fled. Chrétien suffered a cruel irony: in 1975 he turned down Trudeau's offer to control the machine as Quebec lieutenant, suggesting that Marc Lalonde be given the job instead.

In time, from guilt, from loyalty, and in the aftermath of Turner's confusion about language rights, some talented organizers such as Léonce Mercier risked disobeying Lalonde. Chrétien was then able to capture about half the elected Quebec delegates. That gave him a first-ballot total of 1,067 votes in June, about 100 votes short of what he needed to pass Turner. In the end, the crucial difference was made by the ex-officio delegates, the party brass from senators to former ministers, who had an automatic vote. They accounted for about a third of the convention, and they opted overwhelmingly for John Turner, allowing him to win on the second ballot with 1,862 votes to Chrétien's 1,368. In other words, the elites went for the candidate they thought most likely to keep them in power.

At Montecassino Place John Turner finished his speech to warm applause. The crowd didn't seem perturbed by the contradiction between Turner's pledge to open up the party and the sight of the anonymous advisers, organizers, and handlers gathering on the stage to pat the candidate as if he were a quarterback returning to the bench after scoring a touchdown for them. Perhaps not many in this audience had even been in Canada when the old ways for which Turner yearned nostalgically had frozen another minority, the French Canadians, out of Ottawa's back rooms and private clubs. Or perhaps in the political cultures from which many of these people had come—the Catholic countries of Europe and Latin America, the caste societies of Asia, the tribal states of Africa—they had been taught as thoroughly as many Canadians that Turner's "prime-ministerial" appearance was supposed to condition a respectful deference to him as a member of the elite. The Italians, the blacks, and the Vietnamese cheered as they cleared a way for him. Then Turner climbed into the back of a waiting car and was whisked to a private cocktail party, to be followed by a private dinner.

VI

Far from Toronto, in the snowcapped mountains of the British Columbia interior on a brilliant day in May, John Turner's faith came sharply into focus.

He had dropped into Rossland, the mining town where his mother had been born and where Turner had spent the years from three to five with her and her parents, after the death of his father in England and before the move to Ottawa. The place only superficially represented his roots.

The visit was essentially a media event to illustrate his connection to the West. It was a connection that Turner was exploiting for the same reasons that Brian Mulroney had exploited *his* connection to Quebec.

Yet Turner seemed genuinely touched as he strode, in a clutch of puffing reporters, up the steep hill to the quaint family home.

"Stable virtues, simple values," he proclaimed on the veranda of the two-storey frame house with redwood stain and white trim. Across the picket fence the Rossland High School band thumped out the school song: "We are the men of the purple and gold, we're from the mountains rugged and bold, we hold our colours proud and high, we fight, fight, fight, and never say die."

Turner licked his lips remembering the huckleberry muffins of his last visit. He praised the current woman of the house for keeping things so "spick-and-span." He remembered the apple tree on which he used to swing and his walks with his grandfather, who used to stop in for some "suds" after a visit to the barbershop. He recalled his Sunday attendance at the Sacred Heart Church where his grandmother had been organist.

Turner's real roots, though, belonged to a time rather than a place. Born in England, with grandparents from Nova Scotia, a summer place in New Brunswick, one law career in Quebec, another in Ontario, a wife from Manitoba, and a mother from B.C., Turner defined himself by the 1940s when—as billboards in Vancouver boasted at the time—"B.C. has men to match those mountains!"

How tempting for the reporters in his wake to put aside their 1980s scepticism and believe along with him. In Rossland he evoked better, simpler times: clean, white sports like tennis and track; Anglo-Saxon manliness. Yes, good old anglo competence, with appropriate doses of anglo camaraderie, anglo nostalgia, and anglo duty. A return to normalcy and straightforward thinking. Out with those confounding Jesuits and to hell with the frogs! Not that John Turner would ever have thought such a thing—he's too much a liberal and a gentleman. By God, though, he's the type of officer you'd have wanted with you when you were approaching Dieppe.

Belief in simpler times came hard in the 1980s. After Turner toured the Rossland Museum with its artifacts of bygone eras, after he admired the Nancy Greene Room ("great gal") and paused in front of a photograph of Father "Mac" MacIntyre ("great guy"), he picked up a rock in the Cominco Wing and said, "Hey, this rock contains 25 per cent lead and 10 per cent iron."

"Sounds like you," said Val Sears of the *Toronto Star*.

Turner didn't laugh. After he visited the mining relics and saw the hoistman's chair that had been his grandfather's, after he sang the praises of small towns while standing in the sunshine, he was asked by Craig Oliver of CTV, "Since we seem to be dwelling on history today, perhaps you could tell us why you resigned from Mr. Trudeau's cabinet in 1975?"

Here, 2,500 miles and more than two weeks from Trenton, amid happy reveries, John Turner couldn't get away from the question. He couldn't get away from Pierre Trudeau. In fact, he couldn't get away from the 1980s. He had to concede Trudeau's success on national unity, the patriation of the constitution, and peace. The Charter of Rights had altered forever the old notion of parliamentary supremacy, because of the increasing importance of judicial rulings. Quebec was no longer contained by a right-wing autocrat, the West was no longer a sleepy rural society on the eve of a boom, and none of the provinces was any longer just a glorified municipality. In terms of the federal government there was some room to speed up decision making, cut paperwork, and limit the bureaucracy, but Turner's dream of the days before the cabinet committee system when strong, independent ministers ran their own departments was just that, a dream, in an age of complexity and coordination.

"It's a colossal put-on," said Michael Pitfield. "When Air Canada was set up, the big question was whether the stewardesses should be trained nurses. Now such an initiative would involve sixteen or twenty departments. It would have foreign policy implications and industrial policy implications. If someone can suggest ways that all the functions of a modern cabinet can be done better by elected ministers, God bless him. But no one's really talking about that. Everyone's talking about putting the ministers back in their offices, making decisions by themselves and being briefed by their own officials. That's a pipedream."

Gone were the days when C. D. Howe could draw up a plan for the trans-Canada pipeline in a two-page memo. And gone with them were many secret deals, arbitrary and accident-prone decisions, cabals of omnipotent mandarins, ways to protect fiefdoms jealously, failures to mesh programs, and terrible cabinet slug fests. Besides, C. D. Howe and Jimmy Gardiner were neither alive nor living in Herb Gray and Lloyd Axworthy.

Keynesian economics had run amok. The baby boomers were adults now, looking for jobs. It was harder for the nation to live off its resources. Japan and Europe were not in ashes. The scale of foreign investment made it less of a benefit. Boxed in by inflation, interest rates, unemployment, and the dollar, few economists had any new solutions or much consolation to offer beyond the hope for growth brought on by general world conditions. Efforts to control the deficit would have to face realities that had become politically sacrosanct since the 1960s, such as the range of universal social programs and the fiscal transfers to the provinces.

Moreover, since the 1960s Canadians had grown accustomed to considering the government as more than a referee. It had become a weapon, not only in Atlantic Canada (where state enterprise is essential) or in Quebec (where nationalism made a habit of the state) but throughout the country, as demonstrated by the widespread support for Petro-Canada. Even in the business community and the West, government grants, government partnerships, and a government presence in international trade had become the norm, provincially and federally; and many Westerners wouldn't have boasted like Turner of being a director of Canadian Pacific. Turner may have felt that Ottawa shouldn't pick winners and losers, but he had sat on the board of Massey-Ferguson when the Trudeau cabinet helped bail the tractor company out of trouble.

"I've been in public life since 1962 and my positions are clear," he said. "My tenets of classic Canadian liberalism have been consistent all the way through. I haven't moved, though I've responded to changing issues."

However, while he was out of government, the party and the country had moved. "Just give me the facts at any moment," he liked to say. If the facts as given him on Bay Street had made him assess reality more like Ronald Reagan and Margaret Thatcher than Pierre Trudeau, the facts as given him on the campaign trail made him appreciate the reality of Glace Bay and Shawinigan. To undo the legacy of Pierre Trudeau would take as much personal will, cause as much social conflict, and risk as much political support as Trudeau had taken, caused, and risked in building it.

Turner was a determined man with a good sense of what's right and how to get there. He could be tough on himself and a tough manager. He trusted that his style would achieve what Trudeau's couldn't. He would recruit strong and able women with which to surround himself. He would get things done by consensus rather than conflict. He wasn't afraid of new ideas or the exercise of power, and he wasn't liable to be pushed around by polls or criticism. He felt enormous guilt when he had to do something that betrayed his conscience, and he knew he couldn't seek peace at any price.

"One attempts to gain consensus and accommodation," he said, "but if the process is exhausted, then one has to exercise unilateral leadership. Consensus is not an excuse for inaction. It's a procedure for action that meets a wider range of acceptance at an earlier stage. But if one has to take strong resolve that meets with disapproval in some parts of the country, so be it. At least one has tried."

However, as the old ladies in Rossland put it, "He was always such a well-mannered little boy." John Turner didn't like conflict, hardball politics, or sudden change. He was civil, conciliatory, and never reckless. "He's small 'c' cautious, not conservative," a close adviser said. Big decisions came slowly, after every argument against them had been assayed. Sometimes they didn't come at all, in the Mackenzie King tradition of hoping that problems would solve themselves. Grand plans were his aversion. Big talk wasn't worth much if he could promise less and deliver more. He wasn't the type to storm into power by declaring a hundred days of decision. Indeed, he believed that his attentive, competent, passive manner suited the style of government required by the times. After the strains of the Trudeau years, it was time for "velvet leadership" (his expression), nuance, civility, accommodation, and rest. He was Robert Borden and Louis St. Laurent. He was the Restoration and the pause that refreshes.

After the provinces had retrenched, though, after the business community had reinvested, after the worst flaws had been removed from the system, then what? "Do you have the *steel* to do what has to be done?" Turner was asked by an old acquaintance anxious for government reform.

"I think so," Turner replied. "I won't like it, but I think I can do it."

Turner's caution worried those who wanted a counter-revolution as much as it worried those Liberals who thought that economic growth, technological change, international competition, national sovereignty, national unity, and social justice required a central state that continued to ram and prod Canadian society into the twenty-first century. Either way, after the protracted niceties and negotiations with the provinces or the Americans or the oil industry, Turner would have to confront the question that absorbed Trudeau in the last years of his regime: will the important and difficult things ever get done, or won't they?

Turner had an administrative, analytical personality. Those qualities served him well in Justice and Finance, where there were bureaucracies to oversee and specific problems to solve. A Prime Minister, however, must be able to do more than use his skills and contacts to negotiate clean-air treaties or sell subway cars to Singapore. C. D. Howe was never more than a "first-rate second man." Turner's hard work and optimism would undoubtedly ease the tensions among the provinces and the private sector, loosen up the civil service and the cabinet system, improve the mood of the West and therefore of the Liberal party, and bring a reasonable and human dimension to government. But even his closest friends didn't know whether he could rise to history with imagination, boldness, and heart.

God knows, John Turner didn't want to disappoint either history or his friends. And he resented the image that he didn't have a heart. He admitted to crying on occasion, he sometimes showed old friends affection by a kiss on the cheek, he was always patting and slapping and stroking. But he had repressed so much in order to be liked; he had pushed his emotions down into the dark centre of his self, and nothing knew the full force of them except some tennis ball he whacked to kingdom come.

He almost broke down, he said, in the Rossland Museum in front of the portrait of his mother in her egret hat. Turner had just been to see her in the hospital on Saltspring Island where she was ill with Alzheimer's disease, too ill to recognize him or to know that her son was finally going to be Prime Minister of Canada. But he knew what she expected him to do, and he did his duty. He didn't break down. He continued along his tightrope.

In Ottawa, on the eve of becoming leader of the Liberal Party, just a step from the perch where he could relax a moment before the appalling experience that fate had in store for him, John Turner looked across the convention arena and found himself face to face with his old nemesis.

"For the last three months I have met thousands of people across the country and I have listened to them," he declared at the podium. "I have listened and I have learned."

Comfortable in the grandstand, Pierre Trudeau smiled.

SECTION FOUR

Triumph of the Wily

I

Norman Atkins didn't expect John Turner to call an early election. The Tories' campaign chairman assumed that the new Liberal leader would take time to give at least the illusion of freshness to the old Trudeau record by bringing in some new faces and showing some new initiatives. Moreover, Turner needed time to patch the wounds from the convention, regather his energy, and put together an election team. He might even want to savour being Prime Minister for a while and bask in the reflected glory of greeting the Queen and the Pope on their visits to Canada. So, Atkins figured, the vote wouldn't come till November. True, the Liberals were ahead in the polls for a change. Atkins had predicted that would happen as a result of the hype around their leadership race. He felt, however, that his clever, experienced counterparts in the Liberal Party would be no more impressed by such a temporary and artificial high than he was.

But they were. For one thing, many of them had just abandoned their principles, betrayed their friends, and blinded themselves to Turner's evident weaknesses in order to go with a winner. So they were triply convinced that he was the winner the polls now proclaimed him to be. For another thing, they had been down so long that getting their heads above water felt like getting to shore.

Almost all the cabinet ministers and key organizers—with the notable exceptions of Jean Chrétien and Keith Davey—urged Turner to seize the momentum and go immediately into an election. Turner was less certain. He had never believed those who said he would win both the leadership and the election in a walk and was still confused and "bushed" by the ordeal he had just been through. Moreover, his natural instinct was for cautious delay. In this case, however, the tally-ho chorus of his advisers coincided with his fears about a downturn in the economy by autumn. Besides, as one insider said, "Turner was utterly, totally, completely psyched out by Trudeau. In 1968 Trudeau won the leadership, went to the country, and got a big majority, so that's what John was going to do too." He flew from London on July 8 after asking the Queen to postpone her summer visit, and announced a general election for September 4.

Though Atkins was surprised, he was ready. He was fifty years old—"the perfect age between experience and youth," according to his old friend, Senator Finlay MacDonald—and he had been through more than thirty-five campaigns from assistant to the New Brunswick campaign coordinator in 1952 to senior consultant in the Bermuda general election in 1983. After nine months of work with the federal Tories his leader was trained, his team was in place, his computers were installed, and he himself was at the height of his form as the back-room boy *par excellence*. Indeed, all the diligent labours and lucky breaks of his life seemed mere preparations for this moment. Though he had achieved some power and renown in Ontario as the godfather of the provincial Progressive Conservatives' Big Blue Machine, an election organization put together by Atkins and his friends in 1971 and often credited with making that party the most successful democratic institution in the Western world, his strongest interest had been at the national level. In the past two decades that interest had encountered only defeat or rebuff. Now victory seemed near despite the polls, and Atkins enjoyed the full confidence of the leader. He brought to Ottawa the skills to merit both.

However, even his closest associates weren't quite sure what those skills were. By trade he was an advertising man, president of Camp Associates Advertising Limited, founded in 1959 by Atkins's former brother-in-law and

"surrogate father," Dalton Camp. The company's bread
and butter were the tourism accounts from Conservative
provincial governments, yet Atkins left the campaign's advertising to others. "My profession is advertising and my
hobby is politics," he liked to say, noting that he had never
accepted a dollar from the Tories for his organizing. As
campaign chairman he was the spokesman for the team,
yet he constantly apologized for not being very articulate,
sincerely played down his influence, and often admitted
that speeches, policy discussions, and big ideas weren't
his strengths. As don of the Big Blue Machine, whose self-
interest and tight bonding have been compared to those
of a mafia family, he manoeuvred about a notoriously brutal world, yet he exuded sheepishness, had a grin as wide
and heart-warming as a Halloween pumpkin's, and usually sounded both woeful and vulnerable. Heavy, ill at
ease, with a face as big as a harvest moon and a grace to
his step that showed why the former high-school quarterback was still a terror on the tennis courts, he looked enough
like Al Waxman that one wondered if the *King of Kensington*
hadn't wandered by mistake onto the set of *Quentin Dur-
gens, MP*.

One suspected guile, but everyone who knew him well
insisted that what you saw was what you got. "He's more
grandfather than godfather," said Nancy McLean, who
had produced television commercials for the Big Blue Machine since 1971 and considered Atkins her mentor. "He's
mush, he's an open wound, he's extremely sensitive and
easily hurt." Even his enemies admitted that Norman Atkins abhorred manipulation, fled from conflict, and really
did believe that goodness, honesty, and fairness would
prevail in the end.

If so, what use was he in the world of politics?

Atkins's forte was organization, pure and simple: putting together events, keeping an eye on the details, establishing contexts in which the best people available could
do whatever they did best. His greatest strength was his
knowledge of his own weaknesses. Profoundly aware of
what he didn't know and couldn't do, he used his likeability to attract the brightest and most experienced Tories

to a structure in which they could interact and flourish. Atkins was called "the great connector," "the quintessential political quarterback," and "the world's greatest casting director," but his role was best described as coach. He allowed the veterans to express themselves creatively and newcomers to move quickly to their level of competence.

"There was a lot of stuff being done in that headquarters that I didn't understand," Atkins confessed after the election. "But I had the people who did understand."

"Norman isn't the greatest strategist in the world," Nancy McLean said, "but he knows what needs to happen and he can assemble the people to do it. More than doing anything himself, he coalesces and directs and motivates. Like Blanche DuBois, he's always relying on the kindness of strangers. That's why he's never heavy or vengeful or arrogant. Often you help him out of pity because you know he'll feel hurt if you say no."

Allan Gregg, the Tory pollster, agreed. "Norman is a really interesting motivator. He's never threatening or coercive. He *whines*—'Come on, do this for me,'—and usually you do it even though you know that if you say you can't, he'll say, 'Oh, all right,' and go whine to someone else. It's not so much leadership by delegation as by abdication."

His second trick was to get everyone working together by keeping in constant communication, by leaving his door open at all times, by concentrating on the details, and by keeping the essentials in view. His unassuming demeanour actually helped him. A political campaign can't be managed like a business, with rigid orders and arbitrary decisions, because it is a voluntary association in the end. It requires prodding, persuasion, and infinite patience. It requires making sure that everyone feels good about the essentials, recognizing when someone needs a rest or has more to offer, getting rid of those who can't get along with others, and talking out all the difficulties. Everyone has to feel as important yet as dispensable as Atkins himself, part of a larger cause and in the game for greater reasons than self-interest.

"Norman personifies the collegial spirit," Gregg said.

"There's no way you're going to thrive and survive unless he thrives and survives, and vice versa, so you might as well forget about bickering and bullshit and vested interests."

What was often seen from the outside as a sleek machine was, on the inside, a human collection of egos and energy. Thus, for example, in the expense accounts of the advance men who prepared the tours was a category called PACR: "Pissed away, can't remember." Atkins had a great coach's semimystical knack of unifying people into a team, then inspiring that team with spirit. Beer-and-pizza parties were as important to him as all the sophisticated computers, and he insisted that the Ottawa headquarters be covered with photographs and banners to make it less like a space station. By evoking sympathy rather than fear, and service rather than selfishness, he became the Tory Party's Gipper.

Once the organization was assembled and coordinated, Atkins served as a conduit between it and Brian Mulroney. Every week during the campaign Atkins and Mulroney met alone to go over what had to be done in the coming week, to discuss the tour plans, and to rehearse the major themes once more. When speaking with Atkins, Mulroney knew he was speaking in fact with scores—if not hundreds—of key party workers across the country; and Atkins's relative lack of personal ambition and his disinterestedness in policy questions meant that Mulroney could count on him to be an honest broker. Atkins was never a yes man, and occasionally his honesty struck someone with the leader's oversensitivity to criticism as brutal.

Election campaigns are too frenzied and high-pressured for the leader to do much more than go where the organization tells him to go, say what the organization tells him to say, and try to keep out of trouble. He can't be both the rider and the horse. If he hasn't found a team and a set of policies to carry him comfortably by the time the writs are issued, he will be unlikely to find them as he runs from pillar to post. Mulroney learned that lesson during the 1983 leadership race when his hands-on approach nearly ended in disaster. The pettiest details went to him for approval, countless decisions were never made or were soon reversed, and entire strategies were discarded in mid-operation in panic and confusion. By the time of the convention Mulroney received a memo that warned him, "Convention campaign out of control—No direction or focus—No organizational discipline—Will cost a lot more than it should—Currently insolvent," and it included a plea in italics: *"You must stop running this campaign and have some faith in your people."*

Of course, that campaign had been assembled hastily and randomly by necessity only after Clark announced the contest. Mulroney had to use whoever offered to help, many of them had no experience at the national level, and the candidate himself hadn't run for anything since 1976. None of those factors worked to alleviate his bad nerves, his characteristic desire to know everything that was happening, and his basic suspicion that everyone else was bound to screw up if given half a chance. Once he became leader, however, he had at his service the real party professionals, most of whom had been in Clark's team. These were the strategists, the pollsters, the media advisers, the advertising gurus, the advance men, and so on who had developed their crafts in the Tory Party for most of their lives.

The great irony of modern election campaigns is that at the time of most exposure the leader is least himself. While hordes of journalists trail him back and forth from sea to sea, while the public pays closest attention to his words, he has temporarily handed over his power and his personality to others. His very wish might be the law normally, but for these two months he's little more than a travelling salesman with a patter and a suitcase of brushes he picked up at headquarters. As a corollary to that there is another great irony: the infrequent opportunity when the people can participate actively and effectively in the political process is usually the occasion when the choice is least, the debate is least, and therefore the participation is least important.

An up-to-date political organization is more than a group of experts who know how to attract a crowd or feed the press. Just as the medium affects the message and technology conditions the society, the election machine has conceptual repercussions that have more profound significance than whatever it was designed to do. It has, in fact, its own ideology. Brian Mulroney understood all that.

He and Atkins had known each other since the Nova Scotia election in 1960, when Mulroney was a student at St. Francis Xavier and Atkins was helping Dalton Camp help Robert Stanfield remain premier. They used to rendezvous at the Lord Nelson Hotel in Halifax to share information and an excitement about politics. Mulroney's excitement seemed innate. Atkins's had been acquired after years of playing Steppin Fetchit to Camp, whom he had idolized ever since the twenty-one-year-old Acadia University student showed up at the Atkins summer cottage on Robertson's Point, Grand Lake, New Brunswick, in 1941 to court Norman's sister Linda.

In 1952 Atkins, about to be an Acadia student himself, accompanied Camp around New Brunswick for the provincial election. Camp, on leave from a Toronto advertising firm, was then in charge of the Tories' communication program. "I was more taken by Dalton than by anything political or philosophical," Atkins recalled. "Dalton once said, 'If I were an NDPer, Norman would be an NDPer,' and he's right." In fact, both of them could easily have been Liberals, since Camp had begun as one.

Thus, like Don Quixote and Sancho Panza (though more successful), they rambled through the Maritimes in election after election, accumulating experience, contacts, and enthusiasm for the game. Norman missed the Diefenbaker sweep in 1958 after being drafted for two years into the U.S. army (he had been born and raised outside New York City, where his father had gone from Nova Scotia to work as an insurance broker); but at bases in Georgia and Germany he picked up important organizational skills as acting corporal assigned to the supply sergeant. What he learned about looking after the laundry and accounting for every spoon he then applied as production manager in Camp's firm and as general factotum in Camp's political activities.

In 1963 Camp served as the Tories' campaign chairman for the federal election. In 1964 he became the party's national president. At the same time, by his intelligence, his sophistication, his energy, and his openness, he became the focus of those young, urban, upwardly mobile Tories who were disenchanted by what their party had become under Diefenbaker—old-fashioned, thoughtless, fundamentally rural, and ridiculously sectarian. During Camp's cross-Canada "pilgrimage" in 1966 to get a leadership review, he—and Atkins, who was acting as a *de facto* executive assistant—established an informal network of like-minded Tories with skills and networks of their own. Among the network was the Montreal lawyer, Brian Mulroney.

"He was our man in Montreal," Camp said, "one of the only sane, reliable, rational guys there, the soundest, the ablest, and with good connections to the Union Nationale."

"Dalton appreciated him in a political context," Atkins said. "I was more Brian's age and I liked him because he was fun to be with, even if I never saw him for too long."

Despite Atkins's beginnings in provincial campaigns, his focus moved to the national level, first with Camp's presidency of the party and then with Camp's two unsuccessful attempts to become a federal MP in the 1965 and 1968 elections. As campaign manager in both races, Atkins put together a team of young, modern, urban Tories who became known as the "Eglinton Mafia." They used the new canvassing techniques that John Kennedy's organization had introduced in the United States; they shared a moderate, progressive, intelligent liberalism; and they were quickly bound by friendship and battle.

Their strength as a group, when linked to Camp's national network, became evident during the 1967 Tory leadership fight. Camp had been leaning toward Duff Roblin, the Premier of Manitoba, but in a meeting in Winnipeg he learned that Roblin didn't intend to run. As a result, Camp offered his services to Robert Stanfield—and stayed with him even when Roblin changed his mind. Atkins, meanwhile, developed an organization chart for whomever Camp chose to support. Its application became a significant factor in Stanfield's victory.

"I remember walking to Maple Leaf Gardens in Toronto the morning of the vote," Stanfield said. "I was behind a band, and at one intersection I saw another band coming to join us in perfect timing. I doubled up laughing to think of the effort expended to achieve that. I imagine it was one of Norman's responsibilities."

In retrospect, Stanfield's winning of the Tory leadership marked the end rather than the beginning of the Camp machine. Once, when Camp and Stanfield were meeting, Stanfield's wife was passing in and out of the room oiling the hinges and locks. Suddenly she stopped and, wagging her finger at Camp, said, "The best thing you can do for Bob is stay in the closet!" For Camp had become the scapegoat for all the guilt and hostility associated with dumping Diefenbaker. Many in the party didn't like his style or his ideas; many didn't like his powerful cadre; and many didn't like him. "He was always a figure of controversy," said Finlay MacDonald, who had known Camp since the 1953 election in Nova Scotia. His enemies saw him as a smart aleck who had become the fastest draw in the party. There was always someone ready to challenge him at high noon."

Stanfield's first priority was to consolidate the party, which contained a large and ornery segment still loyal to Diefenbaker and far from progressive. Camp and his friends were deliberately kept at a distance. Camp understood, but he was hurt. "Those were difficult days for Dalton," Stanfield admitted. "He must have been very disappointed." In 1968, after Camp lost his second election bid to Trudeaumania, he resigned as party president and began to pull back further and further, away from political involvement, away from the advertising business, away from his marriage to Linda Atkins, and home toward the beautiful countryside outside Fredericton. "I had had enough," he said.

II

"We were all adrift," Atkins said of Camp's semi-retirement to write and reflect, as if describing a death in the family. "It seemed we had nowhere to go, no opportunity to have influence."

Then, in 1970, John Robarts resigned as the Premier of Ontario. His heir-apparent was William Davis, a moderate and a friend of Dalton Camp's. Still, Camp resolved not to get involved in the campaign. It had fallen on Atkins, in the meantime, to maintain the links that would keep Camp's network intact until something interesting came along. Few in the group, including Atkins, had had any involvement in Ontario politics or knew any of the candidates well, but at least this was an occasion to pull together again.

"There were a bunch of battle-scarred, slightly paranoid people," said Hugh Macaulay, a closer adviser to Davis, later chairman of Ontario Hydro and a friend to Atkins, "a kind of mercenary army looking for a fight."

Davis was the logical man to support, but he didn't seem to need help. He didn't return the phone calls offering assistance, and he reeked of the party Establishment. So Norman and the boys decided to back Allan Lawrence. It would be a challenge. It would be *fun*. Camp was uncomfortable with Atkins's decision, but chose not to interfere. And so Norman Atkins stepped out of the shadow of Dalton Camp. Drawing on his lists, his federal experience, and his knowledge of organization, he assembled a campaign that caught fire, fuelled by the anti-brass mood in the party at the time. To many people's surprise, Allan Lawrence came within forty-four votes of toppling Davis.

Ten days later, at the urging of Hugh Macaulay and Roy McMurtry (a member of the Eglinton Mafia who later became Ontario's Attorney-General), a dinner was arranged at the National Club so that Davis could meet with about a dozen organizers, friends and foes, to put the pieces back together in time for the next provincial election. It was the type of magnanimous, professional gesture that

Atkins respected. He had met Davis only twice very briefly; but this night, over dinner and then in a hotel bar, they discovered that they had much in common. Neither liked the War Measures Act, for example, and both liked cigars, boating, football, and Robert Stanfield. Atkins in friendship always became a huge, sloppy, sentimental sheepdog, equally anxious to fetch sticks or give up his life on command. Now Bill Davis became his friend, and Norman Atkins became loyal, as one associate put it, "to the point of lunacy."

Soon after their first conversation, Atkins was able to bring some interesting ideas to Davis, ideas drawn from work done at the federal party headquarters in Ottawa by Malcolm Wickson. A Vancouver lawyer and businessman, Wickson had been hired by Stanfield as national director in 1968. The election that year had been a disaster for the Tories, and Wickson realized that the problem had been more than Trudeaumania. Little had been coordinated or planned. There had been no centralized budget, no polling, no science to the conception or execution of the leader's tour. Print ads, radio commercials, and pamphlets had been produced without reference to each other, and no one had known how to use television. Such improvised chaos was the norm. At the kick-off meeting of the 1965 campaign, for example, John Diefenbaker asked a couple of dozen people gathered around a table, "Well, what are we going to do?" Then he answered himself, "I want to see the people. I'm going to get on a train." And he left.

Wickson and Atkins figured there had to be a better way of organizing an election campaign. They studied the American models. Wickson got access to the Republican National Committee and advice from its chairman, Ray Bliss, who was considered a great political organizer; and he hired a public-opinion research firm from Detroit that did work for moderate Republicans and seemed appropriate for middle-of-the-road Tories. By December, 1970, Wickson, Atkins, and the campaign planning committee produced a document in which responsibilities were divided on paper into little boxes and coordinated into an election team. The idea was to integrate the realities of

modern politics—polling, television, systematic touring—
with a general strategy by means of an efficient organization. The innovation was to link communications with
organization, organization with strategy, and strategy with
opinion research.

"It was nothing very profound," Wickson said, "but
no one had done it before in Canada."

Shortly after the National Club dinner, Hugh Macaulay
asked Atkins what it would take to get him involved in
the upcoming Ontario election. "It won't take anything,"
Atkins replied. "I'll do whatever you ask."

Two weeks later he was asked to be campaign manager. "Sure," he said, and talked with Wickson about tai-
loring their organization concept to the province. Wickson
joined the team that Atkins was recruiting from the Eglinton Mafia, diverse contacts, and fresh volunteers. By a
slow metamorphosis, Camp's network became Atkins's
network. Moreover, the new politics demanded new skills,
and they just happened to be the mundane skills that
Norman Atkins had been practising so cheerfully over the
years. As campaign logistics became as important as policies, as images supplanted ideas, as a single poll gained
the power to silence ten philosophers, the acting corporal
assigned to supplies gradually emerged as the most unlikely commander in Canadian politics.

Between the spring and fall of 1971, he constructed a
formidable organization. Then, with the help of compar-
atively primitive polling techniques, the organization constructed a strategy: to maximize the popularity of the new,
activist leader. All the resources of the campaign were
mobilized to implement that strategy. The advance men
were told to make Davis the focus of the tour arrangements. The print ads featured Davis. The radio spots sang
"Davis will make it go." Davis was the centre of well-
produced television commercials that used music, pretty
pictures, and emotional devices to convey the message.

"It was no longer party workers conspiring to put up
signs or hold meetings," said Hugh Segal, once Principal
Secretary to Premier Davis and then executive vice-president of Camp Advertising. "It was people sitting down as

if to launch a new product, then going about it in a thoughtful, methodological way, matching resources with people and people with ideas."

The result was a great victory for Davis—the Ontario Tories won 78 of 117 seats—and a watershed in Canadian politics. It was also the birth of a legend. Borrowing from the popular nickname of the Cincinnati Reds baseball team, the "Big Red Machine," Claire Hoy of the *Toronto Star* applied the Tories' colour and dubbed Davis's organization the Big Blue Machine.

The immediate effect of that victory was to convince a number of Tories in the federal party that what they needed to win in Ottawa was the kind of people who had just won in Ontario. That suited Robert Stanfield's belief that it was important for the party to establish strong links with Ontario and Toronto anyway. He had always got along well with Atkins, and was one of the first to recognize that Norman Atkins had organizing talents distinct from Dalton Camp's intuitive gifts for public relations. In addition, he probably hoped that Atkins could bring back the Camp machine without the controversial figure of Camp himself. For these good reasons, Stanfield offered Atkins the job of campaign manager in the 1972 federal election. Atkins declined because of previous commitments to Davis, but he agreed to do what he could. He did quite a bit, in fact, particularly in coordinating communications. Perhaps his greatest contribution was to recommend Malcolm Wickson be appointed director of operations and Finlay MacDonald be made national campaign chairman. Both were "connectors" to the Big Blue Machine. Stanfield concurred.

The national campaign was run from Ottawa by MacDonald, but its guts—polling, advertising, logistics, tour direction, and issue identification—were in Toronto. There was even a speech-writing unit headed by Dalton Camp, who once observed that "trying to leave politics is like a Jesuit trying to leave the Church: you never totally succeed." Wickson depended heavily on the Atkins team, fresh and eager from the provincial win and urged on by the Premier's own involvement in the federal campaign. "Davis's boys were like homicidal maniacs freed to fight again," MacDonald recalled. "As a result, they quickly identified with Stanfield, and he became a popular, respected figure with that crowd."

The Conservatives ran a textbook campaign—the first real manifestation of the "new politics" on the national level. Elements of the concept had been used by the Liberals in previous elections, ever since Keith Davey had absorbed Theodore White's *The Making of the President, 1960*, but 1972 marked a new, more sophisticated, more complete phase in campaign organization. Given another couple of weeks and better grass-roots activity in a few key ridings, the Tories might have ousted Trudeau.

They tried again in 1974—this time with Wickson as campaign chairman and Atkins as director of operations—but the party was hung by its pro-West oil policy, Stanfield's support for wage-and-price controls, and his inability to communicate effectively. Worse, the Liberals had regrouped after their near-defeat by adopting many of the Tories' own organizational and strategic innovations. They developed their use of polling; they set up a centralized, in-house advertising agency; and, for emotion and pretty pictures, they highlighted Margaret Trudeau going on about the Prime Minister as a loving guy at party rallies. The old professionals such as Davey, who had been pushed aside by the eggheads in 1972, returned with a new bag of tricks, and they won a majority government. Nobody missed the implications. Image was more important than content; emotional messages were more important than Socratic dialogues about the future of the nation; and progressive policies were more important than raising the real problems that confronted government.

Success and near-success did not bring everyone in the federal Tories around to the methods and personalities of the Big Blue Machine. There still remained an Old Guard of Diefenbaker loyalists (strong enough that they would soon bring down Stanfield). There were people jealous or afraid of the new gang's power, and others who couldn't accept its moderate philosophy or its modern techniques. Moreover, the boys themselves had become rather carried away by their own enthusiasm and confidence.

"They had to be accepted as an arrogant bunch of professionals," Finlay MacDonald said of them. "Sometimes I wasn't consulted about whether the leader was going to Thunder Bay or Split Lip, and I used to joke whether I could get an appointment to see them. That caused tensions, but you had to accept a certain amount of it. If you got on your high horse, then forget it—you weren't going to work with them."

The hostile undercurrents surfaced in 1976, after Stanfield lost the support of the Tory caucus and resigned. Even though Atkins had once argued with him for turning his back on Camp, he had become devoted to the leader in typical sheepdog fashion. He urged Stanfield to stay on and was discouraged by the resignation. In the leadership race that followed, Atkins was sympathetic to his one-time assistant, Joe Clark—and, unlike most people, he thought Clark could win by being everyone's second choice—but he took no real part. "I didn't want to have a federal interest any more," he said. "I didn't have the stomach or the heart for it, and I had enough to worry about in Ontario."

That, however, may be an explanation after the fact. As leader, Clark went out of his way to distance the Big Blue Machine. He had the same problems in the caucus that Stanfield had had in 1968, and he may have been more sensitive to them as a Westerner. He never seemed comfortable with the Toronto boys or their mechanistic, marketing view of politics, and he certainly wasn't prepared to meet their demands for full authority over the organization. Atkins, for his part, was unwilling to play a subservient role. He couldn't be sure he'd be able to do his job as he thought it should be done. Moreover, he worried that Clark's slightly paranoid reluctance to associate himself with smarter people might jeopardize the "open tent" attitude Atkins believed was necessary to attract the best people to a team.

"Norman was prepared to do something at one stage," Finlay MacDonald said, "but not in a half-measured way. Joe clearly gave the impression that the boys weren't needed, so they said, 'Screw it.' "

For the 1979 federal election Atkins was appointed by

Davis to be the link between the Ontario organization and its national counterpart. Clark was informed of that in a letter, but Atkins was called only once and visited only once. According to Clark's campaign chairman, Lowell Murray, Atkins was unenthusiastic when approached and even tried to discourage any of the boys from joining Murray. Only a few did. Instead of an all-out Ontario effort that might have made the difference between Clark's minority and a majority, little happened. "It was as if the body-snatchers had passed through Ontario, it was so dead," said one witness.

In the 1980 election, after the energy-pricing battles between the Clark government and Queen's Park, Davis withheld his support. The Big Blue Machine, which had had its origins in federal politics, had settled down in Ontario. It had expanded its connections, honed its skills, and become more and more involved with the provincial government. Atkins estimated that between 1976 and 1983 he was in Ottawa only four times. "We found a home," he said, "and a leader who understood the approach we enjoyed working with."

III

William Davis's first term had not been considered a success. He moved in a hasty and rather insensitive manner on a number of controversial fronts, such as the imposition of regional governments on Ontario cities, and he was seen as a remote individual surrounded by bureaucrats. There was a touch of scandal involving shady election contributions and building contracts (which led to a commission under Dalton Camp on the funding of political parties), and the press developed an adversarial stance that was new to the province. By 1974 it was apparent that the Tories were in trouble. They lost four high-profile by-elections in a row; they were twelve points behind in the polls; and the grass roots were upset. "Suck in your gut, Daddy," Atkins told the boys as they prepared for the 1975 election, which Atkins was always to judge his most difficult challenge.

About a year before the election was called, Atkins began to assemble an organization, shaping it from a concept on paper to a troop on alert. It had the familiar components: polling, advertising, tour arranging, candidates in place early. At the same time, having a government record to defend, Atkins advised Davis to put more politicians and fewer MBAs into the decision-making process. Polling was used as a way of pinpointing and avoiding problems. A policy committee of fifty or so Tories from around the province was established to meet monthly to discuss directions, difficulties, and organization. The committee executive, including ministers and organizers, began to meet weekly to look at the short-term issues and give advice to Davis, who was now recast as slow, decent, folksy Brampton Billy.

"We were on the run most of the time," Atkins said, "but everyone worked together, no one panicked, and Davis performed well. We turned it around in the last two weeks and won a minority government."

The 1975 Tory victory in Ontario was largely due to the deliberate integration of government action and party machine. In that respect it resembled the 1974 federal Liberal victory, which had been achieved by much the same integration. The lesson wasn't forgotten at Queen's Park. The result was what became known as the Davis style of government: a low-key, gradualist, middle-of-the-road approach that was heavy on consultation, consensus, and public opinion. Leadership was defined as a cautious advancement toward moderate goals. "Make haste slowly" was the motto.

Davis was sometimes willing to act without broad support on issues he believed were right or necessary, from patriation of the constitution to mandatory seat belts. On most matters, however, he was happy to go along with the mood of the province, and he never wanted to get very far ahead of it. For example, though he may have been sympathetic to official bilingualism in Ontario for the sake of national unity—and went further toward it than many in his party would have liked—he refused to go further than the province would comfortably tolerate. While both the party and the opposition were kept in line by a judicious application of rewards and blandishments, Davis's own amiable, obfuscatory personality worked to smother any potential conflicts or sharp debates.

The Davis style was the product of several forces, including the party's heritage since Leslie Frost ("The Great Tranquilizer"), the Tories' minority status in 1975 and again in 1977, and the Premier's own political acumen. But that style clearly encouraged—and was encouraged by—the Big Blue Machine. In essence, the Ontario Conservatives became engaged in a perpetual election campaign. To keep its ear close to the ground and to keep the electorate content, the government incorporated touring, polling, and advertising into governing to a new degree. The mechanisms for contributing to government strategy and policy were broadened to absorb heavier doses of political advice. And Atkins, rather than simply managing a team fielded every four years or so, assumed a greater ongoing role.

"After 1975 he became more involved in the overall strategy of the government and advice on appointments," Davis said. "He wasn't so concerned with the details of policy, but we were good friends by then so he wasn't reluctant to offer advice on almost anything."

Atkins insisted on, and got, direct access to the leader, and he was a regular member of the group of cabinet ministers and party officials who met for breakfast every Tuesday morning at the Park Plaza Hotel in Toronto to advise Davis on current issues. Such was the meshing of government and organization that the people at the breakfast meeting were often referred to, erroneously, as the Big Blue Machine, though Atkins was usually its quietest participant. Indeed, at times everyone from party workers distributing pamphlets to Ontario bureaucrats attending conferences was seen as the Big Blue Machine.

The real machine remained the core team of experienced volunteers who shared a professional concept of winning elections. The core, however, kept expanding. As some of the original associates went on to other jobs—in politics, in the bureaucracy, often in the party organizations of other provinces—Atkins stayed in contact with them. Meanwhile he cultivated the new talent that showed up at each election. "Don't throw away any resources" was one of his slogans, and he made sure no one ever left in pique or got lost by neglect.

"Campaigns are like going to war," he said. "They create strong associations. So we keep in touch by phone or through party functions. I have a policy to try to answer all my calls and to share what I know so that everyone feels included and trusted."

Much of Atkins's power came from his being the friendly spider at the centre of an intricate and extensive web; much of the power that others derived from him came from the inside knowledge he could share and the favours he could do. As his network and his influence grew, the quality of his advice improved. Bill Davis came to understand that speaking to Atkins was in effect speaking to a wide range of informants well placed in the party and the province. That lent clout to Atkins's opinions on issues or appointments. His clout, in turn, strengthened his ability to keep the machine in running order.

In some ways it is more difficult to maintain a successful machine than an unsuccessful one, as the federal Liberals discovered in Quebec during the 1984 election. In a successful political organization, hunger, ambition, and the fun dissipate. Arrogance, complacency, and fatigue set in. The veterans are less likely to move on or be pushed out; fresh blood is less eagerly sought. The dreams of power meet the realities of government, and distance opens up between the grass roots and the party brass. Despite Atkins's eye for new talent and his conviction that a party is strong only with strong riding associations, the Big Blue Machine came to be seen in some quarters as a self-serving clique more intent on protecting the interests of the leadership than advancing the wishes of the membership. "If you haven't got a past with Norman," some said, "you haven't got a future."

The charges of cliquism were for the most part another case of jealousy, ambition, and outsiders wanting to move in. In fact, there was less anti-Establishment feeling at the party's conventions in January and November, 1985, than there had been in 1971, and neither Atkins nor most of his colleagues had the backgrounds or manner of the social elite. The Big Blue Machine was more like a service club, a kind of political Order of Raccoons. It engaged in male bonding of the beer commercial variety, often excluding women from the events where decisions were made and deals cemented; but Atkins as the Grand Raccoon became adept at massaging as many people as possible with the balm of power, from chances to hobnob with the famous to the thousands of jobs, contracts, and goodies left to the discretion of the leader. He consulted broadly, he didn't ignore merit or social justice, and he always remembered that excessive patronage could backfire at the polls.

No, the real problem was that the "new politics" seriously threatened the traditional role of ordinary people in politics. Atkins considered himself just another volunteer and saw his organization simply as hundreds, if not thousands, of party members working for a cause they believed in. But the demand for expert skills and professional methods couldn't avoid undermining old-fashioned participation. Nancy McLean went so far as to describe many of the technical people associated with the Big Blue Machine as "mercenaries in a sea of missionaries," not because they made money from the process (most of them didn't, at least not directly) but because they tended to give their heads more than their hearts. Dalton Camp agreed that polling, advertising, and advance men made politics "less party-centred and people-centred, more money-centred and professional."

Atkins often said that the Big Blue Machine was held together by "friendship, loyalty, and principle." The first two were obvious and only really interesting to those who were in or wanted in. The third was complex and of great significance to Canadian politics. At that level the Machine became an ideology, a way of viewing power and society, more than an address book. Whether in elections or in government, this group of people generally believed in moderate, centrist politics. It used scientific methods as well as networks and intuition to discover where the centre was. It shaped policies to suit that centre. And then it employed all the latest techniques of mass marketing to sell them back to the centre, whence they were derived. From these basic beliefs everything else flowed: the professional cadre of like-minded organizers, incremental change instead of confrontation, consultation instead of action, compromise instead of conviction, publicity instead of argument, circumstances instead of will.

In Ontario under Davis almost nothing was done without a thorough and sober assessment of the political ramifications; and since the province was more left of centre than the Tory Party, so were Davis and Atkins. Whether buying into an oil company to have "a window on the industry" or controlling rents or spending heavily on social programs, there was little the Davis government did that the federal Liberals wouldn't have done, though Davis usually waited for Ottawa or another province to take the initiative so that he wouldn't rock any boats. Even the NDP found it hard to criticize Davis's actions and kept the Conservatives in power during their minority periods. By bland competence, reasonable openness and honesty, and liberal programs that often stopped short of making any waves, Queen's Park became as plump and docile as a glorified municipal government, till many people simply forgot it was there. As a result, thanks in part to the even split between the Ontario Liberals and NDP but in large measure to the organizational and strategic wizardry of the Big Blue Machine, Davis won a majority government in 1981.

"The electoral machine has become a way of governing," said Bob Rae, the leader of the Ontario New Democrats, soon after Bill Davis announced his retirement in 1984. "Wherever the leadership thinks the centre is going, it follows. That makes it very difficult to attack. It also stifles healthy debate and blunts real choice."

"Bland works," Davis once said. It was a legitimate political philosophy, as legitimate as Trudeau's concept of the strategic prime-ministership, and it was based on Davis's remarkable sense of his people and knowledge of his province. Basically, and more than any other region, Ontario reflects Canada's political culture. Once the bastion of Macdonald Toryism, it became the key vote behind Trudeau Liberalism. It may not have liked Trudeau's methods, his personality defects, or his economic record, but on the great issues of state—national unity, centralization, patriation, government intervention—it was more social democratic than classic liberal. Part of the shift was due to urbanization and immigration, which gave traditional Grit centres a new electoral clout and made Toronto a Roman Catholic city full of ridings controlled by New Canadians. Part of the shift was due to Ontario's position in a changing federation and the practical matters that followed from that, such as energy prices, protection, and fiscal transfers. Another part was due to the change in Canadian liberalism from Macdonald to Trudeau. After all, the CCF almost beat George Drew in 1943 and the NDP was the official opposition in 1975. Davis knew that the centre of Ontario was left of centre on the spectrum, so the only way to win was to play to that position.

That truth was reinforced by what happened after Davis retired. At the leadership convention in January, 1985, the traditional, rural, and small-town delegates expressed their displeasure at having been relegated to second place in the leadership's considerations by voting for a rustic, right-wing candidate named Frank Miller. An amiable man who had lifted himself from poverty to millionaire status by hard work, shrewd investments, and salesmanship, Miller didn't blush to wear tartan jackets or call himself "the new Reagan" of Ontario. He was best known for trying to close a number of hospitals across the province when Minister of Health. He favoured extra-billing by doctors and selling off Ontario's share in Suncor; he didn't like rent controls and official bilingualism; and his regular pitch was on the glories of free enterprise.

Miller squeaked in on the third ballot, partly because the moderate candidates had been divided going into the convention, partly because his views reflected those of many delegates, but mostly because the final option was him or Larry Grossman, a progressive, urban Jew. The Big Blue Machine knew that Miller would be a mistake. Many of its members, including Allan Gregg and Hugh Segal, were with Grossman from the beginning, while Norman Atkins assembled another contingent behind his close friend Roy McMurtry.

Miller's victory demonstrated a number of important facts about the Big Blue Machine. Though Atkins shamelessly exploited every personal debt, moral argument, and political reason, he couldn't bring all his associates to McMurtry's camp. They knew that he'd be hurt by their refusals, but they also knew he wouldn't be vindictive. The Machine was not a regiment. It was a free and rather fragile group of individuals who could leave it for the least cause or a higher loyalty. And for all its influence and talent, it couldn't impose its will if the people wouldn't buy the candidates or policies that the organization had to sell. Miller's victory also demonstrated that power alone was not enough to attract the Machine's help. The help was dependent upon moderate policies, personal rapport, and freedom to act as necessary.

The new Premier of Ontario was as aware as every other politician that a modern, experienced organization can pluck victory from the jaws of defeat or come up with a majority in a close election. Miller would have been foolish to throw away such valuable human resources. Immediately after the convention he made polite overtures to Atkins and even asked him to serve as campaign chairman for the approaching election. Atkins couldn't have said no. He had a duty to party unity; his usual conditions of access to the leader and full authority seemed to have been met; and he couldn't risk being held responsible for a poor Tory showing. But the inherent difficulties soon became apparent. Miller wasn't close to the boys, his biases were reactionary, and his own right-wing novices were manoeuvring for control.

Within a week of Atkins's acceptance of the post, Miller changed his mind and appointed Patrick Kinsella instead. Though Kinsella was a veteran of the Big Blue Machine and had been Davis's campaign manager in 1981, he had less conviction about the need for moderation. He saw himself on the party's right and had been Bill Bennett's chief adviser when the Premier of British Columbia intro-

duced his harsh restraint programs in 1983. That was probably why Miller recognized a better chemistry with him
than with Atkins. Atkins's reaction was predictable. "If
the new leader doesn't want the help of the Big Blue Machine," he had said before the convention, "he won't get
it." Now he told Miller, "You've made your decision, Premier. I wish you luck."

As it turned out, Frank Miller needed more than luck.
He needed troops out in numbers. He needed advance
men who could get crowds to public meetings. He needed
media advisers who could take advantage of his folksy
charms and halt his deteriorating image with the press.
He needed strategists who could turn him into a progressive candidate. He needed policies to capture the urban,
immigrant vote. Though some of the party faithful stayed
home out of revolt against Miller's acceptance of Davis's
parting promise to extend the public funding of Roman
Catholic schools, the real erosion of support came from
the Liberals' ability to steal back the left-of-centre constituency between Miller and Rae. On May 2 the Tories dropped
from seventy-two seats to fifty-two, while the Liberals picked
up forty-eight and the NDP got twenty-five. In June, in a
desperate attempt not to lose power after more than forty
years, the Tories introduced a Speech from the Throne
that borrowed blatantly from the promises and rhetoric of
the two opposition parties. In January Miller had said,
"Ontario doesn't need another Liberal Party, Ontario doesn't
need another NDP." Now he said, "If you start on the
right, then go to the left, you end up in the centre." The
centre, however, was already occupied. Through an agreement with the NDP, the Liberals were able to bring down
Miller and form a government. That agreement was probably an accurate reflection of where Ontario's political culture was. Indeed, within a few months Premier David
Peterson even began to look like William Davis.

The full participation of the Big Blue Machine might
not have affected the outcome enough to have kept Miller
in office. However, as in the case of Joe Clark in the 1979
and 1980 federal elections, eliminating the grosser errors
and gaining just a few more seats could have made a dif-

ference. In the end, the product the Ontario Tories tried to sell wasn't as good as the brand the Liberals were pushing with many of the Big Blue Machine's own tricks. A poll taken after the election found that 53 per cent said Frank Miller was a weakness for his party. In August he got the message and resigned. In November another convention elected Larry Grossman as leader. For many traditional Tories, being in opposition overcame their aversion to Grossman and Toronto. And since he was supported by most of the Big Blue Machine, including Norman Atkins, his victory was a signal that it was welcome to carry on. The lesson had been learned: winning elections had become a science more than an art—the right ingredients applied to the right recipes—and to the holder of the magic formula went the spoils.

The importance of the Ontario formula was that, more often than not, the national spoils depended upon it too. In purely numerical terms, the federal Tories usually needed to win most of the province's ninety-five seats in order to overcome the Liberals' historical advantage in Quebec. In purely political terms, Ontario was the swing province and metropolitan Toronto was the swing area of that province. In other words, that was the "market" in which the Liberals and the Tories would be competing most fiercely. Moreover, in ideological terms, it came closest to representing the national market.

As the birthplace of English Canada's political culture, as the heartland of the economy, as the centre of media, as the locomotive of the federation—for better or worse— urban Ontario's thinking had impact far beyond mere population. Brian Mulroney knew that Ontario had denied Joe Clark a majority in 1979 and a victory in 1980. He wasn't going to make Clark's mistake of alienating the Big Blue Machine, either as an election team or a philosophy.

IV

During the federal Tory leadership campaign of 1983, Brian Mulroney telephoned Norman Atkins and asked, "If and when I win the leadership, would you be willing to help me put together an organization for the election and assist me when I'm Prime Minister?"

Despite their friendship, Atkins hadn't supported Mulroney's leadership bid in 1976, because he had seen Mulroney as too hot, too fast, and too inexperienced; and when Joe Clark unexpectedly called the June convention in 1983, Atkins had seen a chance to fulfil a dream that had been nurtured quietly in his mind and heart for a long while: to make Bill Davis the Prime Minister of Canada. Atkins thought that Davis would be the best choice and could win both the convention and the next election. That thinking was often cited as an example of Atkins's loyalty overpowering his good political sense. The federal party was realizing that it couldn't make advances in Quebec without a bilingual leader, and Davis's candidacy was bound to provoke divisive counterattacks from Peter Lougheed, Grant Devine, and the western caucus in Ottawa. For weeks Atkins and his allies appealed to Davis to run, but ultimately the latter's own acumen—coupled with his reluctance to move to Ottawa and take on greater responsibilities—kept him out of the race.

Mulroney's call to Atkins may have been a coy attempt to get support from Davis and a number of influential Ontario delegates during the campaign, but he proved he was serious. On the night he won the leadership, Mulroney met Atkins by chance in the CBC broadcast booth. He asked if they could get together the next day. Atkins agreed, and their general discussion about how Atkins might help led to a couple of phone calls during the summer. That September, after Mulroney won a by-election in Nova Scotia, he again called Atkins, and they met at Kingsmere, outside Ottawa, for four hours. By the end of that meeting Atkins had agreed to be the Tories' campaign chairman for the next federal election.

Mulroney knew there would be resistance from people in the caucus and at national headquarters to the Atkins appointment. There were those who still associated Atkins with Camp and the Diefenbaker leadership review, others who feared the influence of Davis and Ontario or hadn't forgotten the Big Blue Machine's coolness in the 1979 and

1980 elections, and some who expected power to be given to Mulroney's long-time supporters rather than to an outsider. To these tensions were added Atkins's usual demands: he wanted direct access to the leader and he wanted to be free to recruit the best people available, regardless of their past connections. For example, Atkins wanted to use Allan Gregg as the party's pollster, even though Gregg had been a high-profile adviser to Joe Clark in the 1983 leadership race and had incurred Mulroney's strongest hostility. "We were in the shithouse with the Mulroney gang for quite a while," Gregg said, "but we deliberately didn't try to ingratiate ourselves. We left it to Norman to solve the problem, and he did."

It was a tribute to Mulroney's political wit that he was able to overcome his heartfelt fidelity to his cronies and his gut instinct (never forget, never forgive) to get Atkins onside. That open-minded commitment to professionalism was just the gesture certain to make Norman Atkins serve Brian Mulroney as eagerly as he had served Bill Davis. It also allowed Atkins to assemble a team in which talent was the only priority.

Not surprisingly, though it drew on many old adversaries from John Diefenbaker's time and Joe Clark's government (including Lowell Murray), almost every senior post was filled by someone associated with the Big Blue Machine. Besides Gregg, there was Tom Scott, the chairman of the Sherwood Communications Group, who had done the Ontario Tories' advertising since 1971, in charge of the national advertising campaign; Harry Near, a Davis advance man in the 1975 Ontario election, as director of operations; Paul Curley, a veteran of the 1975 and 1977 Ontario elections, as campaign secretary; Jerry Lampert, once the Machine's Eastern Ontario organizer, as co-director of Mulroney's tour; and in various front-room and back-room capacities Patrick Kinsella, Malcolm Wickson, Brian Armstrong, Hugh Segal, Finlay MacDonald, and Dalton Camp.

Shortly after Atkins came aboard in the fall of 1983, there were troubles. The most immediate was a turf fight between the campaign committee and some of the Leader of the Opposition's staff. The fight was partly a struggle for influence, but it was also partly the result of Mulroney's management style of setting up opposing camps, dealing with them both, and hoping never to have to choose between them. There were serious misunderstandings and conflicts, including a plan to set up a second, separate polling unit in Mulroney's office. Atkins's first reaction to power games was to try with infinite patience to talk out the difficulties. If that failed, his second reaction was to walk away. At one point he felt his authority so threatened that he wondered if he could stay. It took Camp and MacDonald to persuade him that he couldn't leave gracefully, that he was being too patient, and that he needed to exert his power.

Ironically, Atkins's abhorrence of confrontation was more often an asset than a fault. Not only did it engender the loyalty and affection that made him so effective in the long run, it permitted him to control the show. Though vulnerable to criticism and sensitive to others, he tended, once he was given *carte blanche*, to plough ahead in the straightforward manner he considered professional. "I wish Norman could take a little water with his wine," Mulroney once lamented, but in the end he gave Atkins what Atkins wanted.

Atkins's second hurdle in planning the Conservative campaign was to make peace with the caucus. Again his way was patience. He went to caucus meetings, made presentations about what he had in mind and what the problems were, visited those Tory MPs who didn't know or trust him, and proved that he knew what he was doing. His guilelessness and good nature served him well. "Those he didn't win, he silenced," Camp said, "and his task was made easier by the Tories' drop in the polls. That caused some people to back off, preferring to let someone else be responsible for driving the bus off the bridge, while it made others recognize the seriousness of doing things well. It also made Mulroney more decisive about allocating particular functions."

Even though Atkins was confident that the Liberals' upsurge during their leadership race was a temporary phenomenon, he never underestimated the problems of breaking the "incumbency barrier," the general bias toward keeping the people in power there because of their experience and all the favours that power can hand out. Often the only chance to persuade people to change their vote is to out-organize and out-perform the governing party in the election campaign. By February, 1984, he had developed his organization chart and had begun to place his personnel in their appropriate roles. He found campaign chairmen in each province and got them to apply his organization concept at the provincial and constitutency levels. He urged that the Tory candidates be nominated quickly and sent out to shake hands immediately. In many ways he simply implemented the same basic organization he had used since 1971, but now he had huge sums of money, scores of veterans, a national range, the most advanced technology, and his own twenty-five years of practice.

While the Liberal leadership contenders were grabbing the headlines throughout the spring of 1984, Atkins took Mulroney quietly across the country, to small towns and grass-roots associations, in order to test his appeal and perfect his campaign techniques. "First of all, we found out that people liked him, so we were competitive," Atkins said. "Then the procedure was to find out what he was comfortable doing and design a campaign around that. A candidate can be 'campaign-conditioned' to adjust to the different demands, but he can't be packaged really. You can't make someone into something he isn't."

True, but you can protect someone from something he is. Gradually, Mulroney's handlers smoothed out his rough edges. Before long Brian Mulroney hardly went out in public without a little flattering make-up on. At great personal sacrifice he even gave up smoking—with the same determination and for the same career benefits that he had given up alcohol—and the weight he gained as a result did as much to solidify his dignity as putting a stop to his furtive, addict-like drags. His more irresponsible flights of hyperbole were checked, his cheaper shots were discouraged, and the Iron Ore Company was less often held up as the model after which the country would be run.

"As a leadership candidate Brian made himself the champion of small business, business, and the ideological right," Atkins said, "but when he became leader and encountered the responsibilities of leadership, and the questions of how to consolidate the party from coast to coast and how to present himself and the party to the public, he found those kinds of ideologies have to be tailored to the realities."

Suddenly, finally, John Turner sprung the election in July. Atkins was surprised but ready to go. "We have a myth to protect!" he yelled to his team.

"To step from the Liberals' headquarters to Norman's offices in Ottawa was to step from the horse-and-buggy age into a jet aircraft factory," Camp said. "He had an awesome, state-of-the-art organization."

There was, for example, an electronic mail system of computer terminals linking together more than two hundred ridings. It enabled Atkins to communicate instantly across the country the same themes, problems, and pep talks he shared with anyone who walked through his open door. In that respect, it was just a technological extension of his old adage that organization is nothing but people and communications. "If you let people know what you have in mind," he said, "they feel like they're participants and therefore they put in the extra effort." At the same time, and for the first time, he communicated directly to the national electorate as *the* spokesman for the Tory machine in the media. He was surprised by how much he enjoyed it and how good he was at it. Talking in front of a television camera was somehow less intimidating than talking in front of an audience.

"Norman proved perfect for the thirty-second clip," Allan Gregg joked, "because he seldom speaks longer than that anyway." In fact, Atkins proved perfect for politics in the television age. With his concern for means rather than ends, with his skills in techniques rather than ideas, and with his emphasis on elections rather than government, he had been carried as if by magic into a position of great influence. But the magic was rooted in the solid, practical base of middle Canada. For all his success Atkins remained without pretension. His office at Camp Advertising was designer-modern in elegant grey, but he marred its modernity with photographs of his wife and three sons, his political saints from Robert Stanfield to William Davis, as well as a portrait of Dalton Camp. His home was a neat bungalow in Markham, a suburb outside Toronto, with landscape paintings by Roy McMurtry in the living room and more talk about sports than politics around the kitchen table. If his domestic life resembled a situation comedy, a combination of *The King of Kensington* and *My Three Sons*, that may have been another case of life imitating art: most evenings Norman Atkins liked to collapse in front of his TV set with the remote-control switcher in his hand and idly flip from station to station.

"Norman doesn't read the newspapers," Camp said, "and he's probably better off for that. He's not influenced by things that *don't matter*. Why should he care what the columnists think? They don't carry any weight. Only the politicians think that columnists carry weight."

As a result, Camp continued, during the election Atkins "was only rarely interested in the grand strategic stuff. It's hard to get a handle on his true genius, but it has something to do with administrative detail. He gets people to confront particular problems, not to generalize or woolgather. He cares that when the leader gets up, the hall is full, everyone has been consulted, the plane has arrived on time, the baggage is there, the bar is set up, the leader is rested and watered and fed and has something in his hands to read. What that something is isn't Norman's business."

In most campaigns the strategy is determined by a group of political advisers, who correlate various inputs, assess how things are going from a reasonable distance, and then recommend words, ideas, and policies to the leader as he zooms from coast to coast using almost all his energy just trying to get up in the morning, give the speeches, answer the questions, stay coherent and pleasant, and not trip up. That was the type of role Dalton Camp had played for Robert Stanfield, Lowell Murray had played for Joe Clark, and Jim Coutts had played for Pierre

Trudeau. Their advice usually dictated where the leader should go, what he should say, and how the advertising money should be spent—really the only three important things that a campaign team can control. In the Tory campaign of 1984, however, the process was reversed.

"At the risk of immodesty," Allan Gregg said, "the research was the strategy. In 1979 and 1980 Lowell Murray had been more the creator than the custodian of the strategy. But Norman's style was to do everything by jungle drum, that is, to get everyone pounding the same beat without anyone deciding this is the beat we're going to play. He had lots of committees, including one called 'Strategy and Planning' that met every Tuesday, but most of them did nothing or were a waste of time. The real strategy was decided in memos from me or before the martinis came out at Finlay MacDonald's place, where Norman was staying. Fundamentally what happened about the tour, the advertising, and the local riding campaigns *became* the strategy, and functionally all the concepts about them came out of the polling data."

Gregg's firm, Decima, polled every night, and by eleven o'clock every morning the leader and the organization were briefed about developing trends and problem areas. Not only had polling become remarkably sophisticated, able to discover the attitudes and values beneath people's intentions and desires, it had become remarkably thorough. Besides doing national polls, Decima tracked twenty-five bellwether ridings in detail every day. By playing the macro- and micro-numbers according to complicated mathematical formulas, it could accurately predict the outcome of the election, find the places that needed a visit by the leader, see what issues sold best in different regions and how best to sell them, figure out what the national advertising should look like, and even determine phrases for the leader's speeches. The findings kept everyone focussed on what was important.

"Norman relied very, very heavily on the numbers," Gregg said. "If people were arguing about what was right or wrong, he'd say there was no point arguing and send us into the field."

For example, because of the extraordinary number of promises Mulroney was making as he criss-crossed the country, the question of their cost surfaced as a major issue in the media and Liberal speeches. In the old, event-driven campaigns someone would eventually have yelled, "We have to do something, we've got to come up with some figures!" Gregg's polls provided a new, sober opinion. They showed that most voters weren't worried about the specific cost. They weren't ignorant, but in the absence of evidence that the promises couldn't be afforded, they were willing to give Mulroney the benefit of the doubt. The result was more discipline, less chaotic reaction, in how the campaign was conducted.

From the data, Decima produced over one hundred memos during the campaign. There was a weekly macro-concepts memo. Regular memos about Mulroney's speeches, his tour, and the advertising program were issued, as well as specific memos about the leadership debates and the women's forum. There were three sets of memos examining the twenty-five tracked ridings one by one, and covering everything from what the local candidates should do to where they should put up their signs. Basically these memos guided the politicians and the organizers through an interpretation of the raw statistics. In many cases the interpretation was what gave Allan Gregg his power. Barely into his thirties at the time, fond of wearing jeans, a T-shirt, a punkish hairstyle, and a diamond earring like the rock musician he once dreamed of being, Gregg was very bright and dynamically articulate. His rapid, confident, often entertaining patter had a postmodern theatricality to match his appearance. His delivery mesmerized like that of a midway salesman pitching the latest gadget that diced, sliced, mixed and crunched—except the stuff Gregg diced, sliced, mixed, and crunched was ideas and numbers instead of carrots and onions.

His data revealed that the one overwhelming issue was the desire for change. Since that could have implied anything, however, Gregg was left to define it more precisely. He found that Canadians were more concerned with changing the *process* of governing than with major new directions in policy. They had had enough of confrontation politics; they wanted Ottawa to deal with their priorities, which were economic, rather than become absorbed in its own preoccupations, such as the constitution; and they wanted open consultations and accountable leaders. In other words, after Trudeau's last wars, they wanted peace. But peace precluded any distressing attacks on the new status quo. Because the old patterns of spending and government intervention didn't seem to have worked too well, the voters were willing to consider new approaches toward job creation and growth, but they weren't ready for new risks, new upheavals, or right-wing attacks on social programs and sacred cows such as Petro-Canada.

These results coincided with—and reinforced—Brian Mulroney's own instincts and talents. As Camp said, the new leader was one of the "sane, reliable, rational" Tories. He was not only philosophically close to Stanfield, Davis, and the Big Blue Machine, he was socially close to many important Liberals. Jealousy and competitiveness may have made him hate the Liberals' condescension, corruption, and phony populism, but the hatred was just a negative expression of flattery, as proven by his imitations. Mulroney hated the Liberals so much because he wanted to be them; or, conversely, he was what he hated. That was obvious in his slick style, which had caused such discomfort to many Tories during the party's leadership race, and it soon became obvious in his policies. Winning the leadership had required him to stress certain phrases, strike certain poses, but Mulroney knew that winning the country required other phrases, other poses. Like Jack he had climbed the beanstalk, rummaged among the giant's things, and run off with the magic formula that had kept the Liberals in power.

"Brian hasn't had two thoughts in his life," a friend said, "but he has terrific Irish instincts." Well before the Big Blue Machine started pumping him with advice and data, those instincts served him brilliantly. They enabled him and his party to dodge the huge traps the Liberals set for them, any one of which could have kept the Tories from victory. In particular, there were the debates over whether Ottawa should act to protect French-language rights in Manitoba and whether extra-billing by doctors should be allowed to jeopardize the health care available to everyone. Knowing the emotional divisions that existed within the Tory caucus on both these issues, the Liberal strategists hoped to force the opposition into revealing itself as soft on minority rights and social programs, so that neither francophones nor lower-income Canadians would be fooled by the dulcet tone of the new leader. Instead, Mulroney hammered his caucus into backing the government's policies.

"I told these guys that it's my way or the way out," he said of his colleagues who resisted his stance on the Manitoba issue. "Hell, what are these guys thinking about? That's what being an opposition party for too long does to you, you tend to confuse prejudice and policies. Bilingualism is the goddamn law of the land! We are either for it or against it, and as long as I'm leader, we are for it!"

Though he had to apply a large stick to his more reactionary MPs, many of whom had supported him for the leadership in order to get rid of that "Red Tory" Joe Clark, he brought most along by simply dangling the fat carrot of power in front of their noses. "This is the way to win," he used to tell them, "and I don't know about you guys, but that's where I'm going."

Mulroney played brilliantly to get himself into the winning position. In fact, he only seriously erred once. Barely a week into the campaign, in the course of what he thought was an off-the-record rap with reporters on his election plane, Mulroney was asked about the controversial patronage appointments Turner had made, most of them on Trudeau's behalf, the day the election was announced. The appointments included sending a gang of seventeen Liberal MPs to various heavens, such as the Senate, the bench, and other secure and lucrative government posts. The most controversial was the naming of Bryce Mackasey as ambassador to Portugal.

Some of the appointments were pay-offs for long or faithful service that Trudeau had to make before he retired. Mackasey fell into this category. He had badgered Trudeau for a diplomatic posting with his own unique combination of Montreal Irish malarky and droopy-eyed beseeching until the Prime Minister of Canada cried uncle. Trudeau did warn him, however, that an ambassadorship could be rescinded as easily as it was bestowed; but after scurrying off and returning, Mackasey told Trudeau that both Mulroney and Turner had promised they wouldn't take it away if it was given. Other appointments were added at Turner's request so as to make room for changes in his new cabinet. Thus, Mark MacGuigan became a judge and Eugene Whelan was promised a new embassy in Rome to let Turner move out two ministers who had run against him as leadership candidates.

Trudeau was fully prepared to make the appointments and take the heat that was expected to arise as a result. However, Turner was worried about losing the Liberal majority in the House of Commons and being unable to form a government. If he called an election immediately, that certainly wouldn't have been a problem. Even if he delayed the election, there were ways to avoid a problem. But Turner was getting poor and conflicting advice that seemed to confuse him. In fact, he dithered from day to day, sometimes saying he would make the appointments, then changing his mind and asking Trudeau to make them. At one point, a cabinet order was drawn up for Trudeau to make them, but at the last moment Turner again changed his mind. Finally, at his own insistence, he signed an agreement with Trudeau to hand out the jobs as soon as it was safe to do so.

It was a wretched mistake. The shameless rewarding of Liberals—particularly Mackasey, whose competence, ethics, and porkbarrelling had been issues of public debate more than once—symbolized what many Canadians found more offensive about the party than its policies. Those same fat faces had been feeding at the trough for so long, they had grown to look upon it as their private preserve. They represented the kind of politics of which many voters had had enough. By appearing to do Trudeau's dirty work, Turner tarred himself with the old brush just as he set out to try to convince people that he rejected the old ways.

Then, on the campaign plane, Mulroney tossed away his wonderful advantage as stupidly as Turner had. "If I'd been in Bryce's position," he was reported as saying, "I'd have been right in there with my nose in the public trough like the rest of them." He added, either of himself or Mackasey (though it hardly mattered), "There's no whore like an old whore."

Neither the language nor the thought came as a shock to those who knew Brian Mulroney. During the Tory leadership race he had demonstrated his high regard for the grease that makes the political wheels go round. He often took an Irishman's delight in the boggy side of human nature. But the electorate still believed in his freshly scrubbed, altar-boy pieties about the evil of patronage. It *wanted* to believe in them. Suddenly he had exposed himself as no better than the last rotten bunch.

"People in the party thought this a bad thing to happen," Atkins said, "and it would have lingered. It was the one place where we might have won or lost the election depending on how we handled things."

The first idea was to lie and say that Mulroney had been misquoted. But that wouldn't have cleaned up the doubts. So, in a dramatic and rare intervention that proved the value of experience and expert advice, Norman Atkins insisted that Mulroney admit he was wrong to have *kidded* about such a serious matter. Perhaps it was astonishing that so many people bought that apology, but faith, hope, and charity prevailed. Certainly Pierre Trudeau had never admitted being wrong about anything, so even a duplicitous admission seemed something. Besides, no actor outside a nineteenth-century melodrama could match Brian Mulroney for contrition: the deeply humble voice, the spanked look, the sincere eyes, and the sad hurt that anyone might question his good intentions. Moreover, since Turner had already blotted his copybook, the public could either believe the Mickey Rooney of Canadian politics or vote for the NDP. In the end, Mulroney kept his promise to the nation (if not to Bryce Mackasey): he denied Mackasey the Portuguese embassy. Then, perhaps feeling cleansed, he proceeded to reward Tories in a spree that angered the nation.

Among the beneficiaries of Brian Mulroney's gratitude was Norman K. Atkins. For the first time since the days of John Diefenbaker, Camp Advertising received a major share of the federal government's tourism advertising account, worth about $24 million. It was merely the first payment of the enormous debt Mulroney owed Atkins for his brilliant and innovative piece of strategy: since you've been caught red-handed, you might as well try honesty.

V

"It was a trap," a Liberal insider said of the Tory general strategy, "and John Turner walked right into it."

If Mulroney's ingenious defences merely neutralized the Liberals' game plan under Trudeau, they gave the Tories an offensive capability under John Turner. Turner's ambiguity on language rights and his Bay Street economic message allowed Mulroney to become the obvious heir to Trudeau in French Canada and for the more forward looking in English Canada. In other words, Brian Mulroney finally succeeded in getting the Tories to the left of the Liberal Party.

The inherent danger for the Liberals wasn't some abstract superstition based on Keith Davey's old shibboleth. It was a concrete threat based on numbers. During the nadir of Liberal popularity in 1982, polls showed that the disaffection was least among the party's basic alliance of francophones, women, and lower-income Canadians. That meant that the party was most likely to regain support from those three groups and *had to* if it wanted any chance of staying in power. No one was under any illusions about how painstaking the task and how uncertain the result would be. With Trudeau there was some hope: he had a magic hold on French Canadians, he had some credibility in pitting himself as a man of the people against the former president of the Iron Ore Company, and his peace crusade was especially well received by women. With Turner none of these was true.

What Turner did have—a new face, a clean record, a fresh approach—he quickly threw away. Most Canadians hadn't paid much attention to his clarifications and rustiness during the Liberal leadership campaign. As the upswing in the polls showed, they were willing to give him a chance to be the agent of the change in process that they desired. In fact, Allan Gregg discovered that the public was "rooting" for Turner. There was still something about Brian Mulroney that many people didn't trust, and Turner was in a unique position to offer both continuity and reform. However, underneath the apparent swing back to the Liberals was an overlooked detail: while more voters were ready to vote for them again, fewer than half were really certain how they would vote and, of those who were certain, the Liberals trailed the Tories. In other words, most people were remaining undecided until John Turner proved he was the agent of change they sought.

"From the standpoint of the Liberal Party," said Angus Reid, a Turner pollster, "the underlying weakness of their vote was, I believe, not fully appreciated. If it had been, I think that both the timing of the election call and the early strategy in the campaign would have been much different."

Indeed, the Liberals suffered a huge loss in the undecided vote in the very first week of the campaign. The patronage pact disillusioned many voters, particularly women, who tended to show a more idealistic view of the political system than men. Also many voters had been discouraged by seeing most of the same old bunch in Turner's cabinet, including Marc Lalonde as Minister of Finance. Turner had been unable to recruit any impressive new talent in such a short time and he had many IOUs to those who had supported his leadership bid, but his excuses only highlighted his inability to put a new stamp on the old inheritance. Worse, he fundamentally misunderstood what the voters wanted.

"The Liberal campaign failed to adequately distinguish between the public's desire for a change in management but not in policy," Reid said. "In the early weeks of the election campaign the Liberal Party was mis-positioned because it appeared to have kept the management and changed the policy." Reid likened the Liberals to a restaurant in decline. The customers' dissatisfaction wasn't with the menu or the quality of the food, but with the arrogance of the staff and generally poor service. They expected a change for the better. Instead, "when the doors were finally opened, many were shocked to see the same waiters and echoes of the arrogance of the former management— chiefly evidenced by the number of tables permanently reserved for special patrons." For those who stayed, the second shock was to see many of their favourite items gone from the menu and nothing very appealing in their place.

At the root of all the Liberals' troubles was John Turner's difficulty in reconciling himself with the Trudeau legacy. Despite what he had learned about the party and the country during the leadership race, he was unable to adjust to the new realities and continued to cling to his outmoded views long after they had been shown a liability. In this he was often misled by his tight circle of advisers, most of whom had been as out of touch with Canadian politics as Turner during the 1970s, many of whom thought the Trudeau Old Guard was trapped in a rigid ideology, and all of whom had a personal interest in dismissing that ideology as a way of displacing its adherents.

"There was a terrible misreading by the guys around Turner that everything related to Trudeau had to be expunged from the party," Michael Kirby said. "Nobody in that group seemed to ask, 'Yes, in some ways the public didn't like Trudeau personally or his economics, but why was he able to run the most successful national political machine in the world for sixteen years?' Instead, they said to ordinary Canadians, to ethnics, to the young, to everyone who had supported Trudeau, 'Boy, what fools you were.' In fact, Trudeau continued to get high ratings. A lot of people hated him and he would *not* have won the election, but he sure would have done better than Turner. Turner had to show people that they could change the government without changing the party, like the Ontario Tories always did. But it was one thing to focus on the economy, it was another to belittle everything the Trudeau government did, to the extent of getting rid of all the pros. Whether we like it or not, election campaigns are professional exercises. By the time Turner brought the pros back in, it was all over. I felt we had been invited to join the Titanic after it hit the iceberg."

In truth, the pros (such as Davey, Goldfarb, Grafstein, and Tom Axworthy) did have input from the beginning, and things might have been better if they hadn't. Not being in charge, they only added to the tensions and confusions already developing between those around the leader and those in the campaign headquarters where Bill Lee, the Ottawa consultant who had managed Turner's leadership campaign, had been placed as head of the first national election he had been involved with since 1972. Unlike Atkins's team, "there was no marriage of egos for the greater good," Jerry Grafstein admitted.

Lee hated Trudeau, Trudeauism, and the Trudeauites. Indeed, after the near-debacle of the 1972 election, he removed himself from politics and Trudeau's fury after advising the Prime Minister to accept blame publicly for the result of his philosophical speeches and constitutional obsessions, announce his retirement, and ask the Governor-General to call on John Turner to form a government. Now, in the summer of 1984, he hit the roof when he discovered that a strategy paper by Tom Axworthy had cost the party $50,000 (Axworthy later returned the money) and another by Goldfarb had cost more than four times that; and he engaged in a vicious, quickly publicized feud with Davey and Grafstein over the work and budgets of Red Leaf Communications, the party's advertising division. André Massé, Turner's communications director, wrote a memo to Lee in which he (Massé) attacked what he considered to be an unaccounted $300,000, unusual salaries and ridiculous cost projections.

As Lee told Finlay MacDonald afterwards, "We started at the precise point of pulling apart where you guys were six months before." Nor did Bill Lee have Norman Atkins's talent for soothing and unifying. He was abrasive, strong-willed, and opinionated. Moreover, he was exhausted from the leadership fight and hadn't wanted to be campaign chairman. To get out of it, he even advised Turner to make Davey chairman, but Davey thought "the optics would be bad." Then Lee suggested John Rae, a vice-president of Power Corporation who had run Chrétien's campaign. Turner was up on the idea after a lunch with Rae, but Rae backed away for personal reasons and Turner didn't pursue him. In the heat of the moment, Turner said (certainly without cause), "Rae will throw the election because that fucking Chrétien still wants to be leader." So Lee was forced into a situation that was soon described as "a zoo," "a disaster area," "a shambles," and "disarrayed panic."

Lee arrived at Liberal headquarters on Ottawa's Bank Street to find virtually nothing ready. That was largely because Tom Axworthy had been planning to run the election out of the PMO if Trudeau stayed as leader. Meanwhile, Turner's eager new team had fired all the Trudeauites in the PMO who knew about Axworthy's election plans. Things were so chaotic, for example, that all the names and phone numbers of the party's organizers in British Columbia were shipped off to the National Archives with Trudeau's papers and sealed for posterity. Then the turf fight began between Lee's budding organization and Turner's gang in the PMO. At various points the PMO denied Lee copies of Turner's speeches in advance and refused to allow Turner's tour director to move into Lee's offices. Soon the new Prime Minister was receiving two sets of briefing books. There were two pollsters (Goldfarb and Reid) providing two different interpretations to sometimes different numbers.

The effect became clearest during the televised leaders' debates. Going into the English debate, Turner heard Keith Davey tell him "to kick Mulroney in the nuts" and Bill Lee tell him "to take the high road." All through the high-pressured situation Turner could hear the two voices arguing in his head. Finally, when the high road didn't seem to be leading anywhere, he launched an attack on Mulroney's patronage statements. That allowed Mulroney to counter with his well-rehearsed indignation about Turner's pact with Trudeau. "I had no option," Turner replied weakly, and Mulroney went in for the kill. "You had an option, sir," he said as he had been told to say. "You could have said, 'I'm not going to do it.' " Given what had really happened and what would happen later, it's impossible to decide which candidate was being more honest or more deceptive in that exchange, but it certainly caused another disillusioned block of voters to slide away from John Turner.

The Liberals' decision to participate in an early debate was another bad move. It gave Mulroney a stature and a momentum he never lost. The decision was forced to an extent when John Turner announced to Lee that he didn't intend to campaign in July. He was tired, he wanted time to brief himself on policies, and he didn't see the need to push with his lead in the polls. Preparing for the debate, therefore, was a camouflage to allow Turner to stay at home; or, as the Prime Minister himself once put it, "Who the hell wants to go to Orillia?"

If the Tories' machine was the model of how-to, the Liberals' operation was an equally instructive demonstration of how-not-to. Because the Liberal organization had coalesced as if by magic in 1980, united in its determination to oust Clark and regain power, everyone assumed that magic could replace hard work. But there was no magic in 1984. Many ridings didn't have Liberal candidates till weeks into the election, and many didn't even have signs up by the end of July. Those that did have candidates had no material or instructions. A polling computer system, similar to the one Gregg used to ferret out and hone in on the key swing vote in each riding, was designed but never put into operation. It, like most of the other failures, was the victim of the party's pathetic financial circumstances. Moreover, unlike Gregg, neither Goldfarb nor Reid was able to commandeer the initial strategy process. Turner himself seemed to have little use for polls, preferring to derive his information *mano a mano* in the old 1960s way. "No one's been able to prove to me that language rights is an important issue," he even said during his leadership campaign, despite all the numbers.

"The pollster was seen as a kind of court jester," Goldfarb lamented, "rather than a reflection of the reality that had to have a response." Thus, to take a small result, the leader's tour was badly planned, with Turner himself getting involved in choosing which ridings he would grace with a visit. He hadn't learned, as Mulroney had, from the mishaps of his leadership run that the candidate shouldn't try to be the hands-on chief executive officer too. Small wonder he found himself covering gruelling distances, facing annoyed reporters, and arriving in half-filled halls.

Taking its tone from the leader, the entire structure valued previous loyalties, closed factions, and elite networks over professionalism and an "open tent" attitude. One of the greatest costs came in Turner's failure to link with Jean Chrétien's popularity. "It is the lack of linkage," Angus Reid found from his studies, "which, I believe, perhaps more than anything else helps to explain some of the electoral failure of the Liberal Party." Whereas Mulroney had worked hard to resolve his conflicts with Clark, Crosbie, and their caucus supporters, Turner hadn't the time nor the will to patch up his differences with Chrétien. Of course, Chrétien was deflated and bitter about his defeat and drove a hard bargain to stay in politics, but he suffered at the hands of Marc Lalonde and André Ouellet, who seemed to carry their animosities from the leadership campaign into their management of the Quebec election machine.

At one point in July Chrétien asked Lee to drop into his office at External Affairs. When Lee arrived, Chrétien evicted his officials in the middle of a meeting and launched into a forty-minute tirade. "People are laughing at me," he shouted. "They're telling me I'm being used to help those guys get back in and then they're going to spit me out! My people are being frozen out in Quebec."

Lee promised to do what he could. He couldn't find Ouellet (because the minister was attending the Los Angeles Olympics!), but he passed on Chrétien's message to Lalonde. "Screw him," Lalonde said. "*We* won and he lost." Meanwhile, Lalonde held a grudge against Lee too. He knew that Lee had advised Turner not to promise Lalonde the Finance portfolio again. Without that promise Lalonde didn't run for re-election. "Don't worry about

Quebec," Lalonde added. "We'll deliver seventy-four or seventy-five seats. Davey always stayed out of Quebec, so you do too."

When Lee reported his conversations to Turner, the Prime Minister said, "Bugger Chrétien. Leave it to Lalonde."

As it happened, nowhere was the collapse of the Liberal Party more spectacular than in Quebec. According to Gregg's polls, a quarter of the province's voters lost their political identity, no longer defining themselves as life-long Liberals, in the ten days that followed the French debate. Mulroney's clear stand on language rights contrasted with Turner's lack of clarity; the debate convinced Quebeckers that Brian Mulroney was obviously one of them and John Turner obviously wasn't; and French Canadians seemed as anxious for a change in process as English Canadians. Not only did Mulroney assume Trudeau's mantle as a federalist and a *chef*, just to be safe he also assumed Joe Clark's strategy of appeasing Quebec nationalism.

For that purpose, he had convinced the Tory caucus to oppose the Liberal government's plan to forbid provinces or their agencies from owning more than 10 per cent of national transportation and pipeline companies. The legislation was intended specifically to prevent a rumoured takeover of Canadian Pacific by Quebec's mammoth pension fund, the Caisse de Dépôt, and it had become a *cause célèbre* in the Quebec media, its nationalist circles, and the Parti Québécois. That and similar gestures, coupled with Mulroney's decision to risk seeking election in Baie Comeau, established the Tories' credibility, while Mulroney's status as a native son, a supplier of patronage, and a defender of minority rights did the rest. The Tories picked up candidates as well as organizers from the ranks of the Parti Québécois.

When John Turner tried to express the same outrage that Brian Mulroney had expressed little more than a year before when known separatists had organized for Joe Clark, Mulroney added his own particular indignation and sorrow to what had been Clark's old defence: these Quebeckers had had a change of heart because of the Tories' sympathetic stance, the third of Quebeckers who had voted

Oui in the referendum couldn't be branded as untoucha-
bles forever, and Ottawa had a duty to negotiate with the
elected provincial government of whatever label for a fair
and honourable constitutional settlement. Gone was all
the table-thumping vitriol about the untrustworthy separatists he had known at Laval; gone was all the convincing
rhetoric about what Quebec should do for Canada. In their
places were sweetness and understanding. If that seemed
like inconsistency or hypocrisy, Mulroney saw it as flexibility or pragmatism. Though bashing the "froggy-froggies" worked well in the Conservative Party, heaping scorn
on the old Liberal confrontations worked better in the
country. His instincts and his polls told him so.

"We could have won with a different campaign," Lalonde insisted, "but we ran a terrible campaign. We took
a lead and we got clobbered. Toward the end we were
dropping a point a day. If the election had been longer,
we would have been wiped out totally. We had only ourselves to blame."

Some Liberals preferred to blame Trudeau, however.
They pointed to the rotten state of the Liberal headquarters
and the bankruptcy of Liberal policy. It was undeniable
that Trudeau took little interest in party matters or that
the energy and clout of the PMO undermined those of the
party executive. However, Trudeau never impeded anyone from putting the party membership list on a computer.
Yet no one did. If anything, the Liberal machine was allowed to decay because Trudeau carried the party to victory on this back, especially in Quebec. The Tories, on the
other hand, had to construct a brilliant organization because that was generally all they had to compete with. It
wasn't until Trudeau departed that the Liberals perceived
how much they had depended on him to raise money,
draw out the workers, and attract votes.

Turner couldn't do the same. His leadership was still
divisive, his speeches were still wooden, and his public
image was still jarring and overheated. He still left a trail
of clarifications, whether to apologize for factual errors or
to explain why he patted women on the bum. Indeed, he
was suffering the fate of the Roman emperor Galba, of

whom Tacitus wrote, "He seemed much greater than a private citizen while he still was a private citizen, and had he never become emperor everyone would have agreed he had the capacity to reign."

By the end of July, in the absence of a popular leader and in the face of defeat, the whole mythic organization began to fall apart. No one would even admit to being in charge on the candidate's plane, because Mrs. Turner had taken to chewing out the staff on it and intimidating Turner into accepting her conflicting advice. On August 3 Lee sent Turner a five-page memo in which he admonished him for trying to run his own campaign and dispersing authority to too many people. "If you don't get the organization in shape quickly, under one person's control," Lee wrote, "you'll be Prime Minister for the shortest reign in Canadian history." Naturally Lee was advancing himself to be the one person in control.

Meanwhile, however, a group of Turner's closest advisers in the PMO, Old Guard pros, and Trudeauites in the cabinet were pressing the Prime Minister to replace Lee with Keith Davey. They felt they needed an architect, not an engineer. Again John Turner felt he had no option. On August 4 he confronted Lee at Harrington Lake, the Prime Minister's summer residence outside Ottawa. Slouched despondently in an armchair, puffing nervously on a cigar, with his eyes hidden behind sunglasses, he told Lee that he couldn't meet the demands in the memo. Then, in one version, Turner informed Lee that he had lost the confidence of the campaign organization and had to go. In other words, as Turner told an adviser later, "I fired him, I fired him, I fired him." In the other version, however, on hearing Turner's refusal Lee wrote out his resignation on the back of the envelope containing the latest disastrous poll from "Gloomy Gus" Reid. Either way, by the end of the meeting Lee was out.

Turner put his arm around him as they walked to Lee's car. "Tell me, Bill, have I sold out to the Old Guard?"

"Yes, John, I'm afraid so," Lee said.

"I just don't know what to do," Turner replied tearfully.

The removal of Lee and the return of "The Rain-

maker"—despite all Turner's rhetoric about "No elites!"
just two months before—caused the greatest drop in Liberal support. If patronage and the debates had begun to
move the undecideds to the Tories, the public revelation
of the party's internal disarray began to make the firm
Liberals think again. Not only was Davey an important
symbolic proof that Turner couldn't be the agent of change,
Turner also lost one of his few assets, his aura of managerial competence. "An organization can't win an election," Norman Atkins often said, "but a bad one can lose
an election." For when the organization itself becomes a
negative issue with the electorate, it's too late to make
anything else the base for a victory.

Keith Davey knew that. He also knew that the critical
time for establishing campaign strategies and policies is
before an election is called, not on the run in the last four
weeks when the party is in a "free fall" in the polls. Once
he raised the spirits of the team, improved the logistics of
the campaign, and worked on the performance of the leader,
his main goal was to try to get the Liberal Party back to
the left as quickly as possible. Far from leaving the party
bankrupt of policies, Trudeau left it with a strong record
and the components for a new agenda. Yet John Turner
and his boys persisted in rejecting both. They wanted to
move from national unity, social programs, and peace to
the economy, and in particular Turner wanted to sound
the alarm about the national debt.

Controlling the federal deficit was a worthy subject and
not necessarily un-Liberal, but every poll indicated that
the vast majority of voters didn't think it was the most
important economic problem. Since there was no consensus and little glory about it, it wasn't an issue around which
to rally the troops, forge a coalition, or stir the masses. In
fact, it disturbed the masses. As Turner said on national
television during the leadership campaign, cutting the deficit "will have to be at the expense of someone." Most
people guessed that "someone" was more likely to be them
than Bay Street. Finally, as well as pushing better issues
into the background, the deficit obsession had the obvious
effect of limiting Turner's ability to make promises. He

even told a strategy committee at the start of the campaign, "We won't make any platform proposals that we can't pay for."

"That was very honest but not very Liberal," Lloyd Axworthy said. "Meanwhile, Mulroney had taken the classic Liberal way of promising everything to everybody at every street corner."

That was true. Mulroney stomped across the country making scores of promises, from restoration of a train service to support for the wine industry to more defence spending. As for the deficit, when he mentioned it at all, he implied in vague terms that it would be tackled by stricter management and the growth which would follow almost naturally from the change in climate brought on by a Tory victory. He didn't talk abut higher taxes, cuts in social programs, or a rethinking of fiscal transfers to the provinces. Indeed, both Michael Wilson and John Crosbie later admitted the Tories hadn't been allowed to talk about the real economic situation in case it let the Liberals regain the left. "There doesn't seem to be an alternative to dishonesty," Crosbie mused with typical exaggeration. Besides, a Decima poll revealed that 74 per cent thought a Tory government should take stock of the situation it discovered in office and then do what's best, *regardless of its promises*. That must have seemed like a licence to lie.

"Promises are always better than no promises," Martin Goldfarb observed. "If you make no promises, the people are in doubt about what you'll do. It's better to have them say, 'You fooled me,' later than not to know where you're taking them."

Before long, Davey had John Turner promising a minimum tax for the rich and saying, "Brian Mulroney is more concerned about free market theory than he is about people." The new strategy was to blend a series of progressive policies with negative attacks on Mulroney's credibility as a "Let's Pretend Liberal" and the "$20-billion Man" with the "hidden agenda." Trust was still one of Turner's few advantages over Mulroney, and Davey intended to play it like he played Trudeau's leadership against Clark in 1980. Liberal television advertisements reminded voters that Mulroney had closed down the town of Schefferville when he was president of Iron Ore, as a way of implying that he would close down Canada if Prime Minister. The approach backfired, however. For one thing, in the absence of any work or consensus on progressive policies, the Liberal campaign became little more than mud slinging. Its sleazy tone reminded people of the Liberals' own hypocrisy and arrogance. Even Turner seemed visibly uncomfortable stepping down from the high plane he had tried to keep since March. Moreover, he himself was as unknown and suspect as Mulroney. In essence, the Liberals only had a front-runner's strategy to trip the runner-up. They had nothing for catching up from behind.

The Tories also had a negative campaign ready, but once they saw that Turner and the Liberals were tripping themselves up, they shelved it for a more positive one.

In 1982 Allan Gregg thought the public mood for change could be satisfied by the slogan, "A new man with a new plan." By 1984, however, he discovered that Canadians were wary of both Messiahs and plans. Using his numbers, he came up with an alternative, "We can *be* better." But when he tested it with his focus groups, he found that it wasn't quite right. People didn't think there was anything wrong with *them*, they were fine, but they did think there was something wrong with what the government was doing and how it was doing it. From that Gregg articulated the wish for change as "We can *do* better together." It was pragmatic, it was conciliatory, it was inclusive, and it was oriented toward process. So that was the message that Norman Atkins kept sending out to all the ridings on his electronic mail system, and that was why Brian Mulroney used to end his speeches by saying, "You help me and we can do it together."

"When I started in this business," Gregg said, "I was Cartesian in the strategy I put forward: there were a hundred things you had to do. In time I became a reductionist: there was one thing, maybe two. When I was asked, 'What do we do this week?' I answered, 'Exactly what we did last week.' The key was to find new ways to do the same thing so that people wouldn't get bored. If you have the right strategy, and if you get the right people to help you find ways to illustrate that strategy, and if you stick to it, boy, you can sure change the numbers."

That wasn't unlike Keith Davey's old adage, "Determine the best issue and make it yours." To make change the Tories' issue, Gregg divided the campaign into two stages: the first was to show that John Turner couldn't be the agent of change; the second was to turn an inclination to vote Tory into a conviction to do so. The Liberals accomplished the first task themselves by the end of July. The second task was accomplished during August by shifting Mulroney from secure ridings to the ridings where there was the best chance for growth and by the $2-million television advertising campaign. The ads were often the only opportunity for most voters to judge Mulroney directly, so Gregg worked part of the day on them with Tom Scott, the veteran Big Blue Machine ad man. Again the design of the commercials and the scripts were influenced by Decima's numbers and tested on focus groups, just like any other advertising job.

"The biggest differences between selling Brian Mulroney and selling soap are that soap doesn't talk and its competitors don't say it's a crock of shit," Gregg explained. "When you're selling soap, you don't have to take in the total environment in which the product is sold. Selling politics requires so much more—the underlying mores and values, the political culture, the credibility of the opposition, the complex attributes of your product, the candidate. In some ways, running a local candidate in a national election is not dissimilar from selling soap. Running the national election is probably the equivalent of establishing an entire corporate image. It needs tons of baggage and a deft touch."

"In a political campaign the only reality is perception, part expectations, part feelings," said Tom Scott. "After seeing Turner in the debates, everyone was asking, 'Is there a Prime Minister anywhere?' So, knowing that Mulroney was a superb television performer, we decided to put him in the window."

"Putting him in the window" meant featuring him up

front in the ads, in which he did nothing fancier than talk straight into the camera about a series of issues. What he said about those issues wasn't the substantial message. The substance was in the lead, "I need help with . . . ," and the finish, "Together we can do better." Besides being vehicles for getting the basic slogan out to the electorate, the ads also spoke to the two major reservations people still had about Brian Mulroney, his glibness and his trust-worthiness. The format let him look like a Prime Minister, sound deep and concerned, and take the high road in contrast to the Liberals' muddy route. Suppressing his usual highly partisan, highly exaggerated, highly facile style, which was at the root of the "trust factor," he projected himself as earnest, informed, caring, and very sincere.

"Trust was a problem for Mulroney, but not as it's traditionally defined," Gregg said. "He hadn't done any-thing bad that could be pointed to nor was there a dis-likeability to which people could impute malevolence. His record was palatable, and he was the right combination of North Shore bootstrapper, businessman, economic con-servative, social liberal, French, English to make a very attractive commodity. But in the context of cynicism and expectations constantly dashed, there was a 'show me' attitude. The ads worked because they showed His Nibs directly telling people that he believed in the same things they did. If we had used others, people would have sus-pected we were afraid to show the real guy, that we were hiding something. On the other hand, as soon as we gave them the least excuse to suspend their doubts, they did."

Gregg and Scott took Mulroney to a hotel north of Toronto and spent a day perfecting his sincerity. Mulroney videotaped the scripts in one room, then went into the room where Gregg and Scott watched the takes on a tel-evision, and the three of them went over the details of what was right, what wasn't right, and what he should do the next time. "I don't know what those poor fuckers in the hotel thought we were doing with the leader of Her Majesty's Loyal Opposition," Gregg said, "but his prog-ress was remarkable. He started off all pumped up and full of himself, like all politicians do—it's less them than their vision of what a politician is—but Mulroney was a quick study, and though he doesn't like anyone else criticizing him, he can be very self-critical. He could see the problems for himself on the TV set, and in effect he became his own director." Twenty-five good tapes were finished by four o'clock, then rushed to Kitchener where focus groups sat waiting to judge them at six. The almost instantaneous feedback was favourable, on the whole, and eight scripts were selected for airing. As Atkins once said, "Brian Mulroney can perform and do a script very well." Thus, the candidate was able to lay to rest the doubts that he was untrustworthy and all surface.

VI

On September 4, the Tories won 211 seats, the largest landslide in Canadian history. The Liberals barely survived as the official opposition with 40 seats, while the NDP came back from the edge of electoral extinction with 30 seats.

In the post-mortems it was clear that Canadians just couldn't face another Liberal government, no matter what cosmetic changes the party might have made. What repelled them wasn't really a question of Liberal policies. It had more to do with the implications for Canadian democracy. If the Tories had lost the 1984 election, they would have entered into new leadership struggles, the outs would have become severely disaffected, and the country might as well have resigned itself to being a one-party state. If the voters merely intuited those implications, they felt a gut revolt against how smug and insufferable the Liberals would have been if their ruse to con the electorate with a recycled, right-wing leader had succeeded. In the past, Canadians frequently returned to the Liberals because the Progressive Conservatives failed to provide an acceptable alternative. Once Brian Mulroney changed that, many people felt liberated to switch their support. In fact, at the risk of indelicacy, as the returns poured in from across the country on election night, carrying off many of the cabinet ministers with whom familiarity had bred contempt, there

was the distinct and rather pleasant sensation that a toilet
had been flushed.

People understood that the Liberals had to lose. That's
why the party would have lost under Trudeau or Jean
Chrétien too. The extent of their loss, however, was due
to John Turner, who single-handedly blew in the range of
sixty seats. He called the election before he or the party
was ready. He fumbled the patronage issue, the campaign
team, the debates, the media, and the patting of women's
bums. He didn't have the instincts (or the advisers) to tell
him to fire Bryce Mackasey, nor did he have the style to
soften his economic message with warmth and compassion. Rather than build on the party's fundamental base,
he managed to offend women, alienate francophones, and
cause lower-income voters to turn to the NDP. He never
realized, as Reid put it, that "his greatest rival was Pierre
Trudeau and not Brian Mulroney." As neither Trudeau
nor Chrétien would have done, he let Mulroney walk away
easily with the left of centre. At times even his closest
friends wondered if John Turner wanted to be Prime Minister. Perhaps his moment of greatest perception came when
he had told Bill Lee at Harrington Lake, "I've screwed up,
I've screwed it all up."

In comparison, Brian Mulroney looked even better than
he was. Though he and Turner shared the same belief in
1960s Canadian liberalism—that is, in elite accommodation, cautious progress, consensual trade-offs, and decentralized power—Mulroney had not been out of touch with
the 1980s. In policy and nuance he moved closer to Trudeau and the "radical centre" than Turner. He didn't even
hide his admiration for Trudeau, publicly calling him "one
of the most impressive political figures in the world." In
fact, though the Tories may have been the "Let's Pretend
Liberal Party" for the sake of the election, Mulroney was
a Liberal in all but label. Even his style was more Liberal
than John Turner's Family Compact aura. Through his
authority over the party and as the representative of the
party, Mulroney was able to get the Tories to the left of
the Liberals. "We were outflanked, that's all," Keith Davey

conceded with regret and respect. "The Big Blue Machine went national and beat us at our own game."

What the Liberal Party and John Turner didn't do for Brian Mulroney, Norman Atkins and his boys did. Their campaign became the latest model in how to fight an election in the television age. The polls, the ads, the speeches, and the platform were churned out with centralized and scientific precision. The spotlight was on the well-trained leader, and his tour was a structure for the media's daily feed. The advance men worked from the same set of instructions as the advertising gurus, and the media was pampered with their every desire—except unstructured access to Mulroney's thoughts. The crowds were large, the local candidates were kept in step, and the content was restricted to promises and platitudes. The very dynamic of the organization guaranteed that ideas, debate, and boldness were replaced by image, blandness, and caution. Money pushed aside the envelope-lickers. Polls pushed aside the thinkers. Optimistic clichés pushed aside hard reality.

"It's sort of sad," Robert Stanfield observed of the new politics, "and it makes a farce of a campaign from a public point of view in terms of the discussion of issues and so on. But a leader hasn't got much choice now. If the other fellow is going to run that sort of campaign, he has to too."

Indeed, as soon as the election was over, the Liberals set about to construct a machine to match the Tories', just as they had done in 1972. Meanwhile, Norman Atkins was predicting that the next election would be fought with even more sophisticated polling and marketing techniques. "The 1984 election was a watershed like the 1971 Ontario election," he said. "The use of high technology changed the approach to organization and required different types of human resources. New ways of targeting voters and their interests are developing that will have terrific impact on campaigns in the future."

As with all questions about technology, the uncertainty rests with the degree to which it really alters society. After all, John A. Macdonald admitted that parties were "merely the struggle for office, the madness of the many for the gain of the few"; and Mackenzie King was the master of obfuscation and guile for the sake of victory. When Pierre Trudeau tried to use elections as a forum for discussion, saying that he was "embarrassed" merely to appeal to people's feelings, he was quickly and rudely enlightened. That embarrassment was one of the few things that Trudeau and Turner had in common. "I just can't play the media game the way Mulroney does," Turner lamented to Davey in the summer of 1984.

In fact, the process didn't change the content substantially. The voters always had high expectations. The parties always made promises. The focus was always the leader. The government would always do whatever it wanted. The implications of the process were profound, however. The centralized machine created a national structure and a national thrust to the campaign. Polling bypassed the elites and the back-room pundits to make the will of the majority clear and specific. The activists and vested interests ignored the party's traditional role as the broker of input and builder of consensus. Instead, they began to develop a direct relationship with the leader and his immediate network. Through television the population also began to develop a direct relationship.

As a result, just as Davis went over his party to the people of Ontario, Brian Mulroney was able to go over his party to the people of Canada. By his direct invasion of their living rooms and their attitudes, he became bound to the voters as if by personal contract. A promise made "up front" on the TV screen, a posture taken with oozing sincerity were not the same as promises and postures half-absorbed through newspapers and hearsay. In effect, the new politics forced the leader to express what he knew the people wanted, and then made it difficult to express anything else once in power. Ironically, while technology allowed politicians to fool the people more subtly, it also enabled the people to read the politicians more subtly. Everyone went along with the game, but suddenly the voters had the promises on videotape and their own terrific instincts about the leader's true nature.

In September, 1984, they gave Brian Mulroney the benefit of the doubt and a chance to do well. He had bought their progressive approach, their desire for a new process, and their commitment to the best in the established ways. Not surprisingly, the people then bought them back. But they made one condition clear: the moment he betrayed their agreement, they'd turn on him without mercy.

SECTION FIVE

Harmony and Prudence Go to Ottawa

I

"Now we don't have to listen to the people," a business executive said to Allan Gregg shortly after the 1984 election. "We have our own government in place for years to do what has to be done."

Though the thought may have been put rather crudely, it reflected the general expectation—and persistent naivety—within much of the Canadian Establishment that September. Slowly, reluctantly, the elites had come to see the realities of modern democracy. Politicians needed to win elections in order to win power; elections were won by bewitching the masses with hopes, images, and expensive promises. That was the game, but it wasn't to be taken too seriously in this case. How many times had potential Tory cabinet ministers told their friends and lobbyists, over dinner or in the course of a pitch for campaign contributions, that their party was ready to make the tough, unpopular decisions once in office but couldn't say so in public before then? And what was more reasonable or customary than to let the people have the election so long as the elites got the government?

Thus, the moment the cabinet was sworn in, men and women who had been public nuisances on Main Street and as common as Jehovah's Witnesses at the front door suddenly vanished into the safety and comfort of huge offices (all in desperate need of refurnishing, it seemed) in buildings as forbidding and impregnable as Gothic castles. There was a disconcerting silence in Ottawa, as if someone had abruptly switched off the continuous oom-

pah-pah of argument, leak, and gossip to which the merry-
go-round of power had been spinning for decades. The
Prime Minister and his staff were holed up in the Langevin
Block trying to get a grip on the levers of state. The ministers were learning their way around their departments,
and Parliament wasn't sitting. The bureaucrats were gagged
by decree, to the point of being barred from social contact
with the media without permission. As a result, the press
was left little to do but rewrite official bulletins. Ottawa
reporters aren't famous for their long memories, but they
only had to think back a month for evidence of the split
between election and government.

"The past few years have seen a veil of secrecy fall
over vast areas of government activity," Brian Mulroney
had said on August 12 in Kingston, Ontario. "If the Canadian people see fit to give us their trust, we will always
give them ours. That means an end to the obsession with
secrecy."

If the Canadian people were out a promise, the elites
didn't suffer unduly. Into the vacuum, providing a pricey
supply to meet a high demand, stepped a number of influential Tories apparently inspired by the spirit of free
enterprise unleashed in the land. In October, for example,
William Neville went from being a key member of Mulroney's transition team (on leave as vice-president of the
Canadian Imperial Bank of Commerce) to chairman of Public Affairs International, a consultant firm, while remaining
one of the Prime Minister's closest advisers. Frank Moores,
the former Premier of Newfoundland who had been instrumental in finding backers for Brian Mulroney's leadership ambitions in 1983, set up Government Consultants
International, which found it could even charge $2,000 for
facilitating a meeting between a Nova Scotia fisherman and
the Minister of Fisheries. And within weeks of the Progressive Conservative victory, a couple of hundred executives paid $950 each to Strategic Planning Forum Inc.—
an affiliate of Advance Planning and Communications,
Norman K. Atkins, chairman—to hear three major cabinet
ministers (Michael Wilson, Joe Clark, and Pat Carney), a
half-dozen Mulroney political advisers (such as William

Neville and Dalton Camp), and more than a dozen high-powered experts (from pollsters to economists to bureaucrats) discuss "The New Government: Players and Priorities."

The two-day conference served to announce the arrival of the Big Blue Machine in Ottawa, smug with success, tightly united by previous adventures, and already peddling influence to within an inch of the law. ("Step right up gentlemen, your ministers are waiting. Nine hundred and fifty dollars at the door, please.") Indeed, the panel sessions themselves conjured up the ghost of Ontario politics past and the ghost of Canadian politics to come, with the audience sitting as dumb as an electorate, mesmerized by the smooth organization, the coquetries of power, and the yak-yak of bland voices. To those paying close attention, the message to the elites was clear: the Tories may have won an historic mandate, but they didn't intend to behave like Ronald Reagan, Margaret Thatcher, or Bill Bennett in British Columbia.

In broad terms, there are two strategies available to a government as it comes into office. In its first year or so it can act purposefully on the unpleasant and controversial issues, hope to see some beneficial effects in the short term as well as the long term, and gradually mend its political fences as the next election approaches. Or it can move with caution and consideration toward its goals, use its authority to develop a consensus about the necessary reforms, and achieve enough to ask the people for more time to carry on its general program. Each course had its fervent proponents among the Tories' policy makers and supporters, but the indications soon pointed toward the triumph of moderation. "This is not Reagan North that he's setting up here," Neville said of Mulroney at the Strategic Planning Forum conference.

Neville was right to personalize his remark, for the mind of the government was to a dramatic degree the mind of Brian Mulroney. Mulroney had staked his leadership on convincing his caucus and his party that he held the winning formula, which in essence was to steal the political centre and Quebec from the Liberals. "The right honourable gentleman caught the Whigs bathing," Disraeli once said of Robert Peel, but he might have said with equal truth of Brian Mulroney, "and walked away with their clothes." Mulroney had known he had only one chance to prove he was right. If defeated, he would probably have been finished. With success, however, he was raised to heroic stature. Most of his MPs felt they owed their seats to his policies and performance; he gained enormous power to advance or retard the careers of cabinet ministers, civil servants, and party members; he had a weakness for loyalty and sycophancy; and no one in his vicinity had better instincts. As a result, in case after case, what Mulroney said, went.

In Mulroney's eyes, September 1984 was less the end of a long road from out to in than the beginning of a long road to staying in. One election didn't matter, he liked to say, "it's the one after that and the one after that which matter more." Whether that was because he needed time to change the direction of the country or merely because he wanted to enjoy the vanities of power until retirement, the implication was profound: his government was going to be managed on a permanent election footing. "The next election begins today," Mulroney told his ministers after they were sworn in, not in two years' time after the strong and odious medicines had been administered.

"Mulroney's style is instinctively Davis's style," Norman Atkins said, "though it may not be the style of those around him. As with Davis, the style can't be set overnight, but ultimately that's what you'll get, even if it takes a second term before the comparisons can be seen. Mulroney is the kind of politician who won't blow his first term in such a way that he won't get a second."

Certainly the first buzz-words of the new government—consensus, consultation, incrementalism, pragmatism—were those of the Davis regime. And from the start there were the same preoccupations with public opinion, media control, and the blending of policy decisions with electoral rewards. Through polls, through advisers and contacts, and through their own extraordinary antennae, both Mulroney and Davis knew that their voters were

to the left of their parties. Therefore, in Ottawa as at Queen's
Park, the leadership had to continually redirect the membership, the caucus, and even many cabinet ministers from
their habitual orientation by means of carrots and sticks.
Mulroney interpreted the task as uprooting the federal
Tories' "opposition mentality"—a self-defeating affinity for
right-wing cant, knee-jerk naysaying, and internal bickering—and replacing it with the more generous, confident,
open-minded attitude of perpetual winners.

"Many of his people still see themselves as outs," said
Hugh Segal, "and that can produce some powerful pressures for the settling of old scores. There are guys in the
caucus and the cabinet for whom vengeance is an acceptable base for public policy. The forces of reaction may have
some sway for a while, but Mulroney is a moderate and
a progressive. It is significant that he supported Trudeau
and Davis on the patriation of the constitution and the
Charter of Rights."

In other words, Mulroney's own propensities reinforced his political expediencies. Though he sometimes
sounded like a classic British liberal (or modern conservative) with his oh-so-sincere paeans to individualism, free
markets, and diffused authority, he was in essence a 1960s
Canadian liberal who valued community (whether nation,
province, or minority group), accepted an interventionist
role for the state, and hoped to promote the central authority by coordinating and coopting the interests of the
various elites. Moreover, unlike John Turner, who seemed
stuck in a romantic Camelot of 1968 (if not 1948), Mulroney
had absorbed some of the lessons of the Trudeau years.
He didn't like the deficits, the conflicts, the extremes, or
the arrogant airs, but he clearly admired Pierre Trudeau
as a national leader more than Joe Clark and he clearly
behaved as if the Liberals were closer to the proper course
than his own gang of reactionaries, misfits, and
stumblebums.

"I was a late bloomer ideologically," he once remarked.
He meant, it seemed, that he only began to bring a set of
ideas to his political aspirations late in the game. But those
ideas about industrial productivity or freer trade were put

on like his new blue suits: they looked good, they were fashionable, and they flattered him. At the end of the day, however genuine or elegant they were, they could be taken off as easily as they had been donned. For Brian Mulroney was a naked pragmatist. As a schoolboy he announced his ambition to be Prime Minister, and even as late as 1976 he seemed to have no other reason to seek the job. It was obvious that his greatest delight came in the rough-and-tumble of the political sport, not in thinking about what he should do if he won the game—beyond, that is, preparing for the next one. His term as president of the Iron Ore Company of Canada gave him enough specific ideas for a slim book, *Where I Stand*, but as soon as he moved from the private sector to the opposition benches to the campaign trail, he demonstrated an awesome flexibility.

"The Prime Minister of Canada is no place for a philosopher," Mulroney said. "If you're going to philosophize, then you should do that in the sanctity of one of our finer universities." In comparison, he described himself as a doer. "I like to listen to people. I get the best advice I can and then act in the interests of the Canadian people. I think that's the only way to function properly."

The long career of Mackenzie King and the turbulent history of Pierre Trudeau both suggest that Mulroney may have been right. Preconceived ideas and the will to implement them usually cause strain and disaffection. So if something ain't broke, why fix it? In fact, even if it is broke, maybe it don't need fixing or will fix itself in time. That's an absolutely valid concept of leadership, and it had the added attraction of suiting Mulroney's character. His reputation was established as a labour mediator (as was King's); he had a distaste for confrontation, despite his love of a good Irish scrap; and he had an insatiable desire for admiration and public love. Above all, he wanted to be seen as a great *manager*, bringing people together and motivating things to happen as Bill Davis had.

As worthy as the concept was, particularly after the failure of Trudeau's human and management skills, it was not devoid of ideology. At the risk of tiresome repetition, pragmatism in Canada is not a neutral, directionless frame of mind. In politics and in government it moves leftward, it encourages intervention, it is progressive, and it checks the wishes of the elites with the wishes of the people. Since the pragmatic in government is not always the same as the pragmatic in politics, they move at different paces and the dichotomy between the policies of in and out develops; but some correlation is necessary if the politicians want to maintain their credibility. Such a correlation takes place the moment a leader decides to run the government like an election campaign. And in Mulroney's case, the thrust of pragmatism was given a push by his own liberal nature.

Some Tories argued that the pragmatic had lost its old meaning. They pointed to the size of the Conservative vote, the longing for change, the rebirth of the entrepreneurial spirit, and the problems within the country as evidence of a mandate to pull Canada sharply back to the right of centre. The question of mandate is one of the toughest all leaders face. With the help of polls, contacts, and instincts they can get a reasonably accurate reading of the mood of the nation toward certain issues and ideas, but they usually have to do more than the Frenchman who cried, "Ah well! I am their leader, I really ought to follow them!" By the special nature of their positions, leaders see more broadly and further ahead than most people, and have the opportunity and the responsibility to manoeuvre their societies away from the dark and toward the light. Even if the public's current thoughts and wishes can be determined, they may not be the best courses of action now or ever. Then what is the *true* mandate? How far can a leader get from the people? How far should a leader get?

"Trudeau was always confronted by the problems of doing what was right and doing what was acceptable in the climate of the times," Jim Coutts said. "His own sense of how fast he could move was more of a rein than his sense of having to balance the various forces within the country."

Even before the 1984 election was over, as the numbers began to turn dramatically in the Tories' favour, Mulroney was absorbed by the questions of mandate. Allan Gregg showed up on the campaign plane not with more data and advice about winning, but to anticipate the public's expectations for a Mulroney government and how to meet them. What had the election been about, after all? Bum patting? Certainly the Tories had made sure it hadn't been about such crucial issues as the deficit or freer trade with the Americans. It had been about change, everyone agreed, but everyone also had a different idea of what that meant. Gregg's definition followed from his work on the party's election strategy: though Canadians were ready to let Mulroney do what he found best, whatever his promises, they were more preoccupied with a change of *process* than of *policy*.

"We interviewed groups until they were coming out our ears," Gregg said. "And we concluded that, unless you changed the inputs into government decision making and allowed labour, business, the provinces, and others to have their say, the outputs would never change. But there is no consensus on what should be done. We're at Point A and people sense we should get to Point C, but there's no agreement on Point B. The people have bought the Conservative agenda, but not the Conservative philosophy."

That advice led to such stage-managed, media-manipulated acts of consultation and conciliation as the First Ministers' Conference on the Economy in Regina in February, the National Economic Conference in Ottawa in March, and a long series of studies, task forces, and policy reviews on major issues. It also undermined the advice of those who urged the Tories to act quickly and boldly. For Gregg's explicit message was that the country wanted and needed a break from high-handed, divisive, willful government. If Mulroney had a personal agenda or if the Conservatives had a hidden agenda, this wasn't the time to spring it on a captive nation. With patience, with gestures of consensus-building, with deliberate control of the news, Canadians might be brought to where the Tories wanted to take them; but if the government imitated the past and pressed ahead dogmatically, without listening, without healing and stroking and trading, all would be lost.

Pushed by his own political instincts, encouraged by his previous successes as a negotiator, aware of the period his neophyte ministers would need to master their portfolios, Mulroney took Gregg's advice and dedicated his first year to the gods of Economic Renewal and National Reconciliation. On that decision rested all the achievements and all the failures of 1985.

II

"There is a general view in Canada that we can no longer live beyond our means as if this picnic were going to go on forever," Prime Minister Brian Mulroney told reporters at the beginning of November, 1984. A moment later, however, he admitted that not everyone was feasting. "We have an unemployment figure which is unacceptable," he said, "and people need jobs." Then he added—not with recrimination or malice, he hastened to point out, but as a sad truth—"This country has been badly managed, badly mismanaged."

The previous June, John Turner had looked at roughly the same economic statistics and said, "I've inherited a bag of shit!" Certainly the numbers weren't encouraging: an unemployment rate of over 11 per cent, which really meant almost 1,500,000 people without work; a federal debt moving rapidly toward $200 billion; an annual deficit of nearly $35 billion; sluggish growth and weak investment following the recession; and the threat of a rising interest rate. Moreover, behind the numbers there lurked disturbing doubts about Canada's future in a changing, competitive world, about the capacity of the nation to pay for its highly cherished redistributive programs, about the equitable development of all its regions, and about the character of Canadian entrepreneurs.

If Mulroney had a clear mandate to do anything, it was to do *something* about the economy. Most Canadians had been shocked, frightened, or brutalized by the recession, and they never forgave Trudeau for his seemingly self-indulgent preoccupation with the constitution in the midst of their bankruptcies, dispossessions, and lay-offs. Ironically it was Trudeau's success with the referendum, patriation, and the Charter of Rights that permitted both Turner and Mulroney to concentrate on the economic issues. For two decades the federal government had had to fight the wars of national unity; but as soon as the imminent dangers were overcome, the Liberals were dismissed like old, boring generals and the Tories garnered the peace. As in any peace, there was a mood as well as an occasion for positive reconstruction.

By coincidence that mood encountered a turn-around in the Canadian economy. It was mostly the result of the drop in interest rates, an American recovery force-fed by military spending and huge deficits, and the stabilization of world energy prices. Since the upswing began under the Liberals, they also gave some credit to their budget policies. Some credit was due them in fairness, perhaps, if only because the party's earlier policies had taken so much blame for the downturn. Fairness, however, rarely applies in the game of politics, for it would involve explanation, nuance, and chivalry. Instead, most people heaped all the bad on the Liberal government and attributed all the good to providence. The Tories did nothing to disabuse them of that perception—just as the Liberals were to do nothing else when they got into opposition.

"For twenty years," Mulroney said during a televised interview, "we've seen a government, in good times and bad, spend more than it took in, live beyond its means, pile on massive debt, while our research and development declined, our productivity declined, our share of world trade declined, the private sector got clobbered, the farmers got it in the neck, as did the fishermen. All the provinces got it. It was constant confrontation and no flowering of the creative genius of Canada."

The impression Mulroney left in speech after speech was plain: Canada's economic woes were caused by the "social democratic-collectivist philosophy" and the "unprecedented profligacy" of the Liberal Party under "the darling of the NDP," because there was "no room in its vocabulary for words like risk, sacrifice, reward, initiative, enterprise, and profit." In contrast, the mere swearing-in of a Progressive Conservative government would create "tens of thousands of new jobs" and "a massive influx of equity capital," because the Tories would bring "a modest degree of sanity into the public expenditures" of Canada and are "committed to the genius of the private sector, the small and medium businessman, the farmer and fisherman, people who make the sacrifices to make this country go."

Part of this was his political ballad; part of it was his tendency to exaggerate; but there was a part that Brian Mulroney believed. He believed that Baie Comeau had been built by risk-taking capitalists and bold individuals, not by "fancy-pants leftists" and civil servants in luxurious offices. He had spent enough time as president of the Iron Ore Company and a director of the Canadian Imperial Bank of Commerce to believe that government regulations, taxes, incentives, and deficits wreaked havoc on the bottom line. Above all, he believed that the simple shift to an attitude of conciliation, cooperation, and consensus would restore the confidence of a "private sector that has been debilitated and crippled by a government bent on extinguishing the entrepreneurial spirit." Confidence would lead to investment, investment would lead to jobs, and jobs would lead to lower deficits, which would create even more confidence.

"There was a time," Mulroney said, "when we were younger and things were better, when many Canadians, I think, looked upon Trudeau's penchant for confrontation as a kind of political theatre. Well, we may still find that more than four hours of Napoleon versus Europe makes a good movie, but we know now that more than fourteen years of Mr. Trudeau versus everyone else makes lousy government."

There is no doubt that Trudeau's adversarial stance toward the business community had had a negative effect. In a series of surveys carried out by the Conference Board of Canada, 55 per cent of nine hundred important executives said that government policies were an impediment to their investment plans in 1981. That was in the midst of the controversies over the NEP. With effort and concessions the Liberals were able to get the figure nearer to 45 per cent in 1982 and 35 per cent in 1983. However, the very election of Joe Clark in 1979 had caused a drop to 30 per cent; the very resignation of Trudeau in 1984 saw a drop to 32 per cent; and the very election of the Mulroney Conservatives prompted a dramatic new low of 23 per cent. The rapidity of these reactions proved that the executives were impressed by psychological factors rather than the implementation of actual policies, but psychology is usually more significant than a tax credit for investors.

On the other hand, the executives stated that government policies, whether real or imagined, were not the greatest impediments to their investment plans. In fact, according to the Mulroney government's own report on investment, which was presented to the Regina first ministers' conference, "In the eight years immediately preceding the recent recession, the share of business investment in total Canadian production was higher than any similar cyclically neutral period of the postwar era. Indeed, between 1974 and 1981, the share of real output going into business investment rose from 13.6 per cent to a postwar record of 16.8 per cent in 1981, and averaged 15.0 per cent for the period as a whole. . . . Although some of our trading partners experienced increasing investment shares in this period, none of them had as large an increase as did Canada." The report went on to emphasize that Canada's weak investment record since 1981 was due to two nonpolitical factors: "first, the interaction between Canada's investment cycle and the severity of the recession, and second, the vulnerable financial position of corporations at the outset of the recession."

In other words, as the report made clear, the important restraining influences on investment in the immediate past and the immediate future were excess capacity, corporate debt loads, weak demand, and high real interest rates. None of them could be turned around by a song, a smile, a pat on the back, or even a government decree. Mulroney knew that, of course, but he was convinced that the first step to improving them was "to create the climate which will be hospitable and productive for national investment capital and for foreign investment capital, because we need it to create the jobs for our citizens."

"Jobs, jobs, jobs" had been Mulroney's favourite cry during the Tory leadership race and the election campaign. He understood the terrible costs to individuals, families, and the whole society of high unemployment, and he understood how the focus on jobs would highlight the Tories' compassion, their progressive image, and his own moral depth. He was less vocal and less strident in public about his party's conviction that the creation of jobs began with a serious reduction of the deficit.

The argument was put clearly by Michael Wilson, the Minister of Finance, at the Strategic Planning Forum conference in October, 1984. "At a time when lower interest rates are not only desirable, but essential to support sustained economic growth and job creation, the national debt poses a major threat and obstacle to lower rates. It encourages inflationary expectations which can put upward pressure on current interest rates. And it increases real interest rates which can crowd out job-producing risk capital and encourage unproductive debt servicing."

Mulroney agreed. "I don't deal with the deficit as something that *per se* I find unacceptable," he said. "I find it unacceptable because it sucks up all of the borrowing capacity of the nation to service a federal debt, thereby driving interest rates up for the small and medium businessman and the farmer who needs that investment capital to create jobs."

Not all economists were on side. In the 1980s the major industrial nations that had the biggest reductions in their structural deficits—Great Britain and West Germany—suffered the biggest increases in unemployment; while the nation that had the biggest deficit increase—the United States—enjoyed the smallest increase in unemployment. Lay-offs, reduced spending, reduced benefits, and higher taxes all had the immediate effect of slowing the economy, diminishing profits, and causing further lay-offs; while some fiscal stimuli did make work, take people from the welfare rolls to the tax rolls, put money directly into the pockets of consumers, and show a marginal advance against the recession. In June, 1985, Mulroney crowed about creating 271,000 jobs in the eight months since his election—"a record number," he said, "a very substantial success compared to anything this country has seen in recent memory." In fact, the eight-month record was held by the last Trudeau government, which created 316,000 jobs in 1982-1983. In either case, economists argued, the deficit went up, not down, and the result had less to do with government policy than with a turn in the world economy and the lowering of U.S. interest rates. Even the Tories conceded that too drastic a slash in the deficit could stall the recovery and cost jobs.

They also knew that any cuts would be in vain if American rates rose—a likely possibility, if the Tories were logical, given Washington's $200-billion deficits. As Mulroney stated baldly, "We cannot have a 'made-in-Canada' interest rate." Wilson chorused, "There's an awful lot riding on the United States." Each increase south of the border would push up the Canadian rate, stifle whatever investor confidence was sprouting, and add to the government's interest payments, which already absorbed about $1 from every $3 Ottawa collected in revenue. As a result, the connection between Canada's deficit and its interest rates seemed questionable at best, non-existent at worst.

However, the Conservatives had other reasons for their emphasis on the national debt. It imposed an intolerable burden on future generations. It stole scarce dollars from productive priorities and social needs, including increased assistance to the elderly, the sick, and the poor. It threatened to spiral rapidly and to such a size that most of the government's revenue would be spent servicing it. It was an iceberg "poised to sink the ship of state," Wilson said. If that wasn't enough, the deficit had become a symbol as well as a peril to the private sector. Businessmen saw it as balance-sheet evidence that governments were incompetent, wasteful, and running amok in the marketplace. If an effort wasn't made to curb the borrowing, then the national economy would go to hell—indeed, the international financial community would send it there—and there would be no logic to investing in such a dismal probability.

After the economists had exhausted their arguments, the psychological factor prevailed in the Department of Finance. Whether cuts in the deficit were a crucial measure or an existential gesture, they were required as "the signal" (to use Mulroney's expression) that Canada was a safe place for investment. "A credible plan to live within our means once again will go a long way toward building business and public confidence," Wilson said, "confidence that will lead to the creation of jobs today."

Business confidence perhaps, but there weren't many indications that the general public gave a damn about the deficit. According to the Tories' own polls, only 3 per cent thought that it was Canada's most important economic problem. It seemed an abstract issue, a Bay Street issue, and it was so complex that even the economists had trouble agreeing on it. People wanted jobs, and it tried their patience to understand why laying off employees, closing down local industries, and cutting back services would create more work. Nor did Mulroney even attempt a good explanation during the greatest opportunity for public education in a democracy, the election campaign. If he spoke about the deficit at all amid his extravagant promises to restore rail services in the Maritimes and help the wine industry in the Niagara peninsula, he spoke about it as a management problem. The Liberals were spendthrifts, the bureaucrats played fast and loose with the taxpayers' money, and the people of Canada deserved better. That seemed fair enough, since almost every voter knew something of Liberal boondoggles and poor postal service, but it was virtually irrelevant.

The federal deficit had little to do with irresponsible profligacy in Ottawa. Of the approximate $100 billion it spent in 1984-1985, more than 20 per cent went to pay off the national debt, almost 20 per cent went to the provinces as prearranged transfers, and almost 20 per cent went to individual Canadians through such social programs as unemployment insurance, pensions, family allowances, and welfare. About 10 per cent went toward defence, which the Tories thought disgracefully underfunded and vowed to spend more on. Most of the remaining 30 per cent was tied up in salaries, reserves, loans, operating expenses, and programs that couldn't be cut quickly or simply. "The cupboard is bare," Mulroney announced shortly after coming into office. It was supposed to be a stinging damnation of the Liberals. In fact, it was an admission that his predecessors hadn't left much fat on the bones of government.

What to do? The cost of paying off the debt was determined by outside forces and liable to grow, so the only solution was to pray for lower U.S. interest rates. Transfers to the provinces couldn't be reduced substantially or soon without jeopardizing Mulroney's wish to reconcile Ottawa and the regions. A task force with the Deputy Prime Minister, Erik Nielsen, and advisers from the private sector was set up to ferret ou the "billions and billions of dollars" of waste, duplication, and inefficiency in the federal government, but the cuts were expected to be politically hard when they weren't politically impossible. General economic growth would help, by raising revenues and diminishing the social burdens, but there had been growth since 1982 and still the deficits had risen. As a result, when Wilson was asked in November, 1984, if the deficit could be checked without a reappraisal of Canada's social programs, he answered, "No. That's why everything is on the table. The bullet has to be bitten."

That raised the obvious and immediate question of universality. This was the principle that every citizen, regardless of income, should be entitled to benefits such as the old-age pension and the family allowance. Universality had been introduced with the programs partly as a *right* of citizenship and partly to avoid a means test, more paper work, and a middle-class backlash. It was popular (as the few, failed attempts by the Trudeau Liberals to tamper with it had demonstrated), but it was expensive. As Mulroney said during a press conference on November 9, 1984, "A legitimate question arises: Are we making proper use of taxpayers' money by giving a bank president, say, at $500,000 or $600,000 a year, the baby bonus? Could that money not be more properly used to assist someone who desperately needs help? I don't know the answer. I am still firmly of the view that the best way to approach this problem is the universal concept. I could, by trade unions, by the private sector, and by informed opinion, be perhaps persuaded to a better utilization of those public funds, but that is what the examination is all about."

The bank president was a typical Mulroney exaggeration, since bank presidents with babies were extremely scarce and the real question was whether middle-class families should receive the baby bonus. That wasn't his most fatal trip of the tongue, however. It had come during the election when he referred to universality as "a sacred trust." His design, of course, had been to appease the worries of the liberal-minded majority about any hidden agenda and shatter the image—"as developed in some of our more sophisticated trendy quarters," he said—that his party was a bunch of "right-wing crazies." Three months later that *handsome* sentiment returned to haunt the Prime Minister and hamstring his Minister of Finance.

Most of Mulroney's promises could be jettisoned without undue embarrassment, since they had been made "pursuant to the availability of public funds"—the verbal equivalent of crossed fingers. "Sacred trust," however, touched upon his credibility, his pride, perhaps his beliefs, and certainly his popularity. Canadians were willing to go along with his cant about the deficit so long as it was confined to better management and control of the patent excesses. The electorate took the Tories at their word when they implied that the problem was rooted in waste and the Liberals. In other words, it was a problem for the government, not for the people.

"There is a big distinction in the public mind between *controlling* the deficit and *reducing* the deficit," Allan Gregg told the Conservatives. "Controlling is good. It means indirect benefits, for if the government is operating better, it will do everything better. But the liabilities of reduction are direct, real, and understandable to the average person. He might get hurt or he might lose a service. The more the people are faced with the hard decisions that fiscal reality needs, the more they may fatigue of the issue. 'If that's what we have to do,' they'll say, 'then forget it. I don't even want the deficit reduced if those are the options.'

"Worse," Gregg continued, "if the deficit becomes the number-one issue of the government while there's less public demand for it, then you'll get, 'This government doesn't share my concerns.' That's death. *The government can't let that happen.*"

If it happened, there would be an alienation similar to the one that occurred when the Liberals rode off on their constitutional hobbyhorse. The effect would be conflict, dashed expectations, and political danger. This came back to Gregg's general analysis: the public agreed that deficits were bad (A), it wanted to see the deficits controlled (C), but it didn't support any harsh or unfair measures to get there (B). Moreover, Brian Mulroney had given his *solemn* assurance—or so it seemed to most voters—that no sacrifices would be required of them.

His desire to win, his desire to be liked, and his desire to imitate Laurier's "sunny ways" caused Mulroney to fall into the same trap he had warned against in a speech in 1982. "One of the great burdens this country has had to bear has been the extravagant optimism of some of our leaders," he said then. "Sir Wilfrid Laurier, for example, proclaimed that 'the twentieth century belongs to Canada.' Our problem is that we believed him, literally. We could peddle our resources to the highest bidder, adopt any social policy of popular currency, display a degree of profligacy in public spending that would cause even the most irresponsible to blush . . . and it did not matter—because we knew, way deep down, that the twentieth century belonged to us." If not this century, Canadians still had smug hope for the next one, not least because of Brian Mulroney's promise of a bright, new tomorrow.

Of course, there were his grim statistics, his dark Irish admonitions, his calls for dedication and restraint, but they were soon swept away by his own style. The day he announced that the picnic was over, for example, he had to defend spending $13,000 to fly Wilson and two advisers by government jet for a five-hour meeting with him in Palm Beach, Florida. In a symbolic gesture he chopped his own salary by about $7,000, then poured more than $100,000 into redecorating 24 Sussex Drive and Harrington Lake.

With one hand his government eliminated several thousand jobs in the federal civil service, while with the other hand it gave its ministers new chiefs of staff at $80,000 a year, doubled the size of the Prime Minister's Office for an additional cost of $2.5 million, and made so much work for Tories from coast to coast that patronage remained a scandal and a joke for the whole year. The deficit continued to be the *bête noire* of every prime-ministerial speech on the rubber-chicken circuit, but the headlines constantly featured his largesse to banks, oil companies, western farmers, eastern fishermen, paper companies, and (last but not least) Manicouagan, the Prime Minister's Quebec riding.

"We plan to do this not only for Manicouagan," Mulroney said as he added $50 million for a new penitentiary to some $100 million spent there by Ottawa since its MP had become PM, "but for all the Manicouagans across Canada."

There were good reasons why a depressed region of high unemployment should receive such help, just as there were good reasons why the banks and the farmers and the paper companies needed assistance; nor would any fair-minded person begrudge the Prime Minister of Canada a nice house and a Challenger jet to relieve the woes of office. Nevertheless, as even the most incompetent public-relations hack would perceive, Santa Claus with his big bag and jolly belly is a poor advertisement for austerity and belt tightening. The thunder of the Tory herd racing for the swill obliterated the cries of "Cut! Cut!" and raised another doubt about the leader's credibility.

Over a lunch one day at Winston's in Toronto a financial power of Bay Street and the party expressed his disgust at how grandiose and extravagant the Tory fund raisers had become. Though he had nightmares about the deficit, he was trying to get federal money for a new opera hall in the city. "That might seem a contradiction," he admitted, "but if they're going to cough up tens of millions of dollars for a *domed stadium*, for God's sake, then I want as much for the opera."

Spending was more than a simple case of buying votes. It touched on the psychology of politicians. They want to be remembered for having built something, for having given something, not for dismantling and cutting back. It was easy for Mulroney to condemn the Liberals for spending rather than saving in the times of prosperity; but if he spent as he did when the country was "broke," one could imagine how he would have spent with a little money in the bank. "You know," he once lamented, "the number of times that I have literally said to myself at night, or said to Mila at night, 'God, think of what we could do without that $36-billion deficit.' "

A moment later he expanded on that thought. "I'm like any other politician or any other reasonable human being. I don't take any pleasure in removing something. I'd like to be doing things for people. That's why I'm here. I'd like to be giving more social security and more benefits to the elderly and more help to the unemployed youth. That's what I'm here for. But the deficit is there, and one percentage point jump in interest payments and all of your sacrifice is wiped out and it's gone."

Michael Wilson, however, didn't seem to believe that politicians are there to spend. He was a rather serious, somewhat earnest, self-restrained kind of guy who had entered the political arena in 1979 directly from the office of executive vice-president at Dominion Securities in Toronto, where he was primarily concerned with corporate finance. His father had been a president of National Trust, Wilson had been educated at Upper Canada College, and so from a tender age he had absorbed the Bay Street creed that the best government was the least government. He had an admirable sense of social compassion and a developing knowledge of political reality, especially after his foray as a candidate in the 1983 Tory leadership race, but he remained convinced that Ottawa should stop "throwing money at problems" and "impeding the private sector's ability to be the engine of growth." Like most businessmen, he was obsessed by the deficit as an economic disaster, a government malignancy, and a political symbol.

Settling into the Finance portfolio, Wilson knew that he had to avoid "hasty, ill-considered actions," which might

give the appearance of a heavy-handed, reactionary government or strangle the weak recovery. He also knew that
he had to send a clear message to the business community
of his purpose and direction. His mini-budget in November, 1984, tried to steer a course between the rock and the
hard place. It announced savings of $4.2 billion, including
almost $300 million from the unemployment insurance
system, $85 million from the CBC, and over $275 million
from capital projects. However, some of the affected expenditures were purely hypothetical, some were only
postponed, and a new $1 billion was to be spent on job-
creation and training programs. More significantly, though
the rate of increase in spending would be lower and the
deficit smaller than they would have been otherwise, both
the expenses and the deficit would be greater in the next
year than in the current year. In fact, Wilson predicted
annual deficits between $34 billion and $38 billion for the
rest of the 1980s.

Tucked into Wilson's November statement was a document called *A New Direction for Canada—An Agenda for
Economic Renewal*. It set out Canada's economic and fiscal
outlook, explored the obstacles to growth, and presented
a number of ideas on eliminating those obstacles. In essence, it was the first step in the Tories' consultative process. "Is it fair to provide benefits of more than $500 per
child to families with income of more than $45,000 a year,
in the face of other pressing social problems, including
family violence and the plight of many single parents?"
the document asked, leaving little doubt about its own
answer. Then, drawing attention to the $11.8 billion in
Ottawa's benefits to the elderly, it stated, "It is therefore
time to examine whether these federal transfer payments
should continue in their present form or whether they
need be redesigned to increase fairness, assist those in
greatest need, and reduce the burdens on the federal
government."

The implications were simple: the Minister of Finance
wanted to begin the debate that would allow him to over-
turn the principle of universality as a means of cutting into
the costs of social programs. "Upper- and middle-income

social programs cannot be afforded today," he said in an interview.

But what about the *sacred trust*? For two months the battle over universality raged in the cabinet, in the press, and in an angry House of Commons. "I think it's a sign of maturity that we can look at programs or a concept that could be forty or fifty years of age," Mulroney said, but he emphasized that universal medicare was excluded from a second look and that any savings would go to the needy, not simply to the deficit. On other days, he pledged "to maintain the integrity of our social programs for the benefit of all Canadians who have contributed to them." Either way, the public differences between Mulroney and Wilson revealed the behind-the-scenes quarrels and confusions. For the sake of his credibility and his popularity, the Prime Minister began to move away from his Finance Minister and eventually blew up at Wilson's dogged attempts to keep alive a debate that had become a personal embarrassment and a government liability.

Finally, on January 28, 1985, the matter was put to bed when the Minister of Health and Welfare, Jake Epp, issued a short discussion paper on social policy. It suggested no changes at all in the benefits to the elderly, whether the old age security cheque, the guaranteed income supplement, or tax breaks such as the age exemption and the pension income deduction. That ruled out selective payments, taxing back the benefits from high-income individuals, or even a special surtax for the wealthy recipients, all of which were seen as infringements on the principle of universality. Similarly, the baby bonus remained universal, though two options were proposed for rejigging the child tax exemption and the child tax credit to help the needy. "Any savings which may result from program changes," the booklet emphasized, "will not be applied to a reduction of the deficit."

There wasn't enough money at stake in Wilson's debate to make or break the national debt, but the defeat of the Minister of Finance was an important indication of Mulroney's strategy. The Tories were still fighting the election, they were still playing to the left of centre, and Brian

Mulroney's instincts were still in charge of the game. Oddly enough, there was evidence that the Tories could have won a fight over universality with some good salesmanship and a little backbone. The polls showed softness on the issue. Even the Prime Minister's *reductio ad absurdum* about the paternal bank president could have been honed into an argument that appealed to the plain sense of Canadians, addressed people's concern about the fair management of their resources, and left the Liberals and the NDP defending the bankers.

"If you can find a pool of public opinion that agrees with what you're saying," Allan Gregg explained, "and if you marshal the arguments fairly and credibly, you *can* move people from the first step to the second and change their minds. I think this is the model this government ought to follow. If it's too tough at the beginning, it will lose political currency and the credibility to do anything. It has to set out directions, as it did in Wilson's November statement, and then get there by mobilizing public opinion in support of those goals while raising the understanding of the means necessary to get there. It gets there by *tacking*."

Mulroney began to go that way. "Is Canada mature enough as a country to engage a debate about the allocation of resources," he asked a television audience in December, 1984, sounding like a faint echo from one of Trudeau's early, naive Socratic dialogues, "given the crying needs of a large number of people in our society who don't have enough to eat and who don't have jobs? I think the answer is yes." In truth, however, he thought the answer was no. As he spoke, he was preparing to turn and run from his first experience of government leadership under fire.

The retreat could have been interpreted as judicious tacking. It showed responsiveness and a liberal nature. "The public appreciates that," Gregg said. "It wants to see the politics of muddling through—*as long as it's sure you're going somewhere by going this way and that.*" That qualification became the bane of the Prime Minister's first year. Being nice was nice; being moderate was nice; but being weak was not nice. Behind the courageous rhetoric of the man who declared publicly that Winston Churchill was his greatest hero, people began to suspect a smaller figure in a Homburg hat who waved a piece of paper to herald peace in our time. Economic appeasement had rapidly become the preferred strategy.

The 1986 census was eliminated in November to save $100 million and then restored. A ferry service in Yarmouth, Nova Scotia, was cancelled but continued operating. The Via rail services were to lose $93 million in subsidies, but several uneconomic runs that had been cut by the Liberals were uncut by ministerial order. The Department of Defence was to suffer a $154-million loss under its funding formula, but more than that was allocated for new uniforms and 1,200 extra troops in Europe. Even threatened environmental studies of gull eggs and caribou herds had their budgets restored. Nor did Erik Nielsen's task force on government spending find it easy to propose savings when faced with cabinet ministers and vested interests ready to appeal to the Prime Minister. The instant there was a rumour that the task force was recommending cuts in programs to the native peoples, for example, the native leaders yowled and the PMO issued a firm denial.

"There's a lot of despondency over in Finance now," one bureaucrat told the *Globe and Mail* in February, 1985. Another added, "There is a strong feeling that the Prime Minister is on the other side, and that feeling has percolated through the cabinet. They have no stomach for the budget process as originally portrayed."

There was also a lot of despondency in the business community when word of Wilson's setbacks reached it. It began a formal and informal lobby to stiffen Mulroney's will before the May budget and urge a $5-billion reduction in the deficit as a strong signal of the Tories' resolve. The campaign succeeded in producing more speeches from the Prime Minister on the "integrity" of the November agenda and many expressions of solidarity with his Minister of Finance. When the budget came down, however, there was more disappointment. True, Wilson announced a deficit reduction of $4.4 billion, but half of that came from November's cuts. Only $455 million came from new program cuts and another $400 million came from new taxes. Even then, the deficit was down only a billion dollars from the $35 billion projected the previous November. Though Wilson had prevented the deficit from exceeding $38 billion, the new figure still made Bay Street shake its collective head. Nor did businessmen miss the point that, although federal spending on programs was reduced from what it would have been otherwise, it still increased by almost $2 billion over the previous year.

"I think the message is there," Wilson confessed of his budget, "that cutting programs is becoming increasingly difficult. Let's be frank. There are political and economic, particularly regional, implications."

On closer inspection there was some good news for the deficit busters in Wilson's estimate that the deficit would drop by $20 billion by the end of the 1980s. The budget papers weren't very explicit about how that would happen, but a secret departmental document revealed that the key lay with the budget's proposal to partially de-index the basic personal tax exemption, old-age pensions, and family allowances. All of these had risen annually at the same rate as inflation. Now Wilson planned to raise them only when inflation went above 3 per cent. The Finance document projected that the result would total $6.4 billion in revenue saved by 1990. The partial de-indexing of pensions alone would yield $260 million within two years and $1.6 billion by the next decade.

To introduce whopping new taxes was bad enough; to do so in such an underhanded fashion was worse; but to reduce the deficit on the backs of the elderly in such a sneaky way was intolerable. It was even worse than intolerable, because it followed an election promise to protect the full indexing of old-age pensions and was accompanied by mammoth corporate tax cuts and a generous exemption on capital gains. Allan Gregg had warned the government that Canadians would accept a tough budget only if it was *fair*. Wilson used the word "fair" and its variations more than a dozen times in his speech. He put in symbolic items such as a temporary surtax for the well-to-do and large corporations, and many taxes were spread to everyone who bought gas, candy, cigarettes, alcohol, or pay-TV services. After the pros and cons had been weighed, however, the Prime Minister found himself being abused by an irate voter on the steps of Parliament. "Hey, Mulroney," she yelled, "I thought you were more honest than that. You really disappointed us. You lied to us. You got us to vote for you and now it's 'Goodbye, Charlie Brown!' Madame is mighty angry."

The battle over de-indexing was the second part of the battle over universality, in some ways. By ruling out the fundamental reform that would give scarce benefits only to the needy, Mulroney had forced Wilson to penalize the poor as well as the rich. Moreover, the first battle had established that there wouldn't be any changes in benefits to the elderly and that any savings in other social programs wouldn't be used to lower the deficit. Above all, the reaction to the retreat on universality had conditioned Mulroney and Wilson to take a tougher stand in the budget and afterwards. Now, and for a month, they stumbled over themselves and each other trying to defend the increasingly indefensible from the opposition, the Tory caucus, editorialists, demonstrations, petitions, Tory premiers, and even (oh, treachery) the Business Council on National Issues.

First, Mulroney resorted to blaming the Liberals for leaving the government in such a fiscal mess. Then Wilson told the House of Commons that he had spoken to some senior citizens, and "many of them have said, 'You're right to do what you're doing, because we are worried about our grandchildren, about that $6,000 of debt that is put on the head of every baby when they're born.' " Even though the "many" might have been a few who had statistics put in their mouths, Wilson vowed that no amount of pressure would force the Tories to back down in the short term. The Prime Minister was as firm. "There will be no change," he advised the House on June 5, though he promised to monitor the impact of de-indexation "to ensure to the extent humanly possible and as quickly as finances permit that no difficulty is sustained by our elderly in Canada."

The political heat continued, however. A week later

Brian Mulroney suggested in the House that the de-indexing of pensions was only a "proposal" that might not have to be put into effect if the economy continued to improve. Not long after that, the Prime Minister sat down with his cabinet to decide how they could surrender without looking like patsies. Some wanted to hold fast; some wanted to maintain the partial de-indexation of pensions while boosting the Guaranteed Income Supplement to the neediest pensioners. Finally, with no consensus in sight and with the issue threatening to distract the government from its agenda all through the summer break, Mulroney got Wilson to announce a complete reversal on June 27. The Minister of Finance only managed to salvage a morsel of his pride and fiscal integrity by imposing extra taxes on corporations and gasoline, but he warned that the government would have to find more revenue after three years to make up the lost difference. Caught between demonstrating strength and displaying pigheadedness, Mulroney had opted once again for harmony and prudence.

"The government, for which I assume full responsibility, clearly, in hindsight, did not proceed in as wise a manner, in retrospect, as should have been the case," the Prime Minister confessed abjectly on June 28 to reporters. "We are not here as emperors, we are in Parliament as commoners, servants of the people. We never contended we were perfect, but we always said we would try and be fair. I think we violated that rule of fairness, as it turns out, and we had to correct it."

It wasn't exactly the "we will fight them in the hills, we will never surrender" school of leadership. However, it had the advantage of allowing Mulroney to shift the blame within moments to the opposition, the media, and the people themselves. "Are we capable of having a mature and reasonable debate in Canada on such an issue? Are we able as a country to recognize that we are caught with a deficit problem which rivals that of countries in serious trouble elsewhere? Do we have the national maturity to recognize that we can no longer do as we please?" Then he gave a sadder, wiser, and franker answer than he had given in the past. "I don't know, but I can tell you that what I've seen so far of public debates at the national level doesn't inspire me with confidence."

After only nine months Brian Mulroney was beginning to see the limits to reason, consensus, and charm. In fact, he seemed to be echoing Pierre Trudeau's despair after the 1972 election that "nine-tenths of politics appeals to emotions rather than to reason." Like Trudeau, Mulroney gave in because, as he said, "I'm a pragmatist and a realist."

III

One battle—or even two battles—does not make a war. Reducing the deficit was only a part of the Tories' general strategy to move the responsibility for growth and jobs from the government to business. "The cuts will be joined and married to a brand new program of fiscal initiatives and so on," Mulroney said, "that will enhance the new climate of job creation that we're trying to initiate."

The aim, the result of his 1960s liberalism, was to de-centralize power away from Ottawa by putting more and more economic decisions in the hands of the private-sector elites. Government would then aid, coordinate, and ac-commodate them for the good of the nation. Jobs would then be *real* jobs, rather than makeshift, unproductive work created at enormous public expense. Investment would then be encouraged to increase and be geared to the mar-ketplace, rather than scared away and wasted on unprof-itable social goals. Entrepreneurs would then be freed from excessive regulation and burdensome taxes, rather than hampered in their manoeuvrability and penalized for the success of their risks. As a consequence, there would be more jobs, more investment, more revenues for social pro-grams, and more entrepreneurs to promote even more prosperity.

Despite Canada's political cultures and unchanging re-gard for the state in general, and despite the impressive growth in gross domestic product and real disposable in-come between 1968 and 1984, Trudeauism became linked with the worst effects of the recession. As a result, the public was open to fresh approaches. "The trauma of the recession caused Canadians to change their attitudes and their behaviour in a very fundamental way," Allan Gregg said. "In a country that had been historically characterized for its pragmatic appreciation of government intervention into the business and private sector, we saw a population ascribing direct liabilities to this form of government initiative. As concern about unemployment increased, support for government spending to create public-works jobs or to assist financially ailing industry as a means of job support dropped dramatically. And in a nation that had always displayed deference to the country's major institutions as the principal solver of individual problems, we saw a population emerge from the recession with a renewed sense of personal powerfulness and individualism."

It was hardly necessary for Gregg to add that, in this context, "an opposition party who had been constantly attacking prevailing government solutions and who adopted a more individualistic and pro-business posture would find favour with the public."

Cautiously, therefore, without frightening people by dramatic proposals or a rush into the unknown, Mulroney felt permitted to pursue this line of thinking in the election and afterwards. Though he toned down some of his more colourful indignation about how the Liberals had tried to "Swedenize" Canada, he continued to play up their statism and its ill effects. He ignored the relative success of the "6-and-5" program as an exercise in controlling inflation by means of voluntary cooperation among government, business, and labour. He blamed the National Energy Program for the West's troubles more than the fall in world oil prices. He highlighted the losses in Ottawa's involvement in Canadair and Canada Post and not the gains in Ottawa's help to Chrysler Canada and Dome Petroleum. He catered to the anti-government prejudices in the business community without mentioning the government's huge tax concessions, its tolerance of gigantic conglomerates and monopolies, and its efforts to promote research and exports.

That's not to imply there weren't serious problems with the Liberals' approach. Once they decided, for pragmatic reasons, "to do what was right" for national unity and the national interest after 1980, they were in danger of losing the acceptable balance between authority and freedom. It was their very conviction that they were right—with God, the people, and eleven years of bad history on their side— that made them dangerous. Because their push was to- ward community, centralization, and leadership, their vic- tims tended to be individuals, locality, and consensus. Trudeau himself recognized that his new emphasis, "The government must be able to govern," could lead to total- itarianism as easily as to a just society.

Trudeau was able to find reassurance by creating his own counterweights and by knowing he wasn't Mussolini. Many people weren't certain about either. Even those who trusted Trudeau couldn't be so sure of his ministers. Freed and revitalized by the spirit of activism that pervaded their last term, some of them picked up Trudeau's worst traits— his Cartesian perfectionism, his disdain for lesser humans, his love of bullying and a good argument—without bal- ancing them against his better characteristics. That seemed to be especially true in the government's relationship with business. Trudeau set the tone with his personal contempt for most businessmen. National purpose, national interest, and the will of the people did the rest.

Thus, often for the best of reasons, the Liberals had set out to handle the business community like they han- dled the provinces, equipped with big sticks and a gross of carrots. Ministers didn't hesitate to threaten chief ex- ecutive officers with laws, orders-in-council, and various forms of state intervention. "You do it," the message said, "or we'll do it." Meanwhile, through the tax system, grants, and other kinds of suasion, companies were encouraged to take decisions or make investments for political and social reasons. In both cases, the market was upset by incursions that weren't productive, planned, or profitable. The clearest example of both techniques at work simul- taneously (and their negative impact) was the Petroleum Incentives Payments grants in the NEP. They arbitrarily favoured the Canadian energy companies over the mul- tinationals; then they lured those companies into exploring on federal lands in the frontier; and the result was little oil and the waste of billions of dollars of taxpayers' and investors' money.

The attitude of the ministers penetrated through the federal bureaucracy, which was already distant enough by history, geography, and mentality from the boardrooms of the nation. "There are only three ways to deal with the private sector," said one very senior official at the time. "Consider it the source of all wisdom, ignore it, or get it before it gets you."

Almost every major businessman in Canada knew what Mulroney meant when he used to say during the Tory leadership race, "You go up to Ottawa to see one of those bureaucrats in their offices, which are usually larger than your factory, and you don't know if they will talk to you or send you out for coffee." Everyone had a horror story about the delays in getting a decision, harassment from Revenue Canada, and the paper-strewn maze of Ottawa. In many ways, the NEP was crucified less by its broad political ambitions than by its destructive bureaucratic details, which showed no sensitivity to the customs and requirements of a corporate balance sheet. The disastrous MacEachen budget in 1981 became the classic illustration of the ignorance and arrogance of officialdom.

Even worse than the departments were all the regulatory agencies that had sprung up in the 1970s, from the CRTC to the Canadian Transport Commission. They added to the time and cost of business decisions, and their corridors seemed impenetrable. Though technically they were accountable to the cabinet or Parliament, the provisions to protect their integrity from political interference meant that it wasn't simple for the corporate old boys to get things done by a call to a deputy minister, a lunch with a cabinet minister, or even a chat with the Prime Minister at a Toronto Club fund raiser. To both Brian Mulroney and John Turner, the agencies became proof that rigid, systematic administration didn't work as well as good old Canadian elite accommodation. Their friends on Bay Street and St. James Street had told them so a thousand times.

The problems of attitude and structure were compounded by the size of the federal government. When it entered the economy as an active player, it came in like an elephant strolling into a vegetable market. Oblivious to the effect of its size or appetite, it caused the small and the intimidated to panic. To promote certain activities or establish a national presence, Ottawa charged into almost every sector and region with authority, cash, and self-righteous purpose. Crown corporations were developed and enhanced long after their original *raison d'être* had been served and forgotten. More and more important decisions were passed up to the centre, where they got lost in the shuffle or made by people who had never seen the product or town concerned. In an environment accustomed to thinking of dollars in terms of billions and unaccustomed to relating those billions to a bottom-line profit, money seemed the least concern. As a result, while all businesses suffered from distortions and insecurity, small and entre-preneurial businesses were particularly nervous. Many looked at the elephant grazing in the marketplace, heard its bellows, and figured the risks were too great and the rewards not great enough.

Of course, some learned to tame and ride the elephant. While many old boys cowered in their leather armchairs and many young hustlers headed for safer ground, a lot of clever individuals and companies cottoned on to the new game as soon as the government created it. Banks such as the Nova Scotia, oilmen such as Jack Gallagher of Dome and Bob Blair of Nova, French-Canadian entrepre-neurs such as Paul Desmarais and Robert Campeau, most of the Ottawa Valley high-tech companies, and a host of others discovered certain advantages in understanding what Ottawa was trying to do. In most cases, they stood apart from their community's cant, bitching, and hypocrisy and tried to cooperate with the politicians, who were after all elected by the people and preoccupied with wider prob-lems than those of Bay Street. However, though their enlightened approach was appreciated and generally re-warded, their appearance on the back of the elephant only served to alienate further those who weren't as fortunate.

The overall effect of government involvement was a vicious circle; and, like a circle, no one knew where it started or where to break it. The government felt the private sector hadn't been doing its job well enough. Therefore, for the sake of the national interest, Ottawa felt it had to step in, one way or another. The more it stepped in, however, the less the private sector felt willing or able to do its job. That made the government feel even more obliged to intervene, and so on. The pertinent questions were: Had the private sector been doing its job well enough? Did the government have to step in to the extent it did? Once in, could the government get out, or would it inevitably be drawn in further?

The election of the Progressive Conservatives in 1984 forced a fresh perspective on these fundamental questions. Indeed, nothing demonstrated more clearly the value of changing the party of government regularly in a democracy. After almost twenty years of continuous Liberal rule, everyone had become fossilized. Liberal ministers wouldn't consider an idea in 1981 because something like it hadn't worked in 1975. Business leaders turned down invitations to work with the government, even as cabinet ministers, because any association with the Liberals was like treason to their peers. Misrepresentations and a litany of personal grudges on both sides stood in the way of establishing better policies or better rapport. With the Tories, the outs got a chance to be in. New players brought new experiences and new energy. Old programs and methods became subject to review, and even if the government opted to maintain them, at least they had been reassessed with a more critical and clinical eye. Rapidly, without altering a law, the word reached every corner of the bureaucracy that officials were expected to "interface" more efficiently and sympathetically with the private sector. Revenue Canada was told by its knowledgeable and amiable young minister, Perrin Beatty, to call off its Dobermans. In short, the mere change brought a beneficial power to heal the wounds of the past.

Mulroney and Wilson built on that power with their pro-business speeches, the Minister of Finance's *Agenda for Economic Renewal* in November, the National Economic Summit in March, and their first budget in May. In addition to the somewhat weakened signal about the deficit, the budget proposed specific tax reductions and tax changes to encourage entrepreneurial risk taking and small-business investment. The catchiest proposal was a cumulative, life-time exemption of $500,000 on an individual's capital gains. Afterwards, Mulroney declared that "the thrust of the entire budget is devoted to people who will take risks, who will go that extra mile, get up that half-hour earlier."

"Certainly," Michael Wilson said, "during the period of time that I was in the private sector, I saw a gradual decline during the course of the Seventies. I saw it imperceptibly and in a very real way. People were just pulling in their horns and saying, 'It's not worth the risk to my capital and taking a mortgage on my house to invest it in my small business.' I think we can turn people on. I think we can give them a sense that there is a real future here.

"We have identified those key areas in the economy where we can motivate the private sector to give us the biggest and fastest response: small business, energy, research and development, trade. What we are trying to do is use a little bit of leverage from the tax system to get the private sector off and running and creating the economic opportunities which will bring the jobs that we have to have to get the unemployment rate down. We can't afford to go the other way. It doesn't work."

That might be good economics in the long term, but it proved poor politics in the short term. The capital gains exemption, which allowed someone to save $125,000 when selling a Picasso as well as creating a job, was swiftly put in juxtaposition to the proposed de-indexing of old-age pensions. Wilson compounded the apparent unfairness by implying that the burden of the deficit had to be placed on the backs of the old rather than the rich because "Canada has an acute shortage of rich people."

If the unfairness were simply a matter of the Tories tossing a juicy bone to their corporate backers, the political problem could have been solved by more judicious pay-offs. The problem, however, was an integral part of the private-enterprise approach. At the same time that businessmen and their associations were calling for a $5-billion

slash in the deficit, either by ending universality or reducing unemployment benefits, they were calling for increased tax breaks for corporations and investors. Indeed,
they argued, the two had to go hand in hand for the approach to work. Thus, William Mackness, a vice-president
of the Bank of Nova Scotia, complained in 1983 about "the
mounting tax burden which has increasingly discriminated
against capital accumulation. As long as Canadian industry is so perilously undercapitalized, there should be little
or no taxation of earnings that are reinvested in the capital
base." (In 1984 he went on leave from the bank to serve
as a special policy adviser to Michael Wilson.)

Yet, by the time the Tories came to power, it was estimated that various forms of corporate tax concessions
cost Ottawa $11 billion in lost revenue a year and had cost
nearly $100 billion since 1976. The effect was to lower the
average federal corporate income tax from 36 per cent of
profits to 15 per cent. Even under the Liberals, the manufacturing sector alone saved more through its breaks than
all Canadians saved through the child tax credit, and individuals bore more than 75 per cent of the tax load. "We
probably deserved more criticism from the socialists than
from business," said Herb Gray, the Minister of Industry,
Trade and Commerce in Trudeau's last cabinet. "In the
context of pursuing national goals, we propped up the
private sector."

Moreover, among those individuals, the system was
weighted in favour of higher-income earners, through a
myriad of tax dodges, to the extent that thousands of wealthy
Canadians who paid no taxes at all became an election
issue with all three major parties. On the other hand,
everyone remembered what the vested interests had done
to Allan MacEachen when he tried to correct some of the
flagrant inequities in his 1981 budget.

Wilson's 1985 budget accentuated those inequities. The
previous November Mulroney had said that raising taxes
wasn't "on the top of the hit parade" because "Canadians
are already paying a pretty hefty bundle for their govern-
mental services." But once he prevented Wilson from
touching universality and other spending areas, some-

thing had to give on the revenue side if a signal was to be sent on the deficit. As it happened, ordinary Canadians were made to give. The federal sales tax was hiked, the gas tax rose, and de-indexing was proposed. Meanwhile, the private sector received its "bit of leverage" to get off and running. The well-to-do received their capital gains exemption, the oil industry received about $2.5 billion from the replacement of the NEP by the Western Energy Accord, and the artful dodgers received a reprieve from the minimum tax promised by Mulroney during the election and as Prime Minister. Basically, money was taken from consumers and given to investors.

At the same time, Ottawa was calculated to be spending between $5 billion and $7 billion on grants, subsidies, and services of all sorts to the private sector. In general, both the Tories and the business lobby proclaimed an aversion toward direct help. Wilson even cut $200 million in November and $250 million in May from industrial development programs, while he shifted government support to the tax system. Direct assistance had come to be regarded as a Trojan horse: it looked like a prize of war, but once accepted, it brought the enemy into the fortified city. While tax concessions were hidden and usually universal, grants and subsidies were obvious intrusions into the marketplace. They allowed the government to set conditions, play favourites, and intervene in the details of corporate decisions. In other words, they promoted the centralization of power in Ottawa.

Moreover, the more sophisticated lobbyists had realized the political damage in the traditional business pattern of asking for deficit cuts and government hand-outs in the same petitions. The contradiction often allowed Liberal ministers to dismiss one or even both. In most cases, however, the Liberals were softer touches than the Tories proved to be, if only because the Liberals needed to buy business support while the Tories inherited it. The more important reason was the economic and political pragmatism the Liberals had learned in government.

The Conservatives learned it quickly. The most illustrative and publicized lesson came early in 1985 when

Domtar requested $117 million from Ottawa's Industrial and Regional Development Program to help pay for the company's $1.2-billion modernization of its paper mill at Windsor, Quebec. According to Domtar, the federal money was needed in order to get another $83 million from the Quebec government, and both grants were needed before the company could undertake the modernization and save seven hundred jobs. On February 21 Sinclair Stevens, the Minister of Regional Industrial Expansion, rejected the application, primarily because Domtar had made a profit of almost $90 million in 1984 and the Windsor project was expected to yield at least a 10 per cent return without a subsidy. "A profitable company like Domtar does not have to turn to the federal treasury," Stevens said. As well, by contributing to a possible over-supply of fine paper, Ottawa would be obliged to assist any other paper producer that asked for help.

The Quebec Tory caucus, the Quebec media, and the Quebec government all howled at Stevens's decision and appealed to the Prime Minister. Clearly votes were at stake as much as jobs. While Mulroney noted that "Domtar's financial situation is better than that of the federal government," he overruled his minister and agreed to seek a formula that would let the project proceed. In early April Ottawa and Quebec announced they would give Domtar an interest-free $150-million loan, which was expected to cost the federal government $38 million over ten years.

A week earlier, during a visit to his riding, the Prime Minister had also indicated that help was coming to reopen the ITT-Rayonnier pulp mill in Port Cartier, Quebec, where thirteen hundred jobs had been lost by the closing six years before. He was looking for private investors, he said, "but in the absence of such a breakthrough, we'll have to act. If we don't meet with enough success in this area, the government of Canada will intervene to ensure that a project that will guarantee an imposing number of lasting jobs in the region."

The forest products industry wasn't unique. Federal money went to a petro-chemical producer in Montreal, a helicopter plant in Quebec and another in Ontario, a heavy oil upgrading plant in Alberta and an aluminum wheel plant in British Columbia, even an auto plant outside Toronto. In October Fishery Products International, the Newfoundland company established as a result of Michael Kirby's task force under the Liberals and 62.2 per cent owned by Ottawa, got another $113 million. In November, after Stevens turned down a grant application from Cominco, Ottawa purchased $69 million worth of preferred shares in the company to help it build a new lead smelter in Trail, British Columbia.

Also in November, in the middle of the Quebec election campaign, the Tories agreed to pay up to $55 million in interest payments over five years as part of a $200-million loan arranged by the Parti Québécois government to lure the Hyundai Motor Company of South Korea into building an auto plant in Bromont, outside Montreal. In the PQ's rush to secure a deal as an election bonus, no one seemed to ask if Hyundai needed the lure. In fact, a company spokesman said on television that "we didn't ask for anything from anyone," and that they would have built the plant for market reasons without the subsidy. But, he added, "you cannot refuse gifts."

Even more controversial and expensive was Ottawa's failed attempt to rescue the Canadian Commercial Bank (CCB) of Edmonton in March, 1985. The federal government lost about $150 million directly and indirectly in the rescue operation it arranged with Alberta and British Columbia, six banks, and the Canada Deposit Insurance Corporation. That wasn't the worst. Because of the emphatic repetitions by the Prime Minister, the Minister of Finance, the Minister of State for Finance, the Governor of the Bank of Canada, and the Inspector-General of Banks that the CCB, and every other Canadian bank, were viable, the federal government was forced to bail out all the uninsured depositors when the CCB and the Northland Bank of Calgary collapsed in September. Whether healthy confidence or blatant incompetence, the cost was around $850 million. In essence, Ottawa spent a billion dollars to clean up the marketplace's mess.

The Prime Minister didn't explain it quite that way.

Instead, he spoke of the need "to come to the assistance of fledgling financial institutions based in Western Canada" which failed "in large measure" because of the climate "induced by the National Energy Program." The Liberals, he added, "are going to have some explaining to do. They created the Charter B banks and they then plunged them into an economic situation in Western Canada and passed the NEP unilaterally that flattened the economy." He didn't mention the fall in world oil prices, the usurious interest rates set by American levels, the bust in Alberta's real estate market brought on by a national as well as regional recession, the effect of Peter Lougheed's own power plays on the Alberta economy, the CCB's disastrous investments in the United States, or even the unsettling connection among the CCB's former president, an ex-director, and the trust company scandals that rocked Ontario in 1983. Indeed, during the government's investigation into the banks' failure, the NEP was proven not to have been a significant factor at all.

It wasn't unusual for the Tories to use the Liberal legacy to account for the glaring difference between their free-market vision and their mounting bills. Often they didn't have to resort to Mulroney's more irresponsible exercises in dissimulation. In most cases it was perfectly clear that the rules and habits of state intervention had profoundly influenced the way the Canadian private sector did business. As in the Domtar case, the first question many executives and entrepreneurs asked when they contemplated an investment was, "Can I get a government grant or tax break or monopoly or protectionist measure to reduce my risk?" Since many of them could, going to the government became as normal a step as going to the bank manager. Indeed, not going to the government was soon considered stupid, as well as a competitive disadvantage, by giant conglomerates, foreign multinationals, anti-Liberal takeover artists, and all their expensive Ottawa lobbyists.

To blame Trudeauism for creating a generation of subsidy addicts was convenient and of some truth, but it missed the greater problem. In more cases than Adam Smith would have cared to hear about, the problem was less the restoration of business confidence than the absence of any confidence in the first place. After all, John A. Macdonald had to hand over public money and large chunks of Western Canada in order to get the CPR built, and even then there was more American gumption and English capital involved than native hustle. Nor were things much different in the 1950s when C. D. Howe (himself born in the bosom of Yankee trade) came to build a trans-Canada pipeline. And in the 1980s when Brian Mulroney decided Domtar couldn't compete in the United States market, despite a 72-cent dollar, without millions of federal dollars it seemed as if things hadn't changed at all.

Canada's business culture was closely related to its political cultures. From the start the lack of sufficient capital, the small population, the huge distances, and a fear of the Americans established financial, legislative, and psychological links between the private and public sectors. There was even a long, pseudo-aristocratic tradition among the educated elites of both French and English Canada that public service was worthier than trade. Well into the 1970s, for example, there seemed more glory and excitement in the Privy Council Office than at Canadian Pacific.

More significant than that, however, was the corporate mentality conditioned by an economic history of natural-resource extraction and foreign ownership. Exploiting and selling resources produced enormous profits for relatively little ingenuity, and a lot of entrepreneurial zeal was concentrated in paper transactions, in moving those profits through various financial institutions for further profits. At the same time, the presence of mammoth British and American concerns in the Canadian marketplace discouraged young and aggressive Canadians from getting into manufacturing, research, and other non-resource or non-financial ventures. In other words, it was rather easy to make a buck, particularly in the decade after the Second World War, without having to take excessive risks. The vast American market was on the doorstep, the world was in poorer shape and had an insatiable demand for Canada's raw materials, there was plenty of money to buy whatever the United States or Europe manufactured, and there was adequate protection for Canadian companies when required.

All these factors produced tendencies that have become familiar by repetition: the closed and cautious clubs, the aversion to risk and innovation by bankers and investors alike, the high rate of savings, the rapidity with which medium-sized home-grown enterprises are sold to foreigners, the drain of brains and entrepreneurial talent to the south, Canada's weakness in expanding into new sectors and new world markets, and so on. "We cannot blame others for our own failures and mismanagement," said Walter Light, the chairman of Northern Telecom, when rejecting the argument that government and tariffs were responsible for the decline in Canada's share of the international market. Instead, he cited the private sector's failure to develop manufacturing industries that could compete around the world, to invest money in research and development, to make products that were better or cheaper than those made by foreign competitors, or to adapt to new technology.

Mulroney himself, in a candid and controversial quote in *Fortune* in March, 1985, admitted as much. "We do not have a very good track record," he said. "Our products have not been of the highest quality. Our deliveries have been lacking in reliability. Our expertise has been in large measure borrowed. Our technology has been purchased. What the hell makes us so special?"

As a consequence, the Canadian economy still depended heavily on the export of food and resources toward the end of the twentieth century. In the meantime, the world demand for raw materials dropped sharply and foreign competition from places such as Brazil (where trees grew faster) and Chile (where copper came cheaper) rose swiftly. Even when Canada could compete, there was a steep price to pay. "Our resource industries are no longer as labour-intensive as they once were," Walter Light said, "and they no longer are creating the new jobs we must create if our young people are to have a future in Canada."

Michael Wilson knew the problems, but he believed that the right climate of confidence, a clear signal on the deficit, and selective tax incentives would begin to meet them. "We think that the private sector will respond and will create those jobs. It's a break from the past. We have said that the private sector has got to do this, not the government."

In the context, his challenge seemed either a long-shot gamble or a long-term haul. Companies needed some guarantees about markets, prices, and profits before they would invest, regardless of the good will emanating out of Ottawa. The harsh reality was that no growth in the foreseeable future could match that of the 1950s or 1960s, when prosperity had made Mulroney's kind of decentralized liberalism practical. In all industrial nations of every political hue, intervention had increased as a pragmatic reaction to the economic turmoils of the post-industrial age. State companies, state money, state partnerships, and state regulations were the general result of trying to help the private sector as well as the national economy through two oil crises, inflation, recession, and the most important shift in technology since the industrial revolution. Even Ronald Reagan wasn't ready to throw the ball back to American entrepreneurs without at the same time throwing them billions of dollars in defence contracts for high-tech research and development.

In Canada there was still an active debate about whether there were enough Canadian entrepreneurs to throw the ball to. Many of the country's best-known businessmen were known for corporate takeovers which, the Prime Minister often lamented, "never created a single job or a barrel of oil" while using up productive capital and driving up interest rates. Many of the country's largest corporations had become huge bureaucracies, headed by CEOs who had got beyond the cares or clutches of real owners. Many of the country's brightest hopes went down in the recession, sold out to the Americans, took themselves or their jobs to the United States, or just couldn't survive in the vicious world market.

Another fundamental problem was regional development. Productivity and competitiveness were rarely enhanced by putting industries into Canada's hinterland, yet for political and philosophical reasons every Canadian government was committed to doing that. Thus, while Wilson finally closed down the heavy water plants in Glace Bay and Port Hawkesbury, Nova Scotia—which he correctly described as "striking symbols of government waste and mismanagement" that cost "more than $100 million per year to produce a product for which there is no demand"—he announced "enriched" tax incentives to attract new investment to Cape Breton.

"Regional development cannot be left solely to the private sector," Brian Peckford, the Premier of Newfoundland, said. "The private sector is extremely weak in most disadvantaged regions. Often private-sector development, even in activities where the region has a comparative advantage, requires a program of facilitative regional development activities by government. Because the private sector is so weak, the tax-based approach, or even the standard grant approach to industrial development, will not bring about any significant measure of regional economic development. These approaches presuppose the existence of a strong, vibrant private sector."

If Wilson had to deviate from his general policy not to intrude in the marketplace's decisions, in order to dissuade industries from clustering in Central Canada, he also had to move some distance from his tax-based approach. As Peckford said, tax breaks don't work if there are no businesses to use them or profits to exempt. Moreover, in all parts of the country, tax concessions tended to assist capital-intensive industries more than labour-intensive ones, to undermine the tax system's effectiveness as an instrument of redistribution and macroeconomic stability, and to reduce the precision with which Ottawa could influence the private sector's decisions. They also made it virtually impossible for Ottawa to discriminate in favour of Canadian companies.

That's why the Liberals had come to prefer grants over tax incentives. In the energy sector, for example, they found that all their tax breaks before 1979 had yielded few results in terms of self-sufficiency and Canadianization. In the NEP, therefore, the PIP grants were designed to boost

both. The same tactic was applied in other sectors. Whenever Ottawa had to step in with a regional development
program or a bail-out, it used the opportunity to set conditions for productivity, modernization, exports, and other
industrial goals. Grants also allowed Ottawa to back "winners" and "chosen instruments" for growth and world
competitiveness. Indeed, it was the very power of grants
that made businessmen—and consequently the Tories—
detest them.

Canadians might have felt more comfortable about the
Tories' deliberate withdrawal from this area if the business
community had shown itself generally more responsive to
the national interest. Even opponents of the capital gains
tax recognized that the 1985 budget's exemption would
cost Ottawa $1 billion per year by 1990 without guaran-
teeing that the money went toward jobs or productive
investments. The NEP had introduced the Petroleum and
Gas Revenue Tax (PGRT), which was basically a royalty
on production rather than a tax on net revenue, because
the energy companies had more or less arranged their
books so as not to show taxable revenue. And as soon as
the Tories got into office, they encountered a classic example of the private sector's worst attitude. In January,
1984, the Liberals had established the scientific research
tax credit, a particularly generous incentive to promote
investment in high-risk research and development. It was
quickly transformed by entrepreneurial creativity into a
"quick-flip" technique of complex corporate transactions,
which produced an uncertain amount of research of uncertain value at a cost to Canadian taxpayers estimated
between $2 billion and $3 billion. When Wilson moved to
check the abuses in October, 1984, investors invented even
more complex transactions to get around the spirit of the
incentive.

"Did you ever expect a corporation to have a conscience," said an eminent British jurist in the eighteenth century, "when it has no soul to be damned and no body to
be kicked?" Yet often it wasn't a matter of conscience. The
business of business is profit, after all, and must remain
profit. But in their dogged pursuit of the profits by which

they are judged and rewarded, businessmen often become blind to the political landscape through which they are tearing. The Canadian Manufacturers' Association helped neither itself nor the Tories' approach by suggesting that laws regarding child labour, minimum wages, and health and safety standards be reconsidered. Nor did Inco help when it threatened to lay off younger workers if older ones didn't accept early retirement, which the Tories had discouraged by making changes to the unemployment insurance program in the fall of 1984 in order to save $90 million in benefit payments. The Minister of Employment and Immigration, Flora MacDonald, even publicly questioned "the behaviour of a company that has returned a substantial profit margin ($33 million in the first half of this year), has done that on the backs of the employees, and is now threatening the employees—and indeed the community—with further lay-offs."

Charles Baird, Inco's chairman, replied that reductions in the company's labour force were merely a response to the "exhortations of government at all levels to improve the competitiveness" of Canadian industry. He was probably right, but his position showed up the tensions and dilemmas in the free-market route. To exalt the private sector as "the engine of growth" was to imply that the vested interests of one social group were worthier than those of any other, including the national community as a whole. Whatever the good reasons for doing so, that spelt political trouble. For the inherent tendencies within Canadian business were toward corporate concentration and huge profits, combined with low wages, low standards, low employment, and regional disparity. Governments, formed by parties and pressed by a wide variety of national and social forces, had intervened repeatedly in the marketplace simply to control those inherent tendencies. Businessmen who asked politicians to do things that might hurt the party's chances in the next election were usually as naive and irrelevant as politicians who asked businessmen to do things that might hurt the company's chances to make a profit.

The silliest and most sensational illustration of this fundamental dichotomy was the tuna scandal at the end of the Tories' first year in power. Basically Star-Kist produced in its New Brunswick plant cans of tuna which government inspectors found rancid and unfit for human consumption. Understandably the company was ordered not to sell the tuna. However, representations were made to the region's MPs, job losses or lay-offs were threatened, and there was a lot of right-wing ranting in caucus and the Department of Fisheries about over-zealous bureaucrats applying the regulations too severely and interfering in the beneficial workings of the marketplace. Ultimately the issue went up to the minister, John Fraser, and he overruled his own officials. As a result, rancid tuna appeared in Canadian stores, people became either nauseous or outraged, the tuna hit the fan in the House of Commons, and the minister was compelled to resign.

In some ways, the tuna fiasco was a minor incident in the life of the government. In other ways, however, it touched upon the government's very soul. When a crowd greeted the Prime Minister on his arrival at a Toronto baseball game with the chant, "Tu-na! Tu-na! Tu-na!," the message wasn't just a tease. It was a reaffirmation that Canadians wanted the state managed well, not dismantled to appease business interests. The same message was sent when Canadians showed an openness toward the deregulation of the airline industry or the privatization of inefficient crown corporations *as long as* services weren't cut and jobs weren't lost. And that was what Canadians were saying when they supported the general notion of getting Ottawa off the backs of entrepreneurs, but wanted acid rain cleaned up and hinterland towns kept open. If corporations insisted on talking about the bottom line, most Canadians could respond with some bottom-line interests of their own: according to one university study, almost one-third of total personal income comes from government wages and transfer payments and since 1975 half of all adult Canadians have been dependent on government for a "significant" proportion of their income.

"While the public had concluded that it was the private

sector that it must look to for solutions to economic problems," Allan Gregg said at the end of 1984, "the public
also began to develop doubts not only about business's
ability to generate these solutions, but also about its willingness to do so. In fact, over the last year there has been
considerable growth in the belief that an unregulated business community would not work in the public's best interest. In fact, I would go further and say that the business
community is close to becoming associated with a double
standard that transmits the impression that the public must
suffer for business to prosper."

That impression was reinforced throughout 1985. What
the budget proposed to take from senior citizens was worth
almost the same amount that it proposed to give to investors under the capital-gains exemption. The same week
that the government bailed out the CCB's depositors, Mulroney told reporters that the social policy debate was closed
because "the country is broke," "bankrupt." According to
every statistic, the large got larger, the rich got richer, the
middle class got stung, and the unemployed got cutbacks.
While the Reichmann brothers of Olympia and York Developments received a tax break worth some $600 million
to help them buy Gulf Canada, the Canadian taxpayers'
$750-million investment in de Havilland's Dash 8 aircraft
was practically given away in a bargain-basement sale to
Boeing of Seattle, Washington, on the eve of profitability.
And while Revenue Canada signalled a bright new day
for corporations, it launched a drive against delinquent
Newfoundland fishermen.

Indeed, the business community seemed to have the
Tories boxed. Every demand was reasonable and useful
within the free-market scenario of long-term good; each
failure by Ottawa to comply seemed to shake business
confidence to its foundations, and thus weaken the entire
strategy. After the budget, business complained that the
deficit was still too high and then it moaned about the
extra taxes placed upon it. There was a great deal of self-
serving in all this, of course. If Pierre Trudeau had arrived
at his classic liberalism from the left, intellectually, and for

the sake of democratic control, businessmen had arrived at their classic liberal rhetoric from the right, pragmatically, and for the sake of "divide and conquer."

However, just as Trudeau had discovered the drawbacks to individualism and decentralization in government, the Tories rejected business's *laissez-faire* liberalism (alias Reaganomics, alias Thatcherism) for their own 1960s Canadian variety. In fact, as evident in the battles over social policy, they even began to succumb to the transformation of view common to almost all who go from being outs to being ins. In short time the requirements of the national interest and the central state became manifest in many areas, and the need to check power appeared less urgent to those who now controlled it.

In the Department of Regional Industrial Expansion, for example, Sinclair Stevens seemed to have undergone a widely noticed conversion from the days when he was known as "Slasher" for his tirades against the federal bureaucracy. Though he still didn't like deficits, he argued that growth was more important than reduced spending; and though he still didn't like grants, he agreed to help Domtar, Hyundai, and a host of others. More significant, impressed by Japan's strategic intervention and the legend of C. D. Howe (behind whose oak desk Stevens sat), he became obsessed with Canada's long-term industrial development. He set out to make Ottawa a major participant in the direction and details of corporate planning. While his approach was heavy on consultation, consensus, and tax incentives, his aim was to involve the federal government in fifteen-year sectoral agreements and specialized agreements with companies in need of capital assistance over a lengthy period. They would require specific commitments, government access to investment plans, and definite quid pro quos—or else, presumably, the companies would either get nothing or be forced to do something. The face was friendlier and the voice knew the proper buzz-words, but Stevens's ideas made his friends in the business community skittish for sounding highly Liberal.

"In the past," Stevens said, "those who run our businesses have often acted as if they had only a limited responsibility to their workers and to their communities when they have to close plants or restructure them. I am a strong believer in free enterprise. But if our free-enterprise system is to survive, it is going to have to face up to its social responsibilities, and rank these higher than short-term greed."

In essence, social responsibility meant the creation of jobs. More than any other indicator, the unemployment rate would show the success of both the private sector and the Tories. Moreover, the judgement would come within four years. "This public is very quick to abandon those in whom it feels it has misplaced its expectations and hopes," Allan Gregg said. "If the public continues to question the activities and public-mindedness of the private sector, then the mandate of the new government will similarly change."

That was the Tories' gamble. Even if their free-market approach brought incomparable rewards in the long term, the party had to survive in the short term. In the short term it faced the reduction in demand that was expected to result from the reduction in government spending, a battered private sector still hesitant to invest and expand until demand and recovery were certain, and strong and aggressive foreign competition. It faced weak markets for resources, the shift from labour-intensive industry to high technology, and the rationalization of work for greater productivity. It faced the retrenchment of foreign companies, the movement of Canadian capital to the United States, and the impact of high interest rates. It faced the perennial problems of regional underdevelopment, an ingrained cultural bias toward saving as opposed to risk taking, and a notoriously cautious business ethos attached for traditional and pragmatic reasons to government assistance.

Working in their favour, the Tories had the spin-off from the American recovery (though no one knew how long that could last), some good economic indicators (most of which were also linked to the American recovery), their own optimism and good will, and the pressure on Canadian business to perform. "For many years," said William Mulholland, chairman of the Bank of Montreal, "business leaders have argued that given a government with a favourable outlook, the private sector would be better at creating jobs and wealth than any public body. This makes good sense, and the time has now come for the private sector, by its actions, to demonstrate that it can deliver."

"This bus is not going by fifteen times," Mulroney told the readers of the *Financial Post*. "The bus is going by now. And what Mulholland was properly saying is that this is the time to get on."

Some more passengers, a little distance, and heading in the right direction would please the government and the private sector, but it was uncertain whether they would be sufficient to please the voters, who tend to share the opinion that "In the long term we'll all be dead." Happy trends and rosy forecasts wouldn't seem cause for public rejoicing if the jobless rate persisted in hovering around 10 per cent (20 per cent in Newfoundland), if more than a million people couldn't find work, and if two-thirds of Canadians continued to live in fear that they or the family breadwinner would lose their jobs in the foreseeable future.

To take the bus through that would require more than luck, charm, and more promises. It would require political will and a determination to persevere at the risk of unpopularity. In his first year as Prime Minister, Brian Mulroney sent decidedly mixed signals to the businesss community about his staying power. His spirit was more than willing, but his flesh seemed weak. If he was ready to subsidize Domtar and Hyundai in year one, what wouldn't he subsidize in year four? Though he showed no end of a patience to consult and seek consensus, overhead hung swords such as make-work projects, central industrial strategies, wage-and-price controls, conditional grants and incentives, and pragmatism.

The Liberals had resorted to those weapons after they had tried the other route, met failure, and had nothing left to lose in terms of private-sector support. The Tories would be tempted to use them because, at heart, they knew that business was a minority with nowhere else to take its vote. It was also an interest group with an annoying habit of demanding its own way in strident terms, with an isolated view of the rest of society's concerns, and with

a ruthless regard for its bottom line. Like all vested interests, it wanted everything but had strict limits as to what
it would give back. Unlike most other vested interests,
which usually understood the costs of their demands, business believed fundamentally that it served the community
best by serving itself first. Thus, jobs would come from
profits before profits would come from jobs. That deep
faith in its own system, which was rooted in the all-too-
human realities of desire and ego, made businessmen wail
louder in prosperity than any welfare recipient in poverty.

By the end of 1985, some of the business community
were issuing thinly veiled threats to invest outside Canada,
to push down the Canadian dollar, and thus to push up
interest rates if the Tories' 1986 budget didn't slash the
deficit to their satisfaction, that is, dramatically and without hurting business's tax benefits. They probably realized, as Wilson himself realized, that this budget would
be "the most critical in this government's mandate," because it was the last chance to be really tough before the
swing toward the next election. However, it wasn't clear
why dramatic cuts would be easier in 1986 than in 1985,
though growth and lower interest rates had taken some
of the pressure off federal spending. "You can't just come
in here with the axe and start chopping away indiscrimi-
nately," Mulroney stated plainly in December, 1985, while
confirming his commitment to a gradual strategy.

Even worse, as far as business was concerned, was the
Tory government's proposal that same December of a minimum tax for high-income earners. In effect, it ruled out
a wide range of tax breaks and incentives, from dividend
tax credits to contributions to retirement savings plans, for
those who earned over $45,000 a year. By changing the
rules in the middle of the game (something the Tories had
vowed never to do) and by soaking businessmen for an
estimated $300 million in 1986, it threw the investment
community into panic and confusion, and prompted a lobbying effort unequalled since the disastrous MacEachen
budget of 1981. In fact, it undermined the confidence and
capacity of the very investors the Tories relied upon to
bolster the Canadian private sector. Yet the more the busi-

ness community became disaffected with Mulroney, the more he would become disaffected with it. Few Prime Ministers retain a belief that it is unreasonable to link private capital with public policy; few acts of state intervention in the Canadian economy were done for any other reason than the lack of a practical alternative; and few politicians can bear giving away power to those who throw rocks in return. By sharing the process with businessmen through consultation and decentralization, Mulroney was also sharing the blame in the event of failure. By giving them enough rope to run free, he was also giving them enough rope to hang themselves.

"I don't have all the answers," Brian Mulroney said of his economic strategy. "Maybe this is wrong; maybe this is not the right way to proceed. If it is not, I guess we will find out about it soon enough. But I'm ready to try. I think this is the way to go. If it turns out that changes should be made, we will make them. But I want to try, and I think we all want to try, that route first."

IV

When Brian Mulroney was a boy, he used to sing for Colonel Robert McCormick whenever the legendary Chicago newspaper tycoon arrived in Baie Comeau to inspect his paper mill. McCormick would summon forth little Brian and reward him with $50 for singing "Danny Boy" or "When Irish Eyes Are Smiling" or (the Colonel's favourite) "Dearie."

"I'd go sing," the Prime Minister later recounted. "I'd perform any song he'd want."

When Brian Mulroney grew up, he was hired by the Hanna Mining Company of Cleveland, Ohio, to sing for it as president of its affiliate, the Iron Ore Company of Canada. In return, he was rewarded with a mansion in Westmount, a membership in the Mount Royal Club, a fishing camp in Labrador, four box seats behind the Canadiens' bench at the Montreal Forum, and a five-year contract with equity and pension benefits that allowed Mulroney to become a politician without having to worry about Mila's shopping sprees.

So he had had some practice in singing for the Yankee dollar when he flew to New York to address the 306th dinner meeting of the Economic Club on December 10, 1984. This wasn't Baie Comeau or even Cleveland. This was Broadway, and Mulroney was going to sing *a capella* where Churchill, Nehru, Kennedy, Khrushchev, and Reagan had been before him. In other words, he had a very sophisticated and powerful audience: fifteen hundred Wall Street bulls and bears disguised for the evening as a mighty herd of penguins, reeking of aftershave and Reaganomics, with a scattering of elegant women and ambitious yuppies thrown in. David Rockefeller was there, chinwagging with His Excellency Stephen Lewis, the former leader of the Ontario NDP whom Mulroney had appointed Canadian ambassador to the United Nations. RCA, Prudential Insurance, *Time*, General Electric, Philip Morris, Citibank, and Goldman Sachs were also there. There was even a large contingent of chief executives from Toronto and Montreal, humming with talk of convertible debentures and winter resorts in the glitzy Grand Ballroom of the New York Hilton.

By way of an introduction, Ross Johnson, a Canadian who was then chairman of the club and vice-chairman of Nabisco, described the "tingling feeling" in his heart at the thought that a former CEO of a multimillion-dollar company had managed to get himself elected Prime Minister of Canada. He remembered accompanying Mulroney on fact-finding missions to "trouble spots" such as Paris, Palm Beach, and Venice. Indeed, his only question was whether Mulroney would be able to run Canada like he ran the Iron Ore Company. "The country should be so lucky," Johnson said, ignoring the fact that Mulroney's best-known success at Iron Ore was the smooth and generous way he had shut down the town of Schefferville, Quebec.

Then Brian Mulroney went to the podium and told about singing "Dearie" to Colonel McCormick for $50 a crack. "So my family became the first Canadian family to benefit directly from American foreign aid," he added. One only had to think of Churchill or Nehru saying something equivalent to realize the national humiliation in the Prime Minister's joke. Mulroney seemed impervious to the implications, however, because he had been conditioned all his life to the benefits of foreign investment.

"I come from a town on the North Shore," he often said, "where the paper mill was built by the *Chicago Tribune*, the grain elevator was built by Cargill, and the aluminum plant was built by British Aluminum. Had it not been for that investment, I and all of my friends on the North Shore would not have had the opportunities that we have had. And so we don't feel in any way diminished by the fact that there has been a cooperative atmosphere to provide economic opportunities in regions where no one else would go. The North Shore was not built by federal civil servants or people preaching economic nationalism from the safety of downtown Toronto."

Therefore, encouraging foreign investment became an important part of his drive for economic renewal and jobs, and that was the fundamental message he brought to New York. For if many Canadian businessmen had felt bullied and buffeted by the Trudeau years, many American businessmen had felt unwelcomed and robbed. The Foreign Investment Review Agency and the National Energy Program had particularly outraged them. The effect, without doubt, had been a loss of faith in—and dollars for—Canada. To reverse that, Mulroney declared before his American audience that "Canada is open for business again." Moreover, without asking for anything specific in return, he promised significant reforms in the two major sources of grievance. FIRA was to be replaced by a new agency called Investment Canada, "whose mandate will be to encourage and facilitate investment in Canada," and the "odious" NEP provision by which Ottawa could take 25 per cent of the energy discoveries made on crown land would be changed. "Canada was not built by expropriating retroactively other people's property," Mulroney said.

The black-tie crowd sprung up to cheer, but it wasn't

certain whether the ovation indicated anything more than delight that a Canadian Prime Minister was again willing to sing for his supper. Like Canadian investors, the Americans appreciated the improvement in the political rhetoric but had to look past it to the economic conditions for growth and profit. They saw the size of Canada's national debt and the problems of reducing it. They saw the jobless rate, the wage levels, the strength of the unions, the social programs, the regulatory systems of both the federal and provincial governments, the excess capacity, the environmental laws, the tax regimes, sluggish growth, uncertain domestic demand, weak export competitiveness, poor productivity, and low resource prices. If there were American capital to spare for investment in overseas resources, why not put it in Brazil or the Pacific Rim, where the wages were low, the product competitive, and the markets huge? The same was even more true for manufacturing. Why should American capital finance a high-technology plant in Canada, with its small population, low duties, and high costs, instead of in the American Sun Belt or South Korea?

Many of the American companies that found reason to come to Canada had already done so, and most of them were financing their further development with Canadian capital. At the same time, because of the relative strength of the American economy and the high rate of return it offered, the United States had become an importer of capital, including hundreds of millions of dollars from Canadian investors. That coincided with a move away from direct investment toward portfolio investment, which tended to be short term, liquid, and global. Finally, even where there was direct investment, there was no guarantee that new capital meant many more jobs. In fact, technology, productivity, and world competitiveness worked against job creation.

When profits and growth looked likely, neither FIRA nor the NEP made many Americans hesitate about putting their money into Canada. When profits and growth looked less likely, all the serenades in Brian Mulroney's repertoire hardly mattered a damn. Mulroney suspected that, of course, but believed that a better atmosphere was the necessary first conditon for long-term benefits. "All we're trying to do is to create the climate which will be hospitable and productive for national investment capital and for foreign investment capital, because we need it to create jobs for our citizens. But I'll acknowledge that no one gives you any guarantees in this business."

Mulroney's approach was made even more uncertain because he couldn't promise Americans the *carte blanche* welcome they seemed to want and expect. Excessive foreign ownership, particularly in sensitive areas such as culture, finance, and energy, harboured real political and economic problems which no Canadian government could ignore. After all, both FIRA and the NEP had been introduced for reasons that were more pragmatic than theoretical, and the purposes of both had been generally supported by the public. Thus, while the Tories made the changes Mulroney promised in New York, they didn't reject the practice of monitoring significant foreign investments or the principle of Canadianization in the energy sector.

It wasn't long before many of the prospective American investors who had emphasized the "fear" in FIRA began to refer to Investment Canada as "ick" in disgust. Though the range and time of the foreign investment review process were reduced somewhat, direct acquisitions over $5 million and indirect acquisitions over $50 million were still subject to approval, as were any investments deemed "sensitive to Canada's cultural heritage and national identity." Foreign ownership of banks, newspapers, and television stations was still restricted, and all major investments had to demonstrate a net benefit to the country under half a dozen criteria. Further, since FIRA's rules had been loosened during Trudeau's last years, to the point where critics felt the agency had lost its teeth and any possibility of expanding to watch the investment performance of existing foreign companies, Investment Canada seemed more a symbolic gesture than a real difference.

The problem with symbolic gestures is that they are usually made at some cost but rarely satisfy the interests which had demanded genuine change. For example, Investment Canada removed the impediments to foreign takeover of the small businesses and high-tech innovators upon which Canada depended for growth and jobs, yet it lost much of its initial good will in the protracted and controversial debate over whether Gulf and Western Industries, the American communications giant, should be allowed to take over Prentice-Hall Canada, the Toronto book publisher, as a result of acquiring its New York parent company, Prentice-Hall. Under new rules established in July, 1985, by the Minister of Communications, Marcel Masse, any direct or indirect takeover of a publishing company had to be approved by Investment Canada, and approval would generally require the new foreign owner to sell control of the acquisition to Canadians "at fair market price" within two years.

Masse's policy was clearly intended to Canadianize a key sector, in which Canadian ownership was a paltry 20 per cent. Indeed, like Lalonde and Chrétien, Masse proved by his energetic will, his interventionist attitudes, his sense of national community, and his insistence on sovereignty to be a prototypical product of his French-Canadian political culture. Once a Union Nationale cabinet minister in Quebec, he arrived in Ottawa and his department in September, 1984. Despite a rocky start in which he intimidated the anglophone cultural community by his arrogant, hands-on style, he quickly transformed his Quebec nationalism into an articulate and fervent Canadian nationalism that made him the darling of artists and protectionists alike. He and his cause suffered a sharp setback in September, 1985, when Masse resigned from the cabinet because of an RCMP investigation into his election expenses. When he was cleared in November, however, he returned to fight Gulf and Western with increased prestige and clout.

The Gulf and Western case was a tough introduction for the Mulroney government into the complex issues of foreign ownership in general and Canadian-American relations in particular. Prentice-Hall Canada was one of the two largest publishers in Canada; Gulf and Western already owned two Canadian publishers and was seeking yet another in addition to Prentice-Hall Canada; and because the takeover had been done long before Masse's policy was announced, the Tories were forced to act retroactively if they wanted to act at all. Moreover, Gulf and Western had extremely powerful allies in Washington and throughout the American business community. As a sign of the seriousness with which the company intended to play, its highly influential lobbyist, Robert Strauss, telephoned the Canadian ambassador to the United States, Allan Gotlieb, on July 30, 1985, to warn that Gulf and Western would adopt a "scorched-earth" response (implying the closure of Prentice-Hall Canada) if forced to comply with the Canadian policy.

A week later Gotlieb wrote Sinclair Stevens, the minister responsible for Investment Canada, to advise him that the policy was being seen as "more radical" than anything the Trudeau government had done to protect publishing and, in some ways, even worse than the NEP. "Unlike the National Energy Program, which set a precise limit of 50 per cent on the Canadianization goal," Gotlieb wrote, "the book-publishing policy has no such ceiling. It is widely seen as a harbinger of what will be done in other areas of communications; e.g. film distribution." Since Ottawa was "in the midst of developing a major campaign in the United States to convince the investment community that Canada is an attractive destination for U.S. investment," Gotlieb emphasized that "the policy could not have come at a more unfortunate time or been less adequately presented."

In truth, no time would have been fortunate and no presentation adequate. There was a basic clash between American and Canadian interests in this situation and almost no room for compromise. If Canada backed down, its cultural integrity would be eroded, other foreign-owned publishers would move to acquire more Canadian firms in order to stay competitive, and the Mulroney government would be seen as caving in to American pressure. Not to back down, on the other hand, would risk the wrath of Washington and American investors, both of whom had the power to do real damage and neither of whom showed any sympathy for Mulroney's predicament. "When it comes down to protecting American interests, the Americans don't play fair," said a senior Canadian diplomat. "If they want something, they don't mind throwing their weight around to get it."

Trudeau had learned that dramatically in 1971 when, without warning or exemption, President Richard Nixon imposed a 10 per cent surcharge on manufactured imports and thereby arbitrarily declared Canada's "special relationship" dead. Nixon's Secretary of the Treasury, John Connally, bluntly told a Liberal cabinet minister that it was appropriate for Canada to pay "a tribute" to the United States. The Liberals' search for a "Third Option" to decrease Canada's dependence on the United States by increasing its trade and commerce with the rest of the world grew out of their shock at Nixon's high-handedness. FIRA, Petro-Canada, moves to bolster the nation's financial and cultural framework, and eventually the NEP were also defensive reactions to specific threats, whether the uncertainty of Canadian oil imports from American multinationals in the event of a global crisis or the unlikelihood of a Canadian weekly newsmagazine while *Time* enjoyed its tax advantage. Trudeau was never a nationalist, but he came to recognize that in the game of nation-states, Canada had to protect its ability to function and survive, particularly in the face of the United States's own nationalism.

Mulroney may have been correct when he argued that the unemployed weren't concerned about "the nationality of the dollar that creates the job but whether the job is going to be created." That only begged the complex question, however: is there a point beyond which the extent of foreign ownership impedes the development of jobs in growth sectors? As demand for Canadian resources fell and the resource industries became less labour-intensive, Canada looked more and more toward specialized manufacturing, high technology, and services for the creation of meaningful work. Yet it was in those very areas that American decision making, American know-how, and American interests placed Canada's development in doubt.

The Tories could not remain indifferent to that doubt. For essentially the same pragmatic reasons as the Liberals, for example, they accepted the goal of Canadianization of at least half the energy sector. To achieve that, Mulroney and his Minister of Energy, Pat Carney, not only promoted the Reichmanns' takeover of Gulf Canada by means of a generous tax break, but made the deal possible by expanding Petro-Canada through the purchase of most of Gulf's refining and marketing assets, including 1,800 service stations, for $886 million. Despite the protests of some members of the party and the caucus about the "asinine" decision, both Mulroney and Carney stressed the national interest.

"I find nothing in my background or in the background of my party that is offended by the role of government in economic development," Mulroney said in August, 1985. "As I remember it, we put together the CBC and the Bank of Canada, to mention but two. The Conservative Party has never been offended by the role of government. Indeed, there's a responsibility of government to involve itself in instruments of regional economic development. When Petro-Canada was formed, obviously there were problems with it, but the Conservative Party never quarrelled with the objectives that were set: the security of supply, Canadian innovation, and so on."

Moreover, when Mulroney moved away from that position to satisfy free-market ideas and pressures, he moved toward economic risk and political trouble, as demonstrated when the Tories helped the oil multinationals with the Western Accord and when they sold de Havilland to Boeing. In the first case, in order to achieve peace with the West and the energy industry, Carney agreed to phase out the Petroleum and Gas Revenue Tax by 1989 and allow the price of oil to float with the market demand. The effect was to give the oil companies an estimated $1.3 billion a year at the expense of taxpayers and consumers, with the hope but no guarantee that the extra revenue would go into job-creating investment. In addition, the multinationals were to benefit equally with Canadian firms and, because "old oil" discovered before 1974 was no longer undervalued in comparison to "new oil" under the NEP, the main winners were the multinationals who had done the least exploration.

Even with a low or declining world price, the profits of the oil companies were expected to rise by as much as 150 per cent by 1990, while their share of net revenues would almost double. Yet the unattractive price would work against the push for exploration and investment that the Tories were counting on as the engine of economic recovery. Worse, perhaps, if the price did begin to soar again by the 1990s, the profit levels of the multinationals would become the same political and economic problem they had been in 1980. Without new taxes and controls of the NEP variety, a good deal of those profits would either leave the country or be used to increase foreign ownership in the Canadian economy. Whatever the short-term advantages of peace, the fundamental questions remained to await further, probably harsher action in the future.

"The industry's very aware I'm going to monitor their activities," Carney said. "We're not laying on hard and fast rules on individual companies, but we will be monitoring on an industry, as well as company-by-company basis."

The de Havilland sale was riskier and more troublesome, because it represented less a gamble for later benefits than a throwing-in of the towel. Coupled with the likelihood of the government selling off its control of Canadair to foreign interests, Boeing's bargain buy raised a political storm as much for the loss of Canadian hopes as for the loss of the taxpayers' investment. Basically the Tories concluded that the government couldn't afford to pump hundreds of millions of additional dollars into the development and marketing of de Havilland's aircraft before the company turned a profit, and they couldn't find a Canadian buyer with the resources and skills that Boeing offered as a huge, world-wide manufacturer. Having to make the classic Canadian choice between the state and the United States, the Tory government chose the latter.

Though the decision may have saved de Havilland's 4,200 jobs and benefitted its Dash 8 in terms of world sales, it also confirmed that the Canadian economy suffered severe disadvantages in the creation and maintenance of skilled jobs, research and development, export opportunities, and growth industries. In essence, the government was saying that the Canadian private sector hadn't the will, capital, or expertise to compete in the critical aerospace sector except as a branch plant, just as previous governments had decided against an all-Canadian car and the Avro Arrow. And while the Tories were willing to gamble billions of dollars on the good will and independent decisions of the multinational oil companies, their faith in the private sector made them unwilling to gamble half as much on the management of Canadian crown corporations. In the energy sector they were prepared to absorb the hefty short-term losses in revenue in the hope of long-term gain, but in the aerospace industry they grabbed a paltry amount of money and sacrificed unknown long-term possibilities in jobs, research, and exports, as well as in profits. The only consistency in their inconsistency was that foreign multinationals did better than Canadian mixed enterprise.

In more cases than not, crown corporations had been established to maintain Canadian control for pragmatic reasons involving the national interest and to provide necessary services that the private sector wouldn't or couldn't provide. Many of them couldn't be sold because, by the nature of their mandate, they were unprofitable. Those that were profitable either had become so at the taxpayers' expense or had public dimensions that couldn't be guaranteed by private owners. To privatize the profitable ones without adequate compensation or regulation was regarded with deep suspicion, as Prime Minister Clark had discovered when he talked about selling off Petro-Canada. To sell them off to foreigners was even worse, as Prime Minister Mulroney discovered with de Havilland.

"What inherent advantage do we have in the aircraft industry?" Sinclair Stevens asked in defence of the deal.

To many Canadians he sounded less like the voice of reason than the voice of doom, condemning them to remain hewers of wood and drawers of water because the state lacked the leadership and the ability to achieve anything else. Stevens seemed to dismiss the fact that governments throughout the world were subsidizing their aerospace sector directly or indirectly because of its importance to their growth. Even in the United States, aerospace companies were heavily sponsored by the massive American spending on defence and space, which was an integrated industrial strategy in everything but name. Nor did he explain how Canadian business would develop the necessary expertise in research, production, and world marketing if its brightest hopes continued to be sold off to foreign enterprises as they had been in the past.

In political terms, the specific decisions regarding de Havilland and Prentice-Hall Canada were complicated by the general movement by the Tories toward closer economic links with the United States. After Trudeau, Canadians were ready for better relations with the Americans, but that stopped a long way short of making the Canadian government a patsy for Washington in either reality or perception. Few Tories understood the dangers and limits of continentalism better than Brian Mulroney. During the Conservative leadership race, for example, he attacked John Crosbie's advocacy of a Canadian-U.S. free trade deal in no uncertain terms.

"This country could not survive with a policy of unfettered free trade," he said in June, 1983. "We'd be swamped. We have in many ways a branch-plant economy in certain important sectors. All that would happen with that kind of concept would be the boys cranking up their plants throughout the United States in bad times and shutting their entire branch plants in Canada. It's bad enough as it is."

Nor was the fate of the branch plants the only problem. The entire manufacturing sector that was built and fostered by Canadian protectionism would be shaken, especially in Central Canada. Canada's cultural institutions, its social and regional development programs, and its capacity to cultivate strong and indigenous entrepreneurs in the areas of services and technology could be jeopardized. Its efforts to expand its trade with the whole world, particularly the dynamic Pacific Rim countries, would be handicapped. Finally, the disproportionate difference in political and economic power between the two countries didn't bode well for Canada's chances of obtaining a favourable deal or maintaining one in the event of bilateral conflicts. "Free trade is terrific until the elephant twitches," Mulroney said in 1983, "and if it ever rolls over, you're a dead man. We'll have none of it."

Mulroney suggested nothing otherwise during the 1984 election. Even when he addressed the Economic Club of New York in December of the same year, his promise to restore "good and sound relationships between our two countries" proposed little more than regular meetings to work on topics of mutual interest, mechanisms to resolve bilateral disputes, and trade liberalization through multi-lateral institutions such as the General Agreement on Tar-iffs and Trade (GATT). However, he did give notice that he had become more open-minded about a special deal with the United States.

"Canadians have some important, even historic, policy choices to make in the near future," he said, "and these choices will be the subject matter of public discussion led by the government. The maturity and self-confidence of our country make it possible for us now to confront issues in a realistic manner, and to examine options that a few years ago produced emotional reflexes that made rational discussion difficult. Nowhere is this more true than on the subject of our bilateral relations with the United States. The U.S. has been and will remain the dominant market for our exports. By 1987 some 80 per cent of Canadian exports to the U.S. will be duty-free. Yet there remain some significant tariff barriers and a growing array of non-tariff measures which impede bilateral trade, including U.S. Buy-American provisions. Proposals for attacking these barriers have included sectoral free-trade arrangements, a variety of private-sector recommendations, and secure market ac-cess. I exclude none of these from consideration."

Then, at the end of January, 1985, James Kelleher, the Tories' Minister for International Trade, began the public discussion with a paper on "How to Secure and Enhance Canadian Access to Export Markets." While the thirty-two page report dealt with all markets, it concentrated on the United States, which accounted for over 70 per cent of

Canadian exports in 1983, fourteen times more than Canada's second-largest market, Japan. And while it considered the status quo in U.S.-Canadian trade and the Liberals' efforts to negotiate sectoral arrangements for better access, it clearly tilted in favour of "a comprehensive agreement which provided for the removal of tariffs and non-tariff barriers on substantially all bilateral trade."

The logic was impeccable. Canada is a trading nation, dependent for a third of its income and more than three million jobs on exports. In the international trade environment it was hampered by declining competitiveness, slow growth, increasing protectionism, high interest rates, global debt problems, fluctuating exchange rates, and uncertain changes in demand and supply caused by new technologies. The outlook was especially bleak for world demand for Canada's resource products because of oversupply and new competition. Therefore, the report said, "it is improbable that the long-term trend toward greater involvement with the U.S. in trade, investment, and access to technology will be reversed."

On that front, however, Canada faced growing protectionism caused by the Americans' record trade deficit, of which Canada accounted for about $20 billion. The United States Congress, pressed by American business interests, was roused to action by the trade deficit's impact on jobs, exports, profits, and the American dollar; and though most of its protectionist stirrings were aimed at the world in general and Japan in particular, Canadian imports in lumber, steel, fish, urban mass transit equipment, hogs, and similar successes were singled out as grievances. Any tariff or non-tariff move against Canada would have harmful consequences for its economy, so that the status quo was considered an untenable position, while the irritation of the American business lobbies had got in the way of any sectoral or step-by-step agreements similar to the Auto Pact or the Defence Production Sharing Arrangement.

According to Kelleher's paper, a comprehensive agreement would remove the threats on both sides of the border and meet less resistance from the Americans or their GATT partners than the sectoral approach. Even if it didn't remove all tariffs and barriers, it would at least assure Canada's exports of their present position. Moreover, and perhaps of greater importance, "only the comprehensive agreement would induce substantial structural adjustment in the Canadian economy. This process would be undertaken as firms adapted to economies of scale and specialization, to increased production and to more intense competition from imports."

In other words, open and guaranteed access to the huge U.S. market would demand the rationalization, competitiveness, and entrepreneurship that artificial intervention had stifled within Canadian industry. Some branch plants would go home, some jobs would be "dislocated," but with time and an opportunity for adjustment, there would spring up in their place efficient new enterprises, whole new sectors, and countless high-value jobs to meet the demands of the expanded marketplace. The prospects in this scenario were for increased employment and productivity, higher real wages and lower consumer costs, and greater investment in Canada.

This was "the leap of faith" advocated by nine premiers, the Canadian Manufacturers' Association, the Canadian Chamber of Commerce, the Business Council on National Issues, the Royal Commission on the Economic Union and Development Prospects for Canada, the American ambassador to Canada, most economists, many influential bureaucrats in the economic portfolios and External Affairs, and a joint parliamentary committee on international relations. Essentially they all maintained there was no other choice for long-term growth.

Among the last to hop on the apparent bandwagon were the Prime Minister and his Secretary of State for External Affairs. Both Brian Mulroney and Joe Clark had expressed public doubts about the economics of the option, and its political implications for the country and the Progressive Conservative Party made them tremble. Mulroney stated time and again that the defeat of Laurier's reciprocity deal in the 1911 election had buried the notion of free trade forever, and despite his optimism in New

York, his intuition told him that the "emotional reflexes" to the issue were still present in the Canadian psyche.

The reflexes weren't just emotional. Companies that benefitted from Canada's protectionism, such as those in textiles, beer, auto parts, furniture, and agriculture, feared the worst for themselves. The trade unions estimated that more than a million Canadian jobs would be threatened or downgraded. The cultural industries wondered how they could survive if inundated by even more American entertainment products. Nor was it clear how a full range of government subsidies, social programs, regional incentives, tax policies, and industrial strategies, all designed to alleviate particular problems in the Canadian economy and all subject to American criticism as unfair trade practices, could be safeguarded. Canadian customs regarding lumber rights and transportation subsidies, Ottawa's grants to the Atlantic fishing industry and Quebec paper companies, and government support for western agriculture were already under attack in the United States.

Though the proponents of freer trade argued that it would eliminate the need for Canadian capital (and, indirectly, Canadian jobs) to move south to avoid being penalized by American protectionist measures, reason wondered whether freer trade wouldn't eliminate the need for Canadian capital (or American capital, for that matter) to create any jobs in Canada. Certainly distance from the major markets, the costs of climate and regional disparity, American advantages in any bidding wars for new industries, and Canada's entrenched redistributive programs, when added to the cautious and branch-plant mentality of Canadian entrepreneurs, seemed to suggest pessimism in that regard. To cite one example, after being built on Bell Canada's telephone monopoly and Canadian government assistance, Northern Telecom began to move its research and jobs to the United States for good economic reasons as much as any fears about U.S. protectionism.

Even when the reflexes were emotional, they weren't less powerful for being so. Canada had been born in a deliberate rejection of the American revolution, its economy had been structured to resist the potent free-market pull of the north-south axis, and the fear of annexation was at the core of the nation's identity. Weighed against the promised benefits was the intimidating paranoia that a binding economic treaty would lead inevitably to commercial and then political union, because the size and strength of the American partner would gradually force Canadians to seek further safety and advantage in that direction. Even if that didn't happen, there was a prevalent worry that increased dependence would restrict Canada's flexibility in terms of trade and foreign policy *vis-à-vis* the rest of the world. The result was a lot of agitated talk among intellectuals, artists, and the media about Canadian sovereignty.

Yet, by the spring of 1985, Mulroney started to come round to a comprehensive agreement, "trade enhancement," "secure access," and all the other euphemisms for freer trade. He was lured in that direction by the investment community, the American ambassador, Peter Lougheed and most of the other premiers, and some important advisers. Catering to them served his economic strategy to encourage the entrepreneurial spirit and American investment, while it advanced his political goal to secure the West and Quebec for the Tories. The alternative would have been to alienate them early in his mandate by turning away from the free-market option and back toward more state intervention, more protectionist policies, and more nationalist postures. Above all, he was infected by the historic proportion of the initiative. Like Trudeau's constitutional package, a comprehensive trade deal with the United States was bold, positive and mature in outlook, and of lasting effect.

His deep reservations seemed to be erased by the time he met Ronald Reagan at the "Shamrock Summit" on St. Patrick's Day in Quebec City. Singing "When Irish Eyes Are Smiling" on the world stage with the President of the United States apparently turned the head of the boy from Baie Comeau and stole his heart away. "He was caught up in the excitement and glamour of it all," a good source told the *Toronto Star*. "It was like a light came on." On the heights where Frontenac had rebuffed the demand of naval invaders from Boston for an immediate surrender by his immortal heroic, "I will answer with the mouths of my cannons," Brian Mulroney agreed "to give the highest priority to finding mutually acceptable means to reduce and eliminate existing barriers to trade in order to secure and facilitate trade and investment flows."

As a result of that agreement in March, Mulroney promised to tell Reagan within six months whether Canada was willing to negotiate a comprehensive trade deal with the United States. After a summer of consultations and studies by the ministers and officials of International Trade and External Affairs, the Prime Minister announced in the House of Commons on September 26, "I have spoken today to the President of the United States to express Canada's interests in pursuing a new trade agreement between our two countries."

Most observers noticed that his short, platitudinous statement was unworthy in vision and rhetoric of a decision of such momentous potential. Mulroney hastened to warn that "Success is not a sure thing" and to accept "the words of prudence coming to us from some quarters on this subject." He ended by declaring, "Our political sovereignty, our system of social programs, our commitment to fight regional disparities, our unique cultural identity, our special linguistic character—these are of the essence of Canada. They are not at issue in these negotiations." Mulroney was right to sound hesitant, however. To trumpet the initiative would have roused its opponents to ask their unsettling questions. It would also have tied the Tories' reputation to an outcome that seemed less and less likely.

First, any deal had to pass through the United States Congress, where Canada's $20-billion trade surplus was already a matter of controversy among some legislators and promised to become more so once brought to the attention of the others. It would be odd if Congress accepted any agreement that wasn't designed to lower that surplus and eliminate U.S. complaints about indirect government subsidies to Canada's lumber and fish exports,

Ottawa's unfair laws regarding the pharmaceutical patents of American companies, or the retroactive "expropriation" of American book publishers under Investment Canada. Yet such an arrangement would clearly harm Canadian interests and infringe on the factors of Canada's essence which Mulroney stated weren't at issue.

Secondly, it was becoming evident that the most powerful force behind Washington's interest in a deal (besides the Reagan administration's ideological desire for a symbol of its commitment to trade liberalization) was coming from the very sectors that most terrified Canadian nationalists, that is, services and information. Many major American conglomerates saw their future, world-wide growth in those sectors, which included banking and investment, advertising, insurance, telecommunications, bio-engineering, data flows, computer software, and the entire range of activities known as entertainment. Not only were these areas in which Canadian companies had some hope to grow and survive in the world market if given a chance, they tended to touch on the sorest points about Canada's nationhood. Even those who considered American ownership of most of Canada's manufacturing and resource industries as beneficial, or at least neutral in effect, recognized that American ownership of banks and television stations was a more dubious matter. Even if ownership wasn't involved, the size and wealth of the American conglomerates raised obvious doubts about the ability of Canadian competitors to exist in an open market and still provide services of unique value to the Canadian community.

That was especially true in the cultural sector, which was why the controversies surrounding Prentice-Hall Canada, the tax status of *Time* magazine in Canada, and the distribution of Canadian films raged as perennial issues. As Mulroney himself said to an audience in Chicago in December, 1985, "When it comes to discussing better trade rules for cultural industries, you will have to understand that what we call cultural sovereignty is as vital to our national life as political sovereignty." He even compared it to the Americans' own obsession with national security.

Because "entertainment" was one of the few fields where the Americans saw a possible advantage in freer trade, however, they pressed to have as little as possible removed from the table before the negotiations started. "I'd be concerned if the term 'culture' is defined in such a way that it would have a dampening effect on the over-all negotiating process," said Clayton Yeutter, the U.S. Trade Representative. "I would certainly hope and expect that Prime Minister Mulroney and Minister Kelleher and others will take a reasonable, rational view of that issue." In other words, culture was an economic matter, all economic matters were up for grabs, and the removal of anything would require a trade-off and could jeopardize the entire deal.

As a result, Mulroney, Kelleher, and Joe Clark tripped over themselves for months about whether the cultural industries were or weren't negotiable. If Prentice-Hall Canada, *Time*, and Canada's many non-tariff barriers to free trade in the cultural field weren't negotiable, then the Americans would quickly lose interest in the process. If they were negotiable, then Canadians would lose interest even faster. The same conundrum applied in questions of social programs, the Auto Pact, regional development, and other government measures that seemed to create an economic advantage for Canadians.

Richard Lipsey, an economist at the C.D. Howe Institute and one of Canada's most ardent proponents of freer trade, stated bluntly that, under an agreement, "some of our cultural support activities would have to go. The straight subsidy would be okay, but straight trade barriers as the Canadian government disallowing advertising expense deductions in U.S. magazines would run into trouble. Also, one big problem for our sovereignty is that our desire to subsidize the less-advantaged areas would be difficult to maintain."

Between March and September, therefore, Mulroney's political queasiness resurfaced. The United States didn't help him by sending a ship, the *Polar Sea*, through the Northwest Passage in August without asking Canada's permission, as a signal that the Americans didn't accept Canadian sovereignty in those waters. The provocation was a public denial of Joe Clark's assertion that "you're going to have more influence on the Americans if you're seen not to be antagonistic." It also raised the latent paranoia within many Canadians about the Americans' grand designs and the viability of an independent Canadian foreign and defence policy under the perpetual threat of economic blackmail. Nor did the warm friendship between Mulroney and Reagan produce much movement by the United States on solving the serious problem of acid rain. Throughout 1985 the polls showed support for freer trade to be dropping among Canadians, and even though it was still a healthy 58 per cent in December, there were strong indications of ambivalence, caution, and vagueness in that number. If Canadians were open to the abstract promise of a deal, they were also ready to run at the first sign of concrete harm.

"It is likely that the higher the profile the issue attains, the lower the degree of public approval will be," said a leaked government memo on how to sell the trade initiative. "The public support generated should be recognized as extremely soft and likely to evaporate rapidly if the debate is allowed to get out of control so as to erode the central focus of the message. At the same time a substantial majority of the public may be willing to leave the issue in the hands of the government and other interested groups if the government maintains communications control of the situation. Benign neglect from a majority of Canadians may be the realistic outcome of a well executed communications strategy."

Hence, Mulroney's "low-profile" announcement in September. Hence, his unsubstantiated but earnest vows that Canada's political and cultural sovereignty would not be sacrificed. Hence, his declaration in Chicago that if the two governments could not strike a deal that would raise incomes, employment, and the standard of living of both countries, "a deal will not be struck."

The second part of the government's strategy was to do some judicious tacking. Just as Mulroney had appointed a prominent NDPer as Canadian ambassador to the United Nations and used his name over and over again to answer criticism of Tory patronage appointments, he tossed out a few sops to Canadian nationalism to distract attention from his basic direction. Thus, shortly before he announced Canada's interest in trade negotiation, his government announced that it wouldn't participate in Reagan's Strategic Defence Initiative (SDI)—popularly known as Star Wars—to develop a defensive shield in space against nuclear missiles. From the equivocal and confusing statements made by Mulroney and his ministers about SDI during 1985, it was clear that the decision had been a tough one. Washington was angry, Canada may have lost high-tech jobs and a research bonanza, and polls showed that a majority of Canadians supported participation, but the Tories feared the political ramifications of joining Star Wars and free-trade negotiations at the same time.

Similarly, to defuse the criticism that the Tories were in Reagan's hip pocket, they rejected the Americans' trade embargo against Nicaragua, launched Masse's publishing policy, beefed up Canada's presence in the Arctic in the wake of the *Polar Sea* voyage, and considered strict guidelines to prevent renewed foreign acquisition of Canada's energy sector. In most cases, such measures were pragmatic responses to the same problems that Trudeau had encountered with the Americans, from the passage of the *Manhattan* through Arctic waters in 1969 to the American invasion of Grenada, from the downside of foreign investment to Washington's hostility to Canada's independent peace inititative. They also allowed Mulroney to assert his "impeccable nationalist credentials" in a political arena where both the United States and Ronald Reagan were viewed with widespread suspicion.

That fundamental suspicion probably doomed the trade talks to failure, however clever the government's strategy might be. Because the impetus on the American side lay with Reagan's own philosophy, the historic "window of opportunity" to secure a deal was only open until 1987, which was also the earliest date by which most observers felt the negotiations could be concluded. It was also the eve of a Canadian election. It seemed extremely unlikely for a Prime Minister of Brian Mulroney's prudence to wish to go into a campaign with all the threatened interests in arms against him, all the nationalists feeding the fires of fear and opposition, and both the Liberals and the New Democrats on the popular side of the issue.

Whatever the polls might have indicated before the debate began in earnest, every politician worthy of the name knew that the winning formula spoke to national survival. Mulroney's drastic cutbacks to the CBC and the Canada Council, his love songs to Reagan for little that was concrete in return, his appointment as trade negotiator of Simon Reisman who had recently advocated diverting fresh water from James Bay to the American Midwest, and his hunger for American capital all exposed him to the old, devastating question, "Who shall speak for Canada?"

In fact, if a trade agreement had the glamour of Trudeau's constitutional reform, it also had all the difficulties. Because subjects and laws of provincial responsibility would be a necessary aspect of the elimination of tariff and non-tariff barriers, Ottawa effectively required the unanimous consent of the provinces for a meaningful deal. The election of Liberal governments in Ontario and Quebec in 1985 made that a virtual impossibility. Even if Mulroney exercised a supreme act of political will and opted to sacrifice his process of national reconciliation by going over the heads of the premiers for the sake of the national interest (another virtual impossibility), he lacked Trudeau's one advantage: there was no consensus among the people that the goal was either beneficial or desirable.

Indeed, the illusion of a growing consensus had been created by the loud and powerful voices of the elites who stood to gain from closer economic ties with the Americans. Almost by definition, the Canadian elites were those who had done well by the protectionist, interventionist status quo. By their very success, however, many of them were exhausting the possibilities of the limited domestic market and seeking secure access to a larger one. That would likely produce greater wealth for them, but it was less certain to produce Canadian jobs, Canadian spin-off industries, or Canadian competition. Whether in its subservience to U.S. capital, its propensity to sell out to American entrepreneurs for a quick buck, its reluctance to invest in regions far from the central markets, or its draining of Canadian profits (often made under quasi-monopolistic conditions) to create work and projects in the United States, Canadian business generally demonstrated that its bottom line had priority over the national interest.

That was appropriate to the rules of the game, but it raised serious problems for the nation. Since there was nothing made in Canada that couldn't be made cheaper somewhere else, freer trade implied lost jobs, lower wages, and industrial stagnation as much as it implied the opposite. Just as whole regions of the country were kept currently by the wealth-producing centres at an enormous cost in unemployment, dignity, and the productive use of money, so there loomed a vision of Canada in which a few huge and wealthy enterprises with "world product mandates" controlled the economy as they saw fit, sold out to foreigners when they chose to, and were in a position to exercise real harm if crossed by government. Indeed, that had already been the direction of Canada since the 1950s. The result, in the opinion of many critics, was the country's stubborn double-digit unemployment, its weakness in high technology and world marketing, its concentrated wealth, its production backwardness, and the louder calls for closer integration with the United States as a panacea.

Mulroney got a mild preview of his approaching trouble in November, 1985, when the Tories lifted the import quotas on men's, boys', and children's shoes after eight years of protection for the Canadian industry. The quotas were said to have cost consumers an extra $500 million; they provoked the fury of the European Economic Community; and there was still a high tariff on imports. Yet the removal of the quotas caused screams in the Tory caucus about the economic and political fall-out, and the president of the Canadian Shoe Manufacturers' Association called the decision "the death of the industry" and its jobs. At the same time the textile and clothing industry was demanding a reduction in imports because of the job losses they had caused (estimated at fifteen thousand in two years) and would cause in future.

"I think that a trade-enhancement program of any kind in Canada would probably meet with an overwhelming degree of ambivalence," Mulroney confessed. "You would get six and you would lose half a dozen, in typical Canadian fashion. 'Whatever you do, hurt him, hurt your neighbour, hurt everybody, but do not touch me. Whatever you do, do not change the status quo.'"

There were some advantages in negotiating, particularly as an excuse to allow Reagan "to go to bat" for Canada against any protectionist legislation coming out of Congress in the next few years, but the achievement of a significantly new trade deal was highly problematic. "It may be that it won't work out," Mulroney admitted at the end of 1985, and he was already prepared to run at the first sight of anything that might look bad for Canada—and for his political hide.

According to most studies and experts, however, the status quo would only lead to gradual decline or economic trauma, whether a long-lasting depression, social unrest, or an unacceptable gap between the Canadian and American standards of living. While the continentalist elites would continue to look to the United States as their salvation, pressing for more integration and moving their jobs and capital south, Canada's history and political culture suggested that most Canadians would turn toward their government for solutions. Since the days of Macdonald's National Policy, that had been the case whenever movements toward reciprocity with the United States failed and times looked tough.

At heart the people trusted their state more than they trusted the Americans, and throughout their history they showed themselves willing to pay a price in dollars, opportunities, and even freedom in order to remain in their inhospitable land. That was their quiet nationalism, and no politician would get very far on a platform of surrendering the nation's sovereignty for a mess of American pottage. To override that reality for the sake of conviction and long-term vision would require a political will and bear a political cost far beyond Brian Mulroney's interest certainly.

Eventually, therefore, the Canadian government would

be thrown back toward multilateral forums, sectoral talks, third options, protectionist measures, and probably the industrial strategies that were interrupted and discredited by the recession before they could be really tested. In fact, in the growing distance between traditional elite accommodation and the wishes of the people that began with the changes and scarcities of the 1970s, the political and economic pressure for state intervention was liable to increase in response to the actions of the disaffected elites.

Regardless of the results of the Mulroney government's trade negotiations, Canada was almost bound to resume its movement to the left in order to find answers for the great question of what its people would do for a living. The inevitable decline of the resource sector, on which Canadians had lived like spoiled children for thirty years, meant inevitable job dislocations, the search for new work and new markets, and the demand for new strategies. They wouldn't preclude some elite accommodation, some role for the marketplace, and some makeshift deals with the Americans (who would still have some cause to wake up every morning and say, as Mulroney advised Reagan to say, "Thank God for Canada. What can I do for Canada today?"), but the thrust would be toward the state as a player and a partner in the economy. To that extent, Mulroney was engaged in a wild goose chase that, after a vague lapse of time, would simply lead back to 1980.

V

Any hope for a trade deal that was meaningful enough to bring economic reconstruction and long-term prosperity was effectively undermined by Brian Mulroney at the end of November, 1985. During the federal-provincial conference in Halifax, he submitted to the demands of the premiers for "full provincial participation" in the negotiations with the Americans. There wasn't final agreement about what that meant, and the matter was sent to further discussions for definition, but it seemed as if Mulroney had given up exclusive federal control of international affairs.

Certainly that's how the premiers interpreted it. To

them the phrase indicated that the provinces could join Ottawa in setting the conditions for the trade talks, guiding Canada's negotiator through his meetings, and approving or rejecting the ultimate deal. "The bottom line is that the negotiator will receive his instructions from the first ministers," said David Peterson, the new Premier of Ontario, in public and in the presence of the Prime Minister, who didn't contradict him. Don Getty of Alberta said, "The negotiating team becomes our team," and Grant Devine of Saskatchewan added, "We are essentially the board of directors that calls the shots."

The implications were obvious. If Simon Reisman required the unanimous consent of every province for every move, the odds of concluding a deal that would satisfy both Ottawa and Washington were dramatically diminished. Peterson was already saying that he would veto any attempt to put the Auto Pact on the table, for example, and his strong reservations about the impact of freer trade on the Ontario economy made him extremely unlikely to accept any far-reaching deal. One Ontario report stated that a third of the province's manufacturing jobs could be threatened by a comprehensive trade arrangement, as branch plants closed down, European and Japanese investors lost reason to set up in Canada, and imports swamped the highly sensitive Canadian industries. Nor, according to the report, did most Canadian firms have the marketing skills or the resources to sustain the level of exports that had been achieved by branch plants supplying their parent companies in the United States.

"Why did a lot of those factories start up here?" Peterson asked. "It wasn't out of the goodness of their hearts. They built here because they had to get behind our tariff barriers to get access to our market. What's to say they can't just beef up production by 10 per cent in the U.S. and close down here? It's going to happen if there's no incentive to be here. We've got higher taxes. It's colder. There are lots of reasons if you're hard-nosed capital, and capital doesn't have any nationality, any particular loyalty."

In practice, of course, the provinces already had an effective veto over a trade deal, since they were second only to the United States government in the range and number of their non-tariff barriers. Eliminating them in areas of provincial jurisdiction would require provincial action; not eliminating them would jeopardize the whole deal. As Joe Clark said, "We can move without the provinces, but we can't conclude without them." That was another key factor in making a deal unlikely.

Mulroney knew that. By agreeing in a vague way to "full provincial participation" in the talks, he seemed to be gambling that the inclusion of the premiers in each stage of the process would only increase the probability of their going along with the final package. That made some sense and may have been his only hope in a rather hopeless situation, but it raised more problems than it solved. In effect, it institutionalized the provinces' authority in areas of federal responsibility, including tariffs, the Auto Pact, and foreign relations, and guaranteed that the debate over free trade would not be a muted one. Far from confronting the real issues of decentralized power in the Canadian federation, Mulroney exacerbated them for the sake of a temporary peace. When he tried to backtrack by insisting that Ottawa's primacy "remains unchallenged and undiminished" as the voice of the national interest, he was immediately confronted by the premiers who had recognized an advantageous precedent when they saw one.

If Brian Mulroney really believed that a comprehensive trade arrangement with the United States was as crucial to the long-term national interest as Trudeau's constitutional reforms had been, then someday he would have to face the tough questions about who speaks for the national interest, who arbitrates in a clash between Ottawa and the provinces, and who decides the will of the people. For the time being, however, he preferred to side-step those questions by painting a rosy picture of the harmony of interests brought about by the good will of reasonable men. To the extent that he was a naive and optimistic conciliator, he believed in that picture. Mostly, however, his instincts and his polls told him that Canadians wanted a reconciliation among their governments after the conflicts of the Trudeau years.

Thus, National Reconciliation joined Economic Renewal as the second pillar of the Tories' first year. Indeed, they were related in Mulroney's mind because harmony would encourage efficiency, cooperation, and investment confidence, while prosperity would foster harmony. No one could fault the honourable intention. No one could say that concerted effort wasn't needed to reconcile Westerners with their national government, to get beyond the animosities that had pitted Ottawa against Quebec City for twenty years, or to restore the faith of Atlantic Canada in its ability to manage its future growth. Yet to affirm the goals was merely to pose the age-old question: how were national unity and national economic well-being to be maintained when confronted by the political greed of premiers, the short-sighted interests of the provinces, and the destabilizing effect of excessive political and economic decentralization?

By September, 1985, the Prime Minister had good cause to brag of his "restoration of civil and productive relationships between Ottawa and the provinces." But if his accomplishment met with less public acclaim that he wanted or expected, the reason wasn't difficult to ascertain. Most observers, and perhaps even most citizens, suspected that there was something flawed, artificial, and above all temporary about his solution. For a year he had simply ignored the fundamental question and given the premiers and the provinces what they demanded.

Nothing better expressed the prevailing sense of unreality than the First Ministers' Conference on the Economy that was held in Regina in February, 1985. As one of the series of public-relations events put on by the Tories to demonstrate their commitment to consultation and openness, it was as long on symbolism as it was short on substance. Even the thickest reporter in the pack couldn't miss the purpose of holding the conference on Valentine's Day, nor did anyone wonder if an extra $2 million was money well spent in frugal times simply to allow the first ministers to sit in a sealed auditorium in Saskatchewan instead of one in Ottawa. To guarantee a love-in, all the sessions were televised and the two most contentious issues in federal-provincial relations (energy pricing and transfer payments) were left off the agenda.

Since all the premiers had access to the same kind of polling results as Mulroney, they all knew that the people wanted them to get down to business and stop bickering. No one was prepared to shatter the romance of "a new era in cooperative federalism," including René Lévesque. "It's been *the* federal-provincial conference," he gushed, "the most enjoyable, the most stimulating, the best that I've seen in eight years or more." Besides, eight of the eleven players were Tories, so they had a vested interest in exalting this meeting above any held under the Liberals.

Above all, the premiers encountered a Prime Minister who didn't challenge them uncomfortably, who seemed prepared to hand over the store for a little peace and quiet, and who didn't ask for anything in return except unstinting praise as a great conciliator. Mulroney himself began the conference by reciting the long list of costly concessions his government had already made to the provinces free of charge. "This list is far from exhaustive," he concluded, "but it is a start." Indeed, he went on to announce a new gift of money and authority for job training, with almost no strings attached.

"I believe in a federalist state you should govern, to the extent humanly possible, in harmony with the provincial governments," Mulroney explained. "It is not always easy, I know, but you should go the extra mile to try and accommodate that, because the process of accommodation ensures that major decisions can then be made in a spirit that allows for economic growth and prosperity."

Basically, Mulroney was talking about the cooperative federalism and elite accommodation of 1960s Canadian liberalism, which Joe Clark had described as "a community of communities" and John Turner had learned from Lester Pearson. As a candidate during the Tory leadership race and the 1984 federal election, Mulroney had borrowed Pierre Trudeau's winning themes of national unity (though qualified and fudged), but once in office he put on the white jacket Clark had worn when serving the premiers. The reason wasn't difficult to understand. Just as Economic

Renewal required rebuilding the confidence of the business elites by quick concessions in "signals" such as government spending and freer trade, National Reconcilation required the immediate appeasement of the provincial elites.

Thus, in March, 1985, Ottawa signed the Western Accord on energy with the three western producing provinces. It was the first step in the dismantlement of the National Energy Program, as promised to the West in the 1984 election, and it was only possible because the Mulroney government agreed to phase out the Petroleum and Gas Revenue Tax. The PGRT was valuable because it brought more than $2 billion into Ottawa each year and taxed net revenue instead of profits, so that oil companies couldn't dodge it through creative bookkeeping. Eliminating it certainly didn't help the federal deficit and probably didn't make a significant difference to the oil majors, whose profits and exploration investments had already started to climb without it. However, the PGRT was an anathema to Peter Lougheed.

From its inception in 1980 Lougheed fought the PGRT on the grounds that it was less a tax than a royalty on production, and therefore an infringement on the provincial ownership and control of Alberta's resources. He personally pressed Mulroney hard before and after the election for a commitment to abolish it, and only compromised to the extent of accepting its gradual phasing out by 1989.

"Three years ago I stood here," Lougheed told his party convention in Edmonton at the time of the Accord, "and I said, 'We moved Ottawa out of the living room and onto the porch.' Friends, we now have Ottawa off the property!"

Not only was the national government prepared to leave Lougheed's "property" despite the cost to all Canadians (who continued to bail out Albertan banks, subsidize Albertan farmers, and give tax breaks to the Albertan energy sector), it was willing to reduce or abandon the incentives for the exploration and development of federal lands. In other words, the focus of energy activity was to shift back to the producing provinces, at the same time that revenue and control also shifted back to the provincial governments. Despite these concessions, Pat Carney had tough battles to get the provinces to limit their own royalties and agree to a new pricing regime for natural gas.

Meanwhile, on the East Coast, Mulroney signed the Atlantic Accord with Brian Peckford of Newfoundland and offered to renegotiate Ottawa's 1984 energy deal with Nova Scotia in light of the new accords. The Newfoundland deal concluded a long and often rancorous search for a compromise between the two levels of government. The main impediment in the past had been the inability of the Peckford Tories and the Trudeau Liberals to agree on who should ultimately control the offshore energy resources. The Supreme Court had decided that Ottawa owned the resources, but politics kept the question alive. Peckford wasn't willing to give up the one great opportunity for Newfoundlanders to develop their economy for their own prosperity and dignity after decades of federal welfare, while Trudeau wasn't willing to give up the principle of national interest after Canadians had shared billions of dollars with Newfoundland when the province was less fortunate.

Once again the significant concession came from the Mulroney Tories. Pat Carney agreed to a joint management board which would, in effect, give Newfoundland control over the crucial decisions about the pace and methods of exploration and development, and over all the other key decisions when Canada was assured of energy self-sufficiency and security of supply. Deadlocks would be broken by a three-person panel, one from each government and the third selected by the Chief Justice of Newfoundland if the two couldn't agree on a chairman. Newfoundland also received financial rights equal to those of the producing provinces that owned their resources. Moreover, its equalization payments from Ottawa were guaranteed not to decrease for more than a decade after its offshore development had begun to pay off.

In essence, the federal government handed over most of its authority and its revenues, despite the fact that the people of Canada owned the resource and were paying almost all the cost of developing it. An independent board, with its power tilted toward the province, had replaced Parliament as the arbiter of the national interest; and in the happy event of an economic windfall, Ottawa would have to make equalization payments to the unluckier provinces without receiving any real help from Newfoundland's wealth.

"If giving away the shop means including Newfoundland in Confederation," Carney said, "I am happy to do it. People forget the total hostility that existed in the regions—the implacable paranoia. Things are peaceful now."

Now, no doubt, but for how long? Without diminishing in any way Carney's excellence as a minister and politician, one might wonder about the centrifugal effects of her accords. Clearly Newfoundland had wanted and deserved as much as the western producing provinces, which had just benefitted greatly from the changes that attracted investment back from the frontier and the offshore; and clearly Nova Scotia wasn't expected to accept anything less than what Newfoundland and the West had gained, particularly since its deal with the Liberals had been based on revenues from the PGRT, PIP grants, and the 25 per cent back-in, all of which Carney was eliminating. If concessions to one region demanded concessions to another, then what about the consuming provinces, the manufacturing centres, the have-not districts? And where was Ottawa going to find the money to pay for its generosity?

In truth, Mulroney's peace was made possible by certain unstable conditions. The war-weary population didn't want to examine the complexities of the deals if that meant more federal-provincial conflicts. Most of the premiers had political, partisan, and economic reasons not to rock the Tories' brand-new boat. The recession had made all the players more realistic in their expectations and more grateful for any advantages. The arrival of new faces in Ottawa and the provincial capitals created a "honeymoon" period in which the old animosities and personality clashes were overcome and new ones had not yet developed. Most of all, as far as the energy sector was concerned, lower world prices had removed the threats of economic and political upheaval that had prompted the NEP.

The world of energy in 1985 looked like the world before the first OPEC crisis in 1973. Supply seemed abundant, prices seemed reasonable and stable, and the combination of supply and price allowed governments and the private sector to work out a *modus vivendi* in an atmosphere of consensus and common purpose. Thus, Canadian oil and gas prices could go to the world price without shocking consumers and industries, and the West could finally be allowed to export energy to the United States without undue concern about Canadian requirements.

However, if world prices rose either sharply or steeply (as logic and most analysts expected them to do before the end of the century), then the old problems would resurface. Huge amounts of money would flow to the producing provinces and the oil companies; Ottawa's share of national revenue would plunge while its obligations to the non-producing provinces would increase; and the conflicts over fairness, sharing, and the national interest would return to the fore because the growth would not be distributed evenly. At that point, regardless of the party in power, Ottawa would have to launch a new raid on the provinces or lose the ability to govern.

In every sector the problems of Canada's economic union were ignored, not settled. Taking the line of the premiers, Mulroney suggested that the country would do well if its regions did well. Unfortunately, however, it didn't follow that what was good for Alberta or Newfoundland was good for Canada. The whole had to be greater than the parts, if only because the federal government had responsibilities and expenses that required a functional degree of political and fiscal authority. Even with Trudeau's sharp turn away from the decentralization of the 1970s, Ottawa's capacity to regulate the macroeconomy, to redistribute wealth, and to control its spending was threatened by the imbalances in the federal system. In the Tories's first year those imbalances were made worse for the sake of the appearance of harmony.

Moreover, for all the talk about freer trade with the United States, nothing was done about the plethora of rules, subsidies, barriers, and boards by which the provinces tried to protect their economies. Every province was guilty of "buy provincial" policies, restrictions on the movement of capital and labour across the country, costly incentives to attract industries, and protectionist marketing regulations. New Brunswick beer could be sold in the United States but not in British Columbia; a town in Quebec had to rip up its new sidewalk for using bricks from Ontario; provincial government contracts gave preference to workers from the province involved; and everything from meat to buses to wine risked penalties when traded across provincial boundaries.

The intent was to promote growth and save jobs in each region, of course, but the result was often smaller markets, higher costs, less efficiency, more regulation, and all the other evils that Mulroney recited about protectionism. It was the natural outcome of provincial self-interest, which was perfectly understandable but somewhat contradicted by the vehement free-trade rhetoric coming from almost all the premiers. Indeed, the Atlantic Accord of which the Prime Minister was so proud formalized a series of regulations that favoured jobs for Newfoundlanders, Newfoundland products, and Newfoundland companies. At the same time Ottawa helped Quebec in its unproductive bidding war for a foreign auto plant, gave up much of its influence to coordinate and override local interests through its regional development programs, and handicapped its own national job-training strategy by tying the strategy's fate to the discretion of the provinces.

Increasingly Ottawa returned to being the writer of cheques, and it seemed reluctant to use its spending power to encourage a national interest in education or break down some of the barriers lest the premiers became annoyed. The Tories had strong grounds for saying that Ottawa had been too arrogant and too remote in its previous intrusions into the regional economies, but abdication hardly prepared the country to take on the world competition in terms of training, productivity, rationalization, research, or planning. Nor did it do much for national unity to have the provinces seen as the agents of creative development while Ottawa was just the ineffectual tax collector. Already in post-secondary education and industrial subsidies, for example, the provinces were getting the lion's share of any political credit flowing from federal spending and Ottawa was receiving most of the abuse for cutbacks.

Brian Mulroney wasn't insensitive to the problem. In fact, his acceptance of provincial participation in the trade talks was partly based on a strategy to force the premiers to confront their own protectionist measures. In other words, since a deal with the Americans was no doubt predicated on the dismantling of many provincial trade barriers, the process of seeking international liberalization could go hand in hand with seeking domestic liberalization. Though the presence of so many players decreased the chances of concluding an important deal with the United States, it increased the chances of having such a deal accepted within Canada if concluded. At the same time it might spin off agreements to strengthen Canada's own economic union.

Basically Mulroney was hoping that an atmosphere of trust, conciliation, and consensus could go a long way in resolving the centrifugal tensions in the federation. Like Clark and Turner before him, Mulroney assumed that the confrontations of the early 1980s had more to do with the personality of Pierre Trudeau than with the dynamics of the system. Undoubtedly Trudeau and the premiers had been imprisoned by their mutual dislike and suspicion, and it certainly suited Mulroney's politics to dramatize that, but he overlooked the lessons of history at his own peril. In truth, the destabilization had come more from Trudeau's decentralization than from his obstinacy, the premiers had demonstrated an insatiable appetite for power once they had a taste of it, and the philosophical approach of every Prime Minister had to face the pragmatic realities of preserving the union.

Thus, the ink was barely dry on the Atlantic Accord before Brian Peckford was lambasting the Mulroney government in public. He wanted more money, more provincial say in Ottawa's regional development programs and more control over the fisheries, and he attacked Ottawa's plan to allow factory-freezer trawlers to fish on the Grand Banks, because they might jeopardize jobs on the island.

"I was quizzical and somewhat perplexed," Mulroney admitted, "to see the Premier of Newfoundland four months after we had concluded an historic accord to the tremendous advantage of Newfoundland and Labrador—at great cost, by the way, to the taxpayers and the people of Canada, but because we thought it was fair and the right thing to do—suggest that we deserved anything but the Order of Canada. It was a bit of a shock."

Meanwhile, after being granted almost every demand from the major (the Western Accord) to the minor (the firing of a junior Ottawa official who had been fingered as one of the leading architects of the NEP), Peter Lougheed publicly pressured Mulroney on free trade and interest rates and privately lobbied him hard. "I can just see him sitting in Sussex Drive and cursing me for what I've done," Lougheed said with a great deal of pleasure. In fact, Mulroney did curse him in April, 1985, when Lougheed became instrumental in the failure of the First Ministers' Conference on the Rights of Aboriginal People to reach agreement about those rights. As Mulroney understood the game of negotiation, he had given Lougheed much and expected something in return. The Premier of Alberta, however, defined concession as his willingness to see the PGRT phased out over time rather than abolished at once.

Nine months after the Regina love-in, the Prime Minister and the premiers met in Halifax in a decidedly less amorous mood. "Federal cuts threaten to spoil Tory honeymoon," read a typical headline. The quarrel concerned Ottawa's decision, as announced in the May budget, to "limit the rate of growth of transfers to provinces to yield annual savings of $2 billion by the end of the decade." Since the transfer payments accounted for almost 20 per cent of federal spending, it had been "appropriate" (as Michael Wilson understated it) to ask if they "should be insulated from policies of restraint." As early as November, 1984, Wilson had decided that they had to be "on the table" if he was to get serious about the federal deficit, though at that time Mulroney once more hamstrung his Minister of Finance for reasons of political prudence by saying, "We have not envisaged any cutbacks" in transfer payments. By May, however, the Prime Minister's back-bone had been slightly stiffened. The rate of growth would be reduced, at an estimated cost to the provinces of $6 billion by 1991, but the actual number of dollars would continue to increase above inflation and the provinces would pick up billions more through changes in Ottawa's tax levels.

When the premiers met in St. John's in August, they forgot their denunciations of the national debt and skipped the fact that transfer payments had emerged in better shape than almost every other area of federal spending. Instead, they attacked the reduction as "clearly inconsistent with maintaining present levels of service, let along meeting projected needs." Then Wilson made them angrier by an-nouncing unilaterally that the reduction would take effect in 1986 rather than 1987, as previously understood. As a result, at the federal-provincial conference in Halifax in November, the premiers accused the Tory government of the Liberals' old sins of high-handedness, intransigence, and foisting Ottawa's political and economic troubles on to the provinces.

Mulroney deliberately chose to hang tough. Not only was he under pressure from Finance and the private sector to do so, he wanted to correct the public impression (as detected by the polls) that he was a spineless jellyfish. "I was listening and I did act," he said when asked why he hadn't responded to the provinces' demands. "I said no."

Still, he seemed shaken by the speed and vehemence with which the premiers punctured his dream of recon-ciliation after the patience and concessions he had given them. "I think everybody knows now, " he lamented in Halifax, "if they didn't know before, that this is a difficult country to govern." Nevertheless, he immediately com-pounded his difficulties and undermined his new-found toughness by conceding "full provincial participation" in the trade negotiations with the United States.

While his strategic purpose was to expedite a deal by getting everyone "to sing from the same song sheet," as he put it, the sharp and well-publicized clashes between Ottawa and most of the premiers about the meaning of participation should have given Mulroney an indication of the unlikelihood of harmony. Even the best personal relations couldn't easily transcend the fundamental tensions between manufacturing regions and resource regions, haves and have-nots, urban centres and rural hinterlands, particularly when competing political interests were added. As Trudeau discovered during the 1970s, participation seldom made decisions simpler, and increasingly expensive gestures of good will rarely bought reciprocal acts of gratitude. Nor was there enough money or power to spread around to obtain the uneasy compromises of Mackenzie King and Lester Pearson.

Thus, the battle over free trade was in the process of becoming as divisive on regional lines as the battles over the constitution and energy prices had been. The opposing sides were already developing hard positions to advance their own interests, and there was less and less room to manoeuvre between Alberta's continentalism and Ontario's protectionism. Yet for Mulroney to take the bull by the horns and override Ontario's caution for the sake of the national interest, as Lougheed had been urging the Prime Minister to do, would require the very same vision of Canadian federalism and political will that Trudeau had espoused (and Lougheed had rejected) when the federal Liberals introduced the National Energy Program and the Charter of Rights. Instead, by accepting Lougheed's old refrain that the national interest was to be decided by Ottawa *and* the premiers, Mulroney in effect handed Ontario a veto over any trade deal with the Americans. Moreover, again thanks to Lougheed in large measure, Ottawa had little legal or moral authority to break a deadlock with a recalcitrant premier by appealing directly to the people.

Ultimately, trying to be a friend to everyone risked becoming a true friend to no one. That was especially evident in Mulroney's relations with Quebec in his first year. During the Tory leadership campaign in 1983 he had catered almost exclusively to Quebec's disaffected Liberals, his crony network, and those looking for the most likely route to the patronage trough. As leader and then as Prime Minister, however, he seemed to adopt Joe Clark's conviction that the Progressive Conservative Party needed to build a more stable base among non-separatist nationalists through a decentralist approach to issues of real and symbolic meaning.

While strong federalists tired of the Liberals and unhappy with John Turner might vote for the Tories with a Quebec leader for one election, in the long run Mulroney had to rely for organization and support on those who weren't likely to return to the Liberals at the first sign of a revival. This anti-Liberal coalition included former members of the Union Nationale, rural Créditistes, and many supporters of the Parti Québécois.

Gone overnight was Mulroney's righteous indignation about the perfidy of separatists. In its place, he held out hope of getting Quebec's PQ government to accept the Charter of Rights, appointed a former member of the PQ as Canadian ambassador to France, and allowed the PQ to announce the construction of the Hyundai auto plant in the course of the provincial election. More significant, in November, 1985, Ottawa reached an agreement with Quebec on the old and thorny question of the province's representation at meetings of francophone nations.

The issue had existed since the 1960s, when Gabon (pressed by France for its own mischievous and geopolitical reasons) bypassed the Canadian government and invited Quebec to send a delegation to a ministerial conference on education. Ottawa reacted by severing diplomatic relations with the small African country and rebuking Paris for encouraging the international ambitions of Quebec's Union Nationale Premier, Daniel Johnson. At the time Pierre Trudeau vowed "to make sure Canada speaks with one voice in the world," because he saw the alternative as the thin edge of the wedge of separation. Again, in 1970, he refused to allow Quebec to be an independent voting member of the Agency for Cultural and Technical Co-operation, which was established as a sort of French-speaking Commonwealth Secretariat, though the province could and did participate in those activities of the agency that concerned provincial affairs. As a result, France wouldn't agree to a summit meeting of francophone nations until Quebec's status was upgraded, and none was held until Brian Mulroney became Prime Minister.

Under the entente reached between him and (ironically) Daniel Johnson's son, the new Parti Québécois leader, the Quebec premier could participate independently in matters of provincial jurisdiction at a summit planned for early 1986 in Paris, though on federal matters he would remain an observer at the side of the Canadian Prime Minister unless invited to intervene. The Quebec delegation would be referred to as "Canada-Quebec" and accompanied by the Quebec flag.

"Never before has the federal government accepted the legitimacy of Quebec's presence at such a summit," Pierre Marc Johnson crowed. "This is an extremely important step for Quebec."

Indeed it was. It signalled nothing less than a return, after the devastating setback of the referendum, to the PQ's initial strategy of a long, slow, step-by-step separation. Each step was to be slight, reasonable, and undramatic, but each step was to lead to a little more power, a little more legitimacy, a little more acceptance until (as Claude Morin told Jean Chrétien) "eventually there will be nothing left." The PQ may have dropped independence as an immediate goal in its vain attempt to win the 1985 provincial election, but the fundamental purpose of the party had not been erased forever.

"The idea that one day Quebec will be sovereign cannot be removed from the mind, heart, spirit, and guts of a good number of Quebeckers, myself included," Johnson admitted during the campaign.

Mulroney was not naive, of course. He knew that Quebec's role at the summit would confer *de facto* special status on the province and boost its image as the homeland of French Canadians, the two notions that Trudeau had spent more than fifteen years battling. So, in a clever move, he also agreed to New Brunswick's participation under the same conditions, because it was an officially bilingual province despite its anglophone majority and unilingual premier. If anyone had any illusions about Pierre Marc Johnson's intentions in signing his entente with Ottawa, they vanished when he attacked Mulroney's deal with New Brunswick as a "hostile gesture."

"I was aware that New Brunswick would be present," he said, "but to the extent that Quebec had a special status. I thought that New Brunswick would be behind the flag of Canada." Describing the equality between the two provinces as "unseemly," he stated, "The reality is that Quebec is the only state in North America controlled by francophones."

In the short term Mulroney had escaped with a neat bit of stick-handling. In the longer term, however, he may have been too clever by half. Powers given to the provinces are rarely retracted without a fight, and powers given to one are usually demanded by all. It wasn't ridiculous to imagine Manitoba and Ontario requesting a seat at a future francophone summit or all the provinces asking for a role at the next British Commonwealth conference. Indeed, the ententes with Quebec and New Brunswick immediately preceded provincial demands for full participation in the American trade negotiations. The only ridiculous thing would be the cacophony of all those Canadian voices as they arrived on the international stage.

Clearly National Reconciliation was leading Brian Mulroney into some rather dangerous waters. It may have been easy for the Prime Minister to agree with the Parti Québécois's assertion that Quebec is a "distinct" society, but that only raised tougher questions. In what ways is Quebec more distinct that British Columbia or Prince Edward Island? What special powers, rights, or privileges should flow from being distinct? The PQ suggested that Quebec should be exempted from the language provisions of the Charter of Rights, for example, while the Quebec Liberals argued for restoration of the province's veto over amendments to the constitution. In his first year Mulroney stuck to happy generalities in order to create an atmosphere of harmony and await the outcome of the Quebec election. Someday, if he was serious about reaching a deal that would cause Quebec to sign the constitutional accord, he would have to confront the same forces that Trudeau had encountered again and again.

In fact, he would have a harder time, because the premiers had cornered Trudeau into accepting a constitutional amending formula that made any significant change next to impossible. Any deal with Quebec would have to pass through that process, which was guaranteed to reject giving any powers or advantages to Quebec without granting equivalent new powers and advantages to everyone else. Against this formidable obstacle, Mulroney was counting on the fairness of the premiers for whom he had already done so much. Thus, Newfoundland and Alberta were to help him bring Quebec back into the fold out of gratitude for what Ottawa had conceded to appease them. But Newfoundland and Alberta had already shown how little gratitude counts in federal-provincial affairs.

All through 1985 some senior officials tried to warn the Prime Minister against surrendering the small amount of turf that Ottawa had captured, inch by inch and at great social cost, for the sake of national unity. They were veterans of all the federal-provincial wars and knew the nature of the enemy. Yet their very experience discredited them in the eyes of the federal Tories. To speak pessimistically and in terms of wars and enemies branded them as closet Liberals pushing the old Trudeau line that Mulroney thought counter-productive. So instead, the officials muted the message to save their own credibility and jobs until Mulroney himself was "broken in" (as one Ottawa bureaucrat phrased it) by the realities. His disillusionment was apparent by November when he finally took a stand against the provinces over the issue of transfer payments. The only thanks he got from Lévesque for a billion-dollar deal with Quebec for regional development was a demand for more money for equalization payments and Domtar; the only thanks he got from Johnson for Ottawa's help to Hyundai was a demand for more money for two paper mills.

Of course, it was entirely possible that the fanatic obsession of Trudeau, the Liberals, and the officials in charge of the federal-provincial dossier regarding national unity both exaggerated and aggravated the problems. Perhaps Canada could bear the economic and political implications of being the most decentralized federation in the world, and perhaps Quebeckers and Westerners would never have been swept away by the ambitions of their provincial leaders. Certainly Trudeauism made compromise and cooperation more difficult. However, it was hard to see how good will would have won the referendum or the constitutional reforms, and it was surely disingenuous of Mulroney to imply that "the separatist government of Quebec dropped its separatist option for the first time" because of the Tories' soft-line approach. The PQ temporarily suspended its quest for independence after being defeated in a bitter, sometimes vicious fight. To suggest otherwise was self-serving distortion of history.

Like Mulroney, most Canadians didn't want to be reminded of past conflicts either. They wanted cooperative efforts to improve the economy, not more confrontations about the constitution. So almost no one worried about the effects of Mulroney's concessions. At the same time the Tories (and national unity) got some lucky breaks, such as the retirement of Peter Lougheed and the defeat of the Parti Québécois by the Liberals under Robert Bourassa, that took the bite out of federal-provincial relations and may have reduced the worst repercussions of Mulroney's surrender. To those who were preoccupied by who should speak for Canada, however, the trend was more disturbing than the details.

For one thing, the Tories seemed to be deferring to the concept that Canada was a compact of the provinces, not of the people. The first ministers' conferences gained formal regularity, while the Prime Minister appeared more influenced by the advice and lobbying of the premiers than of his own regional ministers. Under Trudeau the premiers had advanced themselves by using the argument that the federal Liberals (and therefore the national government) didn't represent the whole country. Mulroney had an opportunity with his widespread mandate to destroy that argument by building up the clout of the regional elites at the centre or by speaking on behalf of the will of the people. Instead, time and again he built up the authority of the premiers in order to avoid a feud.

Secondly, it became obvious that his political strategy was based on locking up the Tory vote in the West and Quebec. If he could do that, he could numerically guarantee Tory victories in Ottawa, independent of the traditional "swing" votes in Ontario and Atlantic Canada, and break forever the numerical advantage the Liberals had held. That made perfect political sense, but in terms of national policy it raised consternation about the results of consistently catering to the two most centrifugal regions of the country. That already was proving to be as expensive to the federal treasury as it was destabilizing to Canada's unity in foreign relations and economic goals, particularly since the interests of the West and Quebec were seldom compatible beyond Ottawa bashing. The arrival of a Liberal government in Ontario increased the temptation for the Tories to play the resource-based, free-trade hinterlands against the industrial, protectionist centre, for possible results that frightened those who believed in the internal and external fragility of the Canadian state.

With prosperity and in the absence of crisis, the elite accommodation of 1960s Canadian liberalism may be the best way to manage Canada smoothly and effectively. Good will would join mutual advantage for common purposes, and the well-being of the parts would add up to the well-being of the whole. In the wake of global challenges, economic dislocation, regional disparity, and provincial ambitions, however, Brian Mulroney and future Prime Ministers would probably have to pick up Pierre Trudeau's arguments about the need to correct the balance in favour of the centre. Once again power would attract power, the practical requirements of getting things done would hold sway, and the demands of the people for federal actions and services would provide the political impetus.

In the end, it was a matter of leadership. Canadians may have wanted an end to the bickering, but they were far from averse to continuing their old habit of voting for one party federally and another provincially. The long period of Liberal rule in Ottawa had destroyed the provincial Liberal parties, but the Tories were barely in office before Liberal fortunes began to improve in almost every province. The pattern seemed a deliberate device by the people to check the power of the elites, to keep all the politicians honest and awake, and to play one level of government against the other for the maximum amount of benefits and entertainment. It also seemed a perverse obstacle course to test the skill and mettle of the leaders.

In essence, Canadians didn't want their Prime Ministers to roll over and play dead at the first sign of an attack from the premiers. They wanted a national vision and an overriding central authority, though the validity of both would have to be demonstrated in routine conflicts with other power centres. That was particularly significant in Quebec, where the electorate continually mystified many analysts by respecting and voting for Trudeau and Lévesque simultaneously. Trudeau's support went beyond his value as a defender of French-Canadian interests and lucrative source of patronage. He was a true *chef*, a strong-willed leader with education, class, and principles. Mulroney, on the other hand, merely behaved as if Quebec's respect could be bought. It was reasonable to conclude that his slide in popularity and credibility in Quebec, despite his boondoggles, his defence of minority rights, and the continued presence of John Turner as Liberal leader, was partially and even primarily *because* Mulroney showed no will, little vision, and less leadership. A premier could get away with that. More was expected from a Prime Minister.

VI

Will, vision, and leadership haunted Brian Mulroney at the end of his first year in power. For all he had done toward Economic Renewal and National Reconciliation, the polls and the headlines focussed on his apparent lack of fortitude and direction. From the left, from the right, and even from sympathetic columnists in the centre, the typical banner read, "It's time for Tories to decide where we're going." Of course, the polls and headlines had accused Trudeau of arrogance and willfulness when the Liberals presumed to do just that, and they were ready to pounce on Mulroney's first incautious act with savage delight, but more and more Conservatives were beginning to recognize that in a no-win situation they might as well do what they thought was right.

In fact, the Tories encountered the perennial questions of leadership: What was their mandate? What were their goals? How far ahead of the people could they get? If the answers simply derived from following the polls, then any half-wit could be a good Prime Minister. However, polls are "the tyranny of public opinion" as much as "the pulse of democracy." Societies need leaders with wider, longer, and wiser perspectives about the future and how best to get there; voters want guidance, structure, and values; and the only truth pollsters never tell their clients is that people don't respect people who listen to pollsters.

"If we're here just to administer," Pierre Trudeau once told his caucus, "we're wasting our years and we might as well let the Tories rule. We're here to try to give direction to the country."

Mulroney and his advisers had been amazed and gratified at how quickly and thoroughly Trudeau slipped from the public's consciousness after such a long period as the centre of national attention. In part, Canadians had tired of Trudeau; in part, his firm decision to maintain a low profile kept him out of sight and out of mind. However, Mulroney fooled himself if he believed that Trudeau's style of leadership had been erased from the public's consciousness any more than had his policies as standards against which the Tories would be judged. The longing for will, vision, and leadership was indicative of the strong sense Canadians had that something important was missing in their new Prime Minister.

There may have been some masochism in that. After all, Trudeau had been provocative, insulting, insensitive, and obsessive. Yet, while he angered and challenged Canadians, he spoke to their deference to authority and national community. They may have resisted and detested uncomfortable change, but at heart they suspected that change had to come. Their resistance merely forced their leadership to make damn sure it really believed in where it was trying to take the nation.

Of course, will for will's sake didn't make much sense either. Despite the opinions of some advisers, there was little point in Mulroney charging ahead at full tilt, stirring up trouble and annoying people, just to show he was tough and determined. Indeed, Mulroney's strategy was to lower the temperature of debate, let sleeping dogs lie, and keep his own skin out of harm's way. After a period of too much will, vision, and leadership, he suggested, it was time for consensus, consultation, and decent management. Muddling through was back in vogue. Grand plans, big ideas, and bold adventures went out the window. That was a perfectly legitimate approach to government, and absolutely logical given the climate of the times, but Mulroney must have wondered at the end of his first year why it hadn't caused him to be garlanded with laurels and loved by his people.

Much of the reason was that many Canadians weren't convinced they were being managed any better than they had been under the Liberals. The economy was doing better, the working relationship between Ottawa and the provinces seemed better, and the worst aggravations from Revenue Canada to the PGRT had been smoothed out, but the improvements were barely noticed in the chaos and confusion surrounding the social-policy fiasco, the budget retreat, the series of ministerial resignations, the tuna scandal, the bank failures, the patronage appointments, the contradictions in policies and statements, and the incompetence of the Prime Minister's own office.

Some of the comedy was forgivable, because it could be attributed to the natural growing pains of a new government with many inexperienced ministers and a good deal to learn. However, more of it was based on serious misconceptions that would continue to undermine the Tory administration if not corrected. They flowed from the myths and exaggerations about the so-called Pitfield system of government management.

At the heart of the myths and exaggerations were some

faulty assumptions: that the system had been designed to centralize power around the Prime Minister, that the system moved power from the ministers to the bureaucrats, that the bureaucrats had been transformed into political partisans, and that ministerial accountability had been replaced by collective responsibility. Acting on these assumptions, both John Turner and Brian Mulroney began to unwind Trudeau's process in order to restore the bright new yesterdays of 1960s Canadian liberalism when ministers were independent, strong, and effective.

Thus, as one of his first and only acts as Prime Minister, Turner dismantled the central ministries for economic and social development, which coordinated the plans, priorities, and spending of the specific departments in their respective areas. Their responsibilities drifted back to the Treasury Board and the Department of Finance, a sweet revenge for Turner who, when Minister of Finance, had lost his battle with Trudeau over the diminution of Finance's overwhelming authority. At the same time the Privy Council Office under Gordon Osbaldeston lost much of its clout with regard to policy analysis and was relegated primarily to the role of supplier of data. Mulroney continued Turner's thrust because of the same distrust of technocratic systems and of Trudeau's civil service.

Immediately, therefore, power in the new Tory government flooded into Finance, where power over economy meant power over the agenda and power over spending priorities meant power over every department, as had been the general case in the 1950s and early 1960s. But Mulroney quickly learned why Trudeau had wanted to check and diffuse Finance's influence. "Otherwise," Trudeau once explained, "the minister there would be as powerful as I am." Moreover, Finance had its own interests to protect as a department of government and its own view to advance in the policy decisions of the nation.

It was instantly apparent that Michael Wilson and his Deputy Minister, Marshall "Mickey" Cohen, were preparing to take a harder line on explosive issues such as the deficit and universality than the Prime Minister thought prudent. Wilson saw himself as the servant of the business community, while Cohen (who had been a high-profile official behind Marc Lalonde and the NEP) seemed determined to prove himself a non-partisan servant of his minister by sounding more Catholic than the Pope. To harness them, Mulroney had to exercise the overriding authority of his own office. Later he even appointed a close and trusted friend, Stanley Hartt, to replace Cohen. Hartt was a bright and able lawyer from Montreal, who quickly earned high marks in the department despite being an outsider, but his main qualification for the job was presumed to be his ability to serve as Mulroney's man on the scene.

It was a short time before the numbers and clout of the PMO ballooned to an extent unmatched since the earliest days of Pierre Trudeau, in order to handle both the political and policy sides of the government. Unfortunately, the key players in the PMO had neither the administrative experience nor the political smarts to instil immediate confidence in their capacity to do the task well.

Most of them were familiar as Mulroney's old cronies, and loyalty seemed a higher attribute than talent. Thus, Bernard Roy became Principal Secretary because his lack of Ottawa knowledge or political connections outside Quebec was far outweighed by his history of intelligent, civil, and dedicated service to Brian Mulroney as a law partner, political aide, confidant, and best man. And thus, despite Norman Atkins's contribution during the election, no representative of Ontario's Big Blue Machine got a post in the PMO. One had been promised, but the Prime Minister's clique (mostly from his Quebec and Nova Scotia days) seemed determined to keep the rewards of victory for itself. Though Atkins remained a valued part of Mulroney's informal network of advisers and though most of the Ontario machine found that Christmas came early in 1984, the Davis retirement and the subsequent defeat of the Ontario Tories under Frank Miller reduced the influence of both Ontario and its political organizers. It wasn't clear whether that caused or was caused by the general Tory strategy to woo Quebec and the West, but it was evident that serious squabbles developed and persisted between the PMO and the Big Blue Machine.

It was strange that Mulroney didn't act to alleviate those tensions in his first year. No one better appreciated the efficacy of an "open-tent" policy; no one had higher regard for the experience and acumen of the Ontario boys; and no one would have more need of their help in the next election. Some insiders attributed Mulroney's attitude to his reluctance to staff his office with anyone whose political instincts were as good as his own. More likely, he owed his loyalists too much to betray them in their long-awaited moment of glory. They had propped him up during the dark times; they understood and tolerated his tantrums and his petty vengeances; and they flattered him with their devotion. Together they were bound by the sense of being underrated outsiders who trusted and respected each other more than anyone else.

Almost at once, as a result, there arose a "bunker mentality" of *us* against *them* that alienated important members of the party, the government, and the media. Because the Prime Minister's staff often served as a private cell before which he could vent his rages, his insecurities, and his frustrations without worrying about his public image as Mr. Civility, an odour of hostility and meanness hung heavy over much of the PMO's dealings with the outside world. Senior bureaucrats had difficulty discovering how to get decisions through the PMO. The press and the party frequently encountered the exclusive, defensive response of people who felt under siege. Even cabinet ministers weren't immune from orders, threats, and insults.

To that weak base was added an impossible work load. Basically, coming into office, Brian Mulroney had little confidence in either his ministers or his civil servants. He saw the former as inexperienced, politically unreliable, and accident-prone (and he had good reasons for seeing that); he saw the latter as Liberals. Therefore, he wanted to keep close watch and tight rein on them by means of his office. But since no one in the office had better experience or instincts than Mulroney, everything began to filter up to him. Soon he was reversing important ministerial decisions from pension de-indexing to grants to Domtar, jumping up in the House of Commons to answer questions about farmers and banks, and making private deals in the corridors just like Lester Pearson used to do.

Within months all the old problems that the Pitfield system had been designed to solve returned with a vengeance. The cabinet committees began to break down because they didn't have enough final authority to make them worth the ministers' time and effort. Instead, more and more decisions were sent up to the Planning and Priorities Committee, which was in effect the inner cabinet chaired by the Prime Minister. But, in the words of one insider, "P and P doesn't P or P," because it was preoccupied with putting out political fires. In fact, no one of any stature in the government seemed to be making plans or setting priorities. The duties taken from the coordinating ministries and the PCO were lost in the bowels of the Department of Finance. The ministers and their departments were too busy with their own immediate trials to bother much about the future or one another. The PMO was running from pillar to post trying to supervise the theatrical media events of its own devising or contain the thousands of unwelcome surprises.

Meanwhile, the Prime Minister was getting swamped by his hands-on approach to government. Because he showed no compunction about overruling his ministers, most of them wanted to play safe and get his agreement first. Because he disliked formal technocratic procedures and wanted to be everyone's friend, everyone tried to corner him for a bilateral promise or an arbitrary trade-off. As a consequence, the strong got an advantage over the weak, dissenting opinions or other options weren't guaranteed a hearing, critical information was left to random phone calls and chance encounters, and senior bureaucrats received conflicting reports about what Mulroney had agreed to. At the same time every vested interest, from native groups to unemployed workers to business executives, publicly demanded meetings with the Prime Minister so that he would do something personally about its latest gripe or wish. To be pushed off to a mere minister was considered worse than useless: it was considered an insult.

Pierre Trudeau had been described as the Sun King,

but it was Brian Mulroney who tended to proceed past hordes of petitioners and say in the manner of Louis XIV, "Je verrai, je verrai." Because of the size and nature of his mandate and because of his hold over his caucus and cabinet, Mulroney had as much personal power as Trudeau at the height of Trudeaumania, but Trudeau had been more insecure about how to get things done and more attentive to the democratic process. While Trudeau had at once started to push power away from himself, Mulroney had started to attract it.

Yet it was not possible or practical to run a modern state as if it were a corporation. Trudeau was infinitely more intelligent than Mulroney, he had surrounded himself with people who were infinitely more intelligent than those around Mulroney, and he was served by a far more efficient organization than Mulroney's, yet Trudeau frequently lost his grip and direction. Of course, some argued that was because Trudeau's system was at fault, that he should have exercised more arbitrary and centralized power, as he did with the constitution and the NEP, but such a strategic leadership only worked when the Prime Minister decided to concentrate on a very small number of crucial issues and delegate everything else to others. Certainly a more presidential style of government required a much better operation than Mulroney had in place in 1985.

Lacking it, Mulroney appeared as out of his depth as he probably was. Flying rather erratically by his political instincts and trying to keep in the centre by swooping back and forth from left to right, he confused and annoyed his ministers, his bureaucrats, and the people of Canada. His improvised inconsistency, his mercurial emotions, his obsession with fighting the last election and then the next one, and his suspicion of ideas seemed to confirm the impression that he had no purpose for power except to keep it.

In part, he was a victim of the anti-intellectualism that swept Ottawa, the Tories, and John Turner after Trudeau. In part, he was trying to bring humanity and human nature back into the process. As a result, reason and coherence seemed to be on holiday or in exile for a while. Ministers went off in different directions, the bureaucracy slipped into a blue funk, and the Prime Minister devoted cabinet time to reviewing his press clippings. Mulroney didn't even hold a daily meeting with his Principal Secretary and the Clerk of the Privy Council, at which he would be regularly briefed on what was happening, his political and bureaucratic chiefs would receive his thoughts in the same way, and there would be some coordination of duties and clash of ideas. As officials passed more responsibilities up to the ministers out of prudence, as the ministers passed more up to "P and P" and the PMO for the same reason, and as "P and P" and the PMO passed more up to the Prime Minister, it was simply a question of time before burn-out, chaos, and crisis would occur.

The burn-out came by July, 1985, after the budget and the subsequent retreat over the de-indexing of pensions. Mulroney and his ministers had been going at full pace since the election the year before, and the cost in terms of fatigue and confusion was obvious to the entire nation. Only those ministers (such as Pat Carney, Michel Côté, and Perrin Beatty) who had gone into their departments with a clear agenda, developed a good working relationship with their bureaucrats, and dodged Mulroney's interference emerged with their reputations improved. The rest tended to flounder in their attempts to set their agendas on the job through task forces and consultation papers, to play policy maker and administrator and politician simultaneously, and to second-guess the ever-changing mind of the Prime Minister.

As their grasp and support slipped in response, the Tories resolved to use the summer break to regain their energy, their sense of direction, and their following. Thus, they decided to march into September with a number of clear and forceful announcements on free-trade talks, the defence of Canada's sovereignty in the North, the refusal to participate in the American "Star Wars" project, and so on, all intended to demonstrate decisiveness, purpose, and a balanced approach to issues. Instead, they marched straight into the accidents that had been looking for a place to happen. It was an unlucky coincidence that the tuna affair and two bank collapses broke in the same month the RCMP revealed it was investigating the Minister of Communications for election irregularities, but no one close to the government was surprised by the resulting chaos.

It brought to mind the remark Robert Borden made as he watched the Parliament Buildings burn down—"What else can happen to this goddamn government?"—but most observers chose to recall the speedy disintegration that overtook the Diefenbaker government after its massive sweep in 1958. In truth, Mulroney was smarter and much more competent than Diefenbaker. A more accurate parallel was the tempestuous period that rocked the Pearson administration, for much the same underlying causes. Modern government was too large and complex to be run out of the Prime Minister's hip pocket, no matter how bright and well connected he might be, yet power would inevitably flow to him if there wasn't a rational system and firm resolve to direct it elsewhere. The pride of the Pitfield system was that the routine affairs of state had carried on in the midst of the FLQ crisis, the OPEC crisis, and the constitutional debates. Now the entire national agenda of the Conservative government seemed to be derailed for weeks by some cans of rancid tuna.

Naturally the tuna was only an excuse for the opposition and the media to attack Mulroney where he was weakest (his egocentric control, his credibility, and his staff of cronies). A reasonable argument could have been made that a decision by the Minister of Fisheries to overrule his officials for political reasons on a relatively minor departmental item was precisely the type of thing that should not have ended up on the Prime Minister's desk for review. If the minister was discovered to have made a mistake, he should have been fired, as indeed he was, but it was lunacy to expect the Prime Minister or even his office to probe into the myriad of decisions made by ministers every day. Yet Mulroney had invited just such an expectation by his own tendency to steal his ministers' authority and limelight.

Ironically, the Prime Minister was in the midst of re-forming his procedures when "Black September" hit. He wanted to reduce the size of the PMO and return a lot of the responsibility for planning and policy analysis to the Privy Council Office. For that purpose, he appointed Paul Tellier, one of the best and brightest young officials from the Pitfield era, as the senior bureaucrat after the retirement of Gordon Osbaldeston. After his insulting references to the Canadian public service and his threats to hand out "pink slips and a pair of running shoes," he had recognized that politicians needed the expertise and collaboration of their officials, that bureaucrats had to be made sympathetic to the objectives of the government for anything to happen, and that sympathy didn't presume partisan politicization. In fact, many senior officials soon praised him for his quick mind, his kindnesses and attentions to them, and his skills in negotiation and conciliation.

However, rebuilding the PCO and improving the links between it and the PMO would only lead back to the bureaucratic control of the 1950s if the cabinet committees weren't revitalized too. Ministerial responsibility and the political domination of departments were worthy goals, but the toughest areas of modern government concerned collective responsibility and the political domination of planning, priorities, and policy. Particularly in times of scarcity, departmental decisions were much easier to make than decisions about trade-offs among departments. If those trade-offs weren't made by ministers in a collective and informed fashion, cabinet solidarity would come apart, the Prime Minister would be forced to adjudicate among competing interests, and real decision-making clout would be picked up by new mandarins in the back rooms and corridors of power. Ultimately someone had to make the tough final decisions. If it wasn't a series of committees of well-briefed ministers, then it would likely be the Prime Minister or his political and bureaucratic staff.

The results of Mulroney's half-measures were revealed by the end of 1985 when Suzanne Blais-Grenier, the Minister of State for Transport, quit the cabinet to protest the decision to allow the sale of a Gulf Canada refinery in Montreal to Ultramar Canada, a British-owned company. The sale meant the closing of the refinery and the subsequent loss of some four hundred jobs. Not only did the controversy involve the sticky issues of foreign ownership, government intervention in the private sector, and regional employment, it was complicated by Blais-Grenier's own reputation as an incompetent minister. She had already been demoted from Minister of Environment and was rumoured to be on her way out of the cabinet, so her resignation was seen as a pre-emptive strike to leave in a blaze of principled glory. Nevertheless, her departure raised a political storm because of her statement that "the real influence of ministers from Quebec in the cabinet's decision-making process seems to me insufficient."

The PMO's reply that the Prime Minister himself was a Quebec minister only emphasized the problem, and no doubt it contributed to the appearance at Mulroney's door of a delegation of workers from the refinery demanding an audience and remedial action. The Quebec press, even members of the Quebec Tory caucus, and eventually the Quebec public were convinced that their interests had been sacrificed for the interests in Ontario and the West, despite all the money and time the Tories had poured into the province for strategic reasons. (Indeed, it was interesting to observe the effect of the reappearance of *bleu* values, in modern form, on the Tories' 1960s liberalism.) Meanwhile, Ontario was feeling victimized by Mulroney's courting of Quebec and the West, and the West was ever vigilant to advantages going to Central Canada. Cases such as Ultramar were bound to be repeated if the decision-making system didn't appease and solidify ministers by participation in patently effective, fair, and open trade-offs.

That would just be more chaos, however. The crisis would come if the decision-making system also didn't force ministers to look past their short-term ambitions to the country's long-term requirements. Such force wouldn't be possible while everyone had too much to do and no occasion to focus on the priorities. In other words, the duties and time of the Prime Minister and his ministers had to be apportioned with greater care and organization, so that the cabinet wasn't stumbling from event to event while the bureaucracy set the overview agenda. By the middle of 1985, voices in the PMO were even mourning the loss of the central ministries and talking of resurrecting something very much like them out of necessity.

Planning and priorities went beyond better management. They addressed the broader question of leadership. Responding to events in a panicky and contradictory fashion didn't just look like sloppy organization; it looked like the absence of any national vision or political purpose. Politics abhors such a vacuum. The people seek dreams, hopes, and excitement as much as competence from their governors, while the politicians quickly gaze past sound administration to glory, history, and greatness.

Indeed, part of Brian Mulroney's trouble at the end of his first year stemmed from his successes as much as his failures. The speed with which he cleared away the more obvious debris of the Trudeau regime left a void that demanded to be filled. Even though there was much that was incomplete and unstable about his Economic Renewal and National Reconciliation, the alleviation of the immediate tensions had both the government and the country asking, "What next?" Neither seemed satisfied by the reply, "More of the same." Even the Prime Minister admitted that beavering away at the deficit wasn't very sexy.

Nor was it enough. In fact, most of Mulroney's successes had been on a symbolic or symptomatic level rather than real or deep. Beneath their rhetoric and hype, the Conservatives deliberately avoided confronting the problems Canada had to deal with before long, whether the economic union, social policy, pension reform, chronic regional unemployment, or rational industrial reconstruction. The Tories denied that, of course, claiming that their budget policies were valid and coherent (if gradual and unglamorous) solutions for the long-term issues, but many of them wondered if bigger and bolder initiatives weren't necessary. To a large degree, free trade had been able to penetrate past Mulroney's caution because of his growing intuition that new ideas of comprehensive and historic dimensions were needed for political and economic benefits.

At the heart of the Tories' leadership troubles was the fact that so many of their ideas focussed on diminishing the national state. It was one thing for an opposition party to attack the size, spending, and competence of the federal government. It was another thing for a party in power to attack itself, in effect. At the immediate level, that meant there were fewer programs and funds by which the Tories could demonstrate that they were creative, active, caring, and constructive. At a subtler level, it suggested that the Tories preferred to abdicate their responsiblities in a confession of their own inadequacy. Each time Mulroney stated that Ottawa couldn't run a regional development program better than the provinces, an aircraft company better than an American multinational, or a western bank better than the private sector, he undermined his own image as the leader of that government.

The Tory policies felt like a void because they were creating one in the centre of the nation's political consciousness. Cutbacks, the decentralization of power, and the tossing of Canada's future hopes to the premiers and the business community and even the American Congress generally didn't respond to the trust, expectations, and demands Canadians had traditionally invested in Ottawa. In the Tory order of things the CBC, the Science Council of Canada, and the Canada Council became objects of abuse and retrenchment, while Boeing, Texaco, and Brian Peckford got financial bonuses and the benefit of the doubt.

Even the harmony and consultation that voters had wanted during the 1984 election soon began to look like meaningless excuses not to act. As Trudeau had discovered in his first term, people wanted decisions more than federal-provincial conferences, business-labour summits, task forces, and endless white papers. As Trudeau had discovered by his fourth term, people wanted national leadership more than concessions to the premiers, *carte blanche* for market forces and the multinationals, and subservience to the United States.

Mulroney's dilemma was that everyone was calling for him to show some will and vision, but only a will and vision of the left of centre would help him in the polls and the next election. While Canada's political culture may have produced a quest for authority and a willingness to defer to it, it also produced a social-democratic thrust. The elites may have been calling for a leader with the will of Margaret Thatcher or Ronald Reagan, but that was precisely the type of will most Canadians wouldn't accept. Therefore, to show any strong will would necessarily alienate either the elites or the people, something Mulroney didn't want to do.

In the past, the best Canadian Prime Ministers had solved the dilemma through a kind of social contract: the elites could maintain their power bases, their wealth, and their influence, and a wide measure of independence, so long as they agreed to pay for the redistribution programs that bought peace and a certain amount of justice. In other words, administrations had been judged by their success in binding the elites and the people in a common purpose. Abundance made the contract possible and rather simple, because there was enough (or at least something) for everyone. Scarcity made it perhaps impossible and certainly difficult, because it provoked conflicts over who would (or should) take the smaller pieces of a shrinking pie.

In the developing struggle Trudeau opted for the people, because of his democratic principles, his personal discomfort with the elites, and the political ambition of his party. In making his choice, he was influenced by certain observations. The decentralism of Canadian liberalism had done a rather poor job in more than a hundred years of forging a united country, partly because majority rule and popular will were checked by the process and partly because many elites found advantage in setting the various power centres against each other. To an extent, the realization of national unity was incompatible with the traditions of elite accommodation because it required the reinforcing of federal institutions and encouraged Canadians to look past their local elites to central authority.

Moreover, because of Canada's colonial history and branch-plant economy, many members of the elites developed attitudes and interests that weren't always in the national interest. When everyone was prospering, that was barely noticeable and hardly an issue. In harder times, however, it became more evident. As the search for wealth became more competitive, for example, there was increased pressure within the business community to sell out to multinationals, move capital and jobs to the United States, or merge into huge conglomerates.

Meanwhile, revolutions in communications, education, and transportation had given the general public a stronger sense of national community and a greater political impact. People were more knowledgeable and sophisticated about the nation's affairs, and polls gave the silent majority a voice much louder than any Ottawa lobbyist's with regard to public policy, whether jobs versus the deficit, government versus the marketplace, or nationalism versus continentalism.

"The most significant trend we picked up during the year right across Canada," Allan Gregg said in a *Maclean's* survey at the end of 1985, "is a growing and potentially dangerous class disparity, in terms of response to common behaviour. This is not a question of class definition but the beginning of class-based thinking."

That was predictable. Those who thought the Liberals' alienation of the elites had stemmed from Trudeau's particular ideology and personality only needed to look to the story of John Turner for proof to the contrary. Turner had come from Bay Street in 1984 with an elitist's conviction about what was good for the country. Not even the dramas of his leadership campaign nor the traumas of the election had really shaken his faith. All through the fall and winter of his first year as Leader of the Opposition, he was clearly out of step with most of his caucus and party advisers. His basic instincts were to agree with Wilson's economic reforms, Mulroney's *mano a mano* approach to the Americans, and the Tories' free-market rhetoric.

As a result, he looked awkward and ineffective in the House of Commons, upstaged by the NDP and his own aggressive back-benchers. Not only was he running well behind his party in popularity at the start of 1985, he was tied with "None of the above" at 11 per cent as best choice for Prime Minister. Few Liberals seemed prepared to help him rebuild the party, and knives were sharpened behind his back in the caucus and back rooms. Some said he would be lucky to survive as leader until 1986. His problems went far deeper than his poor media image, his persistent throat clearing, and his apparent inability to say or think anything that wasn't written on a cue card beforehand.

Basically the Liberal Party needed to win back its traditional support among francophones, lower-income and New Canadians, and women if it hoped to regain power. The Tories and the New Democrats were still working hard to secure those constituencies for themselves by stealing the Liberals' old methods and policies, and if they succeeded, it wasn't impossible that the great Liberal Party of Canada might vanish altogether. Meanwhile, John Turner still appeared preoccupied with making inroads in the business community and the West; he still looked and sounded like a high-priced lawyer from Toronto; he still made clumsy digs at Trudeau and Chrétien in Quebec; and he still didn't understand his own party.

During 1985, however, he persevered with all the nobility and resolution of John the Baptist. He visited the constituencies and the provincial parties, did the "chief-executive-officer-type work" on finance and organization, logged an estimated quarter of a million kilometres, and "listened—God, have I listened," as he put it. Eventually, as he absorbed his briefs and his file cards, his stoic persistence in the face of humiliation and defeat began to earn him some admiration. To it he added by September the benefits of his speech lessons, his media lessons, his French lessons, and a new fighting style prompted by the effectiveness of the party's "Rat Pack" MPs and the findings of a Goldfarb poll in August.

Improvements in his style and the party's administration would not have paid off if they hadn't been accompanied by changes in his thinking (or, at least, in his rhetoric). From month to month and issue to issue, Turner strengthened his emphasis on the role of government, national sovereignty, cultural identity, social justice, regional equality, and minority rights. Pushed by the messages from the grassroots, the polls, and the Trudeauites who had regathered near him, he sought each occasion the Tory government gave him to get onto the left of centre. Concern about the deficit was lost in his more strident demands for jobs; he fought for fully indexed old-age pensions and Canadian sovereignty in the North; he questioned free trade, the Western Accord, and the bank bail-outs; he opposed the sale of de Havilland, "Star Wars," and unfair corporate tax breaks; he spoke eloquently about the food banks he had visited in Vancouver. Boosted by the election of a Liberal government in Ontario (to be followed by one in Quebec) and the end of the Tories' honeymoon with Canadians, Turner's transformation got him a prolonged standing ovation at a party conference in Halifax in November and let the Liberals move to first place in the polls by early 1986.

At the same time, that transformation cost him the respect and support of many of the elites who had backed him in 1984. Like Trudeau, Turner had had to make a choice, and the choice could no longer be easily fudged by friendships, secret deals, nebulous positions, and contradictory stances. In the pinch, the lines were hardening into two clusters of complementary ideas: nationalism, protectionism, and interventionism on the left of centre (where most of the people were) as opposed to continentalism, free trade, and free markets on the right of centre (where most of the elites were). Of course, there was nothing to prove that John Turner would take the same line in power that he was using to get there. In fact, taking a leaf from the Tories' book, he went out of his way to avoid making promises or outlining alternative policies.

"I don't have to come up with those alternative programs right now," he said. "I told the people where I stood. Now I have the duty to prod the government to come forward with its programs. That's my role. My role is to wait for Mulroney to move."

In power Turner would face the same pressures, the same economic statistics, the same long-term problems, and the same cleavages as Mulroney; and he shared Mulroney's wish to win, indecisiveness, weak staffing, and ideological schizophrenia. Out of power, however, he could steal back the winning formula that Mulroney had stolen from the Liberals. As the Tories had demonstrated, power was best won by progressive postures, close attention to the polls and the election machine, the suppression of extreme beliefs among the membership, chameleon leadership, and above all the patience to wait for the incumbent government to stumble with its own failures and fatigue. In the end, the rise of the Liberals in 1985 had more to do with the errors of the Tories than the labours of John Turner, and everyone expected the same would be true if the Liberals won the next election.

While Turner had gained Mulroney's old advantage of simplistic criticism and righteous indignation, it may not have been enough to guarantee victory. With a grip on the West and the odds of keeping enough seats in Quebec as a patronage-dispensing native son, Mulroney had a built-in numerical foundation that Turner would have a great deal of trouble shattering even if he took most of Ontario and Atlantic Canada. Moreover, Turner's history and his aristocratic manner didn't suggest that he could overwhelm the NDP's challenge from the left as he would have to do to negate the Tories' head start. In other words, because of problems particular to the leader, recapturing the winning formula wouldn't assure victory. Not recapturing it, however, would assure defeat.

Indeed, the Liberals' best opportunity would arise if external circumstances and internal pressures forced the Tories to continue abandoning the left of centre. Mulroney believed he could stay there by being Mackenzie King and Bill Davis, but the 1980s aren't the 1940s and Ottawa isn't Queen's Park. Brokerage politics isn't easy when the divisions are too wide for consensus, the trade-offs are too vicious for compromise, and the decisions can't be postponed for another decade. The strength and appetite of other power centres mean that conflicts can't be smothered simply, and the leader of a federal government can't hide from the opposition and the media or originate nothing as routinely as a premier can. Choices have to be made, and each choice means enemies, new tensions, and a public record to defend.

For most of his first year, Mulroney tried to avoid such choices, but he learned that evasion itself was a choice that angered both the powerful interests and ordinary people.

Then he tried throwing one sop to one side and another to the other, but he learned it was human and political nature to accept one's due without thanks while never forgetting what someone else got away with. The most dramatic lesson of his consultation exercises was how polarized were the cleavages between Ottawa and the provinces, business and labour, East and West, the established and the unemployed.

Moreover, because of the Tories' approach to public policy, Mulroney was short of the two traditional means of reducing such cleavages: cash and nationalism. The first restricted his ability to continue buying peace at any price and forced him to seek cheap glory in foreign affairs and symbolic gestures, neither of which confronted the real issues at home. The second limited his ability to inspire Canadians to subsume their particular interests under the national good. Indeed, the Tory thrust toward the individual over the community, "me first" over public service, and competition over altruism undercut the government's chances of rallying everyone together for any purpose, whether the reduction of the deficit or the alleviation of regional disparities. Worse, as the Liberals had often discovered, there was even short-term political advantage in playing one interest against the others.

Centrist politics remained the Canadian way to govern, but the centre itself was unstable and harder to define. "The thing that will get the Liberals back in fastest is if the Tories are perceived as not being in the centre," Bill Neville said. The application and implication of that, however, were at the source of the Tories' conundrums.

However forcefully Mulroney's polls, intuitions, and instincts as Canada's first working-class Prime Minister told him to pull to the left, he was riding a tiger that wanted to go to the right. That tiger consisted of the right-wing members of the party and caucus who had been the base of his leadership victory, the right-wing members of the cabinet who had their own influential constituencies, and right-wing members of the elite who had underwritten the career of the quick-minded, amusing, ambitious kid from Baie Comeau. If Mulroney thought he had tamed the tiger by tossing it the raw meat of power in 1984 and dangling the promise of more in future elections, he discovered that the taste made it hungrier, hornier, and more aggressive.

Brian Mulroney knew what he had to do to win an election, and he had a fair idea of what he had to do to govern well and harmoniously, but he didn't know how to put the two together. The result was his waffling, his "weak knees" (as Lougheed put it), and the revival of the old problem of his trustworthiness. Because he seemed on all sides on every issue, many Canadians harboured fresh doubts about his honesty and integrity, and worried about his opportunism. He looked packaged, confused, and fundamentally soft at the centre, like a man who had unfinished business with his own soul. He could be as smooth, as anecdotal, and as populistic as Reagan, but he lacked the impression Reagan conveyed of moral fibre and determined views.

His political and personal dilemmas were best expressed by his obvious desire to be loved. "I have no enemies, I swear to you, I have *no* enemies," he told a reporter as late as 1983, and that delusion told much about his behaviour as a human being and as Prime Minister. He seemed genuinely shocked that the media would say the same mean things about him that he had been known to say about them, and he seemed sincerely perplexed why the opposition parties attacked him with the same partisan hysteria and lack of civility he had been known to release against them. Respect and votes didn't seem enough. He wanted to croon his way into the hearts of the people, to be as mythic and adored as Kennedy or Churchill, to be lifted on the shoulders of Canadians and history.

If that were the case, Brian Mulroney was doomed to disappointment. "You can calculate the worth of a man by the number of his enemies," Flaubert once observed. Prime Ministers are permitted few friends (and fewer cronies), and it is generally impossible for them to carry on love affairs with their parties, their elites, and their people without being condemned as unfaithful and insincere. That might be especially true in Canada, where the imperfections of its democracy had bred the social custom of mocking, abusing, and discarding leaders. Contradictory demands, countervailing power centres, and a predominant liberalism guaranteed that Canadians would agitate against the very authorities in which they placed their hopes, their confidence, and their futures.

That didn't mean Mulroney couldn't win his next election. No one should underestimate the effect of better economic statistics, the skills and luck of the Prime Minister, the potency of a political machine with money and the benefits of incumbency, the strikes against John Turner as a patrician from English Canada with a shaken party and a credibility problem of his own, or the short-term efficacy of muddling through. Sooner or later, however, Mulroney would have to develop a thicker skin, a taste for wielding a sword in public, and a more coherent vision for the sake of the country as well as his own good. Reacting to every challenge with *ad hoc* policies, quick surrenders, and oversensitive emotions might steal ground from the opposition and buy temporary peace, but it would do little for the structural flaws that every analysis agreed were sending Canada into a gradual decline or toward an impending crisis. In fact, the decline was well under way.

Political will is a neutral thing, of course, but the history of Canadian politics had demonstrated that it is more acceptable and pragmatic in a move to the left than to the right. Any objective study would indicate that on the eve of an election or in the face of a real crunch, the options that leaned toward the state and the nation would prevail over the options that leaned toward the marketplace and the continent, everything else being more or less equal. That's what had happened since the 1950s and why the closing of a Gulf refinery caused more political headaches than the expansion of Petro-Canada. Mulroney understood that a sound Conservative government was probably what Disraeli had described as "Tory men and Whig measures." But Disraeli had also described that as "an unhappy cross-breed, the mule of politics that engenders nothing."

That was Brian Mulroney's nightmare. "I've always had a healthy respect for the Liberal Party," he said. "It's not a party of 28 per cent. It's had a bad go of it in the last election, and I'll try to make sure that it happens again, but I don't take any of that for granted. The Liberal Party has a long tradition of office. It knows how to get there and usually how to stay there, so I think it'll be back knocking on the door. I treat it very seriously."

Mulroney's astute and realistic perception virtually promised that the pendulum would start swinging back to the left sooner rather than later. The Tories had a stake in acting that way, the Liberals had a stake in sounding even more so, and it wasn't unlikely that after the next election the New Democrats would hold the balance of power to force either the Tories or the Liberals to move toward them, as happened in Ontario in 1985. The official connection of the New Democratic Party with the labour unions (which Canadians tend to trust less than business or government) probably condemned it to remaining a 20 per cent party nationally, but with time and without commotion the major parties would probably continue to steal its policies as they had done since the 1930s.

That could cause the absorption of the NDP into the Liberal Party (whose right wing would ally with the Tories presumably) or it could cause the NDP to maintain its effectiveness as the vanguard or "decompression chamber" of new, leftist ideas. Either way the die seemed cast in favour of more interventionism, more nationalism, greater centralization of the federation, and the triumph of the will of the people.

What that meant for the private sector and the provinces, how best to organize and implement such policies, and how to preserve individual freedom and initiative—those were likely to be the great debates of Canada's twenty-first century. If so, they would be fought out with more conflict, more chaos, and more cleavage than Canada was used to. They might even require a leader of unprecedented strength for their resolution, and such a leader was again more likely to come from the left than the right. And then? The crystal ball becomes cloudy. Will and crisis throw all the patterns askew, and political cultures can take some strange evolutions over time. The bomb, environmental disaster, global famine, or a new ice age could make the entire discussion academic, if not mundane.

In the meantime, there was so much to amuse and distract the country. A world's fair was about to open in Vancouver, the Toronto Blue Jays and the Montreal Expos were about to begin another run for a baseball pennant, and Mrs. Mulroney revealed that her husband had no sense of smell. For the rich there was a soaring stock market. For the poor there were fabulous lotteries. And across Canada people huddled in groups in the cold night air to scan the heavens for a glimpse of Halley's comet. The little light hurtling through the universe reminded them of their place in time and space. It linked them to a romantic Canada lost in the past. It linked them to an uncertain Canada rushing up in the future. It even linked them to the wonders of the present, in which a fortunate and rather crazy nation closed one eye and peered into the blackness, still seeking the fault in the stars and not in themselves.

On a Personal Note

My stated intention to highlight the key patterns of Canadian politics in the 1980s forced me on occasion to paint the picture with very broad strokes. More than once, I felt the same way about some of my sweeping statements as the Duke of Wellington did about his ragtag troops when he said, "I don't know what effect they'll have on my enemies, but, by God, they frighten me." Like every rule, every generalization has its exceptions. That is especially true in the world of politics, where inconsistency and dissimulation are often proclaimed as virtues under the guise of open-mindedness and pragmatism. My only defence is that I haven't been unaware of the dangers involved. In many cases the patterns have proved to be useful interpreters, even augurs, of unfolding events. In some cases their value must await future developments. In any case they will have served their purpose if they provoked some thought or raised some hackles.

Certainly none of them was motivated by conscious bias. Unfortunately, since I don't believe that perfect objectivity is possible in the search for truth, I can't speak for the unconscious biases with the same confidence. That bothered me as a reporter. In my experience, people want informed opinions, but they also want some indication of the biases so that they can weigh them in the balance when making their political judgements. Therefore, at the risk of undermining my own conclusions, I thought I should sketch the direction from which I've approached my subject.

I am a male, upper-middle-class baby-boomer, three-quarters Irish and one-quarter French Canadian. Though born in Ottawa, I grew up in Montreal, where (like most English Quebeckers) I learned to look more attentively and more sympathetically to the national government than to the provincial capital. As a student at McGill University in the mid-1960s I had a passionate love affair with Quebec nationalism, full of poetry, song, and *Gitanes* in wine-dark bistros, as exciting and insane as any adolescent infatuation. It passed and I came to believe in the vision of a bilingual and bicultural Canada, but I never developed the hostility and paranoia toward Quebec nationalism that affected so many of the anglophone minority. Though I had to move to Ottawa and Toronto for work in the English-language media, my psychological home remains a piece of land in a beautiful valley 100 miles east of Montreal. It was there, in a small cabin by a brook surrounded by a pine forest, that I wrote this book.

Inevitably my place gives me a Central Canadian perspective, though I have travelled extensively through every province and territory, have immediate relatives on both coasts who aren't shy about correcting my myopia, and have tried to pay particular attention to the voices from other parts of the country. On the other hand, this book is about *realpolitik*. Like it or not, power in the early 1980s was concentrated in Central Canada, so most of my focus is there. Those who feel I haven't done justice to the views from elsewhere might gain comfort and an advantage from a better knowledge of the nature of the enemy. That knowledge is often the most useful beginning to change.

At the age of fifteen I was a crazed devotee of John Diefenbaker and even represented the Progressive Conservative Party, arms akimbo and jowls skaking, in my high school's mock election in 1963. Both the Chief and I came second to the Liberals. As an undergraduate I listened to a history professor outline the political ideas of John Stuart Mill, whereupon I whispered to the friend beside me, "I think I'm a nineteeth-century British liberal." As a graduate student in the Institute of Canadian Studies at Carleton University, Ottawa, I was lured by friends, the times, a concern for my country's independence, and guilt about my privileged background into the Waffle wing of the New Democratic Party.

I was as dogmatic, as strident, and as driven by good intentions and utopian dreams as any other twenty-one-year-old socialist, but even then I realized I wasn't a very good Waffler. I was too much of a loner to feel comfortable in a mass movement, however bright and likeable its members, and too much of a skeptic to accept the obvious contradictions between our ideas and our lives.

This erratic political autobiography reveals, I hope, someone patriotic, fair-minded, more interested in public service than private gain, and deeply disillusioned. In my naive imagination, power was about doing God's work on earth; in reality, it seemed little more than a Stanley Cup final among players who got into the game to do good for others and ended up doing well for themselves.

For almost ten years I remained adamantly apolitical. I hitch-hiked around the world, spending more than six months in Africa and almost a year in India, and returned home convinced that Canadian politics was just so many tempests in an extremely valuable teapot. I barely followed current events in the newspapers, I preferred to talk about literature rather than separatism with Montreal friends, and I voted in a least one federal election for the Rhinoceros Party. The only exception to my indifference came the night the Parti Québécois won the provincial election in 1976. Out of curiosity I went to hear René Lévesque address the victory celebration in the Paul Sauvé Arena. My fascinated equanimity in the face of such emotion and uncertainty was my first clue that I was destined to be a journalist.

Between 1980 and 1985 *Saturday Night* magazine assigned me to do, among subjects as diverse as a cardinal of the Roman Catholic Church and the closing of a mining town in Northern Saskatchewan, four political profiles—which appear here in different form as three of the five sections. I came to them cleansed of any party affiliation, any Ottawa connections, and any solutions for the problems of the world. Working on them gave me a more mature attitude toward the glories of Canada's democratic system; I became more respectful of politicians' labours and more tolerant of their foibles; and I met some very intelligent and articulate people, who showed extraordinary patience in teaching me what they knew. I can't say, however, that I have any more interest in which party gets elected or any more conviction about which policies Canada *ought* to pursue. Indeed, as I said earlier, the purpose of this book is to explore the forces that make party and policy somewhat secondary.

I must admit, though, that I haven't reacted to the personalities of my subjects with the same neutrality with which I reacted to their thoughts and ambitions. On the contrary, as a writer of in-depth magazine profiles I saw it as my role to transmit to those sitting at home in their armchairs how the company of the famous and the mighty *felt*. I was the surrogate, in effect, for those who didn't have the opportunity to follow John Turner for three months across Canada or have breakfast with Brian Mulroney in his home. Approaching public figures with almost no preconceived ideas other than those gathered by everyone who watches the news, I trusted I would see what most people would see if put in the same position.

In most cases I plunged into the lives of politicians for a period of time, sought out their strengths and weaknesses, stayed until everything started to repeat itself, and seldom crossed their paths again except at crowded public functions. Usually I only picked up by hearsay their reactions to what I had written. For months after my article on John Turner appeared in *Saturday Night* during the 1984 election, for example, I got absolutely no indication of how he felt about it. Then one of my younger brothers, who looks something like me, encountered him at a cocktail party in Toronto. "Didn't think much of your fucking article," Turner said to him. To which my brother replied, "It's my fucking brother you don't think much of."

There are two exceptions worth a comment: Jean Chrétien, whom I like as a person, and Brian Mulroney, whose famous charms have never worked on me. Of the politicians I have followed, I found Chrétien the most like his public self in private—unpretentious, frank, funny, shrewd, an odd mixture of confidence and inferiority—and the least carried away by power and success. When I began tracking him in the fall of 1980, I was profoundly suspicious of my assessment and tested it widely among his political enemies, his senior bureaucrats (off the record), and ordinary citizens. The range and depth of his popularity made me consider him a serious contender for the 1984 Liberal leadership when most of the press corps was dismissing him as a light-weight regional candidate; nor was I surprised in the autumn of 1985 by the phenomenal sales of his memoirs, *Straight from the Heart*.

That book was partly the result of my research for this one. When I asked for an interview about his career, he invited me to his cottage near Shawinigan and we talked for several days. Later I told a Toronto publisher about the transcripts, which contained much more material than I needed, and she convinced Chrétien to use them as the basis for a book. I was contracted to help edit the English version while Chrétien laboured on the French. Though I came to wonder if those taken aback by the long line-ups at all Chrétien's autograph sessions hadn't been more blinded by his faults than I had been by his virtues, I have tried to compensate for any distortion in these pages. To those who don't believe that is likely sufficient, I suggest they add a little salt for the true taste of the man.

Where Brian Mulroney is concerned, I suggest they add a little sugar. For he is the one I found the least like his public self in private. I had seen him almost apoplectic with anger and insecurity. I wasn't as tickled by his love of deviousness and showing off as his admirers seemed to be. I didn't think he sought office for any reason beyond his own need for glory. My negative reaction caused me to underestimate him during the 1983 Tory leadership campaign and before the 1984 general election.

To an extent, both of us were too Irish to be deceived by the other's game. I wasn't shocked when a friend joked one day, "Where are your bodyguards?" It seemed that Mulroney, then Leader of the Opposition, had found fault with something I had written about him and spent a portion of a dinner party at Stornoway ranting and swearing, "His time will come!" This story had the ring of truth, because I had once heard him vow vengeance against some other miscreant with exactly the same phrase.

So, quite foolishly, I assumed that people would find

his pious exhortations, his earnest appeals for civility and his sentimental blarney as hard to take as I did. That happened to an extent, in the form of Mulroney's perennial problem with his credibility, but I had let my own emotions overwhelm my judgement about his extraordinary skills as a politician, a conciliator, and a master of disguise. I was so certain he would trip badly on his fatal flaws that I didn't notice he might skate smoothly on his undeniable talents. Now, in the spring of 1986, as more and more of those who were beguiled by Mulroney's songs tell me I might have been right about him, I'm no longer sure.

Expecting so little, I've been impressed by his effort, by his acumen, by many of his underpublicized achievements, and by his quick grasp of the fundamental issues. I think he wasted most of his first year, but his inexperience may have been less a factor than the deep desire of an exhausted nation to enjoy the harmony and prudence he offered. He had serious problems with his staff and the organization of his government, but he's smart enough to fix them before too long. At times, he's too thin-skinned, too short-fused, and too hesitant for his own good or the good of the nation, but his job is more likely to toughen him than to break him. His approach to policy is too partisan and event-driven, but he has the ability to win elections for a long time.

My outstanding doubt is whether he has the capacity within himself to develop into a respected leader who can lift the country, united, sovereign, and prosperous, to the magnificence it could represent in the world and the next century. Those who know him very well say he can grow into the role. If he doesn't, then sooner or later he'll be swept from power onto the dust heap of history, with all his perks and vanities not worth the hardship.

Though the prejudices, the mistakes, and the worst generalizations are mine alone, I owe a debt of thanks to my friends and colleagues in the political press corps who welcomed a novice into their ranks, generously shared their information and insights, and made the rigours of the job such a pleasure: Claude Arpin, Dominique Clift, Mike Duffy, Graham Fraser, Carol Goar, Charlotte

Gray, Richard Gwyn, Sandra Gwyn, David Halton, Bob Hepburn, Mary Janigan, Bruce Little, Charles Lynch, L. Ian MacDonald, David McCormick, Roy MacGregor, Terry McKenna, Don Newman, Peter C. Newman, Jean Pelletier, Val Sears, Robert Sheppard, Jeffrey Simpson, Michael Valpy, Tom Walkom, Pam Wallin, Terrance Wills, and Hugh Winsor. The list isn't complete and doesn't include the many from whose work I learned much, but my thanks is great enough to encompass everyone who helped.

This book could not have been written without the support, the commissions, and the good advice over the past five years from the entire staff at *Saturday Night* magazine. My gratitude reaches far beyond these few words. I would especially like to thank Norman Webster for his vision, John Macfarlane for his unfaltering confidence, Robert Fulford for his brilliant guidance, Gary Ross for his superb work, Tecca Crosby and David Macfarlane for their invaluable contributions, and Nigel Dickson who often did much more than take the award-winning pictures.

At Collins I'd like to thank Nick Harris, Jan Whitford, and my excellent editor, Chuck Macli. Last but not least, a special thanks to Nancy Colbert, the legendary agent who got me into this and saw me through it.

Since 1980 I have talked at length to scores of people, from Prime Ministers to constituency workers, about Canadian politics. Some of them are mentioned by name in the text. By choice or necessity, however, most of them are not. To each I offer my appreciation for their time, knowledge, and kindnesses. I also ask forgiveness for any errors, misinterpretations, or unintended harm. Entering other lives as a reporter is like entering foreign lands as a traveller: one gains some feel for them, but mostly one comes away with a greater sense of one's ignorance.

Index